A
Covenant
with
Color

The Columbia History of Urban Life, Kenneth T. Jackson, General Editor

A Covenant with Color

**Race and
Social Power
in Brooklyn**

Craig Steven Wilder

Columbia University Press   New York

Columbia University Press   Publishers Since 1893
New York   Chichester, West Sussex
Copyright (c) 2000 Columbia University Press
All rights reserved

Library of Congress Cataloging-in-Publication Data
Wilder, Craig Steven.
A covenant with color : race and social power in Brooklyn / Craig Steven Wilder.
p. cm.– (The Columbia history of urban life)
ISBN 0-231-11906-2 (cloth : alk. paper) – ISBN 0-231-11907-0 (pbk. : alk. paper)
1. Brooklyn (New York, N.Y.)–Race relations. 2. New York (N.Y.)–Race relations. 3.
Afro–Americans–New York (State)–New York–Social conditions. 4. Afro–Americans–New
York (State)–New York–Economic conditions. 5. Brooklyn (New York, N.Y.)–Social condi-
tions. 7. Social classes–New York (State)–New York–History. 8. Brooklyn (New York,
N.Y.)–Economic conditions. 9. New York (N.Y.)–Economic conditions. I. Title. II. Series
F129.B7 W56 2000
305.8'009747'23–dc21   99-056462

CIP
Casebound editions of Columbia University Press books
are printed on permanent and durable acid-free paper.

Printed in the United States of America
c10 9 8 7 6 5 4 3 2 1
p 10 9 8 7 6 5 4 3 2

For Theresa Madeline Wilder

Contents

Photo Insert appears between pages 106 and 107

List of Tables

LIST OF MAPS

Acknowledgments

My sisters Terrie Diane Wilder and Gloria Wilderbrathwaite MD remain my closest friends, and my brother-in-law Carlos Wilderbrathwaite has been a dear and generous supporter. John Henry Wilder, Thoven L. E. Pearce, Travis Austin Wilderbrathwaite, Kai Maya Wilderbrathwaite, and Trent Dean Wilderbrathwaite, my nephews and niece, have all sacrificed play time to watch me work and have earned the chance to read their names. Catherine and Kevin Suarez equally deserve my thanks.

This work began as a dissertation under Kenneth T. Jackson in the History Department at Columbia University. He has been a fantastic adviser and friend, a sensitive scholar who was quick to challenge the intellectual rigor of my work and as quick to encourage and defend my rights to experiment with new approaches and ideas and dissent from mainstream thought. Eric Foner, Barbara Jeanne Fields, James Shenton, Manning Marable, Joshua Freeman, Elizabeth Blackmar, Jonathan Rieder, Rosalind Rosenberg, and Marcellus Blount provided invaluable support and advice. Mark Naison, my undergraduate adviser, has been a well of encouragement and friendship. It is fair to say that Mark Naison and Eric Foner introduced me to history, Barbara Fields revealed its rules, and Kenneth T. Jackson taught me to enjoy it. I also thank Lester Wilson, John Ehrenberg, George Sherer, Althea Spence, Jill Vexler and Ellen Shapiro, Lynnette Virginia Diaz, Calvin Holder, and the late Barbara Witenko for their encouragement.

An Adsit fellowship from the board of Williams College funded a sabbatical to complete this manuscript. I extend my appreciation to all my colleagues at Williams, especially Dennis Dickerson, Shanti Singham, Kenda Mutongi, Tim Sams, Kai Lee, Alex Willingham, Stephen Sneed, Sandra Burton, David Smith, Elaine Beretz, James Wood, Charles Dew, Sandra

Zepka, Scott Lewis, Marcella Villada Peacock, Enrique Peacock-Lopez, Lee Dalzell, and Kathleen Crandall. Sharron Macklin and Tanya Salcedo provided countless laughs and critical technical assistance.

I must single out Kate Wittenberg, editor-in-chief of Columbia University Press, for carefully guiding this manuscript. I owe a great debt to the staffs of the Schomburg Center for Research in Black Culture (NYPL), the Society for the Preservation of Weeksville and Bedford-Stuyvesant History, the Brooklyn Public Library, the New York State Library and Archives, the Brooklyn Historical Society, the New-York Historical Society, Howard University's Founders Library, the United States National Archives (DC and New York), the New York City Transit Museum Archives, the Sawyer Library at Williams College, and Columbia University's Butler Library.

It would be foolish and ungrateful not to acknowledge "Pandora" and "Ethiop," the personal computers that have carried this work.

My father's illness left my mother to raise her three children alone in Bedford-Stuyvesant, Brooklyn. She worked two jobs for twenty years to provide for our future. She educated herself and still found time to always attend PTA, scouts, sports, and spelling bees. She is my hero and the most significant role model in my life. This book is dedicated to my mother for the countless sacrifices that I saw her make and, especially, for those that I never saw.

Craig Steven Wilder
March 2000

A
Covenant
with
Color

The Trial of Race

Ever have men striven to conceive of their victims as different from the victors, endlessly different, in soul and blood, strength and cunning, race and lineage. It has been left, however, to Europe and to modern days to discover the eternal world-wide mark of meanness—color!

—W. E. B. Du Bois
(*Darkwater*)

In the summer of 1808 a trial, *The Commissioners of the Almshouse v. Alexander Whistelo (a black man)*, began on Blackwell's (Roosevelt) Island in the East River. Lucy Williams accused Whistelo of fathering her girl child, born January 23, 1803, and then failing to support their daughter; and under state law the commissioners of the Almshouse brought suit against the alleged father. The facts of the case were simple: Whistelo and Williams had a sexual relationship, during the affair Williams also had sex with a white man at least once, Williams bore a child, and Whistelo denied being the father of that child.[1]

A succession of "experts" on race advised the court. Doctors Joshua Secor and Wright Post testified that, since offspring always have a complexion that is intermediate between the mother and the father and since the child in question had lighter skin than her mother, her father would have had to be white. Since Whistelo was a dark man he could not have been the parent. Dr. George Anthon agreed, reminding the court that the child's hair had "every appearance . . . of a white person." Dr. David Hosack stated that he had no doubt that it was the child of "a white man, or a light mulatto man." Edward Miller disagreed, testifying that while the child's skin and hair were like those of a white person, her "thick lips and flat nose are indications of the father's being an African."[2]

Confused by the complexion of the child's skin—which was lighter than

Williams, a "yellow woman," and Whistelo, a "black man,"—the court eventually turned the case over to the Mayor of New York and a committee of officials to decide. A second wave of testimony was given. Dr. Kissam noted that according to "the general rules of experience" this was not the child of a black man. Doctors Hosack, Post, Anthon, Secor, Williamson, Osborne, and De Witt all concurred. Williamson went a bit further, instructing the Mayor that if the child was a black man's then the case was a prodigy, and that "he did not believe that prodigies happened, though daily experience unfortunately proved that perjuries did." The most interesting testimony came from Dr. Samuel L. Mitchell, who offered a lengthy description of the principles of race which, while not fully logical, seemed to awe the officials and prove Whistelo's innocence. But, after dazzling the court with his sermon on color, Mitchell dashed out any hopes of an easy decision by declaring that he believed the court should judge Whistelo to be the father of the child if for no other reason than that Lucy Williams said he was. Under cross-examination, Mitchell amused the court and defended his peculiar declaration with stories of black people who had turned white, emotionally upset women bearing deformed children, and a white woman who gave birth to a black child after ink was spilled in her shoes.

Conversely, Dr. Pascalis assured the court that there were reliable laws of race; the three primary characteristics of the Negro being their curly hair, their dark skin, and the peculiar shape of their legs and feet, particularly an elongated heel. At least one of these signs appeared in racial mixtures. For example, he continued, the French general Rigaud, a mulatto, who "was very handsome and well made" albeit "so dark as to differ little from the true African complexion." On that foundation Pascalis judged the child to be a "perfect mulatto" with no possibility of being fathered by a black man. The court also heard testimony on the processes of racial reproduction. Information was given on whether or not outside stimuli during conception could change the physical appearance of the offspring, whether or not a child could be transformed by a sex act that occurred immediately after conception, whether or not the child's color was a biological accident or the result of albinism, and, most importantly, whether or not this very line of reasoning suggested that black and white people were the same *species*.[3]

Whistelo's attorney concluded that expert testimony could not establish any immutable principles to guide the court. The judges needed a science but the rules of race offered by the experts were gathered from social experience and social mythology. The mayor, delivering the opinion, acquitted Whistelo on the judgment of "the most respectable medical gentlemen in the city," but bolstered that by reasserting the charge that Williams had an affair with a white man.[4]

Science simply could not explain the elusive and diabolic social work of race. It was clear to the judges that the little girl was *black*; and, had the question been at issue, the court could have easily determined whether or not the child was enslaved or free by simply tracing her mother's status. Two hundred years of law guaranteed the solution to that problem. People of African descent were enslaved and those of European ancestry were at liberty, so the difference of skin color captured the gap between the free and the unfree and was available if an individual's class status was unclear. Moreover, since servitude passed from mother to child few people ever experienced such ambiguity.

That there was no scientific basis or tangible proof of its beliefs did not trouble the court or disturb its faith in race; the judges and experts only needed to walk outside to prove that color had meaning. Although servitude was in decline there was still plenty of evidence to mark the difference between black people and white people. If slavery saw the emergence of a race concept, the unaltered social power of white people allowed that concept to keep its currency in the aftermath of bondage. The fact that many people of color remained enslaved, that those who were free were largely without political rights, that virtually all were to be found among the ranks of the poor, and that they remained supplicants before white authority all proved the *nature* of color in society. That too was social evidence; but, without it, these men could never prove race.

Racism was not produced *by* slavery; it was produced *during* slavery. Race arose in defense of the perverse maldistribution of social power through which people of African descent were enslaved as the application of that power came into question. Therefore, racism could, and did, survive even the destruction of bondage. Race shadowed power.

A Covenant with Color is the social history of an idea. It looks at three centuries of social relations in Brooklyn to show that racism is a fluid ideology that expresses the realties of power. Class describes the productive relationships between social actors, ideology is the difference of perspective that those relations necessitate, and power is the medium by which those relations are enforced. By conflating the latter two, it is often erroneously argued that ideology is a historical impetus, e.g. racism causes inequality. Power is the creative force in the construction of racial ideology and the formation of social inequality. The majority, however constructed and contested, exercises the ability to hoard resources, avoid risk, locate burdens, and impose an individual or group will upon the society through economic, political, and physical force. In such a system biological or cultural characteristics can easily be symbolic of social status. And through such antagonistic and dependent relationships, Brooklynites have come to live under a covenant with color.

CHAPTER ONE

Race and Social Power

—

Slavery and the
Evolution of an Idea,
1636–1827

—

. . . a marvelous fore shadowing of the scapegoat role the black was to play in American life is contained in Peter Stuyvesant's explanation of his surrender to the British. The city could not withstand the British siege, he explained, because three hundred slaves, brought in just before the British arrived in the harbor, had eaten all the surplus food. Scarcely any American politician has since improved on this extraordinarily convincing way of explaining American reverses.

—James Baldwin, "Preface," to Roi Ottley and William J. Weatherby, eds., *The Negro in New York: An Informal Social History* (New York: The New York Public Library, 1967).

Brooklyn was founded on the labor of unfree people. Academic debate about the genesis of African bondage in British North America has focused on the agricultural commerce and plantation culture of Virginia, but, as Oscar and Mary Handlin contend, "Negro slavery was not spontaneously produced by heat, humidity, and tobacco."[1] Dutch and English colonization in New Netherland-New York created a dense slaveholding society. Bondage moored the colony from its beginnings as a Dutch outpost. Slavery dictated the use of land, human chattel provided the measure of status and wealth, and servitude was the standard against which free people judged their liberties. African slavery conducted residents through that complicated process in which they invented themselves as not just nations but *races* of people. Bondage shaped the lives and thoughts of masters, yeomen, merchants, statesmen, servants and free laborers. Slave labor sustained the great Dutch, English, and French households of Colonial New York. Brooklyn was, under Dutch rule, under English rule, and in independence, not greatly different from the South in its reliance upon unfree labor and its yield.

Holland was already engaged in an international trade in human beings when one of its vessels, the *Halve Mane* (Half Moon), flying Dutch colors and carrying a Dutch crew, but commanded by an Englishman, Henry Hudson, anchored in a bay south of what is today Brooklyn on September 4, 1609. A few of the indigenous people of the long island that stretched 120 miles to the east came out to meet the ship. Well-clad and polite, the Canarsee delegation, by Hudson's account, was pleased to meet the Europeans. They traded green tobacco for the crew's knives and beads, and in little time the encounter ended.[2]

It was not until 1623 that Holland decided upon a permanent presence in the area in reaction to England's modest colonies, south at Virginia and north at Massachusetts. The Dutch West India Company, formed two years earlier, turned the "few rude buildings" used for fur trading on the island of Manahatta (Manhattan) into a more formal settlement.[3] The colony was named New Amsterdam and the larger province, which at this time existed only in Dutch imaginations, New Netherland. In 1636 a second colony was organized across the eastern river on the near shore of the largest of the islands. The new village was named Breuckelen after a town outside Amsterdam. This island was home to a number of tribes, including the Canarsee, who occupied much of today's Kings County and a portion of Queens. The island was Seawanhaka: the island of the shells.[4]

The same year that Breuckelen was established, the settlement of New Amersfort (Flatlands) began, it was followed by Midwout (Flatbush) in 1651, New Utrecht in 1657, and Boswyck (Bushwick) in 1660. Together they constituted the "Five Dutch Towns," a label which clearly distinguished them from the English clusters chartered at Hempstead in 1643, Gravesend in 1645, Rusdorp (Jamaica, Queens) in 1655, and Middlebury (New Town, now Astoria, Queens) in 1656. The 1645 Dutch encampment at Vlissingen (Flushing, Queens) balanced the British immigration to Jamaica and New Town.[5]

In 1629 the directors of the West India Company laid out the rights and privileges of colonists in New Netherland. Shaped to encourage immigration, the articles exempted settlers from taxes and duties for ten years. Emigrants could depend upon the Company to protect their right to servants, to hunt fugitive bondspeople, and to strictly enforce labor contracts. Eager to populate the area with Christians, West India's directors went further, promising to use their resources to satisfy the colonists' appetite for the enslaved and permitting settlers to peacefully expand into Native territory. The "Freedoms and Exemptions" also guaranteed a defense against foreign invasion.[6]

Peopling a colony was a dangerous business. In the first three decades the Dutch solidified their claim to Long Island by buying tracts of land from the Canarsee and neighboring tribes, by securing servants for Christians and loaning out the Company's bondspeople when labor was scarce, and by pursuing the often conflicting goals of bolstering themselves against the Iroquois nation and the English. British settlers were a welcome buffer against the Iroquois. In 1641 West India enthusiastically received the application of "a considerable number of respectable Englishmen with their Clergyman" to migrate. The consent demanded only an "Oath of Allegiance to the Noble Lords States General and the West India Company" in exchange for freedom of religion, the right to nominate their own officials, and jurisdiction over their own courts. However, the British settlers were not allowed to build forts, for England remained the major foreign threat to New Netherland, and that fear was aggravated by the Company's inability to find Dutch people interested in colonizing. Dutch pioneers were often profiteers who had no desire to become Americans. Freed Dutch servants turned to the fur trade rather than cultivating tracts of land as the Company wished.[7]

Dutchmen who did take to the land frequently laid claim to vast stretches, hoping to profit as the population increased. In 1650 Holland's fears for its colonies were relieved slightly when the island was divided in two: the Dutch in control of the west and the English claiming the east. In 1659, to control land speculation, settlers were given six weeks to improve their holdings or forfeit them. That solution failed. In 1671 the constable and overseers of Breuckelen asked the colonial governor to confiscate and redistribute the land of Charles Gabry. Lying adjacent to the town, the unfenced manor "is not and has not been occupied for the period of the last 15 or 16 years because the owner has gone to Holland or his country." The neighbors charged that the abandoned farm was injuring their property values and they claimed that its attached swamp was a hazard to horses and cows. The petitioners were eventually allowed to purchase the property.[8]

African bondage further complicated social relations between Christian and Native communities. In 1626, writes T. J. Davis, "a parcel of eleven [African] males" were transported to New Amsterdam. Enslaved Africans were critical to the agricultural development of the Hudson Valley and the southern islands. The Company itself was the largest slaveholder in the province, keeping its chattels in "half-freedom" to avoid supporting Africans whose labor was only seasonally needed. In 1659 the Company used the bondspeople of eastern Long Island to build a fort at Oyster Bay and strengthen the Dutch presence. Enslaved Africans were shifted between Long Island and New Amsterdam to meet occasional needs and to build the colony's infrastructure. The Company also dispensed Africans to the minor Christian villages.[9]

Policing servants and enforcing service contracts was one of the most important functions of the colonial administration. By 1640 runaway workers had put their masters "to great inconvenience and expense; the Corn and Tobacco rot in the field and the whole Harvest is at a stand still, which tends to the serious injury of this country, to their Masters' ruin[,] and to bring the magistracy into contempt." The Governor placed a hefty fine on harboring fugitives and imposed a penalty on running away that doubled the lost time. Two years later the problem was worse. Runaway servants from New England and Virginia were entering New Netherland. The Company determined that no migrant could be lodged in the colony until registered with the Director, levied a fine for noncompliance, and made the host responsible for the actions of the stranger. In 1654 the problem remained acute. That year New Amersfort's farmers were employing enslaved Africans to find and capture African runaways.[10]

The introduction of unfree people was the precursor to the destruction of the Native population, an important phase in the colonial mission that sought to reduce the danger of aggrieved, free residents and the potential for volatile combinations of subaltern groups. In 1638 Brooklyn's Dutch farmers petitioned for the right to wage war on Mareckkawich, the Canarsee village, until its residents accepted their subordination. The following year the Company prohibited Indians from acquiring arms and powder in order to cut down on their "mischief." On May 10, 1640 the Dutch purchased all of Canarsee chief Penhawitz's claims to the remainder of western Long Island and they considered the local Natives settlers. But the land transfers took place in the context of growing Christian aggression. During Governor Kieft's War (1639–1644)—a series of violent conflicts sparked by the executive's attempts to subdue and tax the Natives near New Amsterdam—the Canarsee sachem Penhawitz and his men burned European settlements across Long Island. In February 1644 the Christians responded. Captain Underhill led an English militia assault on a small Indian hamlet. The Dutch attacked a larger Native concentration. About 120 Canarsee were killed. In 1655 a company of Indians, probably Mohawk, on their way to battle with tribes on eastern Long Island, sacked Staten Island and then invaded Gravesend. Soldiers had to be brought from New Amsterdam to put down this assault.[11]

Unfreedom was the catalyst of Dutch expansion in the colony, but, as with the British experience in Virginia, that process was lengthy and complicated. In the literature on Virginia, historians have engaged in a lively debate on the relationship between prejudice and the evolution of African enslavement. Three distinct positions have been staked out. The first, captured in the work of Winthrop Jordan and Alden Vaughan, holds that, from their earliest appearance on North American soil, Africans were subject to distinctly different and inferior treatment compared to other people, even other unfree people. The implication is that prejudice advanced the cause of Christian freedom by accentuating the logic of African bondage. Looking at the first decade of the African presence in Virginia, Vaughan argued that the limited sources do not solve the question of causation but they do "show with disturbing clarity that the black men and women . . . held from the outset a singularly debased status in the eyes of white Virginians."[12]

On the other hand such scholars as Oscar and Mary Handlin and Edmund Morgan have read the scanty evidence through the lens of economic determinism and decided that the enslavement and dehumanization of Africans occurred fairly late, so that bondage bred racial prejudice. The first Africans to arrive in Virginia were not slaves but servants, similar in status to unfree Christians, argue the Handlins. Chattel slavery was forged over time and was "not a response to any inherent qualities that fitted the Negro for plantation labor." To that Morgan added a provocative question: if Virginians believed Africans to be distinctly suited for bondage "why did they wait so long" to enslave them? Two compromise positions have been offered. African enslavement was born of economic pressures, asserts George M. Fredrickson, and gave rise to racial prejudice; but, once elaborated, "racism became a force in its own right." Through a subtle distinction, Winthrop Jordan crafted a common genesis by arguing that "both may have been equally cause and effect, constantly reacting upon each other, dynamically joining hands to hustle the Negro down the road to complete degradation."[13]

The evidence from New Netherland also shows that Africans suffered a peculiar degradation from their earliest arrival. On February 25, 1644 the eleven African men who came in 1626 petitioned the Company for freedom. Paulo Angola, Big Manuel, Little Manuel, Manuel de Gerrit de Reus, Simon Congo, Anthony Portugis, Gracia, Peter Santomee, Jan Francisco, Little Anthony, and Jan Fort Orange had each served the West India Company for

eighteen years. As Governor Kieft admitted, they "have been long since promised their Freedom" and had been bound longer than a typical period of
indenture. The African men and their wives were freed. However Kieft clearly
did not view them as equal citizens; for, while he declared "them free and at
liberty, on the same footing as other Free people here in New Netherland," he
imposed regulations on them that were far more severe than those governing
Christians. They were given no exemptions from taxation and duties; in fact,
each man owed West India a yearly payment of "thirty skepels of Maize, or
Wheat, Pease or Beans, and one Fat hog, valued at twenty guilders." Any
African man who failed to meet this special obligation was to be returned to
bondage. Moreover, the West India Company kept legal title to their children,
including those born after the act of manumission.[14] By 1644 New Netherland's
Africans were suffering hereditary servitude for indefinite terms.

Still the question of causation remains. While these differences can be
attributed to prejudice they can also be attributed to the conditions of incorporation: Africans had already been bound, they arrived without foreign or
colonial restrictions on their treatment or guarantees of their rights, and their
captors were also the regulators of their legal status. Africans had few defenses
against a system that was devised to fully exploit all laborers regardless of their
origins. Barbara Jeanne Fields provided a solution to the problem of causation by separating prejudice, a set of attitudes and predispositions, from
race, an ideology that equates social relationships with natural and inherent
human characteristics. The belief that Africans are a distinct, even inferior,
culture or nation is not the historical equivalent of the idea that Africans are
a different racial group. Racism is itself historical, a social product bound in
time. It is important in understanding how historical actors came to view
their social relations, but not itself a tool of analysis.[15]

Prejudice proves fully unreliable as an explanation for African servitude.
A reasonable interpretation of Brooklyn's history will expose that fact.
Because they were prejudiced, seventeenth-century Dutch and English freeholders shunned Africans for European servants. They believed Africans to
be poorer workers, culturally inferior, and physically offensive. Yet, as the
century progressed, the supply of Africans increased while the importation
of indentured Christians declined. Those same prejudices allowed Dutch and
English freeholders to react by seeding their farms with enslaved Africans
while experiencing no sense of inconsistency. Thus, prejudice explains why
Africans were and were not enslaved; therefore, it explains nothing. The

freeholders' attitudes did not drive their actions; their sensibilities proved subordinate to their wants and aspirations. They were the rulers of the people around them, which permitted them to shift the burden of unfreedom at their convenience and to invoke some or all of their biases in defense.

The focus on attitudes has an underlying assumption that prejudice leads naturally to persecution, and greater prejudice to greater persecution. It can, but it need not; when it does, the relationship is not necessarily causal. The political, economic, material, and military factors that intersected to produce African slavery make the question of what people felt largely irrelevant.

Other prejudices existed that did not bring equivalent social exploitation or similar ideological conclusions. From the mid-1650s the Christians of New Netherland, particularly New Amsterdam, openly expressed their "disgust and dislike" of the "Jewish Nation." Governor Stuyvesant tried to ban Jewish immigration to the colony. New Amsterdam put prohibitions on Jews owning real estate and trading. Jews were segregated in daily life and in cemeteries. Those regulations might have survived, according to E. B. O'Callaghan, if not for the pleas of a few Jews among the stockholders of the West India Company. The Company substituted Amsterdam's restrictions on Jews for New Amsterdam's. Jews were banned from military service and a special tax was levied on them to support the colony's defense. New Netherlanders were equally hostile toward Quakers. A 1663 act made it a crime to transport "Vagabonds, Quakers and other Fugitives" into the colony.[16]

The argument for prejudice's causal role holds that Jews and Quakers were not enslaved because they were hated less than Africans; however, if true, the paradoxical situation arises in which a group of people motivated by bias used slavery to draw closer those who they most despised while demanding physical separation from those who they despised less. While it is somewhat logical to imagine that hatred could drive them to draw wealth from the labor of an oppressed group, that decision also meant that an outcast people were introduced into their homes and institutions. Theodore Allen saw a similar illogic when he questioned why historians had ignored Anglo-America's anti-Irish and anti-Jewish sentiments while assigning blame for the enslavement of Africans to prejudice. The belief that cultural animosity drove Africans into bondage is the ahistorical result of our knowledge that Africans were reduced to hereditary slavery. Winthrop Jordan wrote, "something about Negroes, and to lesser extent Indians, set them apart for drastic exploitation, oppression, and degradation."[17] There is another answer: the process that brought the English of Virginia and the Dutch of New Netherland to Africa for a supply of unfree workers was shaped not by their attitudes but by the fact of a preexisting commerce in Africans. A century-old slave trade prepared the labor market in which colonial Christians fulfilled their needs.

The only missing variable is power. Few scholars would defend the Dutch farmers of western Long Island or the English landholders of Virginia against the accusation of prejudice; however, they did not yet project their lives and life chances through the lens of color, nor was such a step necessary. In Brooklyn, as in Virginia, slavery was a function of political economy, not social psychology. As they came to experience mastery over countless human beings, they surely did come to assume their own natural superiority; that was not, however, the product of a predisposition, but rather the result of real social relationships. Brooklyn's free residents racialized their society as their capacity to enslave and persecute Africans crystallized. Racial thought matured as European Americans' power came to shape the *nature* of colonial society. Ultimately, they even mistook that power for genius.

It was not hate but an equally vulgar greed that drove local Christian farmers to enslave Africans. In 1648 Dutch West India opened a trade with Brazil and a slave trade with Angola. The resolution stipulated "that the ships returning may take freight from Brazil; but those coming back from Angola are to bring Negroes to be employed in farming." Four years later the administrators further liberalized the privilege of slaving in response to the colonists' incessant demands for labor: "In order to favor this Plantation the more, we hereby consent on the proposal of the Inhabitants there, that they shall be at liberty to bring in their own ships from the coast of *Africa*, as many Negroes as they shall have need of for the cultivation of the soil." To preserve the Company's interests, a duty was placed on each person so imported, and three years later a tax was imposed on Africans exported from New Netherland.[18]

English conquest brought an even greater reliance upon unfree Africans. On March 12, 1664 Charles II granted to his brother the Duke of York (later James II) all the lands of North America roughly bounded by the Connecticut River to the north and the Delaware River to the south. The frustrated King, who had not been able to ignite a conflict as a pretense for seizing the Dutch colonies, specifically reminded his brother that the grant included "all that Island or Islands commonly called by the several name or names of Matowacks or Long Island," displaying his vague knowledge of the area, "together also with the said River called Hudsons River."[19]

Eager to claim his gift, the Duke dispatched three men-of-war and a transport with 450 troops to New Amsterdam. The British forces met little resistance. Governor Stuyvesant's pleas for assistance were ignored in Holland, which was more concerned with avoiding conflict on the Continent and preserving its West Indian interests than with the costly defense of a far-off colony that had already proved more of a burden than a boom. Stuyvesant chose to console himself by blaming hungry Africans for bringing on New Amsterdam's demise. New Netherland succumbed to the British assault, he explained, because recently imported Africans (who presumably lacked the discipline of the Dutch) had consumed all the colony's provisions. Regardless, by September the greater portion of the Northeast coast of the Americas was joined under English rule and the colony of New York chartered. In November 1683 the British designated as Kings County the independent towns and surrounding lands of southwestern Long Island—including Breuckelen, New Amersfort, Midwout, New Utrecht, Boswyck, Gravesend, and the area that later became Williamsburg. Nearby New Town was added to Queens County.[20]

The Canarsee felt English rule first. Killing off the Native population was also a part of the British formula for growth, tying the Dutch and English in a pattern that Allen highlighted as an early feature of racial systems: "the assault upon the tribal affinities, customs, laws and institutions" of the oppressed. Long Island's indigenous population had been hired, indentured, and enslaved, legally and illegally. But Native Americans were targeted for reduction rather than servitude as Africans became the primary source of unfree labor. When Daniel Denton explored New York in 1670, he accused a mysterious hand for their destruction:

> there is now but few upon the island, and those few no ways hurtful but rather serviceable to the *English*, and it is to be admired, how strangely they have decreast by the Hand of God, since the *English* first set[t]ling of those parts; for since my time, where there were six towns, they are reduced to two small Villages, and it hath been generally observed, that where the *English* come to settle, a Divine Hand makes way for them, by removing or cutting off the *Indians*, either by Wars one with the other, or by some raging mortal Disease.[21]

Men acted far more often than God.

From the colony's earliest days both colonial governments actively attempted to thin the Native population, and while intertribal wars resulted in the deaths of many Natives, Christians often encouraged those wars. In his history of Brooklyn, Silas Wood charged that the Mohawk leveled the Canarsee, but, he added, that this was only after English and Dutch residents promised but did not provide protection to the Canarsee. With that offer, the Canarsee ceased paying tribute to, and attracted the wrath of, the powerful Iroquois.[22]

British governors were committed to slavery as an avenue to colonial success, and Brooklyn's Dutch farmers benefited from the thrust toward unfreedom. In 1664, the year that the English claimed the colony, the Reverend Polhemus, who Governor Stuyvesant appointed to minister to the Dutch residents of New Amsterdam and western Long Island, took time to purchase an African at auction for his Midwout estate. If Holland used servitude to sustain the colony, argues Edgar McManus in his history of bondage in New York, the English, through the Royal Africa Company, used the "colony to implement slavery." The fantastic increase in the population of enslaved Africans in the century after English conquest highlights that fact.[23]

Racism was the effect of the democratic experience of mastery as it took shape under British rule, for it awaited the emergence of a system in which nationality correlated fairly accurately with social position. "Whatever might have been the case with literate members of the ruling class, the record indicates that laboring-class European-Americans in the continental plantation colonies showed little interest in 'white identity' before the institution of the system of 'race' privileges at the end of the seventeenth century," argues Allen. The availability of Africans in an international trade, Dutch West India's and Royal Africa's abetting of that commerce, and the fluctuating supply of European servants helped Brooklyn's residents along the path. As Edmund Morgan writes, other people had already done the difficult work of enslaving Africans.[24] Local farmers only needed to change their behavior as consumers of workers, they only had to react to the labor supply; and, a series of Colonial laws that exploited the absence of British regulations on the treatment of Africans and placed limits on Christian servitude hastened their adjustment.

The burden of the system quickly transferred to Africans. In his history of slavery on Long Island, Richard Shannon Moss found that a 1646 grant of half freedom to Francisco and Anton of Boswyck (Bushwick), who had been petitioning the company for their freedom for more than a decade contains indirect evidence that the two were subject to bondage for life. Lifetime hereditary servitude was secured when the Articles of Capitulation (1664) confirmed Dutch titles to chattels for terms or life. A rush of codes defining the social strata followed English conquest. Immediately upon seizing power in 1664, the Duke of York proclaimed that

> No Christian shall be kept in bond slavery, villenage, or captivity, except such who shall be judged thereunto by authority, or such as willingly have sold or shall sell themselves, in which case a record of such servitude shall be entered in the court of sessions held for the jurisdiction where such masters shall inhabit, provided that nothing in the law contained shall be to the prejudice of master or dame who have or shall by any indenture or covenant take apprentices for term of years, or other servants for term of years or life.

The Duke's declaration put legal proscriptions on Christian bondage while pointing colonists toward Africa as the source of unfree labor. In 1678 Governor Andros of New York complained to the King that there were "but few Serv[an]ts, much [are] wanted & [there are] but very few slaves."[25]

The British West Indies provided New York with enslaved Africans but never enough, particularly as New York's European population became free. Still, by 1691 the continued importation of Africans allowed the colony to pass an act refining and expanding the rights of Christian "freemen." Colonial officials had used religious cleavages to justify the widening liberties of Europeans and the construction of hereditary slavery for Africans; however, by the end of the century many Africans were Christians but not free. Religion no longer explained freedom and unfreedom in the colony because that class division reacted to and resulted from economic, not spiritual, pressures. In October 1687 the Legislature did emancipate a group of "Christian Indians" from Vera Cruz and the following summer it freed and deported several "Spanish Indian slaves professing Christianity." But these were rare occurrences and the fiction that chattel could earn freedom through acts of faith soon disappeared. In 1706 the Legislature acted to encourage the baptism of enslaved people by assuring masters that they should not be "deterred and hindered therefrom by reason of a groundless opinion that hath spread itself in this colony, that by the baptizing of such negro, Indian, or mulatto slave, they would become free, and ought to be set at liberty." To clear up lingering sources of confusion, the act also decided that children of mixed parentage "follow the state and condition of the mother and be esteemed, reputed, taken and adjudged a slave and slaves to all intents and purposes whatsoever." Because the society was also criminalizing sexual relations between African men and Christian women, the legislators assumed that newborns with claims to bound and free parents had *black* mothers.[26]

The period saw biology easily supplant religion as the symbol of social division. Over four decades their language and laws came to confess that Christianity did not sire liberty. Instead, the colonists exploited the increasingly obvious national differences between the free and the unfree. The same process that brought Kings County residents to Africa for their labor also allowed them to fix upon skin color and elevate it above all other human characteristics by suggesting that it had the power to determine social status. In less than half a century color became the primary metaphor for class. Having become ineligible for hereditary bondage, Kings County's Dutch and English residents were only now free to speculate on the biological and cultural faults of those who suffered enslavement.

Bipolar color references did not capture the diversity of the enslaved population. Native Americans were bound in the colony from its founding. Seventeenth-century Dutch governors encouraged a traffic in Indians. On the eve of English conquest, Governor Stuyvesant was personally overseeing the sale of Natives from Long Island to Curacao. English governors also allowed unfree Native Americans to be imported and sold to Long Island and New York residents. These "Spanish Indians" were typically from the Caribbean and were often of mixed ancestry. The 1712 bequest from Jan Meserole Jr. of Kings County to his wife Mary included "Betty, an Indian woman, and her child." Advertisements for runaways also document the persistence of Native-American servitude. In 1746 Jeffrey, a 28-year-old Indian indentured servant of Sampson Crooker, fled his master's Long Island estate. Crooker posted a reward for his return and hinted to bounty hunters that Jeffrey "professes him self to be something of a sailor." Three years later Jack, an 18-year-old "Indian Man," absconded from the Long Island farm of John Petty. Jack was in the company of Toney, the 19-year-old mulatto slave of neighboring John Tuthill. About the same time, Nicholas Bayard of New York City—who also owned English, Irish, and African servants—was seeking the return of James, a 40-year-old "Indian Man Slave," who was suspected to be in the Westchester area.[27]

Masters from a broad region ran advertisements for runaway Irish servants. In 1746 Captain John Riven of Manhattan was seeking the return of Hugh Martine, his "swarthey," 20-year-old "Irish Servant Man." The following year Nicholas Bayard suffered greater losses when his Irishman William Patterson, Patterson's wife, and a third servant absconded. Bayard noted that Patterson changed his name to "John O'Konner." In 1751 a Pennsylvania master advertised in New York for the return of his smallpox disfigured Irish servant, Thomas Kelly. A year later the arrival of "a Snow from Dublin with Servants" calmed local demand for unfree Irish people.[28]

TABLE 1.1

Enslaved Africans Imported to the Province of New York, 1701-1725

Year	Indies	West Coast	African Total
1701–1705	225	24	249
1706–1710	—	53	53
1711–1715	70	170	240
1716–1720	719	379	1,098
1721–1725	379	176[a]	555

[a]117 were from Madagascar.
SOURCE: "Number of Negroes Imported from 1701-1726," in E. B. O'Callaghan, MD, *The Documentary History of the State of New-York; Arranged Under the Direction of the Hon. Christopher Morgan, Secretary of State,* 4 Vols. (Albany: Weed, Parsons, 1849), I: 707.

The overwhelming African majority among the unfree was itself ethnically varied(see table 1.1). From 1701 to 1725, 1,400 enslaved African-Caribbeans were legally sold at New York harbor, the region's premier slaving port. In that same period, one of every three enslaved people brought to New York was from Africa. In December 1744 Samuel Willis of Middletown, Connecticut, was offering a reward for his "well set Angolo" who escaped him with several suits of clothing and a bit of silver money. That month John Thorn of Whitestone Ferry in Flushing was trailing his "new Negro Fellow," Prince, who "can't speak a word of English" but knew to also carry off a gun. In 1785 Joseph Rose of Manhattan was aggressively hunting Amelia, an African woman of the "Chambo" nation, who joined with a servant named Harry and "beat their mis[t]ress very cruelly the night they went off."[29]

Africans were the vast majority of the enslaved, but Native and "Christian" unfreedom persisted. Therefore, color references are a particularly important harbinger of the emerging ideology of race; however, they are unreliable measures of the scope of unfreedom. Frequent allusions to mulatto servants and bondspeople with "Indian" features or blood imply not just sexual relations between free Europeans and enslaved Africans but also the frequent mingling of African, Native, and European (especially Irish) servants. If by law the children of Dutch and African unions were enslaved then certainly the offspring of Africans and the Irish or Africans and Native Americans were subject to bondage for life—and, therefore, functionally black. Christian and Native slavery were in decline but they eroded at the very hour that a greater diversity was being recognized in the nonwhite population.

White racialism crystallized during the Revolutionary era as the promise of liberty came to be unrestrictedly extended to European Americans. That guarantee also exposed the political and social barriers to African Americans' freedom. While the Revolution did not demand universal freedom, David Brion Davis has written, "the crises of the 1760's and 1770's left a sense of expectancy, of an approaching fulfillment, which would be an essential catalyst in transforming abstract ideals into militant antislavery protest."[30] However one views the causation between slavery and race, the focus on that connection creates the expectation that the end of slavery would bring the decline of racism.

Unarguably the Revolution posed a challenge to bondage, but that in no way jeopardized race. In fact, by embellishing racism, the "founding fathers" seized the political benefits of universal freedom while avoiding the social and economic consequences of universal emancipation. Moreover, state emancipation laws were fully consistent with racism. For instance, white New Yorkers had long been concerned about the dangers of enslaved Africans and had even debated schemes for returning to the use of unfree white labor. Increases in the black population resulted from legalized slavery. New York's law makers were optimistic that independence would allow unfettered commercial activity and a general material elevation and they recognized the difficulty of competing with the South for bondspeople. They came to see the Revolutionary moment as an opportunity to racially homogenize the state. Their fears and prejudices led them to concede slavery to the South, put limits upon the number of black people among them, and move to capture the dominant commercial position that England had surrendered.

The growth of slaveholding during the Revolution, New York's long delay in passing a manumission law, and the resistance of the large slaveowning counties to emancipation, contradict the argument that the spirit of liberty was central in New York's motion toward freedom. New York's masters were potent opposition to emancipation. It was not until March 1781, long after the British began uprooting servitude in the state, that the New York Legislature acted to enlist black men in the fight for independence. The English emancipated thousands of black people in an attempt to undermine the colonial economy, and thousands of African-American and white loyalists were evacuated with the British after the surrender. Before their November 30, 1783 deadline for evacuation from New York, England's forces transported more than 3,000 black people to freedom.[31]

Still, the enslaved population in New York State was maintained through importation. Manhattan newspapers ran ads for runaways and auctions. *The Independent Gazette* attracted advertisements from as far away as Pennsylvania. In December 1783 William and Abraham De Peyster were soliciting a "well-recommended" "Negro wench." A Manhattan intelligence office offered "a SMART, well handed NEGRO GIRL" and "an active NEGRO BOY" for sale. Kings County entered the Revolution with a third of its population enslaved and at the dawn of peace the same proportion remained bound and the number of unfree Africans actually increased. Imports continued after the Revolution. New York was already the nation's fifth largest slaveholding state, and from 1786 to 1790 the state's enslaved population increased 12.9 percent. Kings County was even less influenced by the challenge of liberty; in 1791 there were only 46 free black people in the county, proportionately the smallest free black community in the state.[32]

In 1785 the Legislature passed an emancipation law with such severe limitations on African freedom as to immediately create a black caste of permanent, hereditary, but unbound, inferiors. The Council for Revision vetoed the measure. In 1799 New York began a reluctant manumission which was later amended to establish a July 4, 1827 target for universal freedom. The law promoted all people born after July 4, 1799; males could be indentured to age 28, females to 25. The 1817 amendment did the same for those born before 1799. That staggered process allowed New York's masters time to recover the value of their bondspeople; even so, Kings County's representatives opposed every freedom law that came before the Legislature. In 1830, three years after emancipation was to have been completed, 75 black people remained enslaved in New York State. Ten years later four African Americans were being bound despite the triumph of universal freedom. The following year the Legislature passed another law to end slavery in New York.[33]

By the end of the Revolution, Kings County's white residents were convinced that Africans were a distinct race: fitted by nature to be enslaved, incapable of exercising elementary self-governance, and inherently inferior. The evidence for that idea was buried in history, not biology. In short, each tenet of the belief began with events, laws, or behaviors that left ideological imprints of Euro-America's tortured journey to domination. Racism did not preexist slavery, nor was it a simple byproduct of slavery. It evolved in defense of European-American power as one of its manifestations—African enslavement—took shape in a complex and contested social terrain.

CHAPTER TWO

Little Masters

—

Slavery and the
Evolution of a City,
1636–1827

—

RUN away from Barnet Van Deventer, of Flat-Bush, on Long-Island, in Kings County, a Negroe Man named Handrick, alias Hank, of middle stature, had on When he Went away a Linning striped, Jacket, a Pair of Humespun Breeches, a Blewish Pair of Stockings, and an old Pair of Shoes, a good Felt Hat: He speaks good English and Dutch, and tells People he is a free Negro. Whosoever takes up said Negro and brings him to his said Master, or secures him so that he may be had again, shall have 30 Shillings Reward, and all Reasonable charges paid by me, Barnet Van Deventer

—*The New York Evening Post*, September 29, 1746

Wanted to Purchase, TWO healthy BLACK MEN, who can be recommended for honesty, industry and sobriety[;] aged from eighteen to twenty-four.
Apply to Francis Titus.
Williamsburgh, Jan 11.

—*The Long Island Star*, January 19, 1814

Brooklyn's Dutch and English families preferred to view African slavery as tangential to their history in spite of the voluminous evidence of their reliance upon bondage. Through most of the nineteenth and early twentieth centuries descendants of the old settler families published histories in which slavery was ignored, cast as anomalous, or romanticized, each work containing an inner friction resulting from the oxymoron, *gentle slavery*.

Henry Reed Stiles, the most prominent nineteenth-century historian of Brooklyn, helped embed that myth by informing his readers that bondspeople in Kings County were "kindly treated and well cared for." Stiles wrote that each of the several Meserole family farms in Greenpoint was equipped with "its own retinue of jolly negroes in field and kitchen." He made those assertions while simultaneously recording evidence of conspiracies, plots, auctions, murders, and revolts. Drawing on Gabriel Furman's earlier work, the Holland Society's Stephen Ostrander concocted a fanciful bondage with aged Negroes spinning fireside tales for the youngsters of courtly Dutch families; however, to prove that Africans were cherished, he could only note that they fetched a much higher price than cows and other animals. In her history of Flatbush, Gertrude Lefferts Vanderbilt assured herself and her audience that Kings County never sustained the conditions that encouraged a cruel bondage, thus, "it is not probable that slavery ever exhibited its worst features on Long Island."[1] Generations of family and community historians forged the belief that slavery in the Colonial New York was fundamentally different, and *better*, than slavery in the Southern colonies. Their ancestors were portrayed as just men and women on a humanitarian mission to Christianize heathens, and, in an instructive display of their power, they recast the Knickerbocker-Yankee enslavement of Africans as the single kindest act that one group of people ever visited upon another.

The elite families began their tenure in the seventeenth century. On April 16, 1663 Jan Meserole,[2] after emigrating from France to Holland, arrived at New Amsterdam aboard the *Spotted Cow* with his wife, Jonica, and infant son, Jan Jr. The family settled on western Long Island. On October 28, 1663 the Meseroles joined the Reformed Dutch Church and three years later they purchased the New Utrecht farm of Jan Clement. They also quickly acclimated to the business of owning people.[3]

Pieter Praa came at about the same time as Jan Meserole. He was born in Leyden, Holland, in 1655 and during the Dutch reign his family came to Long Island. After the 1664 English conquest of New Netherland, Praa helped found Greenpoint, purchased servants and considerable land, and was appointed magistrate and captain of the militia by British Lord Cornbury. For a time, Praa claimed more bondspeople than any other Kings County resident.[4]

In 1660 Leffert Pieterse—the young Peter Lefferts—left Holland for New Netherland. He settled in Midwout (Flatbush), where by 1675 he had bought a small farm and bondspeople. At the turn of the century, his son Jacobus

Lefferts acquired the land and house at Clove and Jamaica Roads in Bedford Corners which became the traditional family seat, although rival estates were to be found in Breuckelen, Midwout, and the other towns.[5] The Lefferts used marriage and inheritance to stand, by the eighteenth century, as one of Kings County's largest slaveholding family.

TABLE 2.1

Population of Enslaved Africans in Kings County, 1698–1790

Year	Total	Enslaved	% Enslaved
1698	2,017	296	14.7
1703	1,912	343	17.9
1723	2,218	444	20.0
1731	2,150	492	22.9
1737	2,348	564	24.0
1746	2,331	645	27.7
1749	2,283	783	34.3
1756	2,707	845	31.2
1771	3,623	1,162	32.1
1786	3,986	1,317	33.0
1790	4,495	1,432	31.9

Note: This is often Negro population which is a close approximation of the enslaved population.

Source: Evarts B. Greene, *American Population Before the Federal Census of 1790* (1932; Gloucester, Massachusetts: P. Smith, 1966), 92–105.

The average seventeenth-century freeholder was a Dutch man, who held a 20 to 50 acre farm, kept cows, sheep, oxen, and horses, and listed Africans alongside his livestock on official rolls (see tables 2.1 and 2.2). Poorer families and young single men managed to survive on small land holdings, supplementing their incomes with paid work and filling their tables with game and fish. The middling comprised those who held and improved agricultural lands, had a horse and cow, and perhaps acquired a servant. In contrast, the wealthiest local farmers claimed up to 200 acres and a disproportionate share of the bondspeople. In 1667 Jan Meserole purchased his New Utrecht farm which also served as the family home for almost a decade. He focused on getting bondspeople in the following years. About 1675 he bought Teunis Jansen Van Pelt's Key Kuits farm (in the western section of Boswyck (Bushwick) that became Williamsburg), 107 additional Boswyck acres, and the Key Kuits meadow in Greenpoint. There he erected a new family seat. In just over a decade Meserole had become one of Kings County's leading men. The family increased its wealth through marriage, the byproduct of a social savvy that they honed for generations. On November 24, 1682 Jan Meserole Jr. expanded his lands by marrying Marretje Coeverts, the daughter of Bedford's Teunis Jansen Coeverts. (At the time, Ruthgret Joosten's 200 acre farm in New Utrecht was the single largest estate in the county, although families like the Meseroles were rising rapidly.) Jan Jr. and Mary made considerable additions to the holdings. When Meserole died in 1712, he gave his wife title to the Turtle Bay farm on which they lived, two Manhattan meadows, a New Brunswick (NJ) farm, and five enslaved Africans. The Key Kuits properties and its servants went to his sons, Jan III and Cornelius.[6]

There were a few free Africans on Long Island. In 1639 Antony Jansen Van Sale, once a pirate, became the first African freeholder in the area when he signed a ten-year lease on 200 acres in Gravesend. On August 27, 1657, when Governor Peter Stuyvesant charted the town of New Utrecht, Van Sale was one of only two men to be granted multiple lots. The Governor used Van Sale's holdings to help define Utrecht's limits: ". . . lying on Long Island by the easterly Hook of the Bay of the North River, over against Conyen [Coney] Island. . . . Bounded on the westerly side by [the] land of Antony Jansen Van Sale. . . ." Van Sale also owned property in Manhattan. He was married to a Dutch woman and suffered the repeated discriminations of his Dutch and English neighbors. In 1660 Stuyvesant oversaw the laying out of the town of Boswyck for a party of French settlers and one of the signers of its patent was Francisco the Negro, a free man of African descent who had come to New Netherland enslaved.[7] While a few Africans did manage to gain their freedom and acquire land, most of the Africans on the island were bound, and their major roles were house service and farm labor.

The key to production in Kings County was not the farm but the family, not land but labor. Households included a husband, a wife, and four or five children. Families with more than five children were far more common than families with no children; in fact, fewer than ten percent of all households were without children. Youths were useful day-to-day laborers and security for parents in old age. Children constituted 51 percent of Kings County's residents. Enslaved Africans were already a third of the adult population,[8] and they carried a major share of the labor burden.

Single women depended more heavily upon child labor. There were few widowers, suggesting a shorter life span and a higher rate of remarriage for men. In 1698 only a handful of men were raising children alone; in contrast, eighteen women headed households. The widow Martentz of Gravesend, who was mother to seven children and owned a bondsman, was typical of independent women in Kings County, ten of whom were masters. Breuckelen's Barbara Luycas held three bondspeople but had no children, making her quite peculiar. At the other extreme was "Susanna" of New Utrecht who had four children, no husband, no servants, and no recorded surname.[9]

Women who owned people were not rare and slaveownership was more than a means of securing vulnerable women. Gender influenced only the pattern of slaveholding. Single and poorer women had fewer choices of servants and typically acquired them through inheritance so that cultural preferences are less apparent, but wealthier women were likely to have women bondservants. Better Dutch men regularly bequeathed enslaved children (especially girls), women, and the elderly to their wives and daughters; their sons were given adolescents and all adult full hands regardless of gender. Dutch women then passed their bondswomen on to their daughters. In her 1687 will, Christina Cappoens, the widow of David Jochemsen and the mother-in-law of Pieter Praa, secured her daughter's future and disposed of the fettered women she had acquired over her lifetime. She instructed her executors to free her "negro woman, Isebella . . . from all manner of servitude and slaverye [sic]." Cappoens left "all my daily clothes," a ring, a pot, and a kettle to Isebella, and she allowed the servant to keep any bedding already in her possession. The mistress probably believed that she was being kind, but the act had a cruel edge. Ownership of Isebella's daughter, Lysbett, was not relinquished but transferred to Cappoens's daughter "Maria, during my daughter's life, without any contradiction." Upon Maria's death, Lysbett was free to "go where she shall think fitt."[10]

The elite Dutch and English families of Kings owned Africans, advertised for runaways, auctioned human beings, and exhibited the violence, hypocrisy, and immorality that people who systematically exploit other people eventually must display. On the largest estates unfree laborers planted and reaped wheat, corn, beans, peas, and other agricultural products, carted crops, marketed the produce, kept accounts, tended to livestock, cooked and cleaned in homes, and cared for children. Bondspeople built churches, houses, fences, barns, and fortifications, and laid the colony's roads. Servants even helped defend the colony in times of war.[11]

TABLE 2.2

Slaveholdings and African Groupings in Kings County Households, 1698

Size of group	1[a]	2	3	4	5	6	7	8
Brooklyn	12[b]	11	4	3	—	—	1	—
Bushwick	3	5	5	—	2	1	—	1
New Utrecht	8	3	2	2	3	1	—	—
Flatlands	9	5	—	4	1	—	—	—
Gravesend	8	1	1	1	—	—	—	—
Flatbush	12	10	4	3	3	—	—	—
Total households	52	35	16	13	9	2	1	1
Total Africans	52	70	48	52	45	12	7	8

[a] Or number of Africans in household.
[b] Number of households.
Source: Compiled from "Census of Kings County; About 1698. A List of All the Freeholders Their Wives Children Apprentices and Slaves Within the Kings County on Nassauw Island" in E. B. O'Callaghan, MD *The Documentary History of the State of New-York; Arranged Under the Direction of the Hon. Christopher Morgan, Secretary of State,* 4 Vols. (Albany: Weed, Parsons, 1849), 3: 133–38.

By the end of the seventeenth century more than forty percent of Kings County's freeholders owned Africans in spite of the prohibitive cost of bondspeople; moreover, the practices of leasing, lending, and hiring out the enslaved allowed the majority of Kings County farmers to exercise mastery in their lifetimes. In 1698 Pieter Praa of Bushwick owned eight bondspeople and was the most prominent slaveholder in the county. The climate and agricultural limits of the region made the optimum estate smaller than that of the southern colonies. While the size of slaveholdings was less dramatic than elsewhere, local freeholders were equally dependent upon servitude. Judging the place of bondage in Kings County's economy by counting bondspeople is misleading because the demands of agricultural production in a northern coastal colony, not wealth or desire, dictated scale. It is far more important to note that Kings County's elite families held Africans as their major investment, that wealth could be measured more accurately in people than in land, and that the colony constantly sought the importation of more servants. Left unexplained, slaveholding patterns in the county might seem contradictory. Because of the small scale of local agricultural production, 40 percent of slaveholding families had only one slave, but, because of the importance of slavery to the local economy, more than 80 percent of all bondspeople lived in multislave households.[12]

The defense of servitude in Kings County rests on the fact that the holdings were small, that these farmers were little masters in a culture far removed from that of the plantation South and Caribbean; but, for two centuries, slavery in the local towns expanded horizontally and vertically, until most white families owned Africans and the largest holdings had more than doubled in size. A significant portion of the county's white population—by the end of the eighteenth century the vast majority—chose mastery when geography retarded the annual economic gains to be made from enslaved labor. Freeholders sought to improve their financial and social position through bondage despite the limitations of their agricultural lands. There were even a few men who fancied themselves planters and were treated as such by their neighbors. For white farmers slavery was the most secure avenue to wealth and any man who ached to climb the social ladder was inevitably called to mastery. They used Africans, not to flood the world market with cash crops, but to shelter their wealth across generations. They committed to a way of life premised upon the domination of other people, a fact that makes them peculiarly akin to the Southern planter class.

The size of Kings County's largest slaveholdings crept higher each decade of the eighteenth century. After the turn of the century, the marriage of Jan Meserole III and Elizabeth Praa, Pieter Praa's daughter, united two grand slave-owning families. Meserole already inherited the sizable Key Kuits properties in his father's will, and over the following decades he dramatically expanded his estate with the help of his father-in-law. In 1726 Praa sold Meserole the southern portion of a large Greenpoint holding, which was later divided up and given to Meserole's sons, Peter and John, and an in-law. The northern piece of that land was willed to Elizabeth. In 1739 when Praa died, Jan Meserole III became the owner of about three-quarters of today's Greenpoint, Brooklyn. From the family's traditional Key Kuits seat, Meserole shepherded over the Long Island, New York, and New Jersey estates and servants for two decades. He was patriarch of one of the region's most courted families, and, in the inbred Knickerbocker style, he and his heirs arranged unions that repeatedly braided their family name into aristocratic Dutch, English, and French lines.[13]

Bondage regularly intruded into the local residents' most intimate calculations. On August 11, 1707 John Aerson of "Brookland," Kings County, sat down to plot out the disposal of his earthly goods. He gave his wife their home near the ferry, the attached farm, its garden, half the orchard, "a horse to ride, at her pleasure, during her life," two cows, pasture and fodder to keep them, an annual allowance of ten pounds, "and a negro girl" to attend her needs. "Two of the old negroes, Sambo and his wife Mary, are to stay on the farm, and are not to be sold, and they are to have every Saturday afternoon to work for themselves." Excepting these, the patriarch continued, "I leave all my negroes to my . . . sons." In but a brief paragraph Aerson parceled out his possessions to his wife, his daughter, and his four boys, and, with no more emotion than he exercised on his livestock, he decided that *his* Africans would labor the rest of their lives only to look forward to a day when they were aged enough to merit "every Saturday afternoon to work for themselves."[14]

Local slaveholders believed this to be a compassionate way to end their lives. Pieter Praa also thought it humane to consume the productive lives of Africans and then reward them with liberty when age had stripped their value as laborers. In his 1739 will, Praa gave his daughter Annette considerable land in Maspeth Kill (Queens). He excluded "the little island in the said piece of land, which I will my old negro Jack shall have as long as he lives to maintain himself out of it." That the land reverted to the Praa family upon Jack's death was but one problem. Jack was old and feeble enough that Praa was still not certain of his survival. He therefore gave Jack the option of remaining with any of the Praa children and being sustained from the estate. Praa then gave Annette a black child, also named Jack.[15] If these were gestures of justice or contrition, then pity and guilt only conquered Dutch hearts at the end of their (and the Africans') lives.

In 1799 Leffert Lefferts (II) prepared his will and testament at the family estate in Bedford. Dorothy, his wife, was given a yearly stipend of 140 pounds, two rooms in either of the main dwelling houses with access to the kitchen and garden, the use of all silver, china, glass, and cooking ware, and the choice of his furniture. The executors were to supply his wife with firewood and he gave her two horses to ride during her lifetime. Dorothy was also granted "the use and services of my negro male slave called Tom" and "the use and services of my negro female slave called Mary." If Mary, apparently elderly, died before Dorothy, Lefferts instructed his executors to "purchase her another female slave such as she shall choose" out of the estate. Both Africans became the property of Lefferts' children upon Dorothy's death. To his son Jacobus went a 500 pound inheritance, a Queens County farm, house, and meadow, and the enslaved Anthony. His son John received a Bedford, Kings County estate, with farm, house, meadows and woods; the 85 acres including house, farm, and lands at Bedford Pond, Brooklyn; and two lots of woodland in Brooklyn. John also received the Lefferts dwelling house and ground at Cruger's Wharf, Front Street in Manhattan. To his son Leffert Lefferts, he left the cherished Bedford family house and farm, a second Bedford estate, three lots of Brooklyn woodland,

and stretches of meadow in Kings and Queens counties. Leffert and Jacobus were to share a second wharf and estate on Front Street, Manhattan. The patriarch Leffert Lefferts then distributed his horses, cows, oxen, hogs, and remaining Africans, including Little Adam.[16]

In the summer of 1801 Denyse Denyse completed his will. He descended from Teunis Nyssen (de Nyse), a Huguenot-Walloon who, in 1638, emigrated from Utrecht, Holland, to New Amsterdam. Denyse was head of one of the area's oldest Dutch families. He had the largest slaveholding in New Utrecht and a fortune gathered over two centuries. Denyse followed a rather formulaic model for his will. He gave his wife Elizabeth a yearly stipend of fifty pounds, a choice of any room in the family house with any furnishings that she might desire. He instructed his executors to ensure that firewood was cut and left by her door in ample supply and that she be "at liberty to go in the garden or Orchard & take the fruit thereof." He also decided that "Elizabeth shall have the choice of one of my negro Wenches to wait on her." The rest of the estate, including the Africans, was to be divided into thirds. His daughters Ryme and Jane received equal portions, and the final lot was to be divided among the seven children of his deceased son Jaques Denyse. His grandsons Denyse and Gerrit Denyse were appointed executors.[17]

Contrary to Knickerbocker myths, small-scale agriculture did not shelter black families. Local masters had greater reason to rid themselves of the elderly and children because the limits of their workable lands curbed the value of additional labor. They had an incentive to realize such investments in a cash price set by an international market, to transfer these bondspeople to relatives, or to lease them to neighbors. For instance, when Leffert Lefferts willed his Queens County farm and his "Negro man slave called Anthony" to his son Jacobus Lefferts, he noted that Jacobus had already taken possession of Anthony. Similarly, on February 27, 1750 the widow Dina Rapalje bequeathed her valuable Brooklyn ferry farm and all the attached lands and houses to her son John Rapalje and his family. The widow Rapalje did not specify the fate of her servants because John had previously assumed control of the estate and the will simply affirmed prior family decisions; however, by the end of the Revolution, the Brooklyn Rapalje family owned nine Africans and the Flatbush branch held ten. Dutch wills record a general lack of concern about the integrity of black families. Jessica Kross found that in neighboring Newtown, Queens, "slave holdings were broken up at the death of the master. . . . This meant not only a dispersal of the slaves among the white population in each generation, but also the reordering of a slave's social and familial life."[18]

Dutch farmers regularly lent or gave their relatives Africans for domestics or farm work. Family heads then easily appropriated these workers to meet the cyclical demands of harvest while still avoiding their year round support. The Meseroles and Lefferts had holdings that were spread across three counties and at least two provinces so that familial bonds among Africans could figure little in their calculations. These farmers had large families to provide for, and small slaveholdings; thus, even the wealthiest slaveowners could not manage or afford to keep African husbands, wives, and children together. And, over their lifetimes the better men of Kings County actually purchased, owned, and controlled a greater number of Africans than census and local documents record and they inflicted far greater damage on black families than the final acts of their wills confess.

One measure of the destruction was the fact that Africans were typically bought and sold individually. An internal trade moved enslaved Africans across the region. "A Negro Wench, that can do all manner of house-work" is how a 1745 advertisement announced the sale of a black woman. Two years later, a New Yorker was looking to buy a "good Negro Boy . . . of about 14 or 15 Years of Age." In 1748 "a likely Negro Man about thirty-two" and "a likely Negro Man about 26" were being sold along with "a likely young Negro Wench, that can Wash, Iron, Scrub, Cook, or do any Sort of Ketchen [sic] Work." In 1751 an African trained as a cooper and a bondsman skilled as a sailor and a mason were sold by their masters. Slavers arrived weekly at the port of New York. Kings County residents learned of such sales from gossip, posted bills, Manhattan newspapers, and other information about ships arriving at the port. As Jessica Kross has noted, most Long Islanders went to Manhattan to purchase newly arrived Africans.[19]

Slavery in Kings County was intimate, but intimacy did not negate brutality. Small holdings meant that local masters were more dependent upon each individual chattel. Owners and servants usually slept in the same houses, although neither in the same nor comparable quarters; ate the same food, although not at the same table; and worked side by side, although not for the same reasons. The familiarity of masters and slaves in Kings County allowed Africans more opportunities to note the equality of human beings and therefore more solid evidence of the injustice of slavery than servants on large plantations, and that same closeness allowed their owners to react to rumors and reports of conspiracies and rebellions with a more sincere sense of personal fear and betrayal than the masters of large plantations.

The final deeds of the Aerson and Praa wills were products of a system that functioned to erase the familial and social ties of the enslaved and elevate bond-labor as their primary social relation. Slavery necessitated an antagonistic dependency that itself involved a certain social intimacy between owner and enslaved. Intimacy also justified the extraordinary brutality of white people who imagined that the system had been transgressed. As was true throughout the hemisphere, African enslavement in Brooklyn and its neighboring towns was predicated on violence. Masters held the breaking up of families, corporal punishment, mutilation, and death as the ultimate checks on their human property, and Africans reserved running away, sabotage, and revolt as the ultimate defenses against those who treasured them as property. In 1664 Lysbet Antoniosent set her master's New Utrecht house on fire. In hope of striking fear among the servants, the court ordered her to be publicly chained to a stake, strangled, and burned. Her sentence was commuted on the day of execution. In the late seventeenth and early eighteenth centuries, county and town whippers were appointed to ensure compliance with the legislature's prescribed punishments for recalcitrant Africans. A bondswoman in Brooklyn was punished for her escape attempt by having a chunk of one ear cut off and "a large iron padlock" hung through a hole ripped in the other. In 1706 a proclamation from Lord Cornbury to the justices of the peace of Kings County, declared:

> Whereas, I am informed that several negroes in Kings County have assembled themselves in a riotous manner, which, if not prevented, may prove of ill consequence; you and every of you [sic] are therefore hereby required and commanded to take all proper methods for the seizing and apprehending all such negroes in the said county . . . and to secure them in safe custody, that their crimes and actions may be inquired into; and if any of them refuse to submit themselves, then to fire on them, kill or destroy them . . .[20]

In August of that year, Lieutenant Colonel Henry Pilkin of the Kings County militia again ordered soldiers to break up a band of Africans who were gathering rebelliously on Sundays. In Jan Meserole Jr.'s 1712 will, he explicitly gave his wife permission to "sell all or any part" of her inheritance—which included five enslaved people—"as she shall think fitt and convenient." In

1782 his grandson Jacob Meserole, the son of Jan III and Elizabeth Praa, resisted the heady dialogue about liberty and humanity that marked the years of the Revolution by seeking vengeance on his servants from his grave. Jacob Meserole willed a number of Africans to his wife and children. He then sent the servants a clear and stern warning:

> And if any of my Negros shold miss behave and be Disobedient to either my wife or family, then, and in such case, I give my said wife full power, while she remains my widow, to Sell and Dispose any one of my said Negros, or all of them, as She my Said Wife shall think Proper, Either att Publick Vandue or otherwise; and the money arising by such Sail she may lay out for other Negros, which she shall think proper to purchase.[21]

Retribution did not stop Africans from seeking freedom. On March 25, 1712 two dozen white New Yorkers were killed or injured in an uprising, and suspicions of a general revolt swept New York and Kings Counties. The Assembly tried to force freemen to police bondspeople more vigilantly, and the Governor wrote that the only reasonable response was to once again "Encourage the Importation of White Servants." In 1741 mysterious fires in New York led to public paranoia, fantastic attempts to uncover a suspected conspiracy, manhunts through New York and Kings, and trials and executions. Israel and Timothy Horsfeld, two Brooklyn merchants and landowners who emigrated from Liverpool, England, saw several of their valuable Africans put to death for complicity in the Great Negro Plot. Cambridge, owned by Mr. Codweise of Kings, was sold to the Caribbean. The widow Carpenter of Manhattan and Brooklyn lost two bondsmen who were skilled butchers, one was burned at the stake and the other sent out of the colony. Many New Yorkers were convinced that Irish priests had kindled and supported the plot to undermine the Protestant colony and that New York's Africans were in league with Long Island's black population and the Catholic powers, France and Spain. Four white people were put to death in the furor.[22]

Flight was a more common form of resistance than rebelling and conspiring. The great Dutch surnames that today tag Brooklyn landmarks decorated runaway-slave advertisements in the eighteenth century. In 1702 Lord Cornbury sent troops to destroy camps of African maroons who supported themselves by raiding Long Island farms. Africans living among the Natives of Suffolk County repeatedly threatened area farmers. In 1746 Handrick, or Hank, who was owned by Barnet Van Deventer of Flatbush, escaped. Van Deventer instructed all that Hank "speaks good English and Dutch, and tells People he is a free Negro." In 1766 Abraham Schenk of Kings County offered a reward for the return of his valuable servant Jack, who was fluent in Dutch and English and an experienced mill worker. A decade later, as the Declaration of Independence was being signed, Nathaniel (belonging to Henry Wyckhoff of Flatbush) and his brother Jacob (belonging to Jeromus Remsen of Newtown) struck for their liberty to the consternation of both masters. In 1777 Rem Couwenhoven was equally angered when Jaff escaped and renamed himself Jeffrey Johnson. The following year Jacobus Cornell of Flatbush and New Lots offered a five dollar reward and all expenses to the person who returned his English- and Dutch-speaking bondsman Hector. The Revolutionary War added yet another nuance to the problem of controlling the enslaved. In 1783, as the War was being concluded, R. Suydam of "Brooklyne" advertised for his fugitive Peter with a warning to ship captains (undoubtedly British) not to carry off his servant.[23]

The traffic in servants usually ran in the other direction, for Brooklynites were always in the market for human beings and slaving was a major activity in the local area (see table 2.3). Manhattan was a regular destination for slavers and the sprawling Long Island shore became a favorite stop for smugglers who sought to escape customs at New York. "By 1738 Kings County had become proportionately the heaviest slaveholding county in the province, a distinction it retained for most of the remaining life span of slavery in New York," argues Harold X. Connolly. By the American Revolution, Kings County was the state's "slaveholding capital." Because they were so far north, local farmers suspected that Africans transported from the Caribbean or the South were physically inferior or criminals and preferred to buy those carried by local traders or brought directly from Africa. But the Caribbean was a frequent destination and point of origin for Manhattan and Brooklyn ships. Captain Fuerer of Brooklyn was typical of the local slavers who trafficked in a number of goods including people. In the summer of 1751 the *Evening Post* included repeated announcements for vessels arriving from or returning to Antigua, Jamaica, Barbados, the Virgin Islands, Curacao, the Bahamas, the Bay of Honduras, Anguila, and St. Christopher. Ships also regularly arrived from Virginia and the Carolinas. Africans were a precious commodity. On

August 14, 1749 the sloop *Rhode Island* docked at Scuyler's Wharf in Manhattan with "A Fine Parcel of Men, Women, Boys, and Girls slaves, imported direct from Africa" to be sold on board.[24]

TABLE 2.3

Enslaved Africans Brought to New York Colony, Summer 1751

Ship	Date	Origin	Manifest
Sarah	5/1	St. Christopher	Nine Negroes to Hugh Wentworth
Fair Trader	5/2	Jamaica	Two Negro slaves to John Devilson
			Two Negro slaves to James Cox
			One Negro slave to Henry Ludlow
Woolf	5/10	Africa	Sixty-six Negro slaves to Peter Livingston
			Seven Ditto to Ginney Wales
Jolly	5/20	Antigua	Two Negro slaves to D[a]v[i]d Allgeo
			Two Negro slaves to Robert Davidson
Broad Island	5/22	Africa	Thirteen Negro slaves to J[oh]n Livingston
Ruby	5/30	Jamaica	One Negro slave to Thomas Densing
Virgin	6/4	St. Christopher	Four Negro slaves to Henry [illegible]
Sybel	6/23	St. Christopher	One Negro slave to Peter Stuyvesant
			One Negro slave to Henry Beekman
Rebecca	7/4	Africa	Twenty Negro slaves to Garret Cousine
Marlin	7/12	Bermuda	One Negro slave to Joseph Reade
Jersey	7/17	St. Christopher	Two Negroes to Ditto [Peter] Stuyvesant
			Two Negro slaves to Isaac Densing
William & Mary	7/27	St. Christopher	One Negro slave to John Sawyer
			One Negro slave to Thomas Willet
Billy Age [?]	7/29	Virgin Islands	One Negro slave to Richard Durhman[?]
Warren	8/1	Africa	Tenn Negro slaves to Thomas Grenett
Jenny	8/2	St. Christopher	One Negro slave to Ditto [Thomas] Willett
			One Negro slave to John Amory
Fanny	8/14	Jamaica	Five Negro slaves . . . to Lawrence Reade
			One Negro child to John Livingston
Cate [?]	8/14	Jamaica	One Negro slave to Lawrence Reade

Source: Office of the Treasurer, New York (Colony), Manifest Books, Vols. 26–7, in "Reports of Goods Imported to New York, 1740–1775," New York State Archives, Albany.

On the eve of the American Revolution, enslaved Africans were one of the major commodities handled at the port of New York. Ship manifests registered black men, women, and children in lists with casks of rum, pipes of wine, and hogsheads of other liquors. In fact the printed manifest sheets used by New York's tax inspectors put bondspeople first among "the several dutiable Goods and Commodities" that came into port:

[*Captain's Name,*] Master of the [*Type of Ship*] called the [*Name of Ship and Origin*] do swear, that this Manifest is true, and that no more or other Slaves, Wine, Rum, or other distilled Liquors, Shrub, Cocoa, or dutiable Dry-Goods, were on board of the said Vessel when she arrived within this Colony, than those mentioned in this Manifest.[25]

The dominance of Dutch farmers in Kings County explains, in part, the growth and resilience of African slavery in that locale. Kings was by far the most heavily Dutch county in all New York—more than 45 percent of the white population—but daily life was equally influenced by the size and ethnic diversity of its black population. Some bondspeople knew African languages, Spanish, or French, and many spoke English and Dutch because of their daily labors, and it is likely that, in the heavily Dutch areas of the county, enslaved Africans were more fluent in English than their masters. Africans daily moved tons of produce and livestock to the commercial markets on the shores of Brooklyn, Williamsburg, and Manhattan, and they served as a cultural buffer between the parochial Dutch and their somewhat urbane customers. The Old Market in Brooklyn Heights was the primary scene of early trade but a number of specialized markets filled the two shores in later years. Butchers dressed meats and had Africans cart them into Brooklyn Heights or Williamsburg and then ferry them over to their stands in New York's Fly Market. Bondsmen, often trained as butchers themselves, were a regular sight at Fly and carried on much of its business. Markets even served as the sites of black people's celebrations. The Old Market was the scene of Kings County's annual Pinkster celebration, an African-American holiday that coincided with, and played off of, the Dutch Paas festival in the week of Easter. "The village was fairly black with them," wrote Henry Reed Stiles in an attempt at humor, "they came trooping into Brooklyn from the island, men women, and children, sometimes as many as two hundred."[26]

Kings County's farmers maintained their provincialism by becoming more dependent upon black labor, and they provide the best example of why it is impossible to disconnect the region's development from the African presence (see tables 2.4–2.6). In 1790 the Cowenhoven family held 60 bondspeople on farms across the county, the Lefferts claimed 58, the Suydams 49, the Wyckoffs 47, and the Remsens 44. White families even controlled the free black population, who had virtually no option but to sell their labor to local farmers. James Lefferts enslaved 14 black people but still found space on his

New Utrecht estate for a free black worker. His neighbor Nicholas Cowenhoven kept 10 bondspeople and a free person. In Brooklyn, George Remsen had 5 unfree workers and a free person, while his fellow townsman Peter Wyckoff bound 7 people and employed one. John Harnnibal of Bushwick, Elisabeth Thompson of New Utrecht, and Phillis of Brooklyn were the only free black householders. Just 7 of Kings County's 46 free people of color lived apart from white families. That pattern worsened over the next decade. By 1800 well over 60 percent of Kings County's white families enslaved an African, a century earlier only 40 percent owned a servant. Rutgert Van Brunt, Jr., and John Cowenhoven, who tripled their slaveholdings in the prior decade, led all Kings County's masters with 20 bondspeople each, a 250 percent increase over the largest estates of the seventeenth century. In 1800, 70–80 percent of the households in the towns outside Brooklyn included an enslaved African, and, since lending, leasing, and hiring Africans continued, virtually all freeholders experienced mastery. A year later the leading slaveholders in each town were Brooklyn's Peter Bergman, 12; Flatbush's Johannes J. Lott, 16; New Utrecht's Denice Denice (Denyse Denyse), 16; Gravesend's Rutgert Van Brunt, 13; Flatlands' William Vanneys, Simon Lott, Clarick Remsen, and William Cowenhoven, 7; and Bushwick's William Bennett, 11.[27]

Mastery remained a dignified business. In 1806 when the last will and testament of David Van Cotts of Flatlands, an in-law of the Meserole family, was read, Nelly Van Cotts, his wife, received the entire Flatlands estate. Her husband then provided her with an enslaved African, his "black girl [also] named Nelly." Van Cotts' neighbors, the Schencks, who together once owned more than twenty Africans, were also looking to secure their interests in a tightening market for unfree labor. On May 15, 1811 Flatlands' Overseers of the Poor placed a "Black male child named *Peter* as a servant to Nick[olas]. Schenck of Flatlands in Kings County." Peter was indentured until his twenty-first birthday. In exchange Schenck agreed to teach Peter "the duties of a servant" and provide him with sufficient food and clothing that he would not be a charge to the town. Schenck was also ordered to teach Peter to read and to furnish him with a Bible upon his release. In 1819 Schenck indentured an eleven-year-old "black child named Albert as a slave servant to Benjamin Bennit in the town of Flatlands." Albert was to be bound until his twenty-first birthday, two years after New York State Emancipation. He was to be provided a Bible.[28]

TABLE 2.4

Population of Kings County Towns, 1791

Town	Enslaved	Free Black	White
Brooklyn	405	14	1,184
Flatbush	378	12	551
New Utrecht	206	10	346
Gravesend	135	5	286
Flatlands	137	0	286
Bushwick	171	5	364
Total	1,432	46	3,017

Source: *Return of the Whole Number of Persons within the Several Districts of the United States, According to "An Act Providing for the Enumeration of the Inhabitants of the United States," Passed March the First, One Thousand Seven Hundred and Ninety-One* (Philadelphia: Childs and Swaine, 1791), 36.

TABLE 2.5

Population of Kings County Towns, 1801

Town	Enslaved	Free Black	White
Brooklyn	445	196	1,737
Flatbush	341	39	566
New Utrecht	213	39	526
Gravesend	162	11	316
Flatlands	128	13	352
Bushwick	188	34	434
Total	1,477	332	3,931

Source: Census of Brooklyn, 1801. Long Island, New York Census, 1801, Census of Kings County, collection of the New-York Historical Society.

Kings County's white residents frequently worked the technicalities between slavery and servitude in order to hold onto their laborers and their way of life. They transported black people across state lines, intimidated their chattel into continued service, and lied about the ages and terms of their human property. Their reputation was apparently well known for New Yorkers interested in trading in enslaved Africans or finding runaways were increasingly turning to Brooklyn's *Long Island Star* to correspond with their comrades. Simply trading in people, however, paled next to the behavior of Kings citizens. In 1800 the New York Manumission Society charged that Captain Gilford of Flatbush was holding a free black woman from Nova Scotia in bondage. Peter Van Roden of Brooklyn bought Peggy Hull and sold her out of state before she could become free. Justice William Livingston of Kings County asked the Manumission Society to intervene on behalf of Harry, a servant who had been promised his freedom and fifty dollars in his owner's will. John Lott, whose family bound twenty-six Africans on their Flatlands farms in 1790, seized Harry and his purse. The executors of the estate of Eleanor Simmons listed Margaret Ansley as a runaway, although Peter Courtelyou of Brooklyn witnessed her emancipation. (In 1790 the Courtelyous of Brooklyn and New Utrecht claimed thirty-two Africans.) A 24-year-old black woman was "sold for life" at auction in the Old Ferry Market. Administrator William Arnold did not display the bondswoman at the market, but made her available for private inspection in the preceding days, because public auctions were considered distasteful. Jacobus Van Nyun of New Utrecht illegally removed Lydia Hill to New Jersey where she remained enslaved. A store on the Williamsburg border sold a 15-year-old black boy, "strong and in good health." A 10-year-old black girl from Brooklyn was bound out until she was 25, a 15-year term of service offered even though slavery was to end in eight years. By 1820, when bondage was in marked decline almost everywhere else in the state, half of the African Americans in Kings County remained enslaved.[29]

In 1800 Mary McCrea of Manhattan, who traced herself to Dutch Kings and New York counties, used a different strategy to secure her interests in the face of slavery's tenuous future. She indentured Flora, a 28-year-old black woman, and James, her 10-year-old son, to Samuel Sackett for terms of ten and twenty-four years respectively. Two years earlier McCrea had indentured 11-year-old Ophee to William Bodle of New Jersey for eighteen years.[30] Thus, McCrea received cash for her servants, avoided the job of overseeing them, and had the option of continuing to bind them, if legal, at the end of their terms.

Even voluntary manumissions offer contradictory evidence about white people's commitment to bondage. Bernard Oblenis of Flatbush simply released William Thomas, age 26, and recorded his freedom with the clerk. Eve was freed by Flatbush's Allety Oblenis. Similarly John Freeke legally emancipated the 26-year-old Sall. But not all manumissions were this simple. When Hendrick Lott liberated Jude, Flatland's overseers were concerned that the bondsman was too old and no longer self-sufficient. Flatbush merchant John Franklin purchased Harry with a promise that he would be freed after a brief term of service. Franklin then sold

Harry to Thomas Walden of Mount Pleasant for fifty dollars and with no stipulation that the man be emancipated. The guilty merchant later tried to secure Harry's freedom, and both masters eventually agreed to abandon all claims to Harry.[31]

Terms of service in recorded manumissions were a compromise between masters who were desperate to hold on to their human property and increasingly recalcitrant bondspeople. Shane White has persuasively argued that the emancipation law coupled with a worsening economic climate gave Africans the leverage to bargain for their freedom. Running away became an option for a greater number of servants as the free black population increased and the end of bondage grew closer. On June 7, 1819 Nicholas Schenck—whose family had married into the Remsen and Wyckoff fortunes—had his Flatlands neighbor Hendrick Lott witness an agreement that he was making with one of his servants. Schenck promised to free Harry Ferguson in exchange for two years of obedient service and fifty dollars.

> Know all men by these presents that I[,] Nicholas Schenck of the Town of Flatlands in Kings County in the State of New York, do hereby promise for myself[,] my heirs[,] executors and administrators, that in case my Negro-man-slave named Harry Ferguson, *shall faithfully serve me* in his usual occupation as a farmer, and my commands obey, *for the time or term of two years* from the date hereof. *And within the said term pay* unto me, my heirs[,] executors or administrators *the sum of fifty dollars* that at the expiration as aforesaid I will manumit the said Harry from slavery.[32]

If masters skirted the law then so did the enslaved. Absconding became epidemic in the decades before emancipation. In October 1811 George Benson, the 14-year-old slave of Brooklyn's Joseph Fox, escaped. A few months later Fox's neighbor, John Hunter, recorded the flight of his 19-year-old "Negro fellow," Tom, and feared that the former servant might take to the sea.[33]

The War of 1812 presented many opportunities for Africans to solve bondage through flight. "Stop the Runaways!" read Josiah Woodhull and Isaiah Terry's plea for the return of their two bondsmen. Rufus had escaped Suffolk County with Lewis who carried off "a number of his master's shirts and other clothing." Earlier, Hendrick Suydam of Kings County was demanding the capture of Harry, a 25-year-old, who Suydam described as "very artful," "fond of liquor," and a good house servant and farmer. Manhattan's John Rice seemed eager to regain Jane, a 20-year-old "Negro wench" with "large breast[s]." Rice feared that Jane had returned to Flatbush, where she was born. J. J. Cossart was hunting

Mary, a "remarkably short and slim, yellowish complexion" woman who "speaks broken English, and generally smiles when she speaks." Mary fled Foster's Meadow but Cossart was sure that "her French appearance and manner of dressing will detect her." Jaques Cropsey of New-Utrecht, Kings County, warned (British) ship captains not to transport his 20-year-old servant, Sam.[34]

In 1819, a year after the founding of Brooklyn's first independent black church, fugitive Africans seemed to be overtaking the county. Sam Johnson, an enslaved 10-year-old mulatto, liberated himself to the dismay of Cornelius Van Cotts of Bushwick, and a bondsman named Charles loosened himself from the Wallabout estate of Jacobus Lott. Lott forbade all from "harboring or employing said runaway under penalty of the law." Johannes Stoothoff of Flatlands was particularly cross when his bilingual servant Dan, age 22, absconded. What most bothered Stoothoff was that Dan had permission to take leave for one day to look for a new master. Dan did exactly that when he decided to own himself but the arrangement was not to Stoothoff's liking. Similarly, 38-year-old Yaff abandoned the Flatbush farm of Levi Hart on which he was enslaved. John Hegeman of Flatbush suffered the loss of two bondspeople, "a negro wench, named BET, and her boy, named SAM, about nine years old." The 28-year-old mother took with her "a considerable quantity of clothing, and other articles." Abraham Selover of Bedford was so vexed when his 25-year-old bondsman Peet escaped that he asked that hunters return him "or confine him in some jail." Garrit Vanderveer of Flatbush had his Bet, 28, flee (he warned his neighbors not to trust her). while 17-year-old Millane fled Brooklyn's Losee Van Nostrand.[35]

TABLE 2.6

Populations of Kings County Towns, 1820

Town	White Men	White Women	Black People	Total
Brooklyn	3,001	2,972	828	6,801
Navy Yard				366
Bushwick	365	387	182	934
Flatbush	376	357	294	1,027
Flatlands	194	197	121	512
Gravesend	226	199	109	534
New Utrecht	422	379	208	1,009
Totala	4,584	4,491	1,742	11,183

aThe first three columns do not include the 366 people at the Navy Yard.
Source: Alden Spooner, *Spooner's Brooklyn Directory, For the Year 1822* (Brooklyn: Office of the Long Island Star, May 1822), 51.

In 1827 Losee Van Nostrand became a managing director of the new Brooklyn Savings Bank,36 making a personal transition from slaveholder to capitalist that mirrored Brooklyn's maturation into a commercial city. Although bondage created the conditions for the rise of bourgeois culture, it is not easy to imagine that a city could evolve from slavery. On the day that emancipation came to New York State, Brooklyn was less than a decade from its city charter and servitude had shaped its social and political relationships for two centuries. The town had a population of about 10,000 and the population of the county was only twice that number. Brooklyn was little more than a wealthy village, and the region was more impressive in its potential than its reality. Perhaps slavery's most lasting effect was not displayed physically in villages and towns but rather appeared in the Dutch and English residents' insatiable appetite for the fruits of other people's labor.

Unprecedented growth and incredible wealth lie just beyond the horizon as this nobility reluctantly abandoned being a small, isolated master class to become the commercial middlemen of a much greater slaveowning society. The end of servitude in New York State did not bring an end to slavery's dominion.

CHAPTER THREE

"Rugged Industries"

The Commercial Revolution
in Kings County,
1797–1876

In times gone by, they were a kind-hearted, quiet people, fond of amusement, always looking upon the bright side of things, never worrying over
coming misfortunes, but content to live in abiding faith upon a literal
rendering of that Scripture which says: "Take no thought for the morrow.
Sufficient unto the day is the evil thereof. Take no thought, saying What shall
we eat? or, What shall we drink? or, Wherewithal shall we be clothed?"

Thus it happened too often that want came, and improvidence
brought with it many misfortunes; and they have begun to dwindle away
and disappear before the rugged industries in which neither their taste
nor their physical strength enables them to take a share.

—Gertrude Lefferts Vanderbilt, *Social History of Flatbush*

It is not an inconsiderable advantage, either, resulting from The Fair, that
Brooklyn has been made known by it to the country at large, as it was not
before; as a city of wealth, liberality, energy, and great public spirit; young
in years, but rapidly striding toward a foremost place among the foremost
of our great and prosperous American towns. It is not a mere dormitory
for New York merchants.

The Drum Beat
March 5, 1864

On Thursday afternoon, September 1, 1859, Captain Thomas Smith called
the New York Harbor Police to the schooner *Neptune's Bride*, which was
docked at Atlantic Basin in Brooklyn. On board they were shown the decaying
corpse of a black man seated upright atop a freight of turpentine and rosin
with his head bowed to his chest and his right arm resting on a barrel. "It was
dressed in blue shirt and overalls, and on one side was a kettle of soup;
under his head was a small bundle of clothing, and on the other side was a

bag of Indian meal," read the *New York Tribune*.[1] Almost immediately it was deduced that the unknown man was a fugitive from slavery.

A coroner's inquest revealed the details of the death. The young man, about 23 years old, boarded either in St. Mary's, Georgia, or in North Carolina. He was likely from Georgia as the crew attested that the hold was not opened after clearing that port. He hid behind the cargo after it was loaded, the hatches were sealed with him inside, and during transport the deadly turpentine fumes filled the space. The crew, knowing the volatility of their freight, never opened the hold. The man was overcome while taking his meal. When the ship docked in Brooklyn, stevedores unsealed the cargo and were met by a foul smell of unknown source, reported the *New York Times*. While unloading the barrels they discovered the body and "a stampede from the hold took place." *The Evening Post* estimated that the corpse had been decaying for eleven days. It was so decomposed that the frightened crew refused to help with its removal or return to work. A police officer from the Third Precinct in Brooklyn finally convinced some of the men to help clear the remains. The coroner was notified.[2]

It is grimly appropriate that the body of a black man who met one of the many pitfalls of a freedom journey was delivered to one of Brooklyn's busiest ports sealed in a commercial ship. These events might suggest that Brooklyn was a destination for black Southerners who sought freedom; in fact, the corpse was a gruesome reminder that Brooklyn was one of a number of Northern cities that consumed, received, traded, and vied for commercial dominance over the products of slavery. The route that the runaway took connected Brooklyn's economy to that of the South. It was a link that white Brooklynites knew well—they saw slavery's yield enter their city's ports and fill its storage houses and expand its commerce and create its jobs and give rise within it to wholly new classes of men with wholly new relationships to their fellows and change its very physical appearance. White Brooklynites' way of life and their ambitions tied them to the South and, ultimately, to African bondage; and, their economic dependence upon the Southern trade was the catalyst of their belief that nature intended black people for servitude rather than free labor.

Death is not a fitting substitute for freedom yet this man risked his life for liberty; not political freedom, but that fundamental individual hegemony upon which all else rested. A man who was enslaved in Georgia arrived dead in Brooklyn, and his story does not easily fit into Northern or Southern history. It belongs to the greater record of the contest to control and define the labor of Africans in the United States, a history that encompasses both region and race.

This enslaved African was the victim of a struggle for commercial greatness that began during the Revolution. The United States had no London and that fact was not lost to many of those who hungered for independence. They understood that urbanization was the shadow of economic success. They also knew that there were few towns or cities in North America with enough significance to impose their names on the common culture and none with the commercial grandeur to attract free workers. During the 1790s London gained its one-millionth inhabitant while New York City began the decade with only 45,000. The most significant commercial cities of the nation—Boston, Philadelphia, New Orleans, Baltimore, and New York—barely approached the size and productivity of second-tier British cities like Liverpool, Birmingham, Glasgow, and Manchester. In 1776 Adam Smith seized a chance to ridicule the colonials by noting that the populations of Peruvian and Mexican cities "exceed greatly those of Boston, New York, and Philadelphia, the three greatest cities of the English colonies." He did not trouble himself to extend a comparison to England and the Continent.[3]

Brooklyn was so insignificant that its name remained undetermined, wrote a long-time resident, having gone through an evolution that included "Breukelen, Breukland, Breuklyn, Broucklen, Brookland, Brookline, and even Brocklandia." In 1780 when Alexander Hamilton, a New York resident and a graduate of Kings (Columbia) College who fought in Kings County during the Battle of Long Island, proposed a counterattack on Brooklyn to George Washington, he used three different spellings for the target of the assault.[4]

Over time Brooklyn earned a reputation as a major commercial and industrial city, but its path to wealth tied it to slavery for the rest of that institution's history in the United States. "Practically all Brooklynites were against slavery but few wished to make a fuss about it," wrote Ralph Foster Weld in 1950.[5] His assertion was based more on faith than fact. White Brooklynites continued to seek prosperity in the subordination of black people, now in the South. Race remained the ideological medium of social relations because a new exploitative relationship had emerged. Kings County's rise as an industrial center placed its white residents in a dilemma:

their commercial revolution was directly tied to Southern slavery, yet industrial capitalism and its attendant free-labor ideology challenged the primacy of bondage in the nation. Thus, they viewed servitude in complex terms that never allowed for a simple choice between slavery and freedom. They judged bondage against local concerns about urban development, employment, the concentration of wealth, and commercial expansion; regional biases over national banks, currency, tariffs, and Westward expansion; and broader issues like immigration, national growth, and political stability. Immigrant workers recorded their support for slavery in vulgar statements and violent acts. Native-born white Protestants shrank toward an amoral defense of bondage as an issue of property rights, but that was not an abstract stance and to assume that it was is to credit them with an objectivity that they never actually enjoyed. Their loyalty to slavery and the wealth that it produced was affirmed in the decades after emancipation in New York State. Constitutional polemics could bring a moral innocence to the city's relationship to African bondage but the anger and violence with which white and immigrant Brooklynites greeted slavery's detractors proved that they were neither antislavery nor indifferent.

In the decades before the Civil War, Brooklynites shifted their investments from people and land into commercial activities driven by Southern slavery. At the center of this transition was a number of local banks that stabilized the money and credit markets and secured investments. The rise of professional banking was an important step in capitalizing the county's business transformation. Some of Kings County's most prominent families played key roles in bringing savings and commercial banks to the region (see table 3.1). Brooklyn industrialist Whitehead J. Cornell—of the old Dutch, slaveholding Duyckinck and Cornell families—was typical. By 1853 he held a $10,000 stock investment in Brooklyn's Atlantic Bank alone. Brooklyn and Williamsburg followed New York into a banking revolution that culminated, in October 1853, with the opening of the New York Clearing House, an association organized by the major banks to process checks, keep debit and credit ledgers, and drastically reduce the exchange of money and notes between banks. In its first full year of operation the Clearing House handled $5.7 billion in bank transactions and at the close of the Civil War that number exceeded $26 billion.[6]

TABLE 3.1

Slaveowning Families Among the Founders of Kings County Banks

Institution	Date	Select Founders and Officers
Long Island Bank	1824	Leffert Lefferts, pres.; John Vandeveer, Jacob Hicks, Nehemiah Denton, Silas Butler, David Baylis, John and Samuel Gerritson, Barnet Johnson, George Sampson, Gerrit Smith, and John Vanderbilt.
LI Farmers and Mechanics'	1824	Jeremiah Lott, Losee Van Nostrand.
Brooklyn Savings Bank	1827	Adrian Van Sinderin, pres.; Abraham Vandeveer, treas.; Hezekiah Pierrepont, Joshua Sands, Adam Mercein, Losee Van Nostrand, Charles Doughty, Clarence Sackett, Alden Spooner, Thomas Everit.
Atlantic State Bank	1836	John Schenck, 2nd pres.; Peter Cornell, John and Jeremiah Lott, George Bergen, Samuel Smith.
Brooklyn Bank	1836	Sidney Cornell, R. B. Duyckinck, E. D. White, and Thomas Clark.
Bank of Williamsburgh	1839	Bank charter never actually activated.
South Brooklyn Savings	1850	Tunis Bergen, John Skillman, James Van Nostrand.
City Bank of Brooklyn	1850	John Skillman, pres.; James Van Nostrand, Henry Boerum, Garret Bergen.
Williamsburgh Savings Bank	1851	Richard Ten Eyck, Norman Van Nostrand, Nicholas Wyckoff.
Mechanics' Bank	1852	Joseph Johnson, George and John Bergen, Abraham Bergen, Loomis Ballard, Daniel Chauncey.
Williamsburgh City Bank	1852	Richard Berry, William Covert, John Furman, William Pease, Abraham Vandervoort, Nicholas Wyckoff.
Farmers and Citizens' Bank of Long Island	1852	George Vandeverg, Jr., Thomas Van Sant, William Tyson, John Seaman.
Manufacturers' National Bank of New York	1853	Aaron Underhill, John DeBevoise, Edwin Johnson.
Dime Savings Bank	1859	Abraham Beekman, George Bergen.
Nassau National Bank	1859	A. M. White, and Moses Odell.
Kings County Savings Instit.	1860	John Furman, Jeremiah Johnson, Jr.
Dime Savings of W'burg.	1864	George Smith, Silas Brainard, George Nichols.
German Savings Bank	1866	None
Germania Savings Bank	1867	None
Greenpoint Savings	1868	Archibald Meserole, pres.; William Meserole, C. Von Bergen.
Commercial Bank	1868	Alexander Underhill, William Bogert, Job Johnson.
Fulton Bank of Brooklyn	1870	None.
Bushwick Savings Bank	1873	Peter Wyckoff, A. M. Suydam, John Nostrand.

Source: Henry Reed Stiles, ed., *The Civil, Political, Professional and Ecclesiastical History and Commercial and Industrial Record of the County of Kings and the City of Brooklyn, N.Y., From*

1683 to 1884, 2 Vols. (New York: W. W. Munsell, 1884), 1: 619–28; Henry Reed Stiles, *A History of the City of Brooklyn. Including the Old Town and Village of Brooklyn, the Town of Bushwick, and the Village and City of Williamsburgh*, 3 Vols. (Brooklyn: published by subscription, 1867–1870), 2: passim; William H. Smith, comp., *The Brooklyn City and Kings County Record: A Budget of General Information; with a Map of the City, an Almanac, and an Appendix, containing the New City Charter* (Brooklyn: William H. Smith, 1855), 65–70.

Many of Brooklyn's better men quickly learned the lucrative business of being New York's neighbor. Brooklyn was "the first and most important of the modern 'ferry suburbs,'" writes Kenneth T. Jackson. In 1816 it was officially chartered as a village. Within a decade the lords of Brooklyn Heights—Hezekiah Pierrepont, Jacob Hicks, Joshua Sands, David Leavitt, George Hall, Tunis Joralemon, and Adrian Van Sinderen to name a few—who dominated the waterfront and the government, were already imagining Brooklyn as a city and a commercial rival of New York. Dividing up the valuable lands, Pierrepont and his fellows advertised the village's bucolic spaces, river views, and proximity to Manhattan. In 1826 David Leavitt purchased multiple lots at Brooklyn Heights along Columbia, Clark, and Willow Streets. "With Mr. Hezekiah Pierrepont, Mr. Van Sinderen, and perhaps one other, he controlled the land on the waterside, from Fulton Street to about the present Remsen Street," recalled his daughter Elizabeth Leavitt Howe. By 1853 Whitehead J. Cornell held fifty prime Brooklyn lots valued at well over $50,000. Brooklyn's lower costs and taxes attracted Manhattanites. Its shore constantly seduced businesses to leave crowded New York and many companies erected "large, custom-built plants," contend two of the area's historians, where "all the processes of production could be centralized." In the following decades the rest of the shore was slowly filled by the excess trade of New York. Aggressive advertising drew residents like the Manhattan master craftsman Duncan Phyfe, who by 1815 had a sizable investment in Brooklyn realty, and affluent China trader Abiel Abbott Low.7

Hezekiah Beers Pierrepont was unarguably Brooklyn's chief promoter and the first to fully exploit its real estate. He was the great-grandson of James Pierpont, a seventeenth-century New Haven minister and a founder of Yale College. But Hezekiah Pierrepont was a ruined Manhattan merchant—the house of Leffingwell & Pierrepont having been destroyed by piracy—when he met Anna Marie Constable. By marrying the daughter of William Constable, New York State's largest landowner, Pierrepont acquired about a half million acres of upstate property. He purchased a mansion in Brooklyn Heights and immediately moved to the center of local business and politics. He was on the committee that secured Brooklyn's village charter, and, "combining the roles of land speculator and local politician," he governed the planning and development of the village into a city while carefully insuring his own financial success. As chair of a street committee, Pierrepont even employed his own surveyor to create a counter proposal to a village street plan and maximize the value of his holdings. He then drove his plan past his colleagues. Real estate soon became Pierrepont's primary occupation and he and his sons, Henry and William, regularly visited all of the holdings. Pierrepont targeted his investments by gleaning information about transportation improvements, particularly those affecting the Southern and Western commerce through the Erie Canal, the local port, and the wharves. When he died on August 11, 1838 Pierrepont's estate included sixty acres of prime Brooklyn property; the towns of Pierrepont, Lewisville, and Stockholm; and additional lands in Oswego, Jefferson, Lewis, St. Lawrence, and Franklin counties.[8]

Henry Waring, another early business failure, was saved by the Southern commerce. In 1813, at the age of 36, he moved to Brooklyn to partner in a naval store. Waring's investment paid off when he began winning large contracts to transport Southern goods. He dedicated his ships to that trade, and in less than a decade he was one of the better men of Brooklyn. He served a five-year stint as a village trustee. He was a director of Long Island Bank at its founding and one of the first trustees of Brooklyn Savings Bank.[9]

A descendant of the county's largest slaveowning family, Leffert Lefferts enjoyed a far lengthier family tradition of governing Kings County (particularly Bedford and Flatbush) by blending personal interests with the public trust. He descended from two of the county's largest slaveowning families, being born, on April 12, 1774, the fifth child of Leffert Lefferts (II) and Dorothy (Cowenhoven) Lefferts. He finished Columbia College at age twenty and then read law in the offices of Egbert Benson. On April 5, 1800 Lefferts was appointed to his father's former position as county clerk. He conducted the people's business from an upper room in the Lefferts' Bedford Corners (today's Central Brooklyn) home. Five years later he became a commissioner in the chancery. In 1823 Lefferts was appointed judge of Kings County. He began the movement to charter a local bank which bore fruit in the Long Island Bank (1824) under his presidency. By 1847 Leffert Lefferts, David Leavitt, and Peter Schermerhorn were among the handful of Brooklynites worth a half-million dollars, and the Lefferts family, claiming about three-quarters of a million, sat with the Schermerhorns, whose combined wealth was over a million, at the top of the Kings County elite.[10]

In 1809 Samuel Smith left his family's Huntington, Long Island, home and his work as a cooper to come to Brooklyn. His career as an itinerant tenant farmer ended in 1811 when he married Eliza, the daughter of Tunis Joralemon, one of Brooklyn's leading property owners. A year later he paid $6,000 for fourteen acres of Fort Greene land. In 1815 he enlarged his holdings by buying six acres for $3,000. In 1818 $10,000 bought him eight additional acres. In less than a decade Smith acquired real estate that stretched from Fort Greene to Brooklyn Heights and included what would become central commercial and transportation arteries. The latter was guaranteed when Smith was appointed commissioner of highways in Brooklyn, a post that he held for eight years. Smith was also president of the Atlantic Bank and a director of the Brooklyn Bank.[11]

Across the East River, where Brooklyn, even after its city charter was granted in 1834, was being derided as New York's "bed chamber," a "dormitory," or, more insulting to Brooklyn's elite men of wealth, a "woman's city" dominated by residential matters rather than the *manly* art of commerce, concern over the growth and potential of Kings County was already brewing. Gendered descriptions did not eliminate the fact that New York's advantages over Brooklyn were slight and often artificial, nor did they lessen the pull that the self-described City of Churches had on Manhattan's wealthiest families.

The longest lasting of the many conflicts between the two—New York's control of the East River and a large strip of the Brooklyn shore as granted by ancient charters—dated back to the seventeenth century and had sporadically flared ever since. In 1814 the successful voyage of Robert Fulton's steam-powered ferry, the *Nassau*—funded in part by Hezekiah Pierrepont, who anticipated the ferry's impact upon his waterfront lands—sparked the river war once again. "The inhabitants of Long Island, particularly, will find this a most interesting improvement; as the ferries, heretofore, however well conducted, have been inconvenient, and to many a subject of dread," noted the *Long Island Star*. Walt Whitman, who was born on Long Island in 1819 and grew up in Brooklyn, recalled the ferry as one of the passions of his childhood. A lengthy poem to the Brooklyn ferry and its riders, included in Whitman's famous *Leaves of Grass*, described

> Crowds of men and women attired in the usual costumes, how curious you are to me!
> On the ferry-boats the hundreds and hundreds that cross, returning home, are more curious to me than you suppose,
> And you that shall cross from shore to shore years hence are more to me, and more in my meditations, than you might suppose.

By 1840 four ferries joined Brooklyn to Manhattan: the Fulton, the Main

Street, the Navy Yard, and the South. The ferries were connected to each other and to the major roads by horse-drawn omnibuses. (George Johnson was one of the few black men to have worked as an omnibus driver.) Lydia Maria Child, author and abolitionist, innocent of the river wars around her, became a regular ferry traveler during her stays in New York and Brooklyn. She wrote in 1841, "for six cents one can exchange the hot and dusty city [of New York] for Staten Island, Jersey, or Hoboken; three cents will convey you to Brooklyn, and twelve and a half cents pays for a most beautiful sail of ten miles, to Fort Lee. In addition to the charm of rural beauty, all these places are bathed by deep waters."[12]

The old families who held on to Kings County land for two centuries profited handsomely from Manhattan's commercial explosion. Brooklyn Heights, noted Child, was not just heavenly, it had "a magnificent view of the city of New-York, the neighboring islands, and the harbour; and . . . they are never unvisited by a refreshing and invigorating breeze." Land speculation ran wild across the Heights, and farms quickly gave way to streets, lots, and brick row houses. "A few years ago, these salubrious heights might have been purchased by the city [of New York] at a very low price, and converted into a promenade, of beauty unrivaled throughout the world; but speculators have now laid hands upon them, and they are digging them away to make room for stores, with convenient landings from the river." Not all Kings County's residents wanted to be a lesser New York. On a trip to visit the sculptured Greenwood Cemetery—of which Hezekiah Pierrepont's son was a trustee—Child picked up the apocryphal tale of an old farmer in Gowanus who was offered $70,000 for his estate by speculators convinced of Brooklyn's destiny. Underscoring the uneasiness that many residents had with urban growth, the story claimed that

> $10,000 in silver and gold, were placed on the table before him; he looked at them, fingered them over, seemed bewildered, and agreed to give a decisive answer on the morrow. The next morning found him a raving maniac! And thus he now roams about, recklessly tearing up the flowers he once loved so dearly, and keeping his family in continual terror.[13]

Northern Kings County underwent a similar process. In 1827 Abraham Meserole and a small committee of men secured Williamsburg's village charter and had themselves appointed trustees. As in Brooklyn, land speculation was uncontrolled in Williamsburg and Bushwick. In 1851 Williamsburg was chartered as a city. The great coup of Brooklyn's developers was the 1854 annexation of the City of Williamsburg and the Town of Bushwick, making Brooklyn one of the five largest cities in the nation and a key commercial center in its own right.[14]

For families like the Meseroles this brought even greater fortune. In 1726 Jan Meserole III, son-in-law of Pieter Praa, controlled three-quarters of Greenpoint and the family's home at Key Kuits farm and meadow. "There in the old homestead of his Grandfather and father[,] he and his wife Elizabeth Praa lived about forty years, and there his large family of five sons and five daughters were born, reared and married. The daughters all married young men of their native town whose names are recognized among the most respectable and leading families of the town of Bushwick during the succeeding one hundred years," wrote Walter Monfort Meserole of his family origins. The output of these lands alone left the Meserole clan comfortable and well provided for, but with time the value of the properties inflated. "The old 'Key Kuits' farm was oc[c]upied by the emigrant Jan Meserole and his descendants continuously for nearly One hundred and seventy five years," noted Meserole. That succession was broken by the bounty of the antebellum years. In 1850 Abraham Meserole—a clerk at the New York Customs House whose salary "is one paid by the merchants"—and Maria and John Miller (Meserole descendants) imposed a street grid onto Key Kuits and sold it. The family still had major real estate holdings in Kings County well into the twentieth century.[15]

Brooklynites were uncomfortably impressed with the velocity of slavery's wealth in the two cities: the fantastic rise of trans-Atlantic commerce and the results on banking, shipbuilding, insurance, warehousing, and manufacturing. For most white people in Kings County simple material interests more than balanced any moral hyperbole about individual freedom and justice. The money, the goods, the ships, the industry, the smoke, the crowds, the misery, the bustle, the political agitation, the swelling population, the vision of men falling, the stories of men rising, land speculation, and the prosperity of local farmers all made it difficult to see slavery in anything but complex terms. They agreed with George Templeton Strong, the Manhattan attorney and frequent visitor to Brooklyn, who confessed to his diary that "slave-holding is no sin" and "the designs of Northern Abolitionists are very particularly false, foolish, wicked, and unchristian." In 1846 Isaac Van Anden, the publisher of the Democratic, proslavery *Brooklyn Eagle*, ended the brief tenure of its proslavery, Democratic, editor Walt Whitman because of his sympathy for the Wilmot

Proviso, a measure introduced in Congress to bar slavery from any territories acquired in the Mexican-American War.[16] Whitman was fired for not being proslavery enough. After all, given the way that slavery shaped their lives, Brooklynites could hate but still surrender to bondage.

The local business community had definite proslavery leanings. Philip S. Foner, in *Business and Slavery*, exposed the ways in which commerce generated Southern sympathies among Manhattan businessmen, loyalties that spawned political defenses of and financial participation in an illegal slave trade and put New York businessmen in the position of resisting any government efforts to disrupt or police slaving. The New York–Long Island area remained a haven for those trafficking in human beings. As early as 1800 the Standing Committee of the New York Manumission Society was decrying the "very general" practice of cheating the manumission law by transporting "Negroes from this to the Southern states . . . from whence they are reshipped to the West Indies." The city also kept an open door for slave smugglers. "Any day of the week, slaves could be discovered stowed in the holds on board ships docked in New York harbor. They were brought from Africa, the West Indies, South America, and the American South, bound for reshipment to Southern plantations," notes Anthony Gronowicz in his history of pre–Civil War Manhattan politics. Looking at the period from 1857 to 1862, Robert Trent Vinson argues that "New York City enjoyed the dubious distinction of being one of the world's leading slaving ports." Sympathetic federal judges and a bustling economy attracted these unsavory merchants to the Empire City, and from Manhattan illegal ventures were directed, financed, and insured almost unmolested. Official leniency was guaranteed when President James Buchanan appointed Tammany gangster and proslavery thug Isaiah Rynders as United States marshal for the New York Southern District. "Many of the slavers were fitted out in New York City," writes Kenneth Stampp, "and some of their cargoes were unloaded with scarcely any attempt at secrecy." As late as 1861 the *Augusta* was impounded and its crew arrested for illegally importing the enslaved at Greenport, Long Island.[17]

Trafficking in people was a logical outgrowth of an economy fueled by enslaved labor. The product of unfree people's toil fed commercial activity in New York. Local merchants monopolized the export trade of the South. Slavery's yield—especially cotton, sugar, and tobacco—daily passed through their harbor. By the 1820s Southern enslaved laborers were feeding the world cotton market. Within two decades cotton was more than half of the United

States' entire export trade. England was the world's cotton textile producer and the South was its supplier, providing better than 70 percent of all England's staple imports. The South had an even greater command of the short-staple cotton market. However Manhattan financed, transported, and traded the crop and as a result built many of its great financial and futures houses. "From New York's vast capital resources—and the resources that it was able to tap in Europe—came the credit necessary for the operation of the plantation system," writes Harold D. Woodman. New York businessmen controlled the "Cotton Triangle," shipping the crop from Southern port cities to Europe where they exchanged it for finished goods and immigrants, transporting those to New York, and, finally, returning to the South with merchandise from the Empire City. At times the process was reversed and cotton was brought directly to New York where it was stored. Henry Wysham Lanier, in his history of New York banking, wrote that "Cotton was 'king,' indeed, both in New York and in the South: a lot would change owners half a dozen times in a week without leaving the factor's hands." In the antebellum decades warehouses on both banks of the East River were giving space to cotton.[18]

Brooklynites wanted only a piece of the Southern trade that passed through the harbor. In the late eighteenth century Brooklyn and Williamsburg became storage centers for Southern and Caribbean goods. In 1797 Jonathan Thompson—born in Suffolk County, Long Island in 1773—opened the Brooklyn warehousing firm of Gardiner, Thompson and Co. Three years later Thompson was the sole owner of the business. In 1820 President James Monroe appointed Thompson collector of the New York Customs House, a position that he held for a decade and that he used to bolster his investment in the local commercial storage industry. In July 1823 Collector Thompson moved one of the Customs House's stores to a building that he had constructed on Furman Street in Brooklyn. After leaving office in 1829, Thompson took advantage of that new relationship by purchasing riverside property, expanding his old houses, and building new stores. Although commonly called the "White Cotton Stores," Thompson's houses also received large quantities of sugar. Thompson's first major rival was Hezekiah Pierrepont. In 1819 when Pierrepont's gin distillery folded, he attempted to find a business suitable to that prime Brooklyn location. Eventually the Pierrepont stores appeared, winning government and private contracts for cotton and sugar. Among the Kings County sugar warehouses that followed were Roberts stores; Prentice; Woodruf & Robinson; Baltic; Union; and

Schencks. The Fulton stores housed tobacco.[19] Within a generation, Brooklyn's businessmen had snatched the lucrative commercial storage industry.

Warehousing was the embryo of the local commercial revolution. The business fed off the obvious fact that, besides storing goods awaiting inspection at the Customs House, warehouses could hold such commodities while Wall Street brokers negotiated their sale, speculated in their futures, or waited for market changes. An excellent example is available at Brooklyn's Atlantic Docks, a vast stretch of piers and stores that Daniel Richards erected in the Twelfth Ward over the opposition of many New York businessmen. Opened in 1844, Atlantic Docks provided warehouses for new businesses needing waterfront space and sped up the process by which Kings County came to dominate the storage of merchandise passing through the port of New York. One of the immediate results was Brooklyn's absolute control of the profitable business of storing Western wheat and grain. By the Civil War, the Pioneer Tobacco Manufactory, at Atlantic, was storing tobacco being carried through New York, producing tobacco goods, and exploiting the New York Tobacco Exchange by wholesaling through the Wall Street brokerage firm of H. W. Hunt & Co. Moreover, Brooklyn's Empire Stores alone handled 90 percent of the tobacco that entered the city.[20]

TABLE 3.2

Sugar Leaving the Port of New York, May–November 1863

Month	Sugar (lbs.)	Molasses (lbs.)	% of all Commerce
May	2,683,300	1,500,800	27.5
June	2,853,900	1,093,300	37.4
July	2,557,000	807,500	39.6
August	1,703,800	999,700	26.4
September	1,375,200	551,800	13.3
October	2,116,400	886,600	14.2
November	851,800	371,100	14.1

Source: New York State Office of the Auditor of the Canal Department, "Weekly Statements of Canal Shipments," 1863, New York State Archives, Albany.

Sugar bound Kings County's welfare even more tightly to that of Southern and Caribbean planters (see table 3.2). On the eve of the Panic of 1857, and the subsequent depression, sugar was clogging Brooklyn's warehouses. "I have just made a visit to several of the warehouses in Brooklyn—Thompsons, Baxters,

Fords and Pierreponts—I cannot hire any additional stores in Brooklyn, nor elsewhere for sugar and mollases," wrote Herman J. Redfield, collector of the New York Customs House. "There are now eleven cargos of sugar and molasses at the Brooklyn wharfs awaiting an opportunity of being discharged, and I have just been informed that at least fifty additional cargos may be expected in the course of a few days." For at least a decade the Customs House had been keeping sugar in specially outfitted stores at Brooklyn's Atlantic Docks. By 1856 there were six stores at Atlantic but those too were filled. The Secretary of the Treasury gave Redfield permission to rent space at any available yards and to increase security details during the evenings.21

If cotton was king in New York, Queen Sugar reigned across the East River as warehousing accelerated the rise of manufacturing. Brooklyn and Williamsburg flooded the market for refined sugars and syrups of all grades (see table 3.3). That refining dominance began in the early part of the century. William and Frederick C. Havemeyer, London-trained sugar bakers of German ancestry, came to New York after the turn of the century and were hired at Manhattan's Messr. Seaman & Co., which produced sugar loaves. On January 1, 1807 the sugar bakery of Wm. and F. C. Havemeyer opened on a lot at 87 Vandam Street leased from Trinity Church. Within three years the Havemeyer shops expanded to three lots on Vandam and produced 4,000 pounds of sugar loaf each day. In 1841 William Havemeyer left the partnership for politics. Frederick Havemeyer kept the Vandam house until 1856 when he gambled on revolutionary changes in sugar refining occurring in London. The new technology demanded large capital investments, riverside property, and labor, all of which attracted Havemeyer to Williamsburg with its expansive shore and large German working class. In 1856 he established Havemeyer, Townsend & Co. with investor William Townsend. The following year it opened, producing 300,000 pounds of refined sugar each day and unloading tons of cane sugar shipments at its own docks. In 1863 Townsend left the company and it was restructured as Havemeyer & Elder. Other major refineries came to neighbor Havemeyer's. William Dick took on a partner and moved the small Manhattan sugar house that he had opened in 1858 to Williamsburg. Toward the end of the Civil War, and in spite of the lull in sugar demands, Dick brought together the capital to open Wintjen, Dick and Schumaker in a new Williamsburg refinery with a daily capacity of 200,000 pounds. "By 1866 American importers of sugar were sending down agents to the British West Indies to buy sugar on the spot," writes a historian of the British Caribbean sugar industry.[22]

TABLE 3.3

Output of Brooklyn Sugar Refiners, 1857–1876

Refinery	Founded	Daily Capacity
Havemeyer &Townsend	1857	300,000 lbs.
Havemeyer & Elder (formerly H&T)	1863	1,000,000+
Havemeyer & Elder (rebuilt after fire)	1883	3,000,000
Dick & Meyer	1863	900,000
Wintjen, Dick, and Schumacher	1865	200,000
Cuba Sugar Refining	pre-1867	[b]75,000
Long Island Sugar Refining Company	pre-1867	[b]200,000
Burgher, Hurlbut, & Livingston	pre-1867	[b]100,000
Gandy, Sheppard & Co.	pre-1867	[b]100,000
Moller, Sierck & Company	ca. 1868	450,000
John Mollenhauer & Sons	1869	
[a]DeCastro & Donner 1	1870	
[a]DeCastro & Donner 2	1873	1,200,000 (combined)
[a]Greenpoint Sugar Refining Company	1871	1,500,000
Fulton Sugar Refining Company	pre-1876	
Brooklyn Sugar Refinery (formerly LISR)	1876	600,000

[a]Eventually taken over by the Havemeyers.
[b]Estimated from tax assessment of plant.
Source: Henry Reed Stiles, ed., *The Civil, Political, Professional and Ecclesiastical History and Commercial and Industrial Record of the County of Kings and the City of Brooklyn, N.Y., From 1683 to 1884,* 2 Vols. (New York: W. W. Munsell, 1884), 1: 669–672; Monthly List, 1867, July to December, Collection District No. 3 of the State of New York, Internal Revenue Service Tax Assessment Lists, 1862–1917, Records of the Internal Revenue Service, RG 58, US National Archives (New York); Harry W. Havemeyer, *Merchants of Williamsburgh: Frederick C. Havemeyer, Jr., William Dick, John Mollenhauer, Henry O. Havemeyer* (privately published, 1989), 31–41.

Sugar refineries successfully competed for space on the Brooklyn-Williamsburg waterfront and quickly became the county's foremost industry. Havemeyer and Elder was the largest sugar refinery in the world. By the close of the Civil War, it was producing more than a million pounds of sugar a day, 50 percent of the nation's total. In 1865 two Brooklyn refineries—Havemeyer & Elder and Dick & Meyer—produced the bulk of the 733 million pounds of refined sugar manufactured in the United States. That capacity was soon augmented by the Long Island (later Brooklyn) Sugar Refinery on South Street in Williamsburg and the Cuba Sugar Refinery on Gold Street in Brooklyn. In 1873 William Dick increased his investment in refining, opening the new Dick & Meyer with a daily capacity of nearly a million pounds. At about the same time, DeCastro and Donner's two plants and the Greenpoint Sugar works joined the slate of major refineries in Kings County. An almost endless list of minor sugar and molasses plants also peppered the city. In Manhattan's busy financial district, Brooklyn companies like DeCastro & Donner; Dick & Meyer; Moller, Sierck & Co.; and the Wintjen plant kept brokerage offices next to the Havemeyers' three Wall Street firms. By the 1880s 2,600 tons of refined sugar left Brooklyn daily, three-quarters of a million tons each year, and sugar refineries accounted for a third—$59,711,168 of $179,188,685—of Brooklyn's annual industrial production.[23]

In the decades before the Civil War a handful of ambitious and enterprising men became a commercial elite, but the means of their rise made the City of Churches an interested party in the politics of the nation's foremost social question. Sugar grown in the unfree and semi-feudal plantation South and Caribbean transformed daily life in Kings County. In 1823 William Dick was born in Hanover, Germany. He came to New York when he was 22 and entered the grocery business. Dick invested the profits in the sugar trade. By the Civil War, Dick was a wealthy Williamsburg merchant and a major employer of the German immigrant workers of that district. In 1841 William F. Havemeyer left his family's sugar business to enter politics. Four years later sugar money and immigrant votes bought Havemeyer the New York City mayoralty. The sugar barons enjoyed an unprecedented economic and political rise. In 1887 Henry O. Havemeyer brought seventeen plants into the Sugar Refineries Company, a national trust to regulate prices and production. Out of the trust Havemeyer organized the American Sugar Refining Company (1891), a single refinery stretching across the Williamsburg shore.[24] Within a few years the Brooklyn sugar lords were being attacked by anti-monopoly forces in New York State and then in the United States Congress but they had already sparked a commercial revolution that sprang from unfree and quasi-free black labor and a deep loyalty to the party that protected that trade.

From the antebellum period through the era of Reconstruction, Brooklyn's economic health was tied to the misfortune of black labor in the plantation world, and white Brooklynites' economic interests were closely aligned to those of the planter class.

CHAPTER FOUR

Irish Over Black

The Advent of Bourgeois Democracy in Kings County, 1800–1865

In our village and its vicinity, how many of us have been educated in colleges, and advanced into different branches of business; or taken into mercantile houses, manufacturing establishments, & c.?

Are we not even prohibited from some of the common labor, and drudgery of the streets, such as cartmen, porters, & c.?

It is a strange theory to us, how these gentlemen can promise to honor and respect us in Africa, when they are using every effort to exclude us from all rights and privileges at home.

—Henry C. Thompson, J. W. C. Pennington, George Woods (1831)

It is in vain that American citizens attempt to conceal their own and their country's degradation under this withering curse. America is cursed by slavery! WE CALL UPON YOU TO UNITE WITH THE ABOLITION-ISTS, and never to cease your efforts, until perfect liberty be granted to every one of her inhabitants, the black man as well as the white man. We are all children of the same gracious God; all equally entitled to life, liberty, and the pursuit of happiness.

We are told that you possess great power, both moral and political, in America. We entreat you to exercise that power and that influence for the sake of humanity.

—Daniel O'Connell and Theobald Mathew,
"Address from the People of Ireland to their County-men and Country-women in America,"
The Liberator, March 11, 1842

In 1830 Adrian Van Sinderen—the head of the Brooklyn Savings Bank and a descendant of an old, slaveholding Dutch family—became president of the newly organized Brooklyn chapter of the American Colonization Society (ACS), an elite, well-funded, and well-connected association that attempted to solve the problem of black freedom by removing free black people to West Africa. Free people of color vexed and embarrassed a city with strong mercantile ties to the South, and white Brooklynites reacted by forcing black people to the margins of political and economic life. In 1839 an American Anti-Slavery Society examination of the condition of African Americans in the North found them alienated and persecuted. It blamed the ACS and Southern slaveowners for promoting prejudice and discrimination against free people of color under the belief that the example of their liberty encouraged discontent among the unfree. In the free states, noted the Anti-Slavery Society, African Americans were denied suffrage but freely taxed, their mobility was circumscribed, they were restricted from petitioning their legislatures, they were barred from army and militia service, they were excluded from courts as judges, jurors, and witnesses, they were refused admission to schools, and they were segregated in churches and cemeteries.[1] The Colonization Society did wage a prolonged attack on the liberties of free black people; however, it did not represent the core of proslavery support in Brooklyn.

The expanding immigrant working class also came to find its economic, and therefore political, interests in the South. As rapidly as slavery produced a sizable African-American population, the end of slavery unleashed a tide of immigration that drowned Brooklyn's black community (see table 4.1). The commercial revolution in Brooklyn required participation in a social system that fastened black labor in the South and addressed the labor needs of the industrializing North with European immigrant workers. In 1800 one of every three residents of Kings County (32 percent) was black; six decades later, on the eve of the Civil War, barely one of fifty (1.8 percent) Brooklynites was of African descent. Between 1840 and 1860 the black population of Manhattan actually decreased, many of them having moved to Brooklyn; and, while the whole number of black people in Kings grew during that period, their percentage of the population declined.[2] Those demographic changes were a result of a capitalist culture that should have undermined unfree labor relations by competing for marginal workers but instead protected Southern slavery by drawing on immigrant labor.

TABLE 4.1

Population of Kings County, 1790–1860

Year	Total	Black	Black as %
1790	4,495	1,478	33.0
1800	5,740	1,811	32.0
1810	8,303	1,853	22.0
1820	11,187	1,761	16.0
1830	20,535	2,007	9.8
1840	47,613	2,846	6.0
1850	138,882	4,065	2.9
1860	279,122	4,999	1.8

Source: George Edmund Haynes, *The Negro at Work in New York City: A Study in Economic Progress* (1912; New York: AMS Press, 1968), 47.

White Brooklynites, like white people nationally, sustained two distinct relationships to black people. The first, well-known and often written about, comprised the struggle of a small elite to enrich itself by claiming rights to the labor of black people. The other was the participation of a far broader segment of the population in sustaining that persecution in exchange for political and economic liberties. Even poor and miserable white men, those who exercised little real power over black people, save the occasional violent outburst, understood the actual and potential rewards of their group status. The political behavior of Brooklyn's white working class reveals that they better than anyone saw race as a function of power. The ability to enslave African Americans was sustained because distinct interest groups came together under the banner of race.

Critical to slavery's longevity was the incorporation of the industrial working class into the Democratic party. Anthony Grownowicz exposed Tammany Hall's message to vulnerable immigrants and declining artisans, a missive based in the link between Southern bondage and Manhattan's commercial expansion. Anti-bank sentiments put the working class in conflict with the financial and commercial elite of New York and Brooklyn, but that division was soon subordinated to a proslavery consensus. Democrats, especially, shunned nativist ideas of social organization, offered the Irish and German population a party that defended their interest as workers and citizens, and redrew the lines of social division to include immigrants but exclude people of color. Over time the artisans of the Loco Foco party, a splinter from the local Democracy, and the laboring-class supporters of the Democratic machine, moved to a rigid proslavery political position, an unholy alliance with Southern planters that extended the hegemony of slaveholders

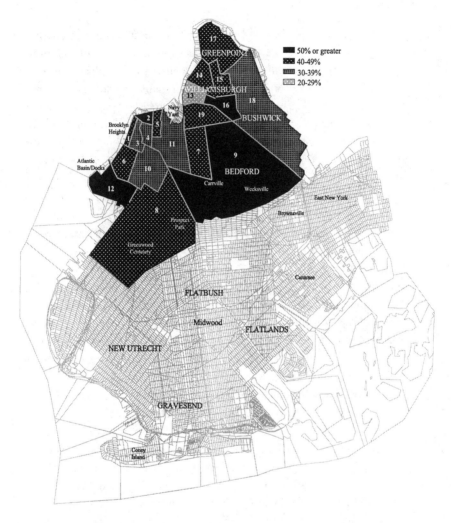

Map 1.Foreign Born Population in Brooklyn's 19 Wards
Source: Constructed by author from data in the *Manual of the Common Council of the City of Brooklyn for 1861-2* (Brooklyn: Goerge C. Bennett, 1862). Base map courtesy of the New York Department of City Planning

in the national government and secured the political and economic position of Northern urban ethnics. "The truth is not," writes Noel Ignatiev, "that slavery made it possible to extend to the Irish the privileges of citizenship, by providing another group for them to stand on, but the reverse, that the assimilation of the Irish into the white race made it possible to maintain slavery."[3]

Brooklynites joined in the proslavery consensus by exploiting the Jacksonian-era invention of unrestricted white male suffrage. White and immigrant voters assaulted the political and civil liberties of free black people and suppressed any public debate of bondage. In the decades before the Civil War the foreign-born population came to dwarf the nonwhite population, and the Democratic monopoly on immigrant votes augmented a Southern-dominant, proslavery national discourse (see table 4.2).

TABLE 4.2
Immigrant Dominance in Brooklyn Wards, 1860

Ward	Foreign-born	%	Black	%	Mulatto	%	Total
1	2,990	43	25	.36	6	.09	6,968
2	4,939	50	47	.48	30	.31	9,819
3	3,667	37	40	.40	8	.08	10,037
4	4,038	34	150	1.2	201	1.7	11,758
5	7,773	44	124	.71	64	.37	17,491
6	11,214	49	85	.37	28	.12	22,720
7	5,162	43	30	.25	20	.17	12,096
8	4,244	46	77	.84	30	.33	9,187
9	9,262	53	530	3.1	59	.34	17,351
10	9,832	39	199	.79	18	.07	25,219
11	8,587	30	786	2.7	30	.10	28,826
12	6,571	59	—	—	—	—	11,086
13	4,175	23	100	.56	9	.05	17,982
14	6,794	44	224	1.4	4	.03	15,476
15	4,431	42	183	1.7	32	.30	10,567
16	11,110	52	325	1.5	357	1.7	21,171
17	3,168	40	2	.03	15	.19	7,946
18	1,651	38	9	.21	—	—	4,317
19	2,917	44	7	.10	21	.31	6,697
Total	112,525	42	2,943	1.1	932	.35	266,714

Source: *Manual of the Common Council of the City of Brooklyn for 1861-2* (Brooklyn: George C. Bennett, 1861), 473.

If in the eighteenth century Irish Catholics were believed to be in consort with Africans,[4] by the nineteenth century abolitionists could regularly complain that the Irish were the most vicious local enemies of African-American emancipation. Africans and the Irish had once been bound across Kings

County, but Irish servitude ended while Southern bondage still posed a physical and political threat to even free black people. The first step in the Irish rise was to eschew their history of servitude and any connections, perceived or real, to Negroes. The distinct definitions of their labor placed the Irish and African Americans on different political trajectories and past similarities and sympathies were buried in time itself.

The political and economic rights of free people of color were being undermined long before the conclusion of New York State emancipation. And, the end of African enslavement overlapped so perfectly with the rise of a racially segmented system of free labor that the potentially revolutionary results of universal freedom were never realized in the City of Churches. Race remained potent because the city's social relations still turned on the subordination of black people. If race first crystallized to protect the power to enslave from the rhetoric of the Revolutionary era, it soon came to symbolize the cohesion of a social majority who used their political dominance to augment their individual rights. That recentering resulted from the Democrats' ability to join the interests of the Southern slaveocracy and the Northern urban working-class. Racial categories expanded and contracted to reflect the new power dynamics, but the continuity of African Americans' persecution provided little reason to ever question the social effects of color. Race survived the end of slavery in Brooklyn because it continued to describe the power that the majority exercised over black men and women.

Irish workers found African slavery and black people to be useful symbols in constructing the conditions under which they expected to live and labor. "Whiteness" was the epithet with which they defined their material and political goals. David R. Roediger has convincingly argued that Irish workers sought to best black workers in the job competition and to underscore their own status as free laborers by reinforcing the racial hierarchy of labor. If the Irish were to lay claim to a status that the antebellum republic respected, they would have to distance themselves from those who seemed ineligible for full freedom. To do so, Roediger concludes, "they had to drive all Blacks, and if possible their memories, from the places where the Irish labored." The rise of "whiteness," adds Theodore Allen, was indicative of societies in which the consolidation of bourgeois rule required the support of the working classes.[5]

The two themes—political realignment and economic competition— merged in Brooklyn where the Democratic machine empowered and protected Irish labor. Out of that relationship came the first political leader to wear the title "Boss." In 1825 Hugh McLaughlin was born on Furman Street in an Irish slum outside Brooklyn Heights. Rudely educated, he discovered his talents and honed his skills on the streets. At an early age, McLaughlin climbed to the leadership of a gang. He apprenticed at a local rope walk (factory) and later opened a fish stand with his brother at the Atlantic market.[6]

Six feet tall and broadly built, McLaughlin was also clever enough with his fists to capture the respect of most men, and that was about all that one needed to go far in Brooklyn Democratic politics. "He came upon the field at a time when the labor element of the party, owing to the famine in Ireland and the European uprisings of 1848, had been largely augmented by immigration, and his vocations had brought him into intimate relations with the working population, among whom he had a wide acquaintance," remembered a contemporary. In 1849 McLaughlin became the underling of the local machine politician Henry C. Murphy. In 1855 his work as a party tough was rewarded when future Congressman George Taylor handed him a position at the Brooklyn Navy Yard hiring civilian employees. "Because of the nature of the work," writes a biographer, "he received the title 'Boss,' an appellation which, although gained outside the field of politics, remained with him in the days when he became political master of Brooklyn." From his Navy Yard post, McLaughlin hired and fired his way to the center of local politics. He lost a bid for sheriff in 1860 but managed to hold the office of register for most of the decade. In the early 1870s he gave up the burdens of keeping office to become the full-time overlord of Brooklyn's Democratic machine. A fellow machine politician remarked, "McLaughlin takes but little interest in politics outside the County. He knows little about State politics, and boasts of it."[7]

By the Civil War immigrants made up 42 percent of Brooklyn's population, and native-born white Protestants were a minority group—a demographic shift that brought about the total transformation of local politics. In 1873 the *Brooklyn Sunday Sun* derided a meeting of the (Democratic) Long Island Club, in which McLaughlin was not a participant, as "play[ing] *Hamlet* with *Hamlet* left out." Twenty years later, the Republican *New York Tribune* continued to warn its readers that

> McLaughlin names the Mayor; the Mayor reappoints the Boss's men as heads of departments; the Boss's men fill the departments with Democratic place-hunters; the office-holders raise a boodle for the reelection of the Boss's candidate for Mayor; and the boodle is used in hiring

the naturalized citizens ground out in Judge Moore's court to vote, for the Boss's ticket, and in employing McKane's swarms of repeaters to violate the election laws. So is the circle of Ring iniquity in Brooklyn squared.[8]

That "Ring" tied Brooklyn's ethnics to the party of slavery, but it also democratized Kings County by challenging the political fiefdom of the Protestant elite. Paradoxically the rise of bourgeois democracy involved a progressive political triumph in the form of white male suffrage and a regressive social revolution in the consolidation of a proslavery consensus. Immigrant Northerners bolstered the national power of slaveholders in exchange for their own political freedom. Or, as Graham Hodges notes, the determination of the Irish to racialize their struggle for equality "came not from any innate prejudice, but rather from cooperation with the existing political system."[9]

The ease of that compromise was exposed in 1854 when Henry Ward Beecher, who emerged in the decades before the Civil War as the nation's leading Protestant minister and Brooklyn's most famous citizen, exchanged articles on African bondage with John Mitchel, editor of the *New York Citizen* and former Irish rebel. In an open letter to Beecher, Mitchel defended African-American enslavement as a humane method of social organization with historical and biblical justification, while chastising abolitionists for perverting the truth of bondage. Mitchel saw no inconsistencies between his proslavery stance in New York City and his earlier revolutionary career in Ireland. "I was actuated by no other principle than intolerance of insolent and ignorant oppression: my principle was simply that *Irishmen* were fitted for a higher destiny and sphere, and that they all ought to feel British dominion as intolerable as I did," he wrote of his limited radicalism. Yet the reign of proslavery in America did not disturb him, for ultimately the subjection of Africans was in the interest of the Southern planter, the Northern merchant, and the laboring Irish. Beecher's response appeared first in the *New York Independent*. He began by dissecting the substance and construction of Mitchel's letter and offering to help the editor construct a better immoral argument in the future. "The Bible has been regarded as a bulwark of oppression by all oppressors," charged Beecher. He then lamented the fall of a man who was once a pillar of the fight against persecution. Beecher called upon Mitchel to use his remaining years to save his reputation and his soul. He warned: "Time, that would have carried you onward, garlanded with achievements worthy of a man living for men, and surrounded by the genial sympathies of loving hearts, now, will drift you to a polar solitude, without love, or sympathy, or pity, or honor."[10]

Another confession of white and immigrant Brooklynites' willingness to benefit from the exploitation of African Americans came during the summer of 1855 when the New York press castigated a Kings County judge for attending a black community picnic. One article mocked the judge by suggesting that he break the other rules of racial etiquette: perhaps have "Cato" or "Scipio" come to his table for dinner, bury black people in white church yards, allow "Sambo" to marry his daughter, force black children into white schools, or let Negroes sit in white church pews. "Why not force Mayors to issue licenses for them to drive carts and hacks, and have equal rights and privileges in all sorts of trades!" the article declared with even greater concern.[11]

Free African Americans' found themselves stripped of political rights and forced to the periphery of urban life. Most white Brooklynites—immigrant or native, Catholic or Protestant, wealthy or poor—were in conflict on all but a single local issue: the subjection of free black people, a cornerstone of proslavery politics. They concurred that their city and county would never be havens for fugitives from slavery, examples of the logic of emancipation, or stages for the war against human bondage. They agreed to sustain slavery and their way of life by exercising their power over black Americans.

The power struggle played out in politics. Before the Revolution, African Americans enjoyed the right to vote in New York State, and in 1785 an attempt to suspend their franchise was vetoed by the Council of Revision, but from that year on a pointed attack against black suffrage began. Property qualifications were strengthened and nonwhite voters were required to show certificates of freedom. Rumors that enslaved Africans were voting and that, when coupled with the ballots of free black men, they were influencing elections made the issue more grave. When the New York Convention met in September 1821 a number of arguments in favor of restricting the franchise to white men were offered. The Negro was declared degraded, immoral, stupid, lazy, illiterate, and barbarous. Peter Augustus Jay, one of a minority of advocates of universal manhood suffrage, insisted that the idea that black people were naturally inferior had long been "completely refuted and universally exploded." Asserting that the constitutionality of the proposal was doubtful, that the majority was attempting to massage its prejudices at the expense of the republic, and that the black population in New York was so small as to make exclusion unnecessary, the forces favoring open suffrage moved the Convention to eliminate the word "white" from the constitution by a vote of 63 to 59. That vote was compromised when a special committee was formed to place restrictions on black voters. The committee recommended a three-year residency and the payment of taxes on an estate valued at $250 above any debts for nonwhite voters, while granting an unqualified franchise to all white men who had resided in the state one year or who had volunteered in the highway or militia service. After a brief debate, the committee's suggestions were accepted 72 to 31. A year later a Brooklyn city directory boasted: "A colored person can vote provided—

1st.—He has been for three years a citizen of this state.

2d.—He has resided one year in the town or county where he votes.

3d.—He has owned a *freehold* of $250 one year before he votes.

4th.—He has been rated and paid a tax on his freehold.[12]

In 1846 the chance to eliminate property qualifications on black voters returned and was easily defeated at the Constitutional Convention. By the same majorities as the 1821 Convention, New York's representatives again dismissed the idea of reducing themselves to equality with black people. A subsequent appeal placed the issue on the ballot for popular referendum in the upcoming state elections. There it suffered an overwhelming defeat.[13] Only a small minority of white men approved of this expression of progress; and, by rewriting the state's constitution, white New Yorkers had managed to go far in silencing slavery's critics.

It was left to Kings County's black population to incubate the struggle against bondage. The African Church was center of black antislavery. On May 19, 1794 Methodism was officially established in Brooklyn, and African Americans were a third to a half of all its communicants. The Sands Street Church, built on the site where Woolman Hickson helped introduce the faith to Brooklynites during the Revolution, had traditionally reserved the "end gallery" for Africans. However, communicants of color ended their relationship with Sands Street when its minister, Alexander M'Caine, publicly sympathized with slavery, authored a proslavery pamphlet, and attempted to charge them ten dollars a quarter for their inferior accommodations. In the fall of 1817 black Brooklynites held a large rally and raised more than $100 for the building of a church. Named the African Asbury Methodist Episcopal Church, it remained for a short while under the pastorate of the Sands Street minister. When ties were severed after the M'Caine affair the church was renamed the African Wesleyan Methodist Episcopal Church, following the lead of the independent church experiment in Philadelphia. On February 7, 1818 Brooklyn's first "black church" was incorporated—with Peter Croger, Israel Jemison, Cesar Springfield, Benjamin Croger, and John E. Jackson as trustees—on High between Bridge and Pearl Streets. From 1820 to 1821 Sands Street's black membership fell from 125 to 6 and its congregation shrank by a third (see table 4.5). M'Caine resigned shortly after the separation and a few seats were reserved at Sands Street for those black parishioners who stayed.[14]

TABLE 4.3

Membership of the Sands Street Methodist Church by Race, 1795–1825

Year	White	Black	Total
1795	23	12	35
1800	34	20	54
1805	44	30	74
1810	170	85	255
1815	138	60	198
1820	202	125	327
1825	408	6	414

Source: Henry R. Stiles, *A History of the City of Brooklyn, Including the Old Town and Village of Brooklyn, the Town of Bushwick, and the Village and City of Williamsburgh,* 3 Vols. (Brooklyn: published by subscription, 1867–70), 3: 704.

"Brooklyn's black churches plunged into the fight for African-American liberation," Clarence Taylor argues. "During the ante-bellum period, they emerged as active agencies in the struggle against slavery, with Bridge Street AWME and Concord Baptist serving as sanctuaries for runaways, and Siloam Presbyterian's creating a fund for the Underground Railroad." At various times each of these institutions harbored fugitives and served as stations on the Underground Railroad.[15]

Willis Augustus Hodges captured the political socialization of black Christianity. Because his new Brooklyn friends were all churchgoers, Hodges began religious instruction and on February 12, 1837 was baptized at Manhattan's Abyssinian Church, "where I now remain a member. I also attended all the abolition meetings." In Brooklyn the Underground Railroad passed through churches and homes. "Children were taught then to neither see, hear nor talk about the affairs in which grown ups were concerned," wrote

Maritcha Remond Lyons, a descendent of one of Long Island's oldest black families. Strangers regularly arrived at the Lyons' house. Her parents actively assisted runaways; in fact, she recalled that "every thinking man and woman was a volunteer in the famous 'underground railroad.' "[16]

The most prominent African to escape to Brooklyn was James W. C. Pennington, born James Pembroke in 1807. In 1829, he ran away from the eastern shore of Maryland. A long and dangerous flight brought Pennington to the North where he "went to New York, and in a short time found employ on Long Island, near the city [of Brooklyn]." He found his life's work while attending classes in the black community's evening schools: "At length, finding that the misery, ignorance, and wretchedness of the free coloured people was by whites tortured into an argument for slavery; finding myself now among the free people of colour in New York, where slavery was so recently abolished; and finding much to do for their elevation, I resolved to give my strength in that direction." In 1830 the Brooklyn Temperance Association was organized to reduce drunkenness and disorder. Benjamin Croger was president, Pennington was secretary, and George Hogarth, a minister and a teacher at the area African school, was a manager. A year later Pennington helped construct the public statement of a convention of Kings County's black residents in opposition to the local ACS's schemes to relocate free colored people to Africa and Haiti. The parents of black children on Long Island felt Pennington's presence through his constant proselytizing to get them to send their youngsters to school. He served as instructor at a new school for Africans in Newtown, Long Island. The fugitive turned teacher attended classes at Yale Divinity School, although its officials would not formally allow him to enroll, and in 1837 was licensed as a preacher in Brooklyn. In the following years Pennington received the degree doctor of divinity from the University of Heidelberg, became a major antislavery spokesman in the United States and Europe, and was installed as pastor of an African church in Manhattan. In 1852, in the concluding remarks to her *Uncle Tom's Cabin*, Harriet Beecher Stowe added Pennington to a list of "individuals [who] have thus bravely succeeded in conquering for themselves comparative wealth and social position, in the face of every disadvantage and discouragement."[17]

If limitations on black suffrage muffled antislavery agitation in politics, the campaign to remove free black people to Haiti and West Africa dampened grassroots antislavery activity by keeping the civil liberties of free communities of color constantly under political attack. During the summer of 1831 Kings

County's black community held a mass meeting at African Hall on Nassau Street, Brooklyn. The urgent issue was the need to counteract the statements and work of the ACS. Henry Thompson chaired, George Hogarth served as secretary, and addresses were delivered by Hogarth, Pennington, and George Woods. The attendees resolved to oppose any attempt to repatriate the nation's free black residents to Haiti, Africa, Canada, or anywhere else. Thompson, Pennington, and Woods were elected to write an address to be published and circulated among the black community in Kings County. The committee assailed the tortured and self-serving logic of the ACS. They pointed out that few black Americans had any first-hand knowledge of Africa, and noted that in order to make their scheme appear logical Colonizationists had to belittle African Americans and cultivate prejudice against them, "which is already one grand reason of our wretchedness." They charged that race hatred closed avenues of life to them, noting that in Brooklyn itself black men were barred from educational institutions and even menial employment as cartmen or porters. They could not find work in the merchant houses and their only business opportunities were in service fields. The public statement demanded that their status as native-born citizens be respected: "Our constitution does not call upon us to become naturalized; we are already American citizens; our fathers were among the first that peopled this country; their sweat and their tears have been the means, in a measure of raising our country to its present standing."[18] In short, they refused to be sacrificed so that white Americans might no longer be irritated by the problem of free Negroes in a slave society.

Willis Hodges, who moved from Virginia to Carrville and then Williamsburg, Brooklyn, was shocked by the racial civilization that dominated the city. "I had expected to find the people of color in free New York far better off than those in Virginia. In the latter state, both bond and free had trades, that is, many of them, and all the skilled work was done by men of color. In New York I found none, or only one here and there." The racial segmentation of labor shaped Hodges's experience in the city. "The first job of work I got was as a laborer on the docks, cleaning away ice, mud and snow, so a gentleman could go across to his ship. I did not get much work the first month, only odd jobs here and there, with small pay, because of which I was low spirited and discontented and began to wish I had never left Virginia."[19]

In the summer of 1831 a black Brooklynite wrote a letter to the *Liberator*, noting the ACS' activities in Kings County, where the organization had been promoting the removal of black people to Africa as the best solution to the nation's race problem. An agent visited Brooklyn twice and "he has been losing the confidence of the Afric-Americans." Almost five hundred black residents attended ACS secretary Gurley's lecture at the Presbyterian Church. As Gurley began to lecture, the sable audience abandoned their segregated gallery seats as readily as Gurley begged them to hear him out. At Gurley's second appearance only two black people, besides this correspondent, attended, "and they were strangers from Canada." Gurley then requested to speak at the African Wesleyan Methodist Episcopal Church but was rejected.[20]

"This correspondent" was Brooklyn's William J. Wilson. A teacher and manager in the local African schools, he contributed to *Frederick Douglass' Paper*, the *Colored American*, and the *Weekly Anglo-African*, writing articles on local and national events under the pseudonym "Ethiop." "I write of course from a private, a very private nook indeed," he once admitted to his audience. For two decades Ethiop's public-private essays, poems, and editorials appeared in the leading black papers of the nation and most frequently in New York's black press. A generation of free African Americans participated in and learned of the major political gatherings and actions of colored people through Ethiop's witty and honest reports. Perhaps his most ingenious offering was contained in a series titled "Afric-American Picture Gallery," which appeared in the *Anglo-African Magazine* just before the Civil War. In it Ethiop takes his readers on walks through an imaginary gallery in which art of various levels of fineness is displayed somewhat chronologically. At times Wilson sits in his easy chair and studies the images; other times he strolls the halls paying close attention to certain pieces. The gallery receives occasional visitors, white and black, who introduce issues important to the community. Ethiop described the space, its walls, lighting, and ambiance in great detail. Couched within the tours are serious dialogues about history, politics, and social issues including vivid descriptions of the horrors of slavery and the slave trade. The gallery was also used to animate prominent historical and contemporary figures, who many black people had neither seen nor heard. For instance, in his first offering Ethiop analyzes "The Last Colored Editor," a painting of the founder of *Freedom's Journal*, in which he adds a brief history of the black press, encourages its support, and credits it with "the linking together of our once scarcely hopeful past with the now bright present." In that same contribution Ethiop describes a picture of a slave ship, a portrait of Crispus Attucks, an African landscape at sunset, and two large paintings of the southern and northern portions of "that mysterious road," the Underground Railroad.[21]

Ethiop also reported the National Colored Conventions. Beginning in 1831

J. W. C. Pennington represented Brooklyn at the first Conventions in Philadelphia and New York. "A public meeting was held on the 27th of March [1832], when Mr[.] James Pennington was duly elected the delegate to the Convention from this village," announced "A Colored Freeman" from Brooklyn.[22]

Pennington and Wilson were active organizers in Brooklyn's suffrage struggle. In March 1837 more than 200 black Brooklynites attempted to bolster their earlier antislavery work by petitioning the state legislature to provide a trial by jury for people claimed as fugitive slaves, to allow manhood suffrage without distinctions of color, and to rid the final vestiges of slavery from the state constitution. Petitions from Brooklyn and Manhattan were sent together. Brooklyn's included the names of 140 black men and 92 black women. The petitions joined those from the black communities of Albany, Oswego, Arcade, Genesee, and other counties. Four years later Williamsburg's black population met to further the cause of universal suffrage:

> Resolved, That we, the citizens of Williamsburg, feeling the injustice of the unequal suffrage under which we labor, do hereby pledge ourselves to use our united exertions to restore an equality of suffrage, and not to cease them until the last link of oppression's chain is broken.[23]

Later, William J. Wilson, Junius C. Morel, and Dr. T. Joiner White of Brooklyn and Williamsburg joined ten black men from New York City to form the Committee of Thirteen. The Committee was organized to oppose the Fugitive Slave Law of 1850, to rebut colonizationists, and to publicize their belief that the actual goal of colonization was to remove the only consistently antislavery population from the nation. "Unknown except to the initiated, a committee of thirteen was formed in our city, each member was pledged to keep the letter but to violate the spirit of the unholy enactment. Without officers, headquarters, passwords or treasury, this band was liberally supported," Maritcha Lyons remembered. The risks that free black people took were incredible, still "any adventurer who had the courage to set out on a life or death journey from bondage to freedom, knew by the 'grape vine telegraph,' New York City would never prove indifferent to his needs in the exigency."[24]

Some hint of black people's militant rejection of colonization came when "a colored citizen of Brooklyn" wrote to Garrison's *Liberator* chiding the Colonization Society for its hypocrisy while not abandoning the idea of emigration. Looking at Canada's Wilberforce settlement, this Brooklynite saluted emigration only when it was a result of the decision of black people not to be ruled over by so-called "freemen, or free tramplers upon the rights of the red and sable race[s]." In 1855 William J. Wilson reported the happenings at the National Colored Convention in Philadelphia, during which Rev. James Morris Williams of Brooklyn organized and presided over the burning of a pro-colonization tract submitted to be read at the convention. By 1859 Brooklyn's Thomas and Robert Hamilton established Manhattan's *Anglo-African*, the first magazine marketed to black people and a sounding board for black antislavery and anti-colonization.[25]

There was a direct connection between black Brooklynites' fight for suffrage and their campaign against bondage. The identification that they made with the mass of unfree people in the South had a real basis in their own self-interest: so long as nine of every ten African Americans were enslaved in the South, black Northerners would be politically dominated by European immigrants and native-born white people, subject to kidnapping by slave traders and bounty hunters, and have the color of their skin remain the badge of servitude. Kings County's black community targeted slavery as a necessary step in its own struggle for equality.

The kidnapping and seizing of free black people and suspected fugitives was common practice in New York State, and Manhattan was the most dangerous region. Slavehunters were hardly unwelcome in a city that financed and protected an illegal slave trade. In March 1834 Henry Scott, a seven-year-old black boy, was dragged from his Manhattan schoolhouse by the sheriff and jailed on suspicion of being a runaway. Children ran from the school screaming "'Kidnapper! kidnapper!" A month later Elizur Wright Jr. reported that eleven African Americans were being "confined in the city prison as slaves." Only five of the eleven—William Miller, James Carter, William Carter, William Scott, and Peter Martin—had been recently arrested. On July 23, 1836 George Jones, "a respectable free colored man," was arrested at work and imprisoned. The following year William Dixon, the 30-year-old choir singer of Zion Church, was seized and jailed. Brought before a justice, Dixon declared, "I am an innocent man. I am a freeman. I have a wife that I love. It is hard to be torn from my family, and thrust into prison like a dog—merely because, being a colored man." Dixon was later beaten for attempting an escape.[26]

Williamsburg and Brooklyn grew more dangerous each year. A week after Congress passed the Compromise of 1850, with its tougher fugitive slave law, James Hamilton Williams (or James Hamlet) of Williamsburg was seized by bounty hunters and rushed to Baltimore to prevent intervention. The

Committee of Thirteen and several prominent local ministers collected funds to purchase Hamlet's freedom. Five days after Hamlet was arrested, the Reverend Charles B. Ray informed 500 black people gathered at Zion Chapel that $800 had already been raised for Hamlet's release. Three days later thousands of white and black New Yorkers gathered at the park next to New York City Hall and heard addresses from black abolitionists William Powell, the Reverend John P. Raymond, Robert Hamilton, and Ray. The Thirteen hosted the mass rally to celebrate Hamlet's return. Following the ceremony, 200 black people escorted Hamlet back to Williamsburg. Robert Hamilton then led a Kings County celebration. African Americans in Williamsburg and Brooklyn followed the victory with public meetings that officially repudiated the Fugitive Slave Act. Still, in April 1852 Horace Preston of Williamsburg found himself falsely arrested for larceny and then offered up as a fugitive slave. Preston was hidden in a Williamsburg jail, prevented from contacting a lawyer, and denied bail. Peter Jay was eventually allowed to represent Preston. The attorney claimed that Preston had been freed by his mistress and was now being illegally claimed by her widower. That response did not impress a court that was uninterested in a fair trial. In fact, the New York lawyer who acted as the master's agent punched Jay in the face for defending his client too well.[27]

The danger of kidnapping united black people from New York and Kings Counties. In 1851 the area's black clergy convened at Manhattan's Bethel Church and Brooklyn's A. M. E. Church. The ministers prayed for the immediate end of slavery. Friends of the enslaved were praised and enemies of bondspeople were rebuked. White Protestant churches were charged with having "failed in this country to extend to us the common sympathies and courtesies of a common Christian brotherhood" and were called upon to recapture the spirit of the "first dissenters" by opposing bondage. The clergy again rejected colonization, and a resolution was passed condemning Henry Clay's opinions on free black people. In the spring of 1851, African Americans from New York, Brooklyn, and Williamsburg issued a startling public announcement. While discussing steps to ensure their continued uplift, a resolution "that this Convention impress on the minds of the young men of this city, and the city of Brooklyn and Williamsburg, to organize military companies."[28]

Free black people also retaliated against Catholicism and immigrants; in fact, people of color seemed fully confident that they would fare well in a comparison with European immigrants. As early as 1831 black Brooklynites were advertising their native-born status as part of their qualifications for full and equal citizenship. Six years later black Manhattan's *Weekly Advocate* announced its intention to see African Americans enjoy the "blessings and privileges" of "native American Freemen." Brooklyn's Peter Vogelsang thought it criminal that men of color were "deprived of privileges granted to European *paupers*, blacklegs and burglars!!!"[29]

During a lecture on Toussaint L'Ouverture at a benefit for Manhattan's Colored Orphan Asylum, Dr. James McCune Smith, who trained many of Brooklyn's black doctors and who lived in the City of Churches for a brief time, assaulted the record of United States slavery and its impact on the nation. He took careful aim at the foreign-born population. The results of the system were visible in the widely different treatment of black people and immigrants:

> Among the many lessons that may be drawn from this portion of history is one not unconnected with the present occasion. From causes to which I need not give a name, there is gradually creeping into our otherwise prosperous state the incongruous and undermining influence of *caste*. One of the local manifestations of this unrepublican sentiment is, that while 800 children, chiefly of foreign parents, are educated and taught trades at the expense of all the citizens, colored children are excluded from those privileges.[30]

Black people were more likely to point out the local results of the political coupling of the Slave Power and the Catholic Irish under the Democratic party. "Foreigners and aliens to the government and laws—strangers to our institutions are permitted to flock to this land, and in a few years are endowed with all the privileges of citizens; but we, *native* born Americans, the children of the soil, are most of us shut out," read one of the *Colored American*'s many editorials on suffrage. The Reverend Samuel Cornish, a founder of Brooklyn's Shiloh Presbyterian Church (1822), co-founded and edited the *Colored American*, which led the charge on the issue of universal manhood suffrage.[31]

Frederick Douglass, having already toured Ireland and the Continent, appeared at the May 1853 convention of the American Anti-Slavery Society at New York and spoke on immigration. Douglass was puzzled that the Irish, "warm-hearted, generous, and sympathizing with the oppressed everywhere" when in Ireland, were "instantly taught, on arriving in this christian country, to hate and despise the colored people." He located the cause of this persecution in a society that rewarded Irish racism with jobs and political privilege.

He accused the Irish of being in league with the ACS and the "slave power."

> While the colored people are thus elbowed out of employment; while
> the enmity of emigrants is being excited against us; while state after state
> enacts laws against us; while we are hunted down, like wild game, and
> oppressed with a general feeling of insecurity,—the American colo-
> nization society—that old offender against the best interests and slan-
> derer of the colored people—awakens to new life, and vigorously presses
> its scheme upon the consideration of the people and the government.

Irish Americans had already rejected Daniel O'Connell's plea that "Irishmen
and Irishwomen! *treat the colored people as your equals, as brethren.*"
O'Connell, one of Ireland's premiere statesmen and Douglass' comrade,
wrote the appeal a decade earlier and claimed that it had 60,000 supporters
in Ireland. It went on to ask Irish Americans to, "by all your memories of
Ireland, continue to love liberty—hate slavery—CLING BY THE ABOLI-
TIONISTS—and in America, *you will do honor to the name of Ireland.*"[32]

The latter request, so simple and obvious a moral call from Ireland,
seemed almost impossible to comply with from the vantage point of the
United States. In their struggle for equality, black Brooklynites continued to
meet the open hostility of European immigrants. In 1855 the Colored
Political Association of the City of Brooklyn and Kings County published a
declaration of its purpose. "This is an association of colored property holders
in Kings County," it began, formed with the intent "to bring them just and
equal rights as *native born* Americans." Willis Hodges was president; Amos
Freeman, vice president; Dr. Peter Ray, secretary; and Elijah Bundick, treasurer. The organization had five hundred members, and insisted that its
membership would triple if the racial proscriptions were removed from
voting. That year the association sent a petition to the Legislature of New York
State that packaged their demand for the right to vote in their history in and
contributions to the nation:

> The undersigned, desire to solicit at your hands, a consideration of the
> disabilities under which we have been, and of the Moral Degradation
> to which we are forcibly subjected, as Citizens of this State, believing
> that the present time affords suitable opportunity for, and that the
> public sentiment is not unprepared, nor averse to, a remedy of the evils
> of which we deem we have just cause of complaint.

We refer to the Anti-Republican Distinction of Color with the Constitution of this State, (art. 2, sec. 1.) recognizes and establishes; and we therefore, most earnestly pray, that your Hon. Body will take the necessary action to provide for an amendment thereto, which will place the Elective Franchise within the reach of all citizens, without regard to complexion.

Many of our petitioners have resided during their entire lives in, and are Freeholders of this State,—their families are permanently located within its boundaries, their social relations are established within its limits, and their entire pecuniary interests are inseparable from its welfare.

As occupants of tenements and rent payers, all of us constitute a share of support of the State Government, without deriving corresponding advantages from it.

Under these circumstances, we feel our cause a just one, and do most earnestly ask a favorable consideration at your hands,

And as in duty bound, your petitioners will ever pray.[33]

While the question of black suffrage was not settled in New York until long after the Civil War, it ranked with abolition at the top of black Brooklynites' antebellum political agenda. In the heated presidential election of 1860 African Americans' Williamsburg Suffrage Club vowed to push for the right to vote. But, white reporters painted the formation of the Brooklyn Elective Franchise Club and eighteen other suffrage clubs among people of color in the county as open attacks on white privilege. On January 16 and 30 Brooklyn's two Republican assemblymen presented petitions from Hodges and 130 black Brooklynites to eliminate property qualifications on African-American voters. The proposal passed the Assembly 70 to 36, despite its rejection by all of Brooklyn's Democratic representatives. On March 17 the measure passed the Senate 17 to 9, with the cities of Brooklyn and New York providing half the opposition. On April 4, when the "Act to Perfect an Amendment to the Constitution Abolishing the Property Qualification of People of Color" was brought before the State Senate, it passed 19 to 3, all of the opposition coming from New York City and the City of Brooklyn. Two weeks later Republican governor Edwin Morgan signed a bill calling for a fall referendum on "Negro voting." In the November 1860 election, white and immigrant Brooklynites viewed the danger of black suffrage with as much concern as they did the candidacy of Abraham Lincoln. They overwhelmingly denied black people the right to vote. More than 140,000 votes stood between African Americans and the franchise, and more than a third of the opposition came from the two great cities in southern New York State.[34]

Toward the end of the Civil War, Henry Ward Beecher took the pulpit at Brooklyn's Plymouth Church and demanded that black Southerners be equipped with the right to vote. In defense of this step, he noted that some black men already voted in New York State and that suffrage was an essential part of liberty. Then Beecher drew a metaphor from the central tension of local Brooklyn politics: "to have an ignorant class voting is dangerous, whether white or black. But to have an ignorant class, and not have them voting, is a great deal more dangerous." Beecher was speaking of the Irish who now "have rights that candidates are bound to respect!" The Plymouth pastor reminded his congregation that black men had earned the ballot through military service and fidelity to the union. Unrestricted male suffrage was also a prophylactic measure to protect white Republicans in the South.[35]

But Negro suffrage echoed peculiarly and uneasily in a city that for four decades had passionately voted to circumscribe black people's rights and a state that disqualified the vast majority of black men from voting. While Beecher saw enfranchisement as the logical result of the conflict and its outcome, most white and immigrant Brooklynites were still not comfortable on that plane of social justice.

CHAPTER FIVE

Hope, Hate, and the Class Struggle

——

The End of
Slavery's Dominion in
the City of Churches,
1827–1865

——

> One would not believe that it was possible for a free people to be so pervaded with the venom of slavery. Almost every organization of the society set itself against this reformation. The family, the school, colleges, caucuses, parties, and legislatures were against it. Churches, consistories, presbyteries, synods, and assemblies were against it. Boards of publication and boards of missions were against it. Bankers and brokers, jobbers and shippers, makers and venders, were against it. Everything was against it. Time after time they killed it. Argument upon argument was hurled at it. Resolution upon resolution was aimed at it. Never was the bell tolled at the death of any rising spirit of revolution oftener than at the death of the rising spirit of anti-slavery.

—Henry Ward Beecher (1860)

A democracy limited by race and gender can easily protect its oppressive foundations from political challenges, but in doing so it tends to elevate the importance of moral discourse. Proslavery Brooklynites were most enraged at those people who dared to expose the ethical problem of human bondage. There were white Brooklynites who supported their black neighbors' anti-slavery struggle; however, white sympathizers were largely formed into a segregated movement. There were two reasons for that social distance: First, most white abolitionists trusted the racial mythology of their age; their anti-slavery beliefs grew out of Christian morality, not social egalitarianism. For instance, Henry Ward Beecher once comforted an audience by telling them that emancipation would not result in a northward black migration because nature had equipped Africans to excel under the sun and heat of a Southern

plantation and not the climate of a Northern city.[1] Secondly, white abolitionists knew that gestures toward racial equality would magnify the violence
and intimidation that they already attracted.

In 1833 Manhattan's Arthur Tappan, a transplanted New Englander and
the head of Arthur Tappan & Company, his brother Lewis Tappan, Joshua
Leavitt, and Elizur Wright Jr., brought their wealth and talents into the fledg-
ling American Anti-Slavery Society. The Society paid agents to reproduce
locals across the North, and set the goal of flooding the nation with the
antislavery message. In December 1833 New York's Beriah Green served as
president and Lewis Tappan as secretary to the National Anti-Slavery
Convention in Philadelphia. Elizur Wright Jr., Abraham Cox, John Rankin,
William Goodell, William Green Jr., and Charles W. Denison of Manhattan
attended and they signed the Declaration of Sentiments.[2]

The reaction against them was harsh. Brutal attacks on abolitionists,
black and white, followed. Tammany and the Loco Focos were at the center.
"I was a witness of that mob, from the hour of its assembling at Clinton Hall,
to its final assault upon the Chatham-street Chapel," recalled abolitionist
William Lloyd Garrison of his 1833 visit to New York City. Encouraged by
reports of the founding of a city antislavery society, white hoodlums pledged
to stop Garrison from speaking anywhere in New York. On Thursday, July 10,
1834 another Manhattan mob stoned the home of Lewis Tappan, proceeded
to his brother's house, smashed in its doors and windows, and burned its
furnishings in the street. Arthur Tappan escaped in disguise while the mob
descended upon his store and broke its windows before being chased away
by Tappan's friends and employees. The violence began earlier, on the evening
of the Fourth, during a meeting of Manhattan's black community at the
Chatham Chapel. The celebration of liberty included the singing of an anti-
slavery hymn:

> When, smitten as with fire from Heaven,
> The captive's chain shall sink in dust
> And to his fettered soul be given
> The glorious freedom of the just!

When white goons interrupted the meeting and attempted to physically
remove the participants from the church a melee occurred. The rioters
roamed the streets for days and at one point were about three thousand
strong. They plundered the African school and the homes of black people on

Mulberry Street in the Five Points area, and tried to destroy St. Philip's (African) Protestant Episcopal Church. According to the *Anti-Slavery Reporter*, the mob promised "to demolish the house of every leading abolitionist, and to exterminate the people of color!"[3]

The Tappans moved to Brooklyn Heights as rumors and threats of violence continued. The atmosphere alarmed Lydia Maria Child who reported from Brooklyn that assassins were everywhere waiting for a chance at Arthur Tappan. Mayor George Hall appealed to the commandant of the Navy Yard to have a detachment of marines ready to assist in Tappan's defense. Men were posted between the Yard and Tappan's house, where the Mayor personally stood guard. Arthur Tappan survived but he and his brother remained targets of brutish hatred. In 1836 Lewis Tappan was sent a black person's ear by a friend of slavery.[4]

As New York outpaced New England many Protestant families, who proved more receptive to the antislavery message, settled in Manhattan and Brooklyn Heights. They dismissed the etiquette that kept slavery out of Northern politics and social discussion. The Beechers were especially vocal in opposing planter power. "Next to John Brown and his sons," James Brewer Stuart recently wrote, the Beechers were "the family most responsible for heightening these Southerners' anxieties." They were already an institution in Connecticut, where Lyman Beecher, the patriarch, and Edward, his eldest son, both ministers, had given their support to the antislavery movement during its riotous genesis. His son Charles also spread the antislavery message from the pulpit. The most lasting of the family's contributions came from daughter Harriet Elizabeth. The 1852 publication of *Uncle Tom's Cabin* made Harriet Beecher Stowe the crier of the white Northern antislavery message. Her audience, a Brooklyn minister later suggested, included "farmers, factory men, merchants and clerks, the miscellaneous mass that make up the millions." Her brother, Henry Ward Beecher, aimed his appeal at a more intellectual crowd, and was honored by Frederick Douglass as one of a handful of "Noble men [who] may be found, scattered all over these Northern States" for his participation in the antislavery battle. So overwhelming was the family's reputation that a contemporary suggested the trinity of humanity comprised "the good, the bad, and the Beechers."[5]

The pivotal moment in Henry Ward's career was his father's appointment to the presidency of Lane Theological Seminary near Cincinnati. Lane became a radical institution under Lyman Beecher. "Beecher is an admirer of Luther,

Knox, Whitfield, and Wesley. His genius is for a leader. His single-handed faith is like that of a host," an editor wrote of the elder minister. His son delivered his first antislavery appeal while a student at Amherst College, and at Lane Seminary he became an activist. There Henry Ward once took to the streets brandishing a pistol to protect antislavery folk during a proslavery riot. In 1834 Lane's students formed an antislavery society; no mean accomplishment since they were within a mile of a slave state and seven of them were the sons of slaveowners. The society grew out of a series of debates and lectures on bondage hosted by the Seminary. The student antislavery society's unrestrained constitution called for "the immediate emancipation of the whole colored race, within the United States; the emancipation of the slave from the oppression of the master, the emancipation of the free colored man from the oppression of public sentiment, and the elevation of both to an intellectual, moral, and political equality with the whites."[6]

In 1847 Henry Ward Beecher was called to Brooklyn to become the first minister of Plymouth Church, the newly established Congregationalist parish at Brooklyn Heights. In 1856 Lyman Beecher retired to his son's Brooklyn home where he died in 1863. Families from New England who came to Brooklyn convinced of the "sin and shame of slavery" organized Plymouth. A group of Plymouth parishioners also began the *New York Independent*, an antislavery paper. The young Beecher, already a distinguished minister in the Midwest, seemed a perfect choice for a fiery upstart congregation. He came expensive. His starting salary was $2,000, rivaling the mayors of both cities. In 1853 a few Plymouth parishioners presented Beecher with $15,000 for a summer residence. Beecher bought a farm in Lenox, Massachusetts, and had a cottage built there. By the mid 1850s Plymouth was paying Beecher more than $16,000 a year.[7]

Beecher's career underscores the problem of white antislavery. The minister viewed abolition as a dialogue between white people, a discourse that objectified and excluded people of color. White abolition also allowed for a certain circus, a detached drama that helped to turn the apathetic into activists. In May 1847 Lewis Tappan shocked many citizens when he invited Henry Bibb, a fugitive from bondage, to lecture to the white Brooklyn Female Academy. A year later Beecher appeared at the Broadway Tabernacle in New York City to help raise money for the antislavery cause. The beneficiaries were two enslaved girls, the Edmondson sisters, whose freedom was to be purchased through a mock auction. When at the end of the evening only $600 of the $2,000 needed to free the girls was raised, Beecher took the stage for a second time and "by his inspiring eloquence and personal appeals" secured the full amount.[8]

Beecher became a regular speaker at the Tabernacle, which was the crucible of antislavery in the two cities. Of it Walt Whitman later wrote, "Here the huge annual conventions of the windy and cyclonic 'reformatory societies' of those times were held—especially the tumultuous Anti-Slavery ones. I remember hearing Wendell Phillips, Emerson, Cassius Clay, John P. Hale, Beecher, Fred Douglass, the Burleighs, Garrison, and others."[9]

Proslavery forces carefully policed the Tabernacle. United States Marshal Isaiah Rynders and a gang of deputized hoods prevented Beecher, Douglass, and Garrison from addressing the Tabernacle audience during the 1850 meeting of the American Anti-Slavery Society. Local papers heralded the thwarting of "Garrison's band of nigger minstrels." Mary White Ovington, who grew up in Brooklyn Heights after the Civil War, remembered her grandmother—who became an abolitionist under the Reverend Samuel J. May of Brooklyn, Connecticut, and later moved to Brooklyn, Kings County, and became a parishioner at Plymouth—telling the story of an abolitionist meeting at which Rynders pulled the speaker from the stage by his beard. One newspaper tagged Rynders' 1850 mobbing of abolitionists as "Five Point[s] chivalry."[10]

Chased from Manhattan the AA-SS contracted to hold its conference at the Brooklyn Lyceum. Fearing violence, the owners canceled when they discovered that Wendell Phillips would be among the speakers. "Wendell Phillips speaks in my church to-night. I want you to be present with a good constabulary force. Let them quietly be scattered over the church, and let the first fellow who opens his mouth to interrupt the meeting, be marched instantly to jail," Beecher demanded of Brooklyn's mayor. "Let us teach New York a lesson!" That night 2,000 people gathered at Plymouth, and the Rev. Storrs of Brooklyn gave the opening benediction before the Anti-Slavery Society.[11]

On May 11, 1853 Beecher was again in New York to speak before the AA-SS. He delivered one of his most radical lectures. The Plymouth pastor at one point called for disunion if left only with the option of an unfree nation, a position that he had severely criticized in his earlier days. He then vowed to fight for the better moral option of universal liberty and national unity. "Christianity is liberty!" he concluded.[12]

The mock auctions and antislavery speeches increased in frequency and vigor. In July 1856 Beecher auctioned Sarah, a bondswoman who "was almost white, had straight hair, and might in a crowd have passed for a white woman. She was about twenty years of age, was neatly dressed, and might be called handsome." Beecher freed Sarah by doing his best impersonation of a true auctioneer. So moved was the audience that "Bank-notes were piled in those baskets, and jewels from women's hands. Those who were near the pulpit laid their gifts at Henry Ward Beecher's feet." The collection plates were filled with cash and gold coins by the end of Beecher's performance. Five hundred dollars would free Sarah, Beecher raised eight hundred that day. At the end of the spectacle, Beecher sighed, "There, Sarah, you are free."[13]

On a Sunday in February 1860, during the symbolic auction of a young woman, an inspired member of the congregation, Rose Terry Cooke, dropped her ring into the collection. Beecher then placed the ring on the young bondswoman's finger, declared it her "freedom ring," and renamed her Rose Ward after the donor and himself.[14]

Beecher's charm was captured by Charlotte Forten, a free black woman, a fierce critic of slavery and discrimination, a teacher in New England, and a teacher in the South Carolina Sea Islands during the Civil War. On Friday night, January 12, 1855, Forten attended a Beecher lecture. In her diary she compared his technique to the clergy of his day:

> This evening [I] attended a lecture by Rev. Henry Ward Beecher of Brooklyn.
>
> The subject was "Patriotism." I thought the lecture extremely interesting, and many parts of it very touching and beautiful. His manner is not at all polished or elegant, but he says so many excellent things with such forcible earnestness or irresistible humor, that we quite forget it. As I had hoped he bore his testimony against the wicked and unjust laws of our land, which it is not *patriotism* to make or to obey. He also eloquently advocated the right of woman to vote; and paid a beautiful tribute to the lovely and noble-minded Lucretia Mott. In listening to Mr. Beecher one feels convinced of his *sincerity*; and we would always rather know that a person *means* what he says, even if we differ from him.[15]

That style made Beecher the most influential minister in the United States.

He was not without his critics. After the Civil War, a contemporary, reflecting on his career described Beecher as a gifted orator with an undisciplined and lazy message.

> His power as an orator was evident, the subtlety of his art and the breadth of his humor were irresistible, but his reasoning was loose, his statements inaccurate, his manner somewhat arrogant, and his dispo-

sition apparently inclined to be demagoguical [sic]. He emphasized himself and all his feelings; appealed largely to the passions of his hearers, evidently forgetting that there was a very large world outside of Plymouth Church, and that reason rules the globe after all.

Even this critic was eventually swayed. Compromising his position, he later declared Beecher to be a sober and good man whose worst flaw was that his heart governed his mind.[16]

"We hazard little in saying that there is no living man in America whose name is more widely known than that of the Plymouth pastor," read the first sentence of the first issue of *Brooklyn Monthly*. But part of Beecher's fame resulted from a deep and general animosity toward his antislavery philosophy; in much of the nation, including Brooklyn, he was infamous. Beecher modestly recalled: "In 1847–48–49 I had become well known. My anti-slavery sentiments began to be well known in New York." His reputation, in fact, escaped New York. "Shall We Compromise?" an article that he wrote in response to Henry Clay's Omnibus Bill (the "Compromise of 1850") was reportedly read twice to the bedridden John C. Calhoun of South Carolina. "The man who says that," Calhoun responded from a thoroughly different vantage point, "is right. Slavery has to go to the wall. There is no alternative. It is liberty or slavery." A better, if unfounded, compliment came when Calhoun charged that Henry Ward Beecher was the real author of *Uncle Tom's Cabin*. In 1856, during the Kansas settlement struggles between free- and slave-state forces, Beecher took the Plymouth pulpit and encouraged his audience to emigrate to Kansas. He announced his plans to equip every free-state man in Kansas with a Sharpe rifle (a.k.a. Beecher's bible) and the Good Book. He then joined with Professor Silliman of Yale to carry out the plan. So well known was the Church and its minister that a later guide to New York instructed tourists seeking to reach Plymouth to "Cross Fulton Ferry and follow the crowd."[17]

A small cadre of white abolitionists guarded the hope that the scourge of slavery could be ended; however, the great mass of white and immigrant Brooklynites loathed radicals, Negroes, and the idea of universal freedom. As Beecher's fame and Plymouth's reputation grew, both the pastor and the church became targets of intimidation and violence for, what George Templeton Strong termed, "niggerophily (or philo-nigger-anthropy)." In 1856 Plymouth Church hosted radical abolitionist Wendell Phillips, who had been refused by virtually every church and hall in the two cities. The event invited so many threats that Beecher instructed the Church's trustees to attend "the meeting with heavy canes," the City of Brooklyn reinforcing them with police protection. Later, a Democratic procession across Brooklyn warned that "Henry Ward Beecher had better stick to the pulpit." On Sunday, June 8, 1856, New York papers announced a white gang's plan to visit Brooklyn, Plymouth, and Beecher that night.[18]

Abolition was soundly defeated in the City of Churches. White Brooklynites did become vexed that Southern slavery required Northern sacrifice. By the 1850s the idea of a "Slave Power"—a Southern aristocracy who demanded political privileges over the rest of the nation to the detriment of other white men—was increasingly real, and Kings County's residents hated the idea of working for them. White Brooklynites were not economic theorists; they rejected only the way that Southern planters affected their lives. Strong captured the subtlety when, after declaring abolition to be a greater sin than slaveowning, he admitted his disgust with "Southern Ultraism." In particular, the planters had earned his wrath, and he excoriated them as "a race of lazy, ignorant, coarse, sensual, swaggering, sordid, beggarly barbarians, bullying white men and breeding little niggers for sale."[19]

While not directly blaming planters for the nation's troubles, Walt Whitman fancied a society in which white men were free of slavery. Like Strong, Whitman was caught between his contempt for black people and his growing resentment of planter privilege. Well on his way to becoming the great American poet, he was influenced by the idealistic "anti-institutional impulse" of the 1850s, writes George M. Fredrickson. For Whitman the existence of political parties explained the continuous social crises that afflicted the nation, and he hungered for a more natural political comity, a "nonpolitical democracy." He came to see the West as the one region of the nation that was untainted, the bountiful preserve of the free white man.[20]

Whitman's schizophrenic career personified Brooklyn's divisions. At twenty-two, he was the editor of a xenophobic, two-penny rag, the *New York Aurora*. Comfortable with the prejudices of its owners, Whitman launched editorial assaults against the growing Irish population of Manhattan. Like many Protestants, Whitman accepted that rapid urbanization, labor struggles, epidemics, and political turmoil, were *caused* by immigrants. When Catholics challenged Protestant domination of the public school system, Whitman blasted the predominantly Irish protesters as "blustering rowdies" and "filthy wretches, whose very touch was offensive to a decent man." He measured their clergymen no more than "sly, false, deceitful villains," and Catholic Archbishop John Hughes a "hypocritical scoundrel."[21]

In 1840 the *Native American Citizen and Brooklyn Evening Advertiser*, launched with Nativist party support, published similar sentiments in Kings County. In time Whitman came to see that the poverty and tumultuousness of the Irish were the symptoms and not the disease. A few years later, as editor of the *Brooklyn Eagle*, his editorials defended the Irish and encouraged their allegiance to the Democratic party. After being fired from the *Eagle*, Whitman edited the *Brooklyn Freeman*, a free-soil paper founded by Judge Samuel E. Johnson in April 1848, which soon became the largest selling penny paper in the nation. Through the *Freeman* he voiced his support for the movement to keep people of color out of the West. In 1851 Manhattan responded with the *White Man's Newspaper*, targeted at the commercial and intellectual element among white Protestants.[22]

By the 1850s Whitman had shunned politics and parties altogether, believing party politics to be responsible for the nation's constant social crises. During the presidential election of 1856, Whitman wrote a lengthy treatise, "The Eighteenth Presidency!" to the nation's mechanics and workers that was not published. "I place no reliance upon any old party, nor upon any new party," he insisted. "As soon as it becomes successful, and there are offices to be bestowed, the politicians leave the unsuccessful parties, and rush toward it, and it ripens and rots with the rest."[23]

No narrow interest was suited to lead the nation and no noble or broad interest ever survived. The national government needed reform from corruption and vice, but no politician offered a cure. Sectionalism and party loyalty were crushing democracy. Elite and moneyed men hoarded power, while "free farmers and work people" had no place to settle and take root. Underneath all this, he suspected, was the failure of the political system. Men were nominated from "lawyers' offices, secret lodges, back-yards, bed-houses, and bar-rooms" or "the venereal hospital."[24] In Whitman's personal revolutions was evidence that the issue of slavery was not a simple choice between freedom and unfreedom but a complex problem that touched the very meaning and order of life.

There were some who would push that conflict to its "logical" end. In March 1858 James Gloucester, the pastor and founder of Siloam Presbyterian Church (African) in Brooklyn, and his wife Elizabeth sent John Brown of Kansas twenty-five dollars "to do battle to that *ugly foe*," slavery. This was not the first time that the Gloucesters had sent Brown money. Two months before

Brown's famous raid of the federal arsenal at Harper's Ferry, Elizabeth Gloucester had contributed to Brown's work. This time Frederick Douglass, who stopped in Brooklyn to see the Gloucesters on his way to Brown, delivered the money.[25] The raid, on Sunday evening, October 16, 1859, was intended to equip the enslaved for a general revolt. Less than 48 hours later a wounded Brown was captured by troops under Colonel Robert E. Lee of Virginia.

The call for mercy was heard from every corner of the North. John Brown of "bleeding Kansas" had become one of the most frightening reminders of abolitionist sentiments that the South could ever have imagined. Before the raid, when Brown had been shopping his scheme among his radical allies, he took time to visit Brooklyn where he likely saw the Gloucesters and Henry Ward Beecher. Now Beecher called for mercy by grabbing the chains that had bound Brown, driving them to the floor of New York's Broadway Tabernacle, and stomping on them during an impassioned speech. Earlier at Plymouth, Beecher stated his position on the Brown affair:

> I deplore his misfortunes. I sympathize with his sorrows. I mourn the hiding or obscuration of his reason. I disapprove of his mad and feeble schemes. I shrink from the folly of the bloody foray, and I shrink likewise from all the anticipation of that judicial bloodshed which doubtless erelong will follow; for when was cowardice ever magnanimous?
>
> If they kill the man, it will not be so much for treason as for the disclosure of their cowardice!

Brown was the victim. He had struggled through the bloody wars to keep Kansas free. He had organized against the political designs of the Southern planters. He knew better than any man the ruthlessness of the Slave Power. Finally, tired of the endless conflicts and unable to compromise, he took direct action. Now, Virginia would victimize him again. It mattered little how accurate this portrayal was, for, as Beecher had done in a single lecture, the North was already writing the story of Brown's martyrdom:

> Let no man pray that Brown be spared. Let Virginia make him a martyr. Now, he has only blundered. His soul was noble, his work miserable. But a cord and a gibbet would redeem all that, and round up Brown's failure with heroic success.[26]

In the aftermath of Brown's raid Wendell Phillips returned to Brooklyn and delivered a lecture, "The Lesson of the Hour," at Plymouth. "You remember the first time I was ever privileged to stand on this platform by the magnanimous generosity of your clergyman, when New York was about to bully and crush out the freedom of speech at the dictation of Capt. Rynders," Phillips said. He reminded his audience that he, not Rynders, was correct. He then delivered a lecture so sympathetic to Brown that it undoubtedly troubled many in his sympathetic audience and attracted the cry of treason from the New York press. "Virginia did not tremble at an old gray-headed man at Harper's Ferry; they trembled at a John Brown in every man's own conscience," Phillips argued. He then called Brown God's school master who was sent to instruct Virginia and the Almighty's High Admiral who is charged with sinking pirate states.[27]

On November 24, 1859 Ms. "H. C." of Brooklyn, who was at Beecher's sermon on Harper's Ferry, wrote a passionate letter to Brown at his Virginia jail cell. She assured Brown that "the Great Northern Heart beats warmly in your behalf," and then captured the same themes as Beecher's speech by asking, "does not the Commonwealth of Virginia foresee that when they have taken your life, and those of your fellow-sufferers, there will rise up twenty John Browns where there was one before, and the ghost of John Brown will haunt them till they let the oppressed go free?"[28]

Two days later "the colored women of Brooklyn" wrote Brown an equally engaging letter. Most noticeable is the way that these women wrote of Brown's raid as an act through which he joined *their* struggle. They saluted Brown for seeing that moral principle transcended material self-interest and told him that his raid had hastened the end of slavery:

> We, a portion of the American people, would fain offer you our sincere and heart-felt sympathies in the cause you have so nobly espoused, and that you so firmly adhere to. We truly appreciate your most noble and humane effort, and recognize in you a Saviour commissioned to redeem us, the American people, from the great National Sin of Slavery; and though you have apparently failed in the object of your desires, yet the influence that we believe it will eventually exert, will accomplish all your intentions. We consider you a model of true patriotism, and one whom our common country will yet regard as the greatest it has produced, because you have sacrificed all for its sake. We rejoice in the consciousness of your perfect resignation. We shall ever hold you dear in our remembrance, and shall infuse the same feelings in our posterity.

We have always entertained a love for the country which gave us birth, despite the wrongs inflicted upon us, and have always been hopeful that the future would augur better things. We feel now that your glorious act for the cause of humanity has afforded us an unexpected realization of some of our seemingly vain hopes.

And now, in view of the coming crisis which is to terminate all your labors of love for this life, our mortal natures fail to sustain us under the trying affliction; but when we view it from our religious standpoint, we feel that earth is not worthy of you, and that your spirit yearneth for a higher and holier existence.

Therefore we willingly give you up, and submit to His will "who doeth all things well."[29]

Brooklyn's black women later supported the widow of one of Brown's men through the New York Liberty Fund, under Ms. Henry Highland Garnet. In January 1860 a Williamsburg, Brooklyn, church held a funeral service for John Copeland and Shields Green, two of Brown's men who were executed after the raid.[30] Copeland was from Williamsburg.

After Harper's Ferry, Brooklyn's abolitionists turned to the election of Abraham Lincoln. In 1858 nationally known Stephen Douglas handed Lincoln fame when the two debated during a senatorial campaign in Illinois. In the election that followed, Lincoln won the popular vote but not the Senate seat because of the distribution of districts. Yet the loser was now a national figure and could command the national stage. In February 1860 Henry Ward Beecher and Henry Bowen, an editor of the *Independent* who funded the building of Plymouth, invited the rising politician to give an address at the church. Lincoln accepted but it was eventually decided that a greater hall, Cooper Union, in the greater city, New York, was a more appropriate location. The day before his Cooper Union address Lincoln took "Beecher's ferry" (the nickname of the Fulton ferry on Sundays) to the City of Churches. "As a small boy, I remember seeing Lincoln on the steps of our home on the Sunday above referred to," recalled Henry Bowen's son. The visitor then went to Orange Street, Brooklyn Heights, and sat in the Bowen pew to soak in Beecher's elegance and drive. The prior Sunday Beecher had auctioned an enslaved Virginian to freedom. But as Lincoln sat in the audience Beecher shunned drama and called on all his oratorical skills for a jeremiad against slavery.[31] The next day Lincoln gave the address at New York's Cooper Union that started him on the road to the presidency.

In the presidential election of 1860 Lincoln took only 43 percent of Brooklyn's vote. Democrats swept the city and drew in the labor vote by painting the Republicans as a wild abolitionist horde. They successfully convinced merchants and entrepreneurs that Republicanism threatened trade with the South, while insisting to the working class that a Lincoln victory meant the death of slavery and the exodus of millions of black workers to the Northern cities. Before election day 30,000 Democrats paraded through New York City carrying images of white abolitionists entwined with "lusty" Negresses. Signs pilloried "amalgamation," "free Niggers," and Lincoln. One local Democratic club carried red, white, and blue lanterns and wore red, white, and blue capes. In the Democratic press the word "nigger" became verb, noun, and modifier as city editors excited citizens against Republicanism. In November 1860 white and immigrant Brooklynites over-whelmingly rejected Lincoln, antislavery, and black suffrage.[32]

Most white Brooklynites saw the election of Lincoln, black suffrage, and disunion in distinctly racial terms because those possibilities threatened to topple relations that they had come to accept as natural. Lincoln won only four of the city's nineteen wards, and of the five outlying towns he won only Flatlands. Theophilus C. Callicot, a representative from Kings County, told the Assembly that "the proposition to put Negroes on a footing of political equality with white men is repugnant to the sense of the American people. They will never consent to share the proud title of 'American citizen' with an inferior and abject race."[33] In but two lines Callicot had repeated that often-spun and sadly ironic story of a people who had declared their natural supremacy but lacked the courage to let it naturally reveal itself.

New York City mayor Fernando Wood—who had Loco Foco roots and whose name unionist Brooklynites soon listed alongside Confederates and hissed by war's end—went further. He played to local commercial interests in a call for New York City to secede. Wood was elected as part of white Manhattan's reaction against John Brown's raid. Now, labeling the Republican party a "venal and corrupt master," positioning Gotham as the Empire City of the Confederacy, and reducing the Union to a mere business arrangement, the Mayor argued that

> Our ships have penetrated to every clime, and so have New York capital, energy, and enterprise found their way to every State, and, indeed, to almost every county and town of the American Union. If we

have derived sustenance from the Union, so have we in return dissem-
inated blessings for the common benefit of all. Therefore, New York has
a right to expect, and should endeavor to preserve a continuance of
uninterrupted intercourse with every section.

Wood then demanded Long Island secession and the formation of "the
republic of Tri-Insula."[34]

In April 1861 the war began and Brooklyn's nationalism was immediately
tested. In Williamsburg the *Brooklyn Daily Times* announced that it received
the news of the attack on Fort Sumter with "a thrill of horror." The editors
later boasted that strongly Republican Germans had dealt with a Southern
sympathizer in the only way possible: "A rope was instantly procured and put
about his neck, and he was dragged out in the street to be hanged to the
nearest lamppost." His life was eventually spared. Brooklyn's mayor tried for
a more peaceful public expression of loyalty in a mass vigil:

Proclamation by the Mayor,
Mayor's Office, City Hall, Brooklyn,
April 22, 1861

The Citizens of Brooklyn are hereby respectfully requested to close
their stores and places of business during the afternoon of Tuesday,
the 23d inst, with a view of affording an opportunity to the clerks
and employees generally, to attend the Mass Meeting at Fort Greene,
and manifest their devotion to the Union in the hour of peril.

SAMUEL S. POWELL, Mayor[35]

Henry Ward Beecher celebrated Lincoln's election in two lectures. The first,
titled "The Sign of the Times," carefully documented how the westward
expansion of slavery divided the nation and how planters and their sympathizers persecuted and silenced abolitionists to protect that growth.
Republican victory meant "that long period, thank God, has come to an
end. The last westward step is taken. I think they will never get any nearer to
sundown than they are now." Two weeks later Beecher told a Boston audience
that people were asking him if the South was going to secede. "I don't care if
they do!" the pastor responded. He saw no room for new compromises or
rehashed discussions; the Republicans were fairly elected and the will of the
people was to be done. "Union for honor, union for truth, union for vigor in
liberty, union for power in free institutions, union for humanity now, and

greater growth—for that I would sacrifice almost anything in life," he asserted. But without those, the union is dead. "Bury the corpse when the soul has gone out of it! Don't keep it to stink above ground!"[36]

Black people in Kings County were even less somber about the national schism. "Colored men, you stand I trust now, only in the commencement of a most wonderful and glorious era in the history of the American people," pledged Rev. Gloucester. Delighting in the threat that the war posed to slaveholders, Gloucester urged black men to force "a crisis hour to a pure virgin liberty." "On the one hand, is but the legitimate throes of the giant slavery to live—on the other, but his own noose in the hands of freemen to strangle." Gloucester continued his appeal to black men through a new paper, *The Colored Patriot*. J. W. C. Pennington demanded an expanded role for black men: "Mark my words, gentlemen, we cannot get out of this terrible scrape, without in some way helping to decide the contest; and I believe that we are on the eve of the grand heroic age of the race, when the last vestige of African Slavery shall be wiped out."[37]

On Sunday evening, April 14, 1861, Henry Ward Beecher took the stage at Plymouth Church and, in muted tones, gave a lengthy sermon to introduce the fact of a war between the states. Moral justice was the theme. The antislavery sentiments that swelled in the prior decades were fueled by righteousness and human compassion, and the method of their expression was the dictate of the Constitution itself.[38]

Even during the War most white Brooklynites renounced any antislavery objectives; in fact, they resisted the idea that slavery was a cause or concern of the conflict. On a ferry ride across the East River, Walt Whitman discussed the war with Mayor Powell, who was convinced that it would be quickly decided. Whitman wrote his brother, Lieutenant George Washington Whitman of the Union Army, assuring him that the South could not last and that all Brooklyn thought the rebellion might be short lived. Beecher, echoing Abraham Lincoln, instructed the First Long Island Regiment (the "Brooklyn Phalanx") on the limitations of a war to preserve the wholeness of the nation, not to end slavery. "Liberty is the birthright of every man, yet yours is not an army of emancipation." However, Beecher continued, if "the slaves avail themselves of the chance to cut and run, that is their lookout—not ours. . . . we do not go South to be anybody's nigger catcher." The pastor raised troops, he raised funds, he counseled and communicated with the President's cabinet, he housed soldiers at Plymouth, and he even sent a son, Henry, to command one of the companies of the First. Every soldier in two companies of the Thirteenth Brooklyn, recalled Whitman, was outfitted with rope to bring back rebels "led in a noose." Abiel Low helped organize the Home Trust of Volunteers of Brooklyn to provide relief for the families of local soldiers. Four Meserole men were among the founders and officers of the 17th Ward Soldiers' Aid Association, formed to assist the families of Greenpoint's 500 volunteers. Still, many Brooklynites were uncomfortable with the implications of the moment. When a black man began to defame the South on a Brooklyn ferry, a white rider instructed him that "now if ever was the time when negroes should keep their mouths shut and when no references to party should be made." Some Brooklynites shed blood, some shed tears, others shed illusions. During that painful first year, white Brooklynites came to accept that slavery was not coincident, that it had to be the central issue of the conflict.[39]

Black Brooklynites had made that clear in their actions and words. On May 23, 1861 they celebrated the sectional conflict and the struggle against slavery by welcoming home the Reverend Alexander Crummell, one of the many black refugees who returned to the United States during the War. He had left New York to attend Cambridge University in England, and after graduating spent two decades as a missionary in Liberia. Before 200 celebrants, Brooklyn's Professor William J. Wilson and the Reverend Henry Highland Garnet, a boyhood friend of Crummell's, gave the introductory remarks. Crummell then took the podium and addressed the audience. "Wherever the black man is, he is my brother, preeminently so. Our race is indomitable; no other race could have undergone the oppression we have suffered and survived. But we have not only survived, but progressed; we have taken hold of the pillars of the country and shaken them to their foundations," Crummell commanded to the applause of his audience. The evening ended with a benediction from the pastor of Bridge Street A. M. E. and a solo from Robert Hamilton.[40]

African Americans were not alone in seeing emancipation as the natural outcome of the conflict. In his 1861 Thanksgiving Day sermon, Beecher warned his congregation not to simply think that emancipation could be declared. The North had to work through the nation's institutions; slavery's destruction could not mean the end of the United States' laws and its principles. Two months later Garrison was at Cooper Union sounding very different. This hour was not greatly different from the radical moment at which New York State ended slavery. "Your Constitution is an Abolition Constitution. Your laws are Abolition laws. Your institutions are Abolition institutions," he proclaimed. It was only the proslavery press and its thugs who retreated from that realization. "Capt. Rynders is not an Abolitionist," said Garrison. "The Bowery Boys do not like Abolitionism." On the eve of the Emancipation Proclamation, a Unitarian convention in Brooklyn declared its support for the President and called upon the nation to do the same.[41]

Instead, social tensions and ethnic rivalries exploded. In Brooklyn, on a Saturday afternoon in August 1862, an African-American man was shoved aside by a white man entering a grog (watered down liquor) shop. The two swapped slurs, then blows. After the white man, Mr. Spaulding, was bested, several white men plotted revenge. On Monday, eight Irish ruffians searched Lorillard's tobacco shop looking for black workers, but only white employees were on hand because everyone else had been sent home by an astute foreman. The rioters, now about thirty in number, then surrounded an adjacent shop owned by a Mr. Watson, who employed an interracial work force of seventy-five people, two-thirds of whom were African American, separated under two foreman, one white, one black. The mob assaulted Watson's factory with curses, bricks, and cobble stones. Soon 2,000 women, men, and children—some intoxicated, all infuriated–were involved. Twenty people of color—five men and fifteen women—barricaded themselves on the second floor where they held off the throng while waiting for assistance. As *The Brooklyn Eagle* later noted, the two policemen on patrol in the area were energetically participating in the violence. The rabble then followed the suggestion of Patrick Canna, another grog seller, "to set fire to the building and roast the niggers alive." Fortunately, police reinforcements quelled the disturbance just as the mob was attempting to torch the building. From Rochester, the sharp pen of Frederick Douglass reported the incident:

> Brooklyn, the city of churches and noble charities, is usually so well behaved, we could scarcely credit the report that a riot had actually taken place there; but a careful and impartial investigation of facts show that the fair fame of our sister city has been sullied by a riotous mob of half-drunken and ignorant white men and women, whose jealously [sic] of the blacks was kindled by a fight . . .

Watson's shop did not reopen and the black employees of Lorillard's were warned that their return to work would bring a second plundering.[42]

A few months later, on January 2, 1863, black Brooklynites gathered at the Bridge Street Church to celebrate the Emancipation Proclamation. Carrying banners that celebrated their antislavery holidays, the audience first heard an address from the Reverend John Gloucester, who was followed by author and abolitionist William Wells Brown. Each member of the assembly agreed to pay a tax of one dollar to support people freed under the Proclamation. The Democratic *Eagle* covered the event under titles like "REJOICE YE DARKIES ALL" and "OUR COLORED 'BREDEN.'" An *Eagle* reporter venomously described the door keeper as "a lemon-colored mulatto" with "long black hair—not wool but hair" and the audience as a "dense mass of colored humanity, packed so close on the benches that a slave trader would scarcely risk the carrying of them." Three days later the black communities of New York and Brooklyn joined with white supporters at Cooper Union for a grand observance of the Proclamation. Among the speakers were the Reverend Henry Highland Garnet, Lewis Tappan, and Professor William J. Wilson. Garnet read the Proclamation. He told the audience that slavery was not dead but doomed, and announced that the black men of the area had offered their military services to the governor. Wilson, seeing the joyous side of the evening, joked that the fall of the press was approaching, for, freed from protecting bondage, the editors would be "looking for some new occupation." The celebration "was a fitting expression of the triumph of the American Union over African slavery," wrote the *Times*.[43]

The Proclamation helped to rejuvenate Henry Ward Beecher. In a Sunday sermon he condemned a rampant commercialism that allowed the strong to dominate the weak. The Plymouth pastor encouraged Lincoln to arm black men and destroy those who profited from the fiendish business of slavery. That summer Beecher went to Europe to recover from declining health. There, although he had promised not to work, he soon delivered a series of town-hall speeches across England to convince Britons that their well-being was with the destruction of slavery in the United States. Although England's economy was faltering because of the shortage of Southern cotton, the British did not assist the Confederacy. Lincoln took note of Beecher's efforts and invited the preacher to the White House.[44]

But most white Brooklynites had already repudiated antislavery and Lincoln. The Irish had long imagined that the end of bondage might bring something like servitude upon them. Already desperately poor and occupying the crudest jobs in the cities, they were faced with the possible freeing of 4.5 million malleable laborers. Brooklyn's Democratic press was openly sympathetic to the Confederacy and spared little criticism of Lincoln. Blatant attempts to undermine the Union were evident. The most frequent tactic was simply unleashing the horrible truth of the conflicts. "The *Eagle*," lamented Whitman during the summer of 1861, "of course, makes the worst of it, every day, to stop men from enlisting."[45]

It did not take much to coax people to treason. On Friday July 10, 1863 the *Eagle* announced the draft quotas for the two cities: New York, 12,500; Brooklyn, 4,600. The cities were to make up for exemptions with a 50 percent increase in the call-up. On Monday July 13, 1863—the day that Hooley's Minstrels were scheduling a performance to benefit Brooklyn's Irish Relief Fund and the day of the draft in the Ninth District of New York City—large numbers of Irish and German workers gathered at Central Park. The *Eagle* reported that the mob voted to resist the draft by force and were led by the local railroad workers and reinforced by the firemen. Marching downtown carrying anti-war, anti-draft placards, "cursing the 'bloody draft,'" some men and women broke into stores, cut telegraph lines, and tore up street rails. They viciously beat police officers who happened into their path, including Superintendent of Police John Kennedy, who "was spotted by a crowd, dragged through the mud and beaten on the head until 'unrecognizable.'" At 10:30 that morning, the firemen of the Black Joke Engine Company, believing that their normal militia exemption should extend to the Civil War, torched the district draft office. An hour later the draft was suspended and the federal papers were removed to Governor's Island. "Jefferson Davis rules New York today," sighed George Templeton Strong, now a member of the Union League Club.[46]

As a result of the Draft Riots, Albro Lyons and his family returned to Brooklyn as refugees. In the 1850s Lyons moved from Brooklyn to Manhattan to go into partnership in William Powell's Colored Seamen's Home. In 1851 Powell had taken his family to England to escape American caste while Lyons ran his business. As proprietor Lyons amassed enough money to move the Home to a larger building and to open a separate seamen's outfitting business. He was also attracting the envy of many a white neighbor. Powell returned to the United States at the beginning of the war. And on the first day of the Draft Riots, Powell's Seamen's house was sacked, Lyons' store was plundered, and a mob descended upon Lyons' home and busted the shutters, broke the windows, and kicked in the front door. The family survived the first attack. Lyons and his wife Mary got their children to safety and then camped out to "protect their property, [and] to sell their lives as dearly as maybe should the need arise." "A lonely vigil of hours passed in mingled darkness, indignation, uncertainty, and dread," one of the children later recalled. The rioters returned. "Father advanced into the doorway and fired point blank into the crowd." Police officer Kelly heard of the attack and appeared at Lyons door sobbing at the spectacle. The following day a third mob proved more successful. Lyons escaped across a fence, his wife was hidden by a German neighbor. In less than an hour the mob demolished their house, stole or destroyed their possessions, and attempted to set fire to what structure remained. The neighbor who assisted Lyons' wife was later given a good beating. That night the Brooklyn police escorted the parents to the Williamsburg ferry where black victims were being transported to Kings County or carried out to the middle of the river for their protection. Mother and children continued across Long Island to New England where Albro Lyons later joined them.[47]

Dr. Philip White also became a Brooklyn resident after the Riots and later served on the Brooklyn Board of Education. White was one of several black men trained in pharmacy by renowned physician Dr. James McCune Smith. White opened his own Manhattan pharmacy near Lyons' business, but local Irish residents protected White's business because he had allowed so many of the poor to pay for prescriptions at their convenience or not charged them at all.[48]

"A Citizen of Brooklyn" wrote the *Eagle* insisting that "the trouble, at present, lies in the exemption clause." Blasting the local abolitionists, he continued, "Mr. Beecher, Horace Greeley . . . or any other man of the . . . class who has been urging on the war is under quite as much obligation to the government as the humblest laborer of New York or Brooklyn, and no sum of money can discharge him from that obligation." That class remained out of the reach of white workers. Instead Brooklyn's white laboring classes chased a black sailor along Hudson Avenue back to the Navy Yard. They visited black peoples' houses. "Pink row, in Canton street, is entirely vacated. It was occupied by colored people," recounted the *Eagle*. "They have gone, no one knows where. The same is the case in some other localities abounding in colored folks."[49]

After Monday the New York rioters were distinctly Irish and African Americans were their particular target. They burned the Colored Orphan Asylum and gangs of thugs randomly assaulted black people, including a nine-year-old boy. "Winding slowly along 34th street into Seventh avenue, headed by a strong police force, came the little colored orphans, whose asylum had been burned down on Monday night. The boys, from two and three to fifteen years of age, followed by little girls of the same ages, to the number of about two hundred each, trotted along," read a newspaper account. The children were followed by black adults who carried bundles of clothing and small pieces of furniture that they had saved from the mob. A police and military guard took them to Riker's Island for protection while holding back the mob with bayonets. Jeremiah Robinson was beaten unconscious and cast into the East River when he was caught attempting to flee to Brooklyn. Tuesday brought the murder of William Williams, a sailor who left his vessel to ask directions. On Wednesday, James Costello, a shoemaker, was "beat," "kicked," "stoned," "trampled," and "finally hanged." Abraham Franklin, a disabled coachman about 23 years old, was caught and stabbed "in the most delicate parts of the body" as others kicked, beat, and bit him. A few people took their heels and ground them into his eyes. They then cut his throat. Franklin's corpse was lynched on a lamppost and then dragged through the streets of Manhattan by the genitals. Ten or eleven black New Yorkers were killed that week. Strong noted that by Thursday a number of other cities—including Albany, Troy, Boston, Hartford, and Yonkers—had draft riots, each inspired by an "Irish anti-conscription Nigger-murdering mob, of the same type as ours." Troops under Brooklyn's Colonel Alfred M. Wood—who was to be elected mayor of Brooklyn in November 1863—were sent to Manhattan to help restore order, and Brooklyn's mayor and other officials again went on night duty with a large police guard to quell the violence in Kings County. Like most of the patriotic members of the Union League, Strong thought it all a "grave business" to be answered "by heroic doses of lead and steel."[50]

On July 17 police sergeant John Rode twice wrote Albro Lyons about the conditions in Manhattan. "I cannot say today what will occur tomorrow," Rode admitted. He tried to help Lyons collect his remaining property by meeting him with a horse and wagon that day but later decided that

> You have better leave your clothing here for a day or two, and every thing will be settled. Then you can come here yourselves and take charge of them. They are all safe here, I will call over and see you this afternoon and then you can come over with me if you want to. I now remain your friend[.]

Rode assured Lyons that three policemen were protecting his house against fire and vandalism.[51]

African Americans were not the only targets of the rioters. The police were frequently victimized along with "well-dressed gentlemen and the houses of wealthy Republicans." Horace Greeley's *Tribune* was sacked and the editor was lucky to escape alive. Even Captain Isaiah Rynders was seeking military protection for his home. After Monday, Irish rioters attacked German and Jewish shopkeepers. On Monday night, local Catholic priests used all their persuasive power to keep a band of rioters from burning the home of the president of Columbia College on the grounds that he was a wealthy Republican. Other Protestant symbols, like the Magdalen Asylum, for aging prostitutes, were also attacked. Manhattan's leading citizens did not easily swallow assaults on their institutions. "For myself, personally," wrote Strong after the riots had ended, "I would like to see war made on the Irish scum as in 1688."[52]

Archbishop John Hughes of New York addressed the mob and called on them to be peaceful. Hughes spoke "as your father" and not as a politician or military man. The disorder had to end because it would soon result in the deaths of many rioters as the police and military forces were strengthened. Yet, even as the Archbishop spoke the basis of the riots was revealed as one person interrupted him with the cry, "Let the niggers keep South."[53]

The victims of the riots—African Americans, the police, the wealthy, Protestants, and the local and national Republican administrations—perfectly captured the extent of Catholic Irish displacement. These were the forces that the Irish saw arrayed against them, and the War to End Slavery only aggravated their hatreds. Slavery had given them their only advantages. They enjoyed the right to vote and a numerical superiority over their black competitors. Now the Emancipation Proclamation threatened to flood the North with more than 4 million freed people, and in the absence of slavery the extension of suffrage seemed more possible. Conscription forced the Irish to participate in the whole affair. In protest they rose up, murdered some of those they thought it benefited, intimidated those who remained out of their reach, and put off the hated draft.

Black Brooklynites assisted victims from New York and organized for self-defense. "The attacks upon the colored people of Brooklyn continue. They are not safe anywhere. They are driven from their homes," reported one paper. The black men of Weeksville armed themselves to fend off attacks and provide shelter to refugees from New York and Kings County. In nearby Flushing the black community alerted the local Catholic priest that they were peaceful but if attacked they would respond by destroying two Irish houses and taking two Irish lives for every one of their houses or lives. There was no violence in Flushing. In a similar show of strength and unity, "most of the colored men in Brooklyn who remained in the city were armed daily for self-defence [sic]."[54]

The reaction in Washington and from the battlefront was severe. "The feeling here is savage & hot as fire against New York," Whitman wrote his mother from the capital during the middle of the bloody week. "I hear nothing in all directions but threats of ordering up the gunboats, cannonading the city, shooting down the mob, [and] hanging them in a body." By now Whitman had seen war and poverty and understood both too well to side with either. "I do not feel it in my heart to abuse the poor people, or call for rope or bullets for them, but that is all the talk here." He contemplated the situation and remained "silent, partly amused, partly scornful, or occasionally put a dry remark."[55]

The Emancipation Proclamation allowed for the use of African-American troops, now more logical since slavery was a target and more necessary in the wake of the anti-draft rage of the North's white laboring classes and the weariness of all. Walt Whitman's letters to his mother often contained the disheartening news of "youngsters" from Brooklyn who had been injured, maimed, or killed. By January 1864, 766 of the 1,000 men in the "Brooklyn Phalanx" were dead. Whitman prayed that conscription would not be reinstated. "I should say it was very doubtful if they can carry it out in NY & Brooklyn." Whitman confided to his mother that if it returned and if his brother Thomas Jefferson Whitman were drafted, he would lecture and borrow to raise $300 for an exemption. In spite of their evangelical racism, white Northerners came to see the use of black soldiers as a godsend. Edward Hogan of Weeksville, Edward Squires, and Peter Vogelsang Jr., the oldest man in the famed Massachusetts Fifty-Fourth Infantry, were among the Brooklynites who enlisted in the Union Army during the War. Vogelsang began as a quartermaster sergeant and rose to the rank of first lieutenant. Dr. Peter W. Ray—who, after the war, kept a Brooklyn pharmacy for fifty years and was a founder of the Brooklyn College of Pharmacy—served in the army as a surgeon. Brooklyn's Joseph Plant, Andrew Smith, and George Williams were serving in the Navy. "There are getting to be *many black troops*," Whitman informed his mother during the summer of 1863, "there is one very good reg't here black as tar—they go armed, have the regular uniform—they submit to no nonsense—others are constantly forming—it is getting to be a common sight." Whitman was encouraged when he saw "mounted negroes" who moved about with an army that "had the look of *real war*."[56]

With men of color now bearing a large share of the war burden, the North moved toward victory and the surrender of General Robert E. Lee in a court house at Appomattox, Virginia in April of 1865. On April 14 at the ceremonial closing of the War, Henry Ward Beecher presided as the United States flag was restored above Fort Sumter, where the rebellion had begun. William Lloyd Garrison, George Thompson, Theodore Tilton, and a member of Beecher's congregation attended. Prior to the flag raising they prayed with 3,000 emancipated black people at Zion's Church. Garrison was given roses, and Thompson addressed the parishioners. At the flag raising, Beecher declared the results of the costly war: the nation was again one, and indivisible; no single state or collection of states were sovereign; and universal liberty was now the foundation of republican government. He turned to the flag:

> It is not the same; it is more and better than it was. The land is free from slavery since that banner fell. . . . When our flag came down, four years it lay brooding in darkness . . . Then rose before it a vision of its sin; it had strengthened the strong and forgotten the weak; it proclaimed liberty, but trod upon slaves. In that seclusion it dedicated itself to liberty. Behold to-day it fulfills its vows! When it went down, four million people had no flag. To-day it rises, and four million people cry out: "Behold our flag!"
> "Hark!" they murmur, "it is the gospel to the poor; it heals our broken hearts; it preaches deliverance to the captives; it gives sight to the blind; it sets at liberty them that are bruised." Raise up glorious gospel banner, and roll out the messages of God![57]

The following day Abraham Lincoln's assassination was reported in Brooklyn. The flags that were flying everywhere in the city were "taken down, or put at half-mast, or draped in funeral serge." Municipal and private offices were closed. Places of entertainment were shut down. Bells rang in an afternoon of remembrance. Meetings were held across the county. Brooklynites even ventured to Manhattan to join New York's memorial procession. But within a couple of weeks of the assassination, Manhattan's Chamber of Commerce was already planning out how the cotton trade would be reestablished and the South's prewar debts met.[58] Lincoln's murder also allowed Brooklynites to recapture their ambivalence toward social justice.

The Civil War finally severed Brooklyn's long relationship to slavery, and, after two centuries, the city comprised people whose lives were shaped by bondage in different and unequal ways. While the War destroyed a mode of persecution, it did not extinguish the benefits of exploitation, nor did it limit white people's power to decide the fate and place of black Americans. Faith in color remained. The wrongs of their past had not been righted and the wrongs of the future were yet to be determined. Black Southerners faced the task of securing themselves against a social system predicated on inequality and injustice; likewise black Brooklynites were particularly vulnerable as the nation matured to capitalism.

The Civil War ended slavery, not the class struggle.

Lieutenant Peter Vogelsang of Brooklyn. The oldest man in the Massachusetts Fifty-Fourth.
Courtesy of the Massachusetts Historical Society.

Brooklyn's Atlantic Docks during the Draft Riots era.
Courtesy of the New York Public Library.

The Brooklyn Bridge and waterfront in 1890.
The New York City Transit Museum Archives, Brooklyn.

An old Brooklyn Heights streetcar.
The New York City Transit Museum Archives, Brooklyn.

Two black youths join the U.S.S. Boston drill at the Brooklyn Navy Yard, ca. 1890.
Library of Congress, Photo and Prints Division, Detroit Publishing Co. Collection.

Brooklyn Ferry.
The New York City Transit Museum Archives, Brooklyn.

Dock workers talking strike, New York, 1911.
Library of Congress, Photo and Prints Division, Bain Collection.

"Hopping from the Trolley." From a series of posed accident photos
that the Brooklyn Rapid Transit Company used for public education.
Library of Congress, Photo and Prints Division.

Girls High School, Brooklyn (ca. 1900).
Detroit Publishing Company Photo, Courtesy of the Library of Congress.

When Harlem was white. White transit workers on elevated structure. In the backdrop is a soap advertisement that prominently features black caricatures, March 4, 1915. *The New York City Transit Museum Archives, Brooklyn.*

Riding to work during the Brooklyn Streetcar strike, August 1919. *Library of Congress, Photo and Prints Division, Bain Collection.*

Downtown Brooklyn, ca. 1940.
The New York City Transit Museum Archives, Brooklyn.

Women boarding the bus to Bedford-Stuyvesant, 1941.
The New York City Transit Museum Archives, Brooklyn.

Two trainees at the National Youth Administration's Brooklyn work center, August 1942.
Library of Congress, Photo and Prints Division, Office of War Information. Photo by Fritz Henle.

Woman employee holding shells at the Murray Manufacturing Co., Brooklyn
Courtesy of the Brooklyn Historical Society.

Mr. and Mrs. Vincent V. Whylie and their five daughters outside their Brooklyn home.
In 1968 Whylie was one of the black men who Jack Star, senior editor of *Look* magazine
interviewed to highlight the problem of union discrimination.
Jim Hansen, photographer. Courtesy of the Hansen estate and the Look Magazine Photograph Collection,
Prints and Photographs Division, Library of Congress.

CHAPTER SIX

The Legacy of Mastery

—

The Rise and
Prestige of Jim Crow
in Brooklyn,
1865–1930

—

At that time—twenty years ago—the darkies were not like they are now by a good deal, in fact they were a great deal more civil and had less trouble among themselves. If you met them on the sidewalk they made way for you, and were not allowed to ride in a public vehicle.

In time the city limits extended; the whites kept buying property and getting nearer and nearer to the darkies, who were driven further out, until at last Crow Hill assumed the appearance it has to-day, all intersected with streets and built up with houses. Now there is as many whites as blacks there . . .

—Policeman Hanft, Brooklyn (1873)

At about 8 P.M. Christmas 1865 Charles White Kellogg—a Brooklynite and the father of actress Fannie Kellogg—arrived in Alston, South Carolina. Earlier that year local residents were frantically holding on to the remnants of bondage. "The Yankee army are advancing upon Spartanburg we fear. They are now destroying Alston and Columbia," wrote Emily Liles Harris as she and other white South Carolinians avenged their losses by maltreating their servants. In the aftermath of the Civil War Kellogg decided to investigate business opportunities in the South. He was in the second month of a seven-month trip when he reached Alston. Homesick and alone on Christmas, he left his hotel room and wandered into a local dance. Almost one hundred black people were in the hall. Kellogg sat down and "paid an Old Darkie 30ᶜ to fiddle." He listened for about an hour and returned to his room. Later that evening he noted the events in his diary as if nothing peculiar had occurred;

in fact, the incident was not extraordinary.[1]

Kellogg objected to the vulgarity of Southern culture and to white Southerners themselves, but he was never offended by the assumption of black people's inferiority. He could even partake in rituals of racial dominance and subordination with which he was both familiar and comfortable. Kellogg proudly documented his habits of referring to black people as "Darkies" and "Niggers," viewing them solely as servants, and suspecting them of crimes. He did not believe in slavery. He did imagine that people of color lived for his convenience or more generally for the betterment of the white race. When Kellogg showed empathy for black people his compassion flowed from a belief that they were wronged by nature, not by other people. While he was emotional upon seeing the ruins of war and the evidence of its human destruction and while he was repeatedly insulted by the hostilities of white Southerners, Kellogg never entertained the thought that perhaps black people should be subservient to no one.[2]

Kellogg was in the South looking to make deals and sign contracts for his Brooklyn oil and soap establishment. He traveled by train, ship, carriage, and horseback. He studied cotton land prices, examined factories, and hunted down investments. History and social policy were secondary concerns. He discovered Civil War sites almost accidentally. He debated national policy between meetings. He entertained the "Negro question" when not otherwise occupied. But from November 6, 1865 when he boarded a train in New York headed toward Washington, DC, to April 7, 1866 when he embarked on a mail steamer that would bring him to Havana, Cuba, and then to New York City, his primary concern was business.[3]

Kellogg was a racist and a fair representative of Brooklyn. He sat between the wealthy and the poor. He saw the Civil War as an inconvenience and its conclusion as the starting bell for the resumption of business. He wanted the rebels of the South to be punished but his greatest desire was commercial reconstruction, and he was more willing to expose black Southerners to the savageries of their white co-citizens than to abandon trade. He was confident in the power of the white majority to determine the political course. Kellogg was a regular Republican.

Charles Kellogg and many white Brooklynites had lived through two emancipation processes—one regional, one national—without being shaken from their belief in the inferiority of black people. The expectation that these Northerners would be freed of such racist convictions is difficult to support given the deep social and cultural roots of these ideas. It can only be sustained by making race a byproduct of slavery or by conflating prejudice and racism. Kellogg may well have been programmed by culture and habit to disdain people of color; however, his racism targeted them for a new exploitation: servile labor and social arrangements devised for a world without bondage. Kellogg's racism was not a residue of slavery and the Civil War, it was that part of his ideological equipment with which he projected and negotiated the future. Few white people imagined that the end of slavery meant the end of their right to decide the application of black labor and most still thought the only appropriate social position for African Americans was that which profited white people.

Race was doing work in postbellum America. White people's power was the constant that tied the antebellum and postwar periods. Race outlived slavery because it continued to describe and defend that imbalance and the resulting social destruction. Perhaps more useful than the legacy-of-slavery paradigm, which describes the disadvantages that African Americans suffered as they emerged from bondage, is its unspoken corollary, the legacy of mastery, or the power of white Americans to eradicate, to perpetuate, or to capitalize on those vulnerabilities. Race, writes Noel Ignatiev of this moment, "came to correspond to the distinction between free wage labor and unfree semi-feudal labor, and between those who had access to political power and those who did not."[4] After all, the resistance of racial discrimination, inequality, and injustice to the recent social revolution wanted desperately for an explanation. And, the moral and intellectual problem of persecuting black people in a society premised upon free labor was no less severe than that confronted when black people were oppressed in a society based upon enslaved labor. Race discarded such ambiguities by shifting the discourse about black America from the problem of social oppression to the assumption of natural inferiority.

"Limited as its accomplishments may appear in retrospect, Black Reconstruction was a stunning experiment in the nineteenth-century world," writes Eric Foner, "the only attempt by an outside power in league with the emancipated slaves to fashion an interracial democracy from the ashes of slavery." Even the perennially conservative George Templeton Strong supported the early radical agenda for the South. With a characteristic white Northern Protestant balance of hope and hate, he admitted, "Niggers seem [to be] helping to reconstruct the South with a degree of sense and moderation I did not expect."[5]

Most white Northerners thought that there were *natural* limitations on the Southern social revolution. Calling freed people tools in a larger game, the *Eagle* blasted carpetbag governments and sided with Southern planters. When the Freedman's Savings Bank failed, an editorial assured readers that its demise was "a glass through which to contemplate the nature of the sympathy for the colored man which certain politicians have made their stock and trade." In reaction to the planned emigration of thousands of black Arkansans to Liberia, the *Eagle* patronizingly offered sympathy for "these ignorant, trustful people," and suggested that it was more humane to locate them on uncultivated lands in the South or West. No mention was made of their coming to Brooklyn.[6]

Black Brooklynites more easily identified with the personal and political goals of black Southerners. In fact, at least eighteen African Americans from Kings County went to teach in the South in decade after the war. William J. Wilson, "Ethiop," spent three years instructing freed people. Mary Wilson, his wife, taught for four years and Anna Wilson, their daughter, for five. Peter Vogelsang, who rose to the rank of lieutenant in the Union Army, stayed in the South for a year to teach. Maria W. Stewart, a widow from the War of 1812 who became quite famous in Boston as an abolitionist lecturer, left her Williamsburg home to instruct in the South for five years. Hardy and Susan Mobley, once enslaved, and their three daughters all taught at freed people's schools.[7]

Black Southerners did not try to punish the engineers of the past; rather, they attempted to secure their economic and political rights. They knew that political freedom was vulnerable unless grounded in independence so they dragged the issue of economic justice into politics. Their claim to a full freedom was expressed in a desire to own land. When land was denied them, they moved to broaden their rights as free laborers, hoping that their future work could be done in dignity and decency. But cotton was the industry of the South and the wealth of the North, and the Negro was its labor. So there was an impassable gulf between the visions of the black Southerners and the visions of their white allies. Reconstruction eventually failed because black and poor white voters resisted having the North dictate a hollow political freedom that guaranteed nothing, while white Northerners resisted the implications of *black equality* in their own states. The political and economic revolutions collided, and black Americans disproportionately suffered the cost of establishing capitalist agriculture in the South. Manhood suffrage was assaulted, black labor was tied more firmly to the soil, and white labor soon followed. As C. Vann Woodward has noted, the South became a colony of Northern wealth.[8]

White New Yorkers' own racial culture curtailed their interest in Southern democracy. In 1869 white men in New York State rejected yet another proposal to remove property qualifications from black voters. A year later the Fifteenth Amendment, intended to create Republican voters in the Reconstructed states of the South, forced equal suffrage upon the men of New York. African Americans held a grand celebration of the Amendment. The Brooklyn Academy of Music was rented and Hiram Revels of Mississippi, the first black man to serve in the United States Senate, was their honoree. Maritcha Lyons read a poem from the pages of the *Liberator*.[9]

Roger Alan Cohen has argued that black suffrage destroyed the radical faction of New York's Republican party. Unrestricted male voting in New York, federal power to intervene in state affairs, and the rule of Reconstruction governments in the South threatened to shift local political relations. White workers came to see free, enfranchised men of color as a direct challenge to their labor position; industrialists saw Reconstruction as a barrier to commercial reunion with the South; reformers viewed Negroes as politically unfit and the battle over civil rights as an obstacle to their political agenda; and local politicians feared that federal authority to regulate voting and intercede in cases of fraud might be used to put reigns on New York's powerful urban machines. It was more than the specter of black suffrage that made white New Yorkers leery of the Fifteenth Amendment and the Force Act of 1870. Of the twenty-six states that had ratified the Fifteenth Amendment, New York had done so with the second lowest percentage of votes.[10]

And, as Woodward documents, it was in New York City that the chain of seedy events began that punctuated the end of Reconstruction with the disputed Hayes-Tilden election of 1876 and the anti-democratic Compromise of 1877. Early in the morning following Election Day 1876 *New York Times* managing editor John C. Reid and William Chandler of New Hampshire woke Zachariah Chandler, Republican national chair, from his bed in a New York hotel and presented a scheme whereby the presidency that Tilden had won could be salvaged for the Republicans. Officials in Florida, Louisiana, and South Carolina rewrote the election results and by daybreak Chandler was declaring Hayes the victor. A new sectional conflict was drawn as Democrats quickly rejected the Republican claim. In the months that followed, solutions were attempted but none succeeded. Eventually a bipartisan coalition of Northern and Southern conservatives brought the crisis to an end. The conclusion accepted Hayes' claim to the presidency, appropriated money to the South for internal improvements, oversaw the withdrawal of federal troops from the former Confederacy, and, as Woodward notes, settled the significant issue of whether the postwar nation would ever again elect an executive without the use or threat of military force.[11]

As black people in the South were reduced to peonage, black people in the North were condemned to caste. The future of Brooklyn's small African-American population was silently decided in the negotiations over the presidency and Reconstruction. In Brooklyn, the Compromise meant the subjection of nonwhite voters to the whim of their white counterparts. When disfranchisement came to the South, 90 percent of the nation's black voters were eliminated and black Brooklynites found themselves at the mercy of a new party system.[12] They were alienated from local and national power and forced to watch their white neighbors define the boundaries of their freedom.

The end of Reconstruction left African-American and white Republicans in the South to the good will of the Democratic party, the violence of the Ku Klux Klan, and outright fraud. Democrats disfranchised the voters of the opposition party. Beginning in Mississippi in 1890 and proceeding through every state of the old Confederacy, various schemes for eliminating Republican votes were enacted. The Democrats then restored their national prominence by reestablishing the ungodly political union of wealthy white Southerners and poor, urban immigrant Northerners.[13]

This system was a national solution to distinct regional problems. In the South, where black laborers were needed in the plantation system, prejudice and politics assumed the Negro to be little more than labor; in the North, where European immigrants did the menial and elementary work, prejudice and politics assumed the Negro to be unfit for labor. The space for a national consensus existed in the regional needs of binding and silencing black workers on Southern soil and spurning and punishing black workers in Northern cities. The violence and fraud used to restrain black Southerners was bolstered by Northern votes and constraints on the upward movement of the North's black citizens—and many Brooklynites found ideological comfort in the accompanying cult of white supremacy. In the logic of the moment, emancipation proved the inherent goodness of white people, while the new injustices marked only the limits of their tolerance.

The Jim Crow South, with its one-party politics, violence, and segregation, had a more than receptive audience in the urban North. In 1882 the *New York Tribune*, disgusted with violence and terror, attacked the Democratic Party for its willingness to profit from anti-Asian violence in the West, race hatred in the South, and ethnic bigotry in Northern cities. In 1889 Thomas McCants

Stewart attempted to build an African-American presence in the Democracy through his Brooklyn Democratic club but abandoned the experiment after six years because of the dominance of Jim Crow Southerners and their sympathizers in the party.[14]

Racial bigotry was rampant in Brooklyn. Weeksville was the largest and best-known African-American neighborhood in the city. White Brooklynites tagged it "Blackville" and an adjacent elevation was dubbed "Crow Hill." A retired white policeman explained the obvious to the *Eagle*: "the woods were at that time full of crows, and it was called Crow Hill, partly because there were a great many crows there and partly on account of the [white] people nicknaming the darkies 'crows,' too." In spite of such animus, the black community used Weeksville and Carrville to organize and support the city's black churches and social institutions. Black Manhattanites utilized these areas for entertainment, worship, and as a symbol of their aspirations. In Weeksville and Carrville, black families owned homes and land, and remained at a distance from their white counterparts. Hunting, farming, and animal husbandry continued in Weeksville longer than they did in the rest of the city, and that often brought the derision of white outsiders; however, residents viewed these as some of the benefits that made the area convenient. "Most of the houses have little patches of garden surrounding them, and although *untidy* and *shiftless* hands attend to them their products in the shape of corn, tomatoes, beans, peas, and what is called 'truck,' are plentiful and well grown. The live stock consists of chickens, geese and goats. They are looked after semi-occasionally, counted in the evening, and the chickens and geese receive a daily allowance of food in addition to what they pick up while foraging in the streets or scratching in a neighboring garden," the *Eagle* noted with the sourness that it reserved for people of color. It went on to describe the area physically: "Nature has kindly done her best to make the place picturesque. It is all hills and hollows. The hills are the highest, and the hollows the deepest of any in the city." Weeksville's streets wound to and fro with so little resemblance to a grid that contractors and developers were infuriated with the very appearance of the place.[15]

Weeksville regularly attracted white hostility, especially as white realtors began planning middle-class developments in Central Brooklyn. The *Eagle* charged "Crow Hill" with being a center of amalgamation houses where "black and white would assemble together in disgusting orgies." Liquor flowed abundantly. The people ran "low groggeries" and traded in "mangy, half fed and wholly savage" animals. Police officer Hanft, stringing together stories of white men who grew rich selling cheap liquor and establishing gambling shops with tales of black men's propensity for violent razor and club fights, insisted that the area was not safe for white people to travel. As proof he offered the experience of a group of ten or eleven *decent* white people who went up to Weeksville on the Sabbath "to make fun at the darkies. In about five minutes the entire village was in arms, the women covered them with slops, and the men made them beat a hasty retreat. One of the whites pulled a pistol out and shot at a darkey; he missed his aim, but was knocked down with a stone before he could take another. The infuriated negroes set on him with razors then and nearly cut him to pieces."[16]

Some black Brooklynites tried to distance themselves from the poorer members of their community in order to avoid racial hostility. Mary White Ovington recalled that her dressmaker, a West Indian woman, "assured [her] positively that she was not a Negro" although "her face was dark." This woman's comment was not an indication of her racial identity but a warning that, despite the color of her skin, she shared little history with black Americans. By 1905 Brooklyn's Samuel Scottron—the grandfather of actress and singer Lena Horne—was blasting the Southern newcomers in an essay with the paradoxical title, "Little Prejudice in New York City." He called black migrants uncouth and ill-bred and argued that "*these people* have added somewhat to our troubles." The public schools would "polish" the migrants, he continued, as they had the "red-eyed, rum-drinking Neg[r]oes, full-bloods, Negro-Indians and half-castes" of earlier years. "If there is any lower specimen of human kind than the Negro-Indians that Long Island was infested with years ago, he ought to be put on exhibition." Scottron then assured his readers that the Southern migrants would also assimilate or die off.[17]

Scottron typified the elite people of color, who reacted to the advent of two-tier democracy by trying to define themselves as a distinct social group worthy of greater liberties. They were loyal Republicans, conscious of their past in the city, anti-immigrant, and careful stewards of colored institutions. They championed the cause of a people who were stripped of political power; paradoxically, doing so while seeking social distance from that group. These Brooklynites claimed ownership of the national culture and engaged in unrestrained celebration of their rise in the face of discrimination. Their ranks included families who distinguished themselves from the mass of poorer black Brooklynites by wealth and education, light skin, and mixed ancestry.

Maritcha Remond Lyons, a descendent of one of Kings County's oldest families of color, was meticulous about mentioning the Shinnecock tribeswomen in her father's lineage and her maternal grandmother, a "distinctly poor white of English descent."[18] They were not race traitors but rather they sought to establish a social middle ground, a racial purgatory from which they could captain their fates unburdened by the history and hostilities of white people and unfettered by the poverty and vulnerabilities of black New Yorkers.

That elite also possessed an esoteric history which included some contempt for the white aristocracy because its success was tied to bondage; however, it also incorporated a mild assessment of servitude in New York. Maritcha Lyons was convinced that "such bondage as we are more or less conversant with did not exist in early colonial times." In fact, slavery in New York affected not just black people but "many Indians and some whites." Inventor, editor, and historian Samuel Scottron, agreed. Revolutionary-era African schools were evidence of a "cordial and fraternal feeling existing between the two races." Scottron argued that the slaveowning Knickerbocker and Yankee families of old New York "differed widely" in sentiment from the planters of the South. Lyons even belittled New York State emancipation: "the few affected by the edict soon passed without leaving any traditions." Truth be told, neither author ever pursued a heritage in bondage, rather they pointed to—and exaggerated—the historical importance of that "class styled 'free people of color'" in New York to explain their culture.[19] They reserved the claim to *real* slavery for the black poor in their city and for the mass of black Southerners while themselves shunning any history of servitude and its attendant dishonor.

Among the black blue-bloods were families whose ancestry reached Colonial Long Island. The Lyons traced their lineage back to the eighteenth century. Their earliest documented relative was George Lyons Sr., of Dutch and African heritage, born on Long Island about 1750. He married a Native-American woman—likely Shinnecock—and they had six children. Albro Lyons Sr., his grandson, was a member of the New York African Society for Mutual Relief (NYASMR) and a leading figure in Brooklyn's black community. Albro's daughter Maritcha became an assistant principal in the Brooklyn school system. Albro Lyons Jr., a graduate of Brooklyn's Pratt Institute, was a druggist by trade. The births of the family's children were attended by the better-known black physicians of Brooklyn—James McCune Smith before the Civil War, Susan Maria Smith McKinney after, and Verina Morton Jones in the twentieth century. The family held membership in St. Philip's and the other leading black churches of the two cities. Marriages were conducted by New York's most prominent black ministers including Manhattan's Peter Williams Jr. and Brooklyn's George Frazier Miller. Family events were attended by the political and social elite. And a Lyons family plot at Cypress Hills cemetery reunited the family in death and emphasized their station in life.[20]

The popular press was clearly aware that the city housed a community of middle-class, well-educated African Americans who laid claim to a lineage that few white Brooklynites could equal. In December 1873 the "gentlemen of color" of the Widow's Sons Lodge held their annual reception at Gothic Hall. The *Brooklyn Sunday Sun* was impressed with the grandeur, the variety of "blondes and brunettes," and the elegant clothes and styles of the celebrants. In the middle of the evening an Irishman named McFadden entered to sell flowers to the guests and had to be removed. The *Sun* took public pleasure in his ousting and also relished the fact that many of the ladies of color were sent home in carriages driven by "Irishmen dressed in livery."[21]

In the 1880s James Weldon Johnson's romance with the Metropolis began among this group. Johnson recalled the impact of riding the ferry and crossing the Brooklyn Bridge to the "great city" during visits to his aunt Sarah's in Williamsburg. Her husband, William C. H. Curtis, was trained as a jeweler and made a comfortable living manufacturing paraphernalia for secret societies. The young boy marveled at the splendor of their beautiful brick and brownstone home, where T. Thomas Fortune and Fred Moore— editors of the *New York Age* and the latter a local politician—were among the many prominent guests. "This house seemed to me palatial, and I regarded my uncle as a very rich man." At the turn of the century, after graduating from Atlanta University, Johnson moved to New York and continued to mingle among the "Brooklyn set:"

> When I came to New York to live, there was not such a thing as "society" among the colored people who lived in Manhattan.... cultivated Negroes living in Manhattan had, for many years, necessarily been going to Brooklyn for the social intercourse that is confined more or less to the people one knows or knows about. Forty years before, there had been a general exodus of the better-off Negroes from Manhattan to Brooklyn. For some years still farther back, there had been the steady lure of the better opportunity to buy homes on that side of the East River; but the Draft Riots in 1863 precipitated a wholesale migration. A number of

these older families in Brooklyn were positively rich; their money, made in the days when Negroes in New York were successful caterers, fashionable dressmakers, and the janitors of big buildings, having come down through two or three generations. I knew a family in which, after the death of the parents, four children were left around sixty thousand dollars each in cash and securities, besides valuable real estate.[22]

Johnson eventually married Grace Nail, the daughter of Tammany's black ambassador John B. Nail.[23]

A minor immigration of educated British West Indians enhanced the black middle-class. Overcrowding in Barbados led to a flood of emigration after British Emancipation. That scattering occurred mostly within the Caribbean; however, by the 1890s a small community of affluent Barbadians and other British West Indians were purchasing handsome homes in Bedford and the St. Mark's district of Brooklyn.[24]

"It has been in Brooklyn for the past three generations that the well-to-do colored families with their children have chiefly been found," Mary White Ovington wrote in 1911. Better-off black Manhattanites began moving to Brooklyn in the 1850s and that movement increased after the Draft Riots. African Americans purchased land and homes, organized themselves through clubs and societies, educated their children, and attempted to live the "American dream" in spite of many white people's objections. In the years that followed the Civil War they regularly vacationed across the United States, in Europe, and in the Caribbean, sent their children off to prestigious colleges, and fought to transform the political culture of the city.[25]

The African-American elite brought dramatic changes to religious life, notes Clarence Taylor. Black churches began to move away from the religious emotionalism of the antebellum era for a more urbane, Christian intellectualism, with formal ceremonies, classical music, aesthetic architecture, a trained ministry, and a growing respect for materialism. Churches crusaded against illiteracy and immorality. As literacy and learning were social goods they also became religious goods, necessary to fill the new role of the Christian which included more than fiery devotion. Church societies provided libraries and classes, sponsored lectures, debates, hosted writing and speech contests, and publicized race issues.[26]

The Howard Colored Orphan Asylum typified the new thrust. "An old blind colored man, led by a little boy, came to our church once a year to ask for money for the Howard Orphan Asylum," remembered Mary White Ovington. He was, in fact, much more than an old, blind, colored solicitor. The Reverend William F. Johnson almost single-handedly established Brooklyn's Howard Colored Orphan Asylum. The Asylum was organized to care for African-American children in 1866 and was incorporated on September 7, 1868. It supported more than fifty children at a time without government aid. By 1899 the Asylum's buildings at Dean Street and Troy Avenue were appraised at $35,000.[27]

TABLE 6.1

Black Population of Brooklyn, 1860-1930

Year	Total	Black	% Black
1860	279,122	4,999	1.8
1870	419,921	5,653	1.3
1880	599,495	9,153	1.5
1890	838,547	11,307	1.3
1900	1,166,582	18,367	1.6
1910	1,634,351	22,708	1.4
1920	2,018,356	31,912	1.6
1930	2,560,401	68,921	2.7

Source: George Edmund Haynes, *The Negro at Work in New York City: A Study in Economic Progress* (1912; New York: AMS Press, 1968), 47. Bureau of the Census, *Negro Population, 1790-1915* (Washington, DC: Government Printing Office, 1918), 822; Id., *Negroes in the United States, 1920-32* (Washington, DC: Government Printing Office, 1935), 62; Id., *Census of Population: 1910*, III: 230-1; Id., *Statistical Abstract of the United States, 1961* (Washington, D. C.: Government Printing Office, 1961), 25.

The black elite blamed migrants for caste discrimination and many of the social programs they sponsored assumed racism's cure was to civilize poor people of color. In fact, the growth of Brooklyn's black population was quite modest (see table 6.1). In 1865 only 5,000 of Brooklyn's 250,000 citizens were of color; by the end of the century, the total population had quadrupled to a million but the black population numbered fewer than 20,000.

The source of the growing racial animosity was national, not local; thus, the growth of the city's black population amplified but did not cause racial hatred. In 1901 Theodore Roosevelt accidentally exposed the popularity of Jim Crow in Brooklyn. On the night of October 16 President Roosevelt caused an uproar by dining at the White House with the "Negro leader" Booker T. Washington. News of the dinner was met with immediate condemnation. White Southerners were outraged by this affront to their history of racial subordination and segregation. To protect the president and Tuskegee Institute, Washington journeyed to New York City, refused interviews, and avoided attention over following days. But as the incident grew stale, notes Washington's biographer, "an unscrupulous reporter for the Brooklyn *Eagle*, a pro-Southern Democratic paper, made up a bogus interview with Washington" and breathed a few days of life into the scandal.[28]

Before and after their 1898 Consolidation,[29] Brooklyn and New York were Jim Crow towns. Discrimination suits in the early decades of the twentieth century forced local courts to construct a policy on the legality of segregation. While the courts tended to side against overt segregation there were enough exceptions to leave African Americans fearful and segregationists hopeful. Hospitals routinely separated patients by color, many moderate and pricey restaurants refused to serve black people, and many theaters had segregated seating.[30]

In 1915 George E. Wibecan, the Republican leader of the Sixth District and a Bedford resident, successfully sued a restaurant on Washington Street in Fort Greene, Brooklyn, that refused to serve African Americans. But the incident was an ominous sign. "Then too, I could not forget that even in New York," remembered W. E. B. Du Bois of his move to the city five years earlier, "with its unrivaled facilities for a center of world thought and culture, it was nevertheless no heaven for black folk. Negroes were not welcome to its hotels and restaurants nor to most of its clubs or organizations."[31]

While at times laughable, the decisions of New York courts clearly revealed the intent of social segregation. In 1918 Arthur Cohn, a white man denied service by black waiters in a Harlem restaurant, fell victim to an extraordinary manipulation of logic. Justice Whitaker, writing for the majority of the Appellate Division of the State Supreme Court, informed Cohn that the waiters had refused to serve him not because he was white but rather because his companion was black. The court then threw out the case of the sensitive plaintiff. A year earlier a Long Island City jury just as cavalierly dismissed the case of Joseph Grey, a black man who was refused accommodation at a Rockaway hotel.[32]

When four African Americans, including a Yale graduate, a probation officer, and an Urban League and NAACP official, won a $500 award against a Manhattan coffee house that Jim Crowed them, reaction was sharp. "The triumph of the insistent four," a *Times* editorial blasted, "will not change the fact that white sentiment here is overwhelmingly against the close association of the two races in places of public entertainment." Warning that the victory should not encourage other black people to assert their citizenship lest the ire of white people be sparked, it concluded: "Everybody has rights that it is unwise to exercise." Judge George W. Simpson of Manhattan agreed. Frustrated at the litigiousness of people of color and their general refusal to accept their "place," the Judge chastised a black man who was arrested for arguing after a white woman called him a "nigger": "There are too many of your kind in Harlem who want people to believe they are not negroes by taking offense when they are called negroes. Nigger means the same thing as negro." Joseph Manning, the defendant, was fined thirty dollars for disorderly conduct.[33]

At Rockaway Beach, Long Island, Joseph and Jennie Millhauser lost the fire insurance on their bathing house because they catered to nonwhite people. The Millhausers defended themselves by pointing out that many businesses accepted black patrons and even solicited them. "There is a man on the other side that has a sign on the outside of his place with an Irish name that not only sells refreshments to colored people, but is doing a trade in parking their cars. That's an old trick—a Jew runs a place and puts an Irish name on the outside," exclaimed Mr. Millhauser. He insisted that he had endeavored to keep his establishment white. "We have been driven to take in colored people," said a contrite Ms. Millhauser.[34]

Conditions were as bad outside New York City. Hattie Mead, a town clerk in Putnam County, had twenty Klansmen escort a white man and a woman of "partly colored blood" from her home when they announced their plans to marry. That same summer a white woman in Camden, New Jersey, was declared mentally incompetent and removed to a home for the "feeble-minded" after applying for a license to marry a black man twice her age. Almost simultaneously State Senator Griswold of Poughkeepsie was piecing together a bill to outlaw miscegenation in New York State.[35]

"I have been informed that several meetings of the Klan were held in this city, at which full regalia was used, consisting of a gown and a mask," warned Judge Francis Mancuso of the New York County Court of General Sessions. "Because thirty-seven languages were spoken by New York City's six million residents," writes Kenneth T. Jackson in his history of the urban Klan, "only one million of whom were white native-born Protestants, Imperial Wizard William Joseph Simmons described Gotham as 'the most un-American city of the American continent.'" After the Armistice in 1918 the Ku Klux Klan moved to take advantage of a recession aggravated by more than 10,000 layoffs at the Brooklyn Navy Yard. In July 1921 a klavern was established in Brooklyn, following the initiation of the Manhattan Klan a month earlier. A minister at Calvary Baptist in Manhattan publicly evangelized for the Klan and gave them headquarters in his church. By December 1922 the twenty-one klaverns in New York City had a combined membership of 150,000. Canon William Sheafe Chase of Brooklyn's Christ Episcopal Church hailed the Order as the defender of political virtue and the rule of law. The man who stood in the pulpit that Henry Ward Beecher made famous, Plymouth's Reverend Newell Dwight Hillis, insisted that every white citizen who was not stained by Romanism should support the Empire. On a Sunday in December 1922, at Brooklyn's Washington Avenue Baptist Church, "a man clad in the robes and hood of the Ku Klux Klan walked slowly up the center aisle . . . mounted the platform" and addressed the congregation. "This order was called into being to meet the need of the times. It is organized to down lawlessness; to uphold Protestantism and to oppose the grabbing of the world's trade by the Jew," the guest began. He then pilloried the destruction of public schools by Catholics and declared the Empire's commitment "to maintain the supremacy of the white race."[36]

New York City's residents proved fairly intolerant of the Klan since most of them were its targets. The dramatic increase in the Empire's activities north of the Mason-Dixon reacted to a perceived threat that foreign-born people and their offspring posed to the Anglo-Saxon nation. In the Metropolis, the Empire focused on Jews and Catholics and immigrants from Eastern and Southern Europe. In 1923 the state legislature passed the Walker Bill which forced publication of the membership lists and regulations of "unincorporated associations." Mayor Hylan's steady assault on the Klan led to the discovery of Klansmen in the police department. The district attorney received hundreds of names of members, and authorities disrupted Klan meetings in Brooklyn. The *Brooklyn Eagle* joined in attacking the Klan's vicious anti-Catholic and anti-Semitic stances, but seemed unconcerned that the Empire was pathologically anti-black. The Reverend H. H. Proctor, an African American and the pastor of Nazarene Congregational Church, made a statement against Christian support for the Klan by preaching before a white congregation. Still, the Klan thrived in the suburbs of Long Island, winning town and county elections, and slipping into the routine of life.[37]

African Americans were not successful at curbing racialism in Brooklyn.

Encouraged by newspaper headlines like "German Measles Invades Navy Yard," Brooklynites gossiped constantly about conspiracies among them. Because the Germans, it was reported, were cultivating resentment toward the nation among the nonwhite population, state and federal agents searched the New York offices of the *Crisis* and interrogated its staff. After the war, the government consistently claimed that part of the threat of communism was its revolutionary agitation among Negroes.[38] Already believing that black people were inferior and a threat to their economic security, many white Brooklynites were easily seduced into believing that black people were also a danger to national security.

New York State's legislature, shocked by the communist revolution in Russia, followed the national government by probing into radical plots among its citizens. Of particular interest to the lawmakers was the growing militancy of some civil rights leaders, like A. Philip Randolph, and Brooklyn's Mary White Ovington and the Reverend George Frazier Miller. Ovington and Randolph applied "communistic principles" to labor organizing when they encouraged a class consciousness that transcended petty race prejudice. Miller was accused of spouting socialist ideology from the pulpit, penning articles in radical journals, and trying to place black people "upon the lofty pedestal of independent activity." (In fact, only a year earlier St. Augustine's had a minor scandal when two vestrymen publicly rebuked Miller for preaching socialist doctrine from the pulpit, jeopardizing the reputation and future of the church through his public connection to Bolshevism, and bringing the whole congregation under suspicion by acting as a contributing editor to "a radical Socialist magazine, 'The Messenger.'" The two dissenters eventually resigned.)[39]

One of the most convincing claims of the propaganda spree was that the Germans had somehow increased the northward migration of African Americans to undermine the political order of New York City. Between 1914 and 1915 the war in Europe reduced immigration to the United States by almost a million, just as American industry mobilized for the conflict. The National Urban League estimated that 1.2 million black migrants moved to the North from 1915 to 1928. Between January and June of 1917 alone, argued the *Crisis*, a quarter million African Americans left the South. As Du Bois informed his readers, there were also push factors: "the movement began because of floods in middle Alabama and Mississippi and because the latest devastation of the boll weevil came in these same districts," while mob violence in Georgia and South Carolina gave an additional spur to relocation.[40]

The roots of the Great Migration were of course deeper than the immediate crises. African Americans' westward and northward trek began immediately after the Civil War, and that movement increased with the failure of Reconstruction. By 1910 half of New York State's black population was Southern born.[41]

The migration was intensified by recent events, but those events did not start it and their conclusion did not draw it to a close. "In 1923, some of my friends I was working with and I decided to catch the boat and travel up to Philly," recalled a young man born on South Carolina's Sea Islands. "We stopped there, worked one month. Didn't like it. Came on over to my brothers in Brooklyn." Southern planters organized to hold their labor. As Du Bois wrote: "They mobilized all the machinery of modern oppression: taxes, city ordinances, licenses, state laws, municipal regulations, wholesale police arrests and, of course, the peculiarly Southern method of the mob and the lyncher." The North was equally confused. White men who labored to keep black workers out of unions and trades saw industries courting people of color to fill the wartime gap. Somewhat upset that "black papers" were praising and assisting the movement, a 1916 *Times* editorial dismissed the *New York Age* as "a newspaper much read among negroes" which "naturally contends for the right of the race to better its conditions industrially by filling the positions left vacant by the drift of labor into the munitions trade." "It is the whites who are worrying." "These are happy days for the colored brethren," the editorial concluded.[42]

Like most Northern papers, the *Times* ran frequent stories about the implications of the changing demographics. As peace was being declared in Europe, Harlem was being touted as the new capital of black America. Between 1900 and 1930 Brooklyn—which became the most populous of the boroughs in the 1920s, ending that decade with 2.5 million citizens—saw its nonwhite residency triple to nearly 70,000. Although *suffering* fewer nonwhite people than Manhattan, white Brooklynites were concerned that their borough housed more black people than Queens, Staten Island, and the Bronx. Long Island, "where many of them settled," also saw concern.[43]

In 1930 42 percent of all black Brooklynites were born in the South Atlantic states—in fact, Virginia and the Carolinas alone provided 34 percent of the borough's black population—and 16 percent were foreign born. West Indians were the vast majority of Brooklyn's foreign-born black communities and they quickly challenged the leadership of the native-born elite. Both political parties preferred native-born black candidates because of their more acceptable educational credentials and community recognition. George Wibecan was the quintessential black politician. He belonged to one of Brooklyn's leading families, he graduated from Boys High School, and he studied law at Columbia. But, the political terrain was rapidly shifting. By 1918 the *Club Democrata Puertorriqueno* was operating in Brooklyn under Joaquin Colon. Carlos Tapia and Luis F. Weber later became the Puerto Rican spokesmen of the Brooklyn Democratic machine. Black West Indians sought representation in the local Democracy because of native-born black people's stronghold on the local Republican machine. Viewing the Republicans as hostile, black Caribbeans fought for a permanent presence in Brooklyn and Manhattan's Democratic machines.[44]

Caribbean immigration—skewed toward the more educated by discriminatory United States policies and the financial and bureaucratic barriers confronted by the poor, the illiterate, and the unskilled—brought sharper cultural distinctions, different routines of life, a queue of new political issues, and a struggle to define "blackness" (see table 6.2). In *Brown Girl, Brownstones*, novelist Paule Marshall provided a sadly comical scene in which a member of Brooklyn's Association of Barbadian Homeowners and Businessmen proposes that the term "Barbadian" be replaced with "Negro" in the organization's title. "Then, as rain comes in the West Indies—without warning, to lash the earth in a helpless hysterical deluge—their indignation broke with the same fury." Black native-born New Yorkers were themselves fluent in a host of stereotypes about the growing foreign-born population. While the stereotypes were contradictory and often silly, the divisions and tensions that they described had real meaning. In 1930 Ira De A. Reid, of Atlanta University, estimated that a third of the black professional population of New York City was foreign born. British West Indians had their primary impact upon Harlem, but that was not necessarily comforting to those black Brooklynites who exercised influence in black Manhattan. Similarly, an immigration of somewhat skilled Caribbeans, however poor, was no comfort to the common class of black New Yorkers who were victims of birth-to-death exclusion from skilled trades, apprenticeships, and occupations. Rufus Murray, a humble West Indian immigrant, became the founder and president of black New York's most prominent benevolent society and credit union. In 1898 Murray was born in Barbados. He was educated and trained as a blacksmith in Barbados and Trinidad. At age twenty-two Murray emigrated to Cuba and then to the United States. He followed Marcus Garvey, worked as a door-to-door salesman, and then formed a partnership with another immigrant, F. Levi Ford. In the 1930s Murray, Ford, and several other West Indian men founded Brooklyn's Paragon Progressive Community Association and, later, the Paragon Progressive Federal Credit Union. Murray served the organization as president, vice president, director, editor of the *Paragon News*, and a part-time teller, and in doing so became one of the most recognizable figures in black Brooklyn.[45]

TABLE 6.2

Native-born, Migrant, and Immigrant in Brooklyn's Black Population, 1910-30

Year	Native born[a]	Migrants	Foreign born
1910	39%	49%	11%
1920	35	44	19
1930	30	49	16

[a]Born in New York State.
Source: Bureau of the Census, *Negroes in the United States, 1920-32* (Washington, DC: Government Printing Office, 1935), 32-5.

The rise of Latino communities of color further complicated racial politics in the borough. On November 18, 1922 Fred Moore's *New York Age* began a Spanish-language page edited by Dr. Bernardo Ruiz Suarez and directed at the "Hispanic-American community of the colored race." "When I reached seventeen years of age I went to San Juan, borrowed twenty-five dollars for the fare and disembarked on one of the steam ships which sailed weekly, named *Jacinto*," recalled Homero Rosado. He was one of many Latinos who came to work at Brooklyn's waterfront. The American Manufacturing Company brought Puerto Rican women to work in its Brooklyn rope plant, provided housing for them in North Brooklyn, transportation to and from work, chaperones from respectable Puerto Rican families, and recreation. In the following decades the small worker enclaves of Manhattan and Brooklyn became the centers of New York City's Latino communities.[46]

White New Yorkers rarely noticed ethnic distinctions among people of color, instead they viewed these disparate migrations as a single formidable wave that had to be controlled. Social segregation became the rule. In the spring of 1920 an overwhelming majority of the seventy-nine seniors at

Girls High School in Bedford voted to "draw the color line" and bar the six black girls in their class from the prom. The seniors, it was explained, objected to the possibility that their classmates' dates might try to dance with white women. Yolande Du Bois, the daughter of the eminent editor of the *Crisis*, was one of the six victims. W. E. B. Du Bois immediately intervened, and superintendent of high schools John L. Tildsley let the belles of Girls High know that if the event were not open to the whole class it would be canceled. A second vote was held, and the seniors decided for inclusion. Notably, six girls voted to cancel rather than integrate the prom.[47]

Five of the six black girls purchased tickets to the dance. On Friday, April 23, 1920, two limousines brought seven African-American couples and a chaperon to the Hotel Margaret for Girls High School's senior prom. The colored celebrants kept mainly to themselves. Yolande Du Bois was the center of attention. In all, the evening was marked only by its blandness. The white girls remained safe—not a single swarthy suitor molested them. The *Brooklyn Eagle*, disappointed that the event was integrated, titillated its readers the following morning with the headline: "NEGROES FROLIC AT GIRLS HIGH DANCE." The announcement was far more sexy than the story, so the reporter emphasized the presence of white women and black men at the affair. Exposing the fact that black men were the specific targets of this attempt at segregation, the correspondent invoked an interesting blend of gender and race:

> Eight negroes and an equal number of young colored women attended the dance given by the senior class of Girls High School last night at the Hotel Margaret, the affair, so far as known, being the first dance in the boro at which the color line has not been drawn.

Apparently *Eagle* readers, who needed help to comprehend integrated dances, understood the difference between "young colored women" and "negroes." Unable to find fault with the dress, style, or behavior of the black participants, the article mentioned that they "exchanged dances among themselves, even to the extent of some mild shimmying" but finally had to admit that "there was no unpleasantness." The *Age* responded: "Contrary to general reports published in the white metropolitan dailies there was no evidence of ballroom segregation."[48]

A number of students did not attend the dance. The most interesting of the absentees was Gwendolyn Bennett, the author of the commencement song, who later became a Harlem Renaissance poet. She, admitted the school's principal, "never expressed any desire to attend the prom." Three years later, Bennett contributed a poem to *Opportunity* that included the autobiographical lines:

I want to feel the surging
Of my sad people's soul
Hidden by a minstrel-smile.

Bennett later graduated from Pratt Institute and studied art in Paris.[49]

In the late nineteenth century Brooklyn's public schools had made moderate steps toward integration. In 1882 Mayor Seth Low appointed the first African American, Dr. Philip S. White, to serve on the Board of Education. The attorney and local Democrat Thomas McCants Stewart took the "Negro chair" on the Board in 1891 and remained until 1894, during which time he fought for a new school in the Weeksville-Carrville area. Under Stewart's prodding Colored School No. 2 in Weeksville was officially desegregated and renamed Public School 68, although it continued to be taught and attended by black people. In 1893 Stewart got the Board of Education to build Public School 83, to house the area's children regardless of color. From 1894 to 1898 Samuel Scottron, whose turn-of-the-century writings decried the deteriorating position of black labor, sat on the Brooklyn Board. In 1901 statutory school desegregation was achieved in New York State following Governor Theodore Roosevelt's initiatives.[50]

Attempts to re-segregate the public schools gained momentum as Brooklyn's black population increased. In 1923 African-American teachers were informed that they would be kept apart from white guests at a dinner at the Hotel Astor honoring the commissioner of the Board of Education. The black educators were given the option of sitting in a segregated section or not attending. They did not attend. In the fall of 1926 officials at Public School 35 in Bedford announced that the Glee Club was to be segregated because voices did not harmonize across racial lines. The principal then instructed what was now the black boys' choir to sing only "mammy songs" and tunes from the South.[51]

Schools were not alone in policing the color line. Estelle Benson, a black woman, was victim to a more wicked abuse of authority. She was punched, knocked to the ground, dragged through the street, and threatened with a revolver when she declined to "go out" with a uniformed white police officer in Brooklyn. Patrolman Thomas McAuliffe asked the woman to get into his patrol car. She refused and the assault began. A white woman who witnessed the beating and attempted to intercede was herself battered.[52]

Located at the heart of Brooklyn, Bedford was at the center of racial turmoil. Here, the in-migration of African Americans and the relocation of the white middle class led to uneasy community and institutional transitions (see table 6.3). St. Augustine's Protestant Episcopal on Lafayette and Marcy Avenues, under the Reverend George Frazier Miller, was one of many houses of worship that the growing nonwhite population purchased.[53]

TABLE 6.3

Ethnicity in Select Bedford and Stuyvesant Health Districts, 1920

Health District	Native white	Black	Other	Foreign white
18 (north)	2,494	393	4	9,973
19 (north)	3,374	358	4	10,132
20 (central)	7,091	916	24	5,263
21 (central)	6,399	412	6	4,454
28 (central)	12,400	1,160	19	4,485
30 (central)	9,679	763	12	4,523
29 (south)	8,701	185	12	4,322
36 (south)	5,845	4,144	9	4,343
52 (south)	2,376	2,341	5	6,615

Source: Welfare Council of New York City, *A Survey of Work for Boys in Brooklyn* (Brooklyn: Welfare Council, October 1932), 228-31.

In 1922 the Reverend Thomas S. Harten made Holy Trinity Baptist Church at Dekalb and Franklin Avenues a stage for protest activity. Harten immediately chose police brutality as a theme of his activist ministry. He later became the organizer of the National Equal Rights League. By the 1930s local Democratic boss John H. McCooey was soliciting Harten's support.54

When in 1928 Federal Judge William Atwell declared from his bench that "white and colored people cannot live together," a thousand protesters gathered at Holy Trinity. The statement came during the sentencing of a white woman accused of selling liquor. Although no black people were involved in the case, Judge Atwell decided that the white defendant was induced to crime by her black neighbors. A year later the Brooklyn Bar Association reprimanded the judge.[55]

Similarly, organized religion continued to embrace Jim Crow more than a century after the issue of slavery caused the first racial division of Brooklyn churches. In September 1929 Bedford drew national attention when the white minister of St. Mathew's Episcopal Church at McDonough Street and Tompkins Avenue instructed the black members of his congregation to take their spiritual business elsewhere. Emeline Munt, an African-American woman and a parishioner at St. Mathew's, recalled that "the rector soon after the start of the services got up and started to read from the church bulletin. He said he wanted to direct special attention to a paragraph in the bulletin about Negroes." The minister then declared: "St. Mathews' [sic] Church doesn't want the Negro's money. We have a couple of Negro members, but we don't want any more." Some white people in the audience gasped at the proclamation, a black woman rose from her pew and walked out in tears, and a black man sat with his head bowed. The church bulletin listed the black Episcopal churches in the Bedford area, and discouraged black people from attending St. Mathew's. Earlier, the Reverend William St. John Blackshear attempted to quietly remove parishioners of color from St. Mathew's. The Reverend George Frazier Miller recalled, "Mr. Blackshear asked me himself to call upon his colored parishioners with a view to having them attend St. Augustine's and I refused." The *Eagle* reported that Blackshear sent a letter to each black member:

> My dear parishioners—
>
> Following out the plan of my administration in this parish in regard to acceptance for membership in the parish of colored people. I am publishing in our first bulletin a notice to that effect.
>
> I trust that you will recognize our motives underlying this policy, and will realize that it in no sense refers to you who are already members of my parish and who are already very dear to me, but it governs the subject as to the acceptance of any new members.
>
> Hoping you will receive this in the spirit in which it is intended, and wishing for you always God's richest blessing, I am,
>
> > Faithfully,
> > YOUR RECTOR.[56]

The NAACP and other African-American organizations immediately condemned Blackshear, as did clergy of almost every religion and denomination. Many embarrassed Brooklynites noted that Blackshear was a Texan and quickly pointed to his Southern ways, few mentioned that Blackshear was also a Harvard graduate with Northern ways. Dr. George E. Haynes, of the Federal Council of the Churches of Christ in America, demanded that mainstream religious institutions condemn and censure Blackshear. Walter White of the NAACP promised to go after all those who helped "to spread the virus of race hatred." Bedford's radical George Frazier Miller declared Blackshear "a gross misfit" and urged him to return to Texas. The Reverend H. H. Proctor of Nazarene Congregational stated that he was disgusted by Blackshear's attempt to enforce Southern sectionalism on Brooklyn while reminding black Christians that this was further reason to support their own churches. The Reverend J. Stanley Durkee said that Blackshear had "turned his back on Jesus." An insulted Blackshear announced that he was "a friend of the negro race," who acted only to ensure that he did not "take away support from the two churches for colored people in this neighborhood." Yet, the Reverend did not back away from his assertion that his was "a white church for white people, and I intend to keep it so."[57]

James Weldon Johnson of the NAACP wrote to Episcopal bishop Ernest Stires of Long Island asking that Blackshear's "un-Christ-like practice of Jim Crow Christianity" be censured. The contemplative bishop enjoyed "the greatest affection and a warm paternal feeling for our colored brethren"; however, he thought that the only issue in the Bedford affair was the "tactfulness or lack of tactfulness of Mr. Blackshear's action." William Pickens, an NAACP field secretary who lived only blocks from the church, wrote to thank Reverend Blackshear for giving moral support to his decision to sleep on Sundays. Capturing the cynical mood of many black people, he continued:

> . . . whenever I began to weaken and to yield to the respectable idea of going to church, the Devil, the ever-present ally of my lazy bones, would whisper to me in my bed of Sunday drowsiness: "Don't go. They don't really want you there. The preachers talk about 'universal brotherhood,' but they are hypocrites and liars."

A few weeks after the incident the vestrymen of St. Matthew's delivered a brief statement approving of the Reverend's stance and declaring themselves in "harmony" with the decision.[58]

Few could resist the furor. Representative Fiorello LaGuardia—whose support of Chicago congressman Oscar DePriest against segregationists in the House of Representatives endeared him to African Americans—stood in front of the statue of Abraham Lincoln at Union Square and insisted that "Christ would have hung His head in shame" over the Brooklyn fiasco. Black people from all over the area made a point of attending St. Mathew's. On Sunday, September 22, 1929 at least eleven people of color were present. Emmy Hadley explained, "I live near this church and will not walk to any other." T. A. P. Morton, who lived at No. 12 Utica Avenue, made the long march across Bedford to see if anyone was bold enough to put him out. Forty-two church leaders from the Metropolitan area, calling themselves the "Conference of Young Churchmen," made a public objection to exclusion and "confess[ed] a more general guilt and perplexity" over the nation's rising prejudice. The Protestant Episcopal Church scored Blackshear, and a number of churches issued public invitations to nonwhite worshippers. In early October the Episcopal bishops gathered at Atlantic City to discuss the excitement in Brooklyn. By then Bishop Stires was far less arrogant about the incident and Blackshear was claiming that he had only discouraged colored attendance at the church and that his earlier declarations were only part of a personal effort "to advance the kingdom of God among the negro race." By September's end he was accusing the press of having begun and fueled the controversy with a "Plague of Lies."[59]

Perhaps the most appropriate response came from waiters who Jim Crowed Blackshear at his favorite eatery. The minister and his party of five were seated but a black waiter declined to serve them. An angry Blackshear called upon the head waiter, also black, and was again snubbed. The pastor then demanded that the restaurant's managers, who were white, act. They refused. Blackshear and his party exited.[60]

However, many Brooklynites silently saluted Blackshear's deed and a few gave public praise. Monsignor John L. Belford, of the Church of the Nativity (Roman Catholic) in Bedford, said that Blackshear "deserves applause for his honesty." "Should we see symptoms of an invasion or should strange negroes become numerous, we would not hesitate one minute to tell them to go to their own church and to exclude them if telling was not effectual," he continued. "Negroes love to make their way into white neighborhoods, white schools and white churches," Belford decreed. "When there were a few, they could be tolerated, not only because they were few but because they behaved themselves. When they became numerous, they became noisy, impudent, arrogant and abusive." He held to his stance although the cardinal eventually rebuked him. On Sunday, October 14, 1929 Blackshear received more effective support when twenty-five Klansmen in regular attire attended service at St. Mathew's to stiffen the Reverend's resolve and to handle a group of one hundred African-American protesters who were rumored to be coming from New England.[61]

The happenings in Brooklyn even made the *Crisis*. Four years earlier, in 1925, Du Bois wrote of the Catholic church to a priest, "it is the greater shame that 'nigger' haters clothed in its episcopal robes should do to black Americans in exclusion, segregation and exclusion from opportunity all that the Ku Klux Klan ever asked." Now Du Bois, disturbed by the braiding of religion and racism in Brooklyn, argued that while Blackshear "may be a blunt and tactless fool . . . he is doing exactly what his church has done for 250 years, and, in this policy, the Episcopalians have been followed by the Catholic Church of America, and, in later years, by the Methodists, Baptists, and Presbyterians." Torn between its lofty claims and its common constitution, the church consistently "writes itself down as a deliberate hypocrite and systematic liar." "And so Bishop Stires cannot find a thing that he can do." Du Bois pointed readers toward history:

> In the past, the Church has opposed every great modern social reform; it opposed the spread of democracy, universal education, trades unionism, the abolition of poverty, the emancipation of women, the spread of science, the freedom of art and literature and the emancipation of the Negro slave. When the reform was gained, the Church righted itself, led usually by some sc[h]ismatic and heretical part of itself, came over on the Lord's side and usually did not hesitate both to claim a preponderant share of the glory of the victory and again to emphasize its super-natural claims.[62]

Although the hatred displayed by the Reverend Blackshear might seem surprising in the City of Churches, it was an unavoidable consequence of white Brooklynites' definition of freedom, which demanded that people of color be barred from full participation in the society in order to guarantee white citizens a surplus of opportunity. Black people could not be oppressed in life but equal in thought, excluded from labor yet respected in discourse, or exploited in national politics while being admitted to national principles. White ethnics did not have to be hateful people to do hateful things. They only had to know that in all their working days they had not met a single moment when everyone prospered. The solution was obvious, for all knew that black people were politically vulnerable and subjected and that their rights as laborers were already violated. In the face of scarcity, white Brooklynites combined with their fellows to grab opportunities. They fought to keep the best jobs and the best places to live. Exercising such power was already a part of the routine of life. When they met with success, they could not forget how easily their victories could be taken away; how there were people beneath them fighting to rise and people above them who did not care about their falling. Since those above could not be touched, they braced themselves more firmly against those below. They grew angry that the contest had no end. They came to accept that the city would ever be estranged and that the divisions of today were to be the divisions of tomorrow. If their consciences played against them, they told themselves that the world was tending toward exclusion anyway, that their actions only ushered in the inevitable, and that maybe Negroes were slightly less human than themselves.

It seemed so irresistible that, as life in the city became divided by color, most came to accept that God too was a separatist.

CHAPTER SEVEN

Fruit of the Class Struggle

—

Labor Segmentation
and Exclusion
in Brooklyn,
1865–1950

—

There was a fundamental and basic difference, as marked as that which
in one soil produces beautiful roses and in another grows rank weeds.
Widely different must have been the social atmosphere which prroduced
[sic] Robert Toombs, John C. Calhoun, Alexander Stephens and Jefferson
Davis, from that which produced Wm. Lloyd Garrison, Wendell Phillips,
DeWitt Clinton, John Jay, Charles Sumner and John Andrews; a difference infinitely wide. Truly we know a tree by its fruits. Social systems as
well as soils will express themselves in fruits.

—Samuel R. Scottron

"For a good tree does not bear bad fruit, nor does a bad tree bear good fruit.
"For every tree is known by its own fruit."

—Luke 6:43–4

On the evening of June 6, 1944 sixteen black women trolley drivers pulled
their cars off line or refused to report for work. Nostrand Avenue had three
idle trolleys, the busy Utica-Reid route lost eight, two Flatbush cars were
missing, and Tompkins Avenue was short three. The action protested threats
and violence against black transit workers in Brooklyn. The spark was an
assault on driver Lillian Oliver. Only three nights earlier Oliver had exchanged
words with a white woman who boarded her Flatbush Avenue car. Two white
men intervened. Ninety witnesses saw the men attack Oliver and strike her
in the face. She defended herself with a switch iron. Oliver was standing alone
on the street when the police arrived. She declined medical attention and

refused to give the officers the iron that she used in the altercation. She was then jailed for disorderly conduct. Black women at the Flatbush Depot organized the June 6 wildcat strike. The following day they and representatives from the *Amsterdam News* and the Women Voters Council met with Spencer Hamilton of the Board of Transportation. Hamilton insisted that it was more efficient to replace black women drivers than to provide them protection, even at night, and that the war emergency required that everyone sacrifice. In a report to his superior, Hamilton boasted that he had not granted the women any "special privileges." The strikers were not fired; however, the episode was recorded in their employment files. The Brooklyn branch of the National Association for the Advancement of Colored People (NAACP) provided Oliver's defense. She was allowed to return to work and eventually exonerated. Over the following weeks two other Brooklyn trolley drivers were victimized. Gadson Goodson was assaulted and pulled from his moving car. A white retired police officer then beat Goodson in the street. A white man battered Mary Gaskin aboard her trolley while the passengers robbed her. The Brooklyn NAACP responded with a special Trolley Operators Unit and an October cabaret and dance at Smalls Paradise to establish a "Protection Fund" for the drivers' defense. A letter from Unit chairman Charles H. White read: "The race rioting now going on in Philadelphia CAN HAPPEN HERE IN BROOKLYN against Negro trolley operators. Become an effective opponent of race prejudice by becoming a Senior Member of the National Association for the Advancement of Colored People."[1]

A year before the public assault on Lillian Oliver, Mayor Fiorello LaGuardia's office received an anonymous phone call from a white woman "complaining that the Mayor and the city are employing too many colored people in the subways." The woman insisted that there were ten black people for every white man. Black workers were lazy, inefficient, and a danger to the public welfare, she continued. The complainant sent similar remarks to Governor Thomas E. Dewey. A year after Oliver's victimization, Spencer Hamilton told the Board of Transportation that nonwhite workers avoided weekend shifts and had poor attendance records because of "too many night social functions" but "otherwise they are reasonably competent." The contradictions of that statement were aggravated by his report that black laborers were disciplined in no greater proportion than white.[2]

Not even the national crisis kept white Brooklynites from violently reacting to black people's encroachment into jobs from which they had been excluded, and public outrage and official callousness protected a labor advantage that these citizens had demanded for better than a century. The rise of Jim Crow in Brooklyn might establish an irrational pattern were it not concurrent to this methodical struggle to subordinate black people as workers. Social segregation and labor exclusion gave experiential and material meaning to white supremacy and both emanated from white Brooklynites' ability to use the state to translate their group status into individual privilege. What emerged from the Civil War was a limited democracy, freed of slavery, but still fully dependent upon the exploitation of minority populations. It was defined by a two-party, single-philosophy system of social dominance that stabilized white communities by destabilizing communities of color.

Some historians have used the prevalence of racism as evidence that the United States was less class conscious than Europe. The class struggle as documented in England by historians from Friedrich Engels to Charles Booth to E. P. Thompson was not repeated in the United States because here racial identification overwhelmed class stratification. For these historians, the caste system and all its racial trappings are proof of the classless society.[3] Yet, racism does not negate class consciousness; race is the ideological product of class. White workers had come to believe that self-selection was necessary to their well-being, so they used the political monopoly created by their numerical majority in the local labor pool and the disenfranchisement of black Southerners to pursue that goal. It seemed a rational response to a system in which people appeared to rise and fall on something far less rational than individual effort. In theory, the worker competition inherent in capitalist culture was supposed to make those who toiled more fit; in fact, it rarely resulted in anything more than their desire to eliminate their competitors. Black workers were the most vulnerable laborers and, thus, the most thoroughly excluded. Race prefigured Brooklyn's labor markets against black people long before there was a significant migration of black Southerners to New York. It was not good enough to expel people of color. Left to that white Brooklynites would ever be haunted by the deed, because people who had once been competitors were now antagonists, coiled waiting to strike. Black labor had to be degraded if the triumph of exclusion was to be an advantage to white people.

Segregation as a social ideal was born in white labor's attempt to secure its position through exclusion. Brooklynites had always accepted that their world was strictly divided into social classes; they had not insisted that those relations have spatial expression. In fact African Americans' nineteenth-century campaign against the etiquette of racial subordination overturned many aspects of social segregation, but the twentieth century brought its return as well as the reordering of the social geography of the borough. At the turn of the century W. E. B. Du Bois noticed that black people's physical isolation in Philadelphia was "more conspicuous, [and] more patent to the eye" than other urban groups,[4] and that was becoming true in every great city.

By the Civil War the broadening of the city's industrial base and the tremendous growth of its white laboring population marginalized Brooklyn's African-American workers. Two-thirds of 260 black workers listed in an 1865 city directory were laborers, laundresses, seamen, porters, and white-washers. The enclaves at Weeksville, Carrville, and the Navy Yard supported a core of servants and craftsmen. The maritime industry provided many men with craft work and the chance to go to sea. Laundry work dominated the time of black women while black men served their neighbors as gardeners, carmen, drivers, hairdressers, cooks, waiters, coachmen, stewards, and porters. The black settlements allowed for some entrepreneurship. Five black tailors were operating. There were four barbers, including Weeksville's Francis Myers. Men also worked as teachers, shoemakers, machinists, and painters. Interestingly, the city supported a black penman, carpenter, engineer, paper-hanger, chairmender, metal smith, and the herbalist Doctor Burton. Robert Jackson, a drygoods dealer, had his operation in the Navy Yard district. Henry Johnson kept a grocery shop downtown. While women had fewer chances at skilled labor, Brooklyn counted several black dressmakers and seamstresses and two black women nurses. Perhaps the most interesting of the working women was Mary Smith, a photographer who lived across from the Navy Yard.[5] This working-class sustained a small professional stratum of doctors, lawyers, journalists, ministers, teachers, and merchants.

Black women's opportunities to work were narrowing although their earnings were critical to sustaining their families. A turn-of-the-century federal study of women laborers assigned only four job categories to black women but thirty to white women (see table 71.). By 1900 most of Brooklyn's adult African-American women were in the job market and 85 percent of black working women were laundresses and domestics. In contrast only half of white immigrant women were domestics and less than 10 percent of white native-born women, with two native-born parents, did that work. That concentration forced personal sacrifice. Two of three black women domestics were single and three quarters of the single women lived with their employers or in boarding houses. Forty-one percent of the black married women who entered the job market had to accept such accommodations. African-American women remained the preferred servants among the city's wealthier white families. An 1880 advertisement in the *Eagle* for a chamber-maid not only designated race but specified that any applicant be "a light colored girl." The servants who occupied this tier of jobs had elevated service to a profession; however, middle-class white families did not stick to racial traditions of hiring servants, rather they recognized the greater availability of immigrant women and tailored their racial logic to the supply. In the following decades the *Eagle* advertised the changes in demand for maids, nannies, cooks, and laundresses: "competent white girl," "experienced white girl," "neat white girl," "Scandinavian girl," "young white girl," "reliable white part time girl," "white woman," "two white girls," and "nice, clean white girl." Only among the rich did black servants survive as a symbol of status; for the middling, servants were selected more democratically. Advertisements usually gave the order of preference as American, German, or Swedish. The first reflected their nativism, the latter two were somewhat determined by supply. Black women were demanded in greater proportions than their population justified because of their disproportionate availability for such work. Interestingly, Irish women were rarely requested and Jews and Italians were even less desired. Laundress adds often singled out women of color.[6]

TABLE 7.1

Black Women's Occupations in Brooklyn, 1900

Category	No. Employed
Dressmaker	213
Laundress	1,001
Servants/Waitress	2,850
Other Occupations	454
Total	4,518

Source: Bureau of the Census, *Statistics of Women at Work* (Washington, DC: Government Printing Office, 1907), 270–71.

The concentration of native- and foreign-born black women in unregu-lated, unprotected, and unorganized domestic service jobs made them "the most oppressed section of the working class." Each morning black women gathered at the "slave markets" of the Bronx and Brooklyn—street corners abutting middle-class districts where white housewives with pennies to spare for domestic help inspected black women day workers. In her novel, *Brown Girl, Brownstones*, Paule Marshall described the Barbadian women who swarmed "the train to Flatbush and Sheepshead Bay to scrub floors. The lucky ones had their steady madams while the others wandered those neat blocks or waited on corners—each with her apron and working shoes in a bag under her arm until someone offered her a day's work." A historian of Brooklyn's Paragon Progressive Community Association recalled that the plight of black women in Brooklyn's "slave markets" helped push the organization's founders toward economic nationalism. In 1937 the National Negro Congress pioneered a short-lived Domestic Workers' Association.[7]

In 1873 a local paper provided a look at the life of a poorer black woman as it examined the work of a "colored clairvoyant" who made her living telling the fortunes of white folk. Ms. Wilson—who the *Sun* described as so old that the oldest (presumably white) resident of Brooklyn recalled that when her grandmother was a child she knew "Mrs. Wilson"—lived downtown in a small house in the black community of Hart's Alley off Bridge Street. "Hart's Alley is a collection of little tenements, whose front doors are reached by ricketty [sic] flights of steps." Wealthy white gentlemen from New York, white ladies seeking husbands, and white sporting men in need of lucky numbers and wagers gathered in the anteroom of the Wilson home. They sat with a handful of black people in a hall decorated with pictures of General Meade in battle, a ballerina, a chart of the steamboat *Continental*, a bird cage with canary, a mirror, and a picture of Lincoln. An album filled with portraits of black ladies and gentlemen rested on a table.[8]

In 1876 Theophilus Gould Steward, the pastor of Bridge Street A.M.E. Church of Brooklyn, glimpsed into the lives of black Brooklynites as he paid unannounced visits to the homes of his parishioners. The wealthy lived in imposing houses that were decorated with such niceties as pianos and often included private libraries. The modest majority lived in humbler homes that they labored to keep tidy and decorated with pictures of John Brown, Charles Sumner, Bishop Richard Allen, and Abraham Lincoln. In contrast to his experiences in the South, Steward was now pastor to a congregation with stark class distinctions.[9]

Black Brooklynites' loyalty to Republicanism brought them only a sliver of government patronage and did little to relieve their plight. In 1881 Brooklyn's black Republicans took the occasion of President Garfield's assassination to reassert their fidelity to the party and to restate their political expectations and goals. At a meeting of the Kings County Colored Club, with T. A. Barnswell presiding, the following resolution was passed:

> As true and loyal representatives of the colored branch of the Republican party of the City of Brooklyn, we desire to express our profound sorrow for the death of the President, and while we lowly bow in sorrow and sadness before the Divine will who has laid this great affliction upon us, we are ever mindful that He doeth all things well. We are also thankful that the noble successor to the highest honors which the nation can bestow, is one who has ever been a lover of humanity, a champion of equal rights, *and particularly a true and tried friend of the colored American citizen in defense of his rights*; and we do hereby accord to him our highest confidence; we share likewise largely in the universal sympathy for the bereaved wife and children of the late President.[10]

Neither party supported black candidates for local offices because Brooklyn had no predominantly black districts and the aspirations of its black citizens were more easily channeled through political clubs like the citywide United Colored Democracy and the Kings County Colored Citizens Republican League. In 1887 James Mars, president of the latter, made an unsuccessful bid for the Assembly (Third District); in 1900 Fred R. Moore lost a race to represent Brooklyn's Eighth District. W. T. R. Richardson, a native of St. Kitts, helped found the pro-Tammany United Colored Democracy, and leaders like John Nail, Tammany's envoy to the black community, were anointed by the machine, given a few patronage posts, and directed to collect black votes.[11]

Local Democrats actually doled out more patronage to African Americans than Republicans did; however, those positions were overwhelmingly in the same dull, unskilled labor that black workers were confined to in the private market. The white working-class' demand for a privileged labor position limited all political rewards to nonwhite voters. In 1897 Tammany leader Richard Croker promised the black voters of New York and Brooklyn patronage in proportion to their numerical strength; and, between 1897 and 1913, Democrats provided more than 800 jobs to black workers. However, more than 600 of the black hires were drivers and sweepers in the Street Cleaning Department and virtually all black municipal workers were menials and common laborers. Kings County's District Attorney, Coroner, and

Register each employed one black clerk and the most prestigious municipal job that a black Brooklynite could acquire was as a teacher in the public schools that served black children.[12]

While black and white people viewed each other through the lens of race, the most striking difference between them was the absence of an ordinary black working class. In every Northern city, African Americans were caught in an atypical job market in which they could be doctors and lawyers but not plumbers or builders; maids and porters but not secretaries or clerks. W. E. B. Du Bois objected to these barriers when he observed in Philadelphia in 1899 "all those young people who, by natural evolution in the case of the whites, would have stepped a grade higher than their fathers and mothers in the social scale, have in the case of the postbellum generation of Negroes been largely forced back into the great mass of the listless and incompetent to earn bread and butter by menial service." Maritcha Lyons blamed the declining status of Brooklyn's black workers on the desperation of immigrants. The days when "work was always in waiting for any and everyone who wanted it" and when it was possible to make "money with limited capital and by slow degrees" were gone, she lamented.

> Opportunities for getting a liv[e]lihood having become restricted, many of our people were compelled to accept less congenial employment and lower compensation. Discrimination in [the] apprenticing of our boys, the pernicious caste exclusion by rising labor unions, combined to develope [sic] a triangular conflict with cupidity, caste and callousness.[13]

Inventor, historian, and editor Samuel Scottron of Brooklyn also saw a connection between immigrant workers and the segmentation of labor. He thought that the Irish "assumption of ownership, power and authority" through politics had resulted in a "war upon the Negroes." Scottron continued:

> . . . the Irish captured at a very early day the whole police department, the aldermanic chamber and the courts of justice, by their political activity; and they took to themselves the public employments, street cleaning, ditch digging and janitors in public buildings. They took to themselves stevedoring, car and cab driving, hod carrying, bricklaying, fruit peddling and rum selling, and early assumed the tone and demeanor of those whose fathers had discovered or invented everything in sight, and had left them the patent right.

He then argued that the Irish also attempted to use their political power, with differing degrees of success, to control competition from Italian and Jewish immigrant workers.[14]

While European ethnics displayed tremendous hostility toward each other—which explains the peculiarly segregated labor market of New York at the beginning of the twentieth century, with its stereotyped Irish cops, Jewish garment workers, and Italian laborers—exclusion was most effective when African Americans were its victims. Unions often found it necessary to include new European immigrants, but rarely thought it prudent to reach out to people of color. Even municipal unions and agencies systematically barred black workers. By 1910 Brooklyn had few black police officers while Manhattan had none, the Fire Department was segregated, and black doctors and nurses were not hired in most public hospitals. The city's first African-American police officer was from the Brooklyn system. About 1892, before Consolidation, Paul H. Lee joined the Brooklyn City Police Department. He remained on the force for four decades. By the turn of the century the handful of African-American officers were allowed to patrol the streets. Black cops were not permitted on patrol until 1911. Samuel J. Battles was the first black man to do uniformed patrol. A somewhat legendary figure among black New Yorkers, Battles rose from foot patrol to sergeant's rank and then became "brass." By 1929 there were ninety black men and two black women in the NYPD. The Fire Department excluded people of color more efficiently than any other major municipal union or trade. By 1929 no women and only five African-American men had entered the ranks of that brotherhood. Before their prominent role in the 1863 Draft Riots, white firemen established a tradition of racial exclusion. By the early twentieth century, Julius Crump—who was born enslaved in Virginia in 1842 came to Brooklyn in 1867 and volunteered as a fireman—was the only black person to parade with the Flatbush firemen.[15]

Private unions had an equally egregious record. A 1910 survey found only 1,358 unionized black workers in all of New York City. Of the trades and trade divisions listed by the Central Federated Union in New York State, 102 had no black membership. As late as 1930 less than one-twentieth of black laborers were organized while one-fifth of white laborers were union members.[16] While it is frequently suggested that people of color were less unionized because they were unskilled; in fact, black workers were less skilled because they were not unionized.

As Louise Venable Kennedy has noted, New York City unions barred African-American labor more effectively than unions in other major metropolitan areas,[17] so black workers at times sought to undermine organized labor in order to overcome these barriers. The late nineteenth century offered many occasions to seek revenge on Brooklyn's white unions. "There were numerous strikes on the elevated lines, along the water front, in the breweries and construction trades," writes Henry Coffin Syrett. Widespread job stoppages in the city accompanied the national struggle for the eight-hour day. In 1895 the Knights of Labor led a bloody trolley strike in Brooklyn. Thousands of city police, company security guards, and National Guardsmen brawled in the streets with striking workers. Soldiers opened fire on the rebellious laborers and even charged at them with bayonets.[18]

Ira DeA Reid encouraged the "colored press" to direct its readers' dollars toward businesses that hired black people, a tactic that got fifty black men hired in a Long Island shoe factory. It was more common for black laborers to enter trades as replacements for striking white workers. In August of 1901 the influential *Colored American Magazine* declared a steel strike to be "a boon to the black people." The editors were excited to bursting at the prospect of black scabs taking the strikers' jobs because union barriers left them to form "an alliance of the capitalist and the Negro North and South against the reactionary forces that would govern intelligence and wealth by mere numbers and disregard of law." In 1905 T. Thomas Fortune's *New York Age* blasted the stupidity of a local transit strike. During the summer of 1912 a strange combination of black scabs and student volunteers from Columbia University and other local colleges helped break the Hotel Worker's International Union strike in Manhattan. A Brooklyn longshoremen's protest ended when "Negroes were imported from the South as strike-breakers." The struggle on the docks, writes Sterling Spero, began in 1855 when African-American laborers were used to replace Irish strikers. "Strikes in 1899 and 1907," continues Spero, "further strengthened the Negro's position on the New York water front." The fall-off of immigration during World War I made black laborers more important. In 1919 black workers were again used as substitute labor on the Brooklyn shore. In 1930 Local No. 968 in Brooklyn had a membership of 1,200 of whom 1,000 were African American, but the full integration of waterfront did not even begin until the 1950s when a split within the white unions forced one side to merge with the black local.[19]

There were attempts to remind workers of their common interests. James

Wallace, an African American and a representative of the International Union of Pavers and Rammersmen, tried to diversify his organization by organizing people across the state. Similarly, the Association of Colored Employees fought to make unionizing efforts more inclusive. Mary White Ovington began organizing African Americans out of necessity. In 1910 Ovington worked to ensure interracial cooperation in a shirtwaist makers' strike. Three years earlier, during the white Ladies Garment Workers strike, she contracted the services of a more experienced organizer for a unity meeting of black and white women at Bridge Street Church in Brooklyn. The Central Labor Union asked all Brooklyn's churches to observe "Labor Sunday" and called "upon all within and without the church, both empoloye[e]s and employers, to recognize and to study the present complex social and industrial situation, and so to act, that justice and fraternity may increasingly dominate our industrial life." In November 1917 A. Philip Randolph cut his teeth by organizing the United Brotherhood of Elevator and Switchboard Operators. In Brooklyn and Manhattan, African Americans enjoyed a monopoly in such work and within three weeks the organization had 600 members. Three years later Randolph founded the Friends of Negro Freedom to unionize migrants, protect tenants, and "elevate the race" in New York City.[20]

African-American businesses were another response to the community's exclusion in the labor market. Brooklyn had a cadre of well-to-do, well-educated black businessmen, who catered to a largely black clientele. They were often leaders of secret societies, state clubs, and uplift organizations. T. Thomas Fortune, who published the *New York Age*, was a leader of Booker T. Washington's National Negro Business League. Another member, Fred Moore, headed the Afro-American Investment and Building Company which used subscribers' savings to provide mortgages to local families. Subscriptions were only a dollar and the company held over $25,000 in real estate. John Connor ran the elite Royal Cafe, which "only a few white cafe's can surpass it in beauty or in up-to-date service." William Pope was proprietor of the rising Square Cafe. Professor B. H. Hawkins owned property in South and the New National Hotel and Restaurant in Brooklyn. Early Taylor, a graduate of Tuskegee Institute, owned a tailoring establishment downtown where he produced clothing and had a cleaning shop. George Harris was black Brooklyn's leading undertaker. Yet as late as 1930 Brooklyn had only ninety-four black-owned businesses, with combined net sales of just $500,000, forty-eight full-time employees and two part timers (see table 2.7).[21]

TABLE 7.2

Black-Owned Businesses in Brooklyn, 1930

Type	Number
Candy stores	7
Grocers	20
Meat Markets	2
Other food stores	2
Dry goods	1
5-and-10	1
Garages and repair	9
Other automotive	4
Men's/boy's clothing	1
Women's apparel	1
Other apparel	2
Antique shop	1
Cafeterias	1
Lunch rooms	9
Restaurants	4
Lunch counters	2
Electric shop	1
Lumber dealer	1
Cigar stores/stands	2
Jewelry stores	2
Florist	2
News dealer	1
Optician	1
Pharmacy	3
Printer	4
Undertaker	1
Second-hand stores	9
Total	94

Source: Bureau of the Census,
*Negroes in the United States,
1920–32: Retail Business*
(Washington, DC: Government
Printing Office, 1934), 36–40.

The Brooklyn labor struggle also provided a chance for white progressives like Mary White Ovington to engage questions of racial justice. She attended Radcliffe while W. E. B. Du Bois was at Harvard, but the two never met there. After graduation she spent seven years as the head worker of Brooklyn's Greenpoint Settlement House. Inspired by a Booker T. Washington lecture to the Social Reform Club in 1903, she applied for and received a fellowship from the Committee on Social Investigations to study the Negro in New York. She began the research in 1904 and published it as *Half A Man* in 1911. When the grant was first awarded, Ovington sent a letter to W. E. B. Du Bois seeking to confer with him. "I am not planning to go into an investigation simply for the sake of adding a few more facts to what is known of conditions among Negroes in poverty in New York," she assured him, "but with the hope of helping to start social work among them." One of Ovington's long-range goals was to establish an African-American settlement house in Manhattan. Crediting Du Bois as her inspiration, she concluded, "you see, you have talked to me through your writings for many years and have lately made me want to work as I never wanted to work before."[22]

Du Bois invited Ovington to attend a conference at Atlanta University, where she met the "man who could write inspired prose and who had dared to counter Booker T. Washington." And there began one of the great partnerships in the struggle for the equality of Brooklyn's African Americans. Ovington later wrote of Du Bois:

> Among the distinguished Negroes in America, none is so hated by the whites as Burghardt Du Bois. And for an excellent reason. He insists upon making them either angry or miserable. So great, moreover, is his genius, that it is impossible to read him and not be moved. Anger or misery, according to the disposition of the reader, comes from his merciless portrayal of the white man's injustice to the black. He exposes a system of caste that eats into the souls of white and black alike.[23]

The effort to secure a place for African-American labor was broader than a few lasting friendships suggest. In 1905, following yet another anti-black riot in Manhattan, Samuel Scottron and realtor Philip A. Payton, Jr. reestablished the Citizens' Protective League. That same year Dr. William L. Bulkley, the African-American principal of a public school in Manhattan, helped Ovington and Scottron establish the Committee for Improving the Industrial Conditions of Negroes. Six years later it merged with the Committee on Urban Conditions Among Negroes and the National League for the Protection of Colored Women to form the National Urban League (NUL). By that time at least five Brooklynites were active, including Scottron, Ovington, and Verina Morton-Jones, MD, a black woman who headed the Lincoln Settlement in the African-American enclave at Fleet Place in Brooklyn.[24]

The fight for economic justice was never popular. After Ovington met some of the "well-established colored families" ("the Petersons, Mars,

Wibecans, and others") they formed themselves into an informal group "calling itself the 'Cosmopolitan Club.' " They held regular meetings in the homes of Brooklyn's white and black elite where they "discussed various phases of the race question." A contemporary described the group as "distinctly socialistic in all of its views." They opposed all concepts of racial superiority and were committed to eradicating ignorance and prejudice about color. "The Society deprecates the policy of effacement and non-resistance to oppression which has never improved the condition of any down-trodden race and has only made the oppressor bolder," an observer concluded.[25]

A typical club event brought a surprising response that underscored the national consensus on race. Oswald Garrison Villard was invited to address the Brooklyn group. "We secured the restaurant," Ovington recalled, "sold tickets, and when the evening came, sat down at a pleasant gathering of quiet, well-dressed people—and to be well dressed in public in those days meant to be inconspicuously dressed." The modest gathering drew great attention. Reporters worked their way into the restaurant and the following day "the storm broke." The meeting was scored as the work of "degenerate whites." The intellectual and religious themes of the evening were forgotten in the controversy over the sacrilege of interracial meals and social equality. Congress even discussed the issue and "as we fell below the Mason and Dixon's line, our sober dinner became an orgy." One paper made specific mention of sable men who had previously dined at Ovington's home, another described an older white woman who was reportedly "leaning amorously against a very black West Indian."[26] At seventy, she probably was leaning but the lusting was likely imagined.

It was against this social machinery—which worked as well in Brooklyn as it did in Birmingham—that the militant Niagara Movement was formed in the century's first decade. The name came from the place where Du Bois convened a group to respond to the racial polarization of the society. In 1908 a second meeting was held at Storer College in historic Harper's Ferry, Virginia. Here, Mary White Ovington, reporting for the *New York Evening Post*, watched Dr. Owen M. Waller, who moved to Brooklyn from South Carolina and became a physician and rector of St. Luke Protestant Episcopal Church, "reverently walk barefooted over the rough grass and stones" where John Brown led his glorious raid. In May 1910, from these convocations, the NAACP was established. Du Bois went to New York as Director of Publications and Research, or editor, of the Association's independent organ, the *Crisis*. In 1914 a Brooklyn chapter of the NAACP was established after Du Bois and Villard spoke to a gathering at Concord Baptist Church.[27]

"The colored people in New York are more Jim Crowed, politically, than in many Southern cities, although they have the ballot and vote," black Republican leader George E. Wibecan wrote in an essay on Brooklyn associations for the 1915 National Negro Exposition. The Henry Highland Garnet (Republican) Club, founded in 1898, held forums and lectures on the condition of the race in the South, and on one occasion even filled the Brooklyn Academy of Music with the borough's best citizens to hear Virginia's James H. Hayes. In 1914 the Citizens' Club was organized to monitor

> all attempts to deny to the colored people any of their rights, and to create an environment where the leading men might get together and consider or discuss questions of mutual benefit; to watch or shape such legislation as would tend toward their progress; to study conditions of the poor, and plan to remedy them; to oppose men in public office, irrespective of party, who are unfriendly to our interests or unfair.

The Citizens' Club hosted W. E. B. Du Bois, Joel Spingarn, and other prominent guest lecturers. The Frederick Douglass Club also sponsored lectures from leading African Americans. In December 1912 Brooklyn's League's Forum was organized to sustain Brooklynites' appreciation for "the best authors of the race." Among the largest of the local associations were the Sons of Virginia and the Sons of North Carolina. The Charleston Club, the Convivial Club, and the Comus Club, established in the early decades of the century, were also active socially. The Bachelors Club of Brooklyn held the "most elaborate and exclusive" public functions, replacing the older Ugly Club as the zenith of black social life.[28]

Social organizations often addressed the economic and political needs of black Brooklynites. The Society of the Sons of North Carolina began in the 1890s when a group of Brooklyn's black men pooled their money to bury a pauper from their native state. As a result a permanent organization was formed to provide relief to the ill and distressed and burial aid for widows. The Sons began with twenty men; by 1925 it had more than 400 active members. It owned a three-story building on Bridge Street in Brooklyn where its meeting were held. Among its notable members was political insider George Wibecan.[29]

Black organizations acted as employment and migrant aid associations, a function that the "colored YMCA" perfected. In 1901 the push for a black

YMCA began and it bore fruit a year later when Dr. William L. Bulkley got hundreds of interested citizens to pledge their support and George Foster Peabody to buy and equip a three-story building on Carlton Avenue. Bulkley served as the Association's first chairman. The "colored Y" offered "pleasant parlors, a reading room, a library with excellent books, magazines, daily and weekly papers; a room for games and a limited number of nicely-furnished rooms for men," in addition to "educational classes, Bible class, religious meetings, literary society, glee club and orchestra, employment bureau, baseball club, and other features to attract and help young men."[30]

By 1905 an African-American branch of the Young Women's Christian Association (YWCA) was established on Lexington Avenue in Brooklyn. Offering a more limited menu of services than the men's association, it focused on courses to prepare women, particularly migrant women, for work. Students could even defer the cost of their education since "skilled labor is in demand, for which good wages are paid, and the training in these various courses will increase the wage-earning ability of the student, this will be considered a loan, for which, after completing the course and employment is secured, a return to the Association of a stated sum, which may be paid in installments, will be required." Easily the most ambitious of the Association's listings was a class in home nursing that provided students with a rudimentary education in anatomy, physiology, and medical science. More typical was training in cooking and kitchen care, serving, laundering, a housemaid course, seamstressing, and a nursemaid course. Essentially, the YWCA exposed the central contradiction of black women's economic lives: their earnings were necessary to their families and communities yet their economic opportunities remained severely constrained.[31]

The black elite's desire to see the swift assimilation of the resident poor and Southern migrants defined the social work of Brooklyn's black institutions. In 1905 the Howard Colored Orphan Asylum announced its plan to add a building for industrial training. In 1907 Scottron and four leading ministers visited one of the evening industrial schools that Dr. Bulkley established in Manhattan, hoping to re-create the experiment in their borough. Scottron was concerned that "Jews and Italians are picking up everything that is offered free, while the colored people shun the schools necessary to their elevation." More alarming were "leaders among the people [who were] so blind as to persuade them to let these things pass." He found the situation "awful and discouraging." The planned Brooklyn industrial school was to have an impressive queue of offerings: "carpentry, practical electricity, care of boilers, janitor-engineering, mechanical drawing, architectural drawing, bookkeeping, common school subjects, embroidery, millinery, dressmaking, flower making, stenography, typewriting, and domestic science."[32]

A few black West Indian associations appeared in nineteenth-century Brooklyn; however, the black foreign-born were more frequently absorbed into the political and social clubs, societies, and churches of native-born black New Yorkers. In the first decades of the twentieth century the growth of Caribbean immigration to the United States allowed for the emergence of independent organizations tuned to the particular needs of black immigrants. That in-migration resulted from a more regular maritime trade with the West Indies, the emergence of the Caribbean as a vacation site, and the United States ascendance as an imperial power in the region.[33]

By 1909 Brooklyn's West Indian Forum was offering political and cultural events and holding regular meetings at 349 Bridge Street. Caribbean benevolent and progressive associations—such as the Barbuda Progressive League, the Grenada Benevolent Association, and the Jamaica Progressive League—primarily sought to help black immigrants find work and housing and adjust to New York (particularly Harlem); organize relief efforts to respond to crises in the West Indies; encourage trade between the United States and the Caribbean; and reinforce cultural connections with the islands. In 1920 the St. Vincent Benevolent Association was established. It preserved familial and cultural links and provided the island with relief and assistance. The Association was also a harbinger of the growing complexity of black politics and black ethnicity in Brooklyn. As Joyce Toney has asserted, "a combination of kin and friendship ties blurred the barriers between the two societies, and increasingly, St. Vincent would appear to be just another section of Brooklyn."[34]

Brooklyn's size allowed black people a wide range of leisure activities despite social segregation. Fraternities, sororities, lodges, and clubs organized comedies, dramas, and musicals. Professional and amateur sports were open to the public through local, regional, and national conferences. Larger sporting and cultural events were held at rented gyms and armories. The Brooklyn (later Newark) Eagles offered professional "Negro League" baseball. The West Indian Cricket Club had two squads competing in an integrated regional league with segregated teams. Students from black colleges toured with glee clubs, theater groups, and athletic teams. Various societies and institutions hosted lectures. Churches offered socials and dances for men and women of courting age. Literary societies arranged book clubs, debates, and speeches. The colored Y's held children's carnivals. And newspapers passed along information about which beaches, pools, and parks were open to and safe for nonwhite families.[35]

In the early 1920s the Brooklyn Urban League (BUL) united with Lincoln Settlement for a more pointed attack on racial inequality. The League offered support services for unmarried girls (particularly migrants) and travelers' aid; a children's health clinic; clothing, food, rent, and funeral relief; Christmas baskets; home visits for courts, schools, and charities; childbirth and childcare classes; Big Sister programs; conferences and public meetings; and a housing department. Lincoln Settlement provided a summer playground; kindergarten; daycare for working women; Boy's and Girl's Clubs; visiting nurses; Sunday school; Red Cross; and meeting space for lodges and societies.[36]

Black Brooklynites were clearly divided on the issue of separate social, economic, and political organizations. Most people recognized them as a necessary response to a racially exclusive society. They understood that these adjustments had allowed their most vital needs to be met. Still, on some level, the fact of a separate institutional life seemed to legitimize or, at least, accept exclusion. A running debate on the use of community's resources for self-help versus fighting the rise of Jim Crowism marked black political discussions.

African-American institutions could attack segregation and still address the community's problems. Churches responded to both the spiritual and the political goals of their parishioners. Social organizations transformed themselves into agencies for uplift and equality. Schools offered job training courses. Societies helped place workers and relocate migrants. Brooklyn's black blue-bloods even came to recognize the need for united action. However, these efforts met with marginal success, for the subordination of African-American workers became more pronounced as the borough's black population increased.

Few white Brooklynites looked forward to economic competition with nonwhite workers and most were hostile to the challenge of social justice. In 1915 Brooklyn's R. S. King wrote in a brief letter to the *Eagle*: "There has been too much bragging about the negro's one-sided advancement." "Under the condition for which neither the white man nor the negro is responsible, while it may seem a sad decree, it is a fact that the negro is what he is, and where he is, and is helpless to be otherwise, it matters not however much attempt is made to cultivate them." King anticipated the logic of Gene

Barbish, a white deputy sheriff from Austin, Texas, who wrote Mary White Ovington during the 1919 race riots to condemn "negro loving white men" and to defend white Southerners' right "to attend to our own affairs."[37]

The Brooklyn Urban League fought to guarantee the opportunities that King thought wasted. While the League provided important social services it did not organize an industrial department until the early 1920s. Its staff had helped people find work on an *ad hoc* basis as they were informed of openings and approached by job seekers. In 1919 the League became proactive, interviewing factory managers to locate those industries that were open to black labor.[38]

In the summer of 1923 the BUL mailed more than a thousand questionnaires to employment officers at Brooklyn factories and stores. It was able to place black men in service and menial positions and black women in service and clerical work; however, in spite of the Urban League's optimistic outlook, the employment market for nonwhite workers remained narrow and unstable (see table 7.3). Black men proved particularly vulnerable. As BUL's own reports reveal, employment for African-American men was shaped and controlled by white workers' demand for service and manual jobs as the better job categories expanded and contracted.[39]

On the eve of the Great Depression the League admitted the impact of employment discrimination. "It is a familiar sight to the average New Yorker to see white men employed as elevator operators, bellboys, waiters, janitors, and messengers, where 16 years ago there would have been no thought of such a transition," lamented BUL Industrial Secretary Henry Ashcroft. While describing the efforts of its nursery and daycare center, the League pointed out the growing importance of paid work for black women. In 1929 attendance at the League's daycare and nursery facilities ran well over 5,000 children a day.[40]

TABLE 7.3

Brooklyn Urban League Adult Job Placements, 1929, 1931

	1929 Men	1929 Women	1931 Men	1931 Women
New Applicants	234	330	533	515
Openings	165	444	73	209
Placements[a]	128	333	60	133

[a]Includes temporary and permanent placements.
Source: Brooklyn Urban League-Lincoln Settlement, Inc., Annual Reports, 1929, 1931 (Brooklyn: privately printed, 1929, 1931).

By 1929 the BUL was seeking jobs outside menial service, encouraging black applicants to take civil service exams, and denouncing the fetters that restricted them to the bottom rung of the occupational ladder. In the early years of the Depression, Henry Ashcroft was able to get the Emergency Work Bureau to establish Registration Station No. 32 on site at the Brooklyn League. It would place at work 2,000 men of every race.[41] The League's efforts to assist black workers failed; and, as the Great Depression settled upon Brooklyn, federal work relief proved to be a greater salvation to white labor than to black.

Black workers suffered not just discrimination, but total labor market segmentation. Brooklyn's subway and surface transit industries were systematically segregated. Unions barred black people as members and transportation companies only hired black workers for crude labor positions. In response to George Schuyler's queries in 1927, the president of the Brooklyn-Manhattan Transit Corporation (the BMT subway system) admitted that the "companies employ comparatively few Negroes in our general office, and we employ none as motormen or conductors." Earlier he mentioned, "the porter service ... consists of practically all Negroes." In the 1930s, when the Brotherhood of Railway Trainmen moved to organize New York City's other privately owned subway system, the Interborough Rapid Transit (IRT) workers, 170 black employees risked losing their jobs because of the organization's color bar. Although Mayor LaGuardia refused to negotiate with the Jim Crow union, black workers remained unprotected. The BMT and the Independent Subway (IND) (a city-owned operation) refused to hire people of color except as porters, watchmen, and laborers. In 1938 the BMT came under attack for its outrageous hiring practices and a company spokesman admitted its guilt, simply stating that since the economic downturn the company had not done much hiring anyway. On the eve of World War II the Brooklyn chapter of the National Negro Congress accused the borough's Board of Transportation of discriminating against black workers in hiring and promotions. With no pretense at fairness, the Board directed the complaints to the Municipal Civil Service Commission. In the mid 1930s one of the first cracks in transportation industry exclusion came with the Transport Workers Union's decision to begin unionizing black porters in Brooklyn (see table 7.4).[42]

In January 1941 the Brooklyn Council of the National Negro Congress met with the Board of Transportation to discuss opening positions on Brooklyn bus routes to black drivers. Several months later Malcolm Martin wrote the Board to complain that no African-American drivers had been hired and that seventy openings for ticket agents were been given to "new people" instead of "Negro porters who, on the basis of seniority, were entitled to promotion." Those black rapid transit workers who were not porters were still concentrated in the ranks of menial and unskilled labor. In January 1943 only 1,703 of the industry's 36,570 employees were black,[43] and African-American applicants were routinely denied employment or tracked into servile jobs.

TABLE 7.4

Porters as a Percentage of Black Rapid Transit Employees, 1942

	IRT	BMT	IND
Porters	356	207	260
Other	62	159	251
% Porters	85	57	51

Source: Report drafted by A. T. Bennett, Clerk, and John C. Laffan, Personnel Clerk, dated 24 April 1942, New York Board of Transportation Records, Discrimination 1938–1963, Box 18, File 1, New York City Transit Museum Archives.

Race was a critical factor in determining the occupations of women working in rapid transit (see table 7.5). In December 1944 there were 2,158 white women and 1,058 black women working under the Board of Transportation. White women received a far broader range of professional and administrative employment. The Board of Transportation hired black women in fifteen categories while white women enjoyed thirty-two. Moreover, women of color were massed in the least desirable jobs, a fate from which most white women were spared as displayed by their minority status in such occupations in spite of their greater overall numbers.[44]

Transit companies were willing to forge racial divisions whenever their employees did not. One of the more divisive issues that the integrated Transport Workers Union faced was the extent to which it would fight discriminatory hiring practices in the industry. "Non-discriminatory union practices," argues Joshua Freeman in his history of the TWU, "meant little if blacks could not get transit jobs or could get only the lowest-paying and most demeaning work." Ultimately, African-American workers were forced to battle discrimination with the assistance of civil rights organizations, but with only sporadic union support, for the companies consistently manipulated the fears of the union's majority.[45]

Fred Johnson, a black Brooklynite and a member of the local Sign Painters'

Union, met a harsher fate. He spent thirty years in a union that was working to oust him. In 1925 he was indefinitely laid off without reason. The National Urban League took his case.[46]

TABLE 7.5

Distribution of Women by Race in Common Rapid Transit Jobs, 1944

Title	White	Black
Car maintainer	8	2
Car cleaner	29	111
Clerk	323	19
Maintainer's helper B	11	18
Maintainer's helper C	11	4
Office Appliance Op.	130	5
Railroad Clerk	1,116	411
Railroad Porter	35	237
Stenographer	167	4
Stock Assistant	16	5
Street Car Operator	25	164
Telephone Operator	110	1
Typist	76	13

Source: Office of the Personnel Clerk, Board of Transportation, "All Females (White) by Classification as of December 31, 1944" and "All Females (Negro) by Classification as of December 31, 1944," New York Board of Transportation Records, Discrimination 1938–1963, Box 18, File 2, New York City Transit Museum Archives.

Utility companies were also marshaled against African-American workers. Mayor LaGuardia's Commission on the Harlem Riots uncovered the utilities' bar against black labor. While large monopolies like Brooklyn Edison were decreasing their work forces at the beginning of the Depression, it and the borough's other major utilities actively nonetheless discriminated throughout the period. In 1938 the New York State Temporary Commission on the Condition of the Urban Colored Population, under State Senator Jacob Schwartz of Brooklyn, investigated racist hiring policies at Consolidated Edison and New York Telephone. Six years later New York Telephone hired twenty-six black women as operators after the federal Fair Employment Practices Commission (FEPC) began a probe into the company's hiring policies. Anti-Semitism at Brooklyn Union Gas, Consolidated Edison, and New York Telephone led to a 1946 grand jury investigation into those companies' policies. Brooklyn Union Gas was then slapped with another suit for violating the rights of Jews, African Americans, and Italians. "The method of recruitment of personnel admittedly utilized by the company insured the perpetuation of the original racial and religious composition of the personnel and was effective insulation against the population changes in the area," argued the Commission Against Discrimination, a Brooklyn watchdog group.[47]

The exclusion of people of color by constitution and custom were important tools in establishing white rule in labor unions; equally important was limiting the pool of qualified black candidates. "Opportunities for apprenticeship training in special trades have shown greater restrictions than the trades themselves," warned the National Urban League (NUL) in 1930. If kept from training few black workers would ever be able to challenge restricted unions. The Urban League's study of four national trades painted a bleak picture. Between 1890 and 1920 the number of African-American apprentices in blacksmithing and carpentry dramatically declined while the gains in painting and masonry were unimpressive. Thirty years after the NUL's study of black labor, a National Association for the Advancement of Colored People (NAACP) examination found that little had changed (see table 7.6). "Underlying the absence of Negroes in significant numbers from skilled-craft employment is their almost total exclusion from apprenticeship training programs," the study concluded. By 1950 less than two percent of the nation's 112,000 apprentices were black.[48]

TABLE 7.6

Black Apprentices in Various National Trades, 1950

Trade	All Apprentices	Black	% Black
Auto mechanic	3,600	90	2.50
Bricklayer	6,510	270	4.14
Carpenter	9,930	60	0.60
Electrician	9,360	90	0.96
Machinist	14,550	60	0.41
Other mechanic	6,720	210	3.12
Plumber	11,010	90	0.81
Building Trade	3,690	150	4.06
Metal working	7,170	150	2.09
Printing	14,160	180	1.27
Other Skilled	11,610	450	3.87
Unspecified	13,440	90	0.66

Source: Labor Department, National Association for the Advancement of Colored People, *The Negro Wage-Earner and Apprenticeship Training Programs: A Critical Analysis with Recommendations* (New York: NAACP, 1960), 10.

In a city that daily generated injustice and daily levied its burden there could be little motivation for the ruling elite or the laboring masses to entertain questions of social justice. Together white Brooklynites exposed the Janus face of democracy: it was at once an instrument of individual rights and a tool of social dominance.

CHAPTER EIGHT

The Covenant of Color

Race, Gender,
and Defense Work
in Brooklyn,
1930 to 1945

The problems facing the Negro workers as well as those facing other minority groups must be faced squarely by all of us active in the defense program if our democracy is to live and thrive in a world threatened by hostile, aggressive, undemocratic forces.

—Brooklyn Coordinating Committee on Defense Employment

If we suggest that Negroes, as they achieve employment opportunities, should become integrated as far as possible into organized labor, it is because past experiences have shown that gains so made are more permanent than those which are purchased at the price of placing Negroes between employers and labor unions. As in the case of the demand for trained workers, the importance of labor organizations seems destined to continue after defense production has passed.... Patterns are being established in our economy today which will be with us for at least a generation.

—Robert C. Weaver

At the close of World War II black Brooklynites were marching through the Bedford-Stuyvesant area demanding a permanent Fair Employment Practices Commission. A diverse group of leaders warned a crowd gathered at Boys High School that the return to peacetime production would bring rising unemployment, greater racial antagonism, and violence. The Brooklyn Non-Partisan Citizens Committee for F.E.P.C., an umbrella association, organized the mass meeting.[1] However, the attempt at coalition politics was not nearly broad enough to impact the segmentation of Brooklyn labor or to reverse a decade and a half of relentless exploitation. Public and private employers were committed to marginalizing nonwhite workers. During the War, black Brooklynites made a major contribution to defense production but they did not enter into the skilled trades in large numbers after the conflict. Defense contractors favored women as replacement workers, ensuring that black men would find it nearly impossible to turn their wartime training into lasting opportunity. Sexism wedded racism as women acquired skilled jobs that they were ineligible to keep and black men were kept from jobs that they might hold. Ultimately, black workers' wartime fortune did not upset the peacetime racial hierarchy. When the War ended, federal money continued to boost employment in Brooklyn through trades that remained exclusive. After more than a decade of depression and war, African Americans' job opportunities had changed little and white Brooklynites had tethered themselves more tightly to the idea that paid work was a right of race.

White Brooklynites responded to the Great Depression by fully exercising their power over people of color. If the racial division of labor brought the ideology of segregation to Brooklyn, the Depression brought more dramatic social schisms as Brooklyn's white workers clung to race as the primary mechanism for distributing economic burdens. African Americans' future was determined when white laborers reacted to the industrial collapse by snatching jobs that were once unacceptable and by hoarding government-funded employment and training programs. The segregated labor patterns of private industry were repeated in public employment. New Deal funds flowed into the borough to relieve unemployment, but black workers received no immediate benefits since that money inflated building trades and defense industries that excluded people of color. The Brooklyn Navy Yard's roster of employees swelled and its production elevated a number of related industries, but the Yard was always the preserve of white men. Long after World War II the racial segmentation of labor continued. Local, state, and federal discrimination reinforced private market segregation to make the work experiences of black and white Brooklynites radically unequal.

The Great Depression aggravated the fears of working-class New Yorkers, and local Democrats took advantage of the turmoil. For the first time in Brooklyn's history, African Americans were dependent on public relief in greater proportions than their white fellows. Discrimination against black workers in government employment programs contributed heavily to that imbalance. By October 1933 more than 687,000 New York City residents were on relief, and 78,262 of them were African American, almost a quarter of the city's black population.[2] Brooklyn Democrats used federal relief to reward their constituents. Employment programs floated party faithful through the crisis while hardship dragged others to the Democratic way.

The Brooklyn machine was busy with needy citizens, but the Depression and an uneasy relationship with the Roosevelt administration curtailed the local Democrats' ability to distribute jobs and relief. In 1933 the *Brooklyn Eagle* gave its readers a lengthy description of the machine process. Rows of job-seekers and favor-pleaders waited to greet Democratic boss John H. McCooey when he arrived at work. "It's the daily routine," said the boss. "If you came down any day that I'm here it would be the same." In the early years of the Depression local Democrats were impotent. "Boss John H" could offer his constituents only kind words and advice. Even with the party in control of the White House, the machine had to wait for the appointment of Democrats to head patronage-rich departments like the Post Office and the Internal Revenue Service before it could fill those bureaus with its voters. The *Eagle* took pleasure in the local Democrats' difficulties and paraded the story under the headline: "Hear the Hooey With Boss McCooey As Men With Sobs Get Words, Not Jobs."[3]

Brooklyn's overtaxed private charities were the first to recognize the long-term social impact of economic depression. In March 1931 the Women's Fund Committee to Provide Relief for Unemployed Single Women and Girls was soliciting volunteers through the borough's churches. Charities received requests for food, clothing, and shelter. Streams of patients who could no longer afford private care poured into public hospitals. In 1933 philanthropist Frederick Pratt, of Pratt Institute fame, called a meeting of private charities to reorganize relief efforts. "It is appalling," said Douglas Falconer of the Brooklyn Bureau of Charities, "to realize that in Brooklyn we have 250 social agencies appealing simultaneously for support." Falconer made a call for a complete restructuring of relief. There were 4,400 families on the rolls of the Bureau of Charities, which by December had distributed a record quantity of food and funds.[4]

"The NRA [National Recovery Administration] brought little or no relief to the Negro worker; and in many cases . . . increased hardships," wrote Lawrence Oxley, the Department of Labor's specialist on black employment. The New Deal failed African Americans. The federal legislation excluded agricultural and domestic workers from its protective regulations, allowed regional policy differences that often worked to impede black people's access to relief and employment, and failed to protect black workers from employers who used the codes to whiten their labor forces. "Barriers to wartime jobs were greater in the North than in the South," noted Robert Weaver in agreement. In New York City the old preserve of "Negro jobs" was disappearing as white people grew desperate for employment. A National Urban League report warned of "considerable shifts" in the black population and a "growing restlessness" among them. "In both Brooklyn and New York City," the League continued, "there has been an influx of outsiders to make a bad situation worse." The League of Struggle for Negro Rights (LSNR) established a branch in Brooklyn to respond to these conditions, and the Brooklyn Urban League/Lincoln Settlement began a number of initiatives to collect and distribute necessities and relieve some of the signs of poverty. Black church organizations, like the Society of St. Monica at St. Philip's Church in Bedford, distributed relief to impoverished families and children.[5]

Surprisingly, Democrats still struggled to attract African-American voters in New York. In 1932 200 angry black voters visited McCooey to protest his failure to support the Reverend Thomas D. Harten's candidacy for a local office. McCooey assured them that his actions were purely political and promised to attend a meeting of the Roosevelt-for-President Club at Harten's Holy Trinity Church as a gesture of fidelity. A month later Democratic incumbent Mayor John P. O'Brien was on Fulton Street and Rockaway Avenue in Brooklyn "facing about 2,500 screaming, arm-waving Negroes" who interrupted the spiritual message at a Major Devine (later Father Divine of Harlem) revival to hear his political plea.[6]

Local Democrats were more successful at winning over African Americans than was their national ticket. Black citizens needed the services of the municipal government so compromises and coalitions based on self-interest were always possible; however, the national slate struggled among African-American voters even in the face of an economic decay that affected black people more severely than other ethnics. Of all the Assembly Districts in New York City, Franklin Delano Roosevelt fared worst in Manhattan's Harlem and Brooklyn's Bedford section, both containing the largest concentration of African-American voters in their boroughs. Four years later many black voters continued to distrust Roosevelt and the Democracy. A month before the election, the Colored Womanhood of the State of New York, whose leadership included Brooklyn's Maria Lawton and Camille Rodman, denounced

Roosevelt for his complicity in racial discrimination. These were probably the same black women who picketed outside the Democratic National Committee headquarters while wearing veils and carrying signs that read: "In Memoriam. Sixty lynchings under the New Deal."[7]

During the Depression a cadre of Brooklyn's black West Indians came to power with the Democracy. In 1931 Nevis-born, Brooklyn-raised Bertram L. Baker established the United Action Democratic Association in Kings County. Within five years Baker had gained 39 seats on the Kings County Democratic Committee. In 1939 he was appointed Deputy Collector of Internal Revenue. Ten years later he won a seat in the Assembly and became the first black official to be elected to a state or city seat outside Harlem.[8]

The March 1931 arrest and subsequent trial of nine young black men in Scottsboro, Alabama, injured the Brooklyn machine's attempt to attract black voters. The courts of the solidly Democratic state managed to move eight of the nine "Scottsboro boys" from arrest to trial to sentencing in a few months. The absence of supporting evidence and a shabby and hasty application of justice for the alleged rape of two white women brought protests from around the world. In the years of trials, appeals, and retrials that followed, African Americans came to view Scottsboro as a dangerous threat to their lives; Northern politicians saw a chance to appeal to black voters through a new sectionalism; Communists found an opportunity to wedge into the black community and tap its revolutionary cord; and established organizations like the NAACP spied a vast challenge to their leadership by reds, rioters, and reactionaries.[9]

Scottsboro generated significant protest activity in New York City. In Harlem there was a struggle between the NAACP and the leftist International Labor Defense (ILD) to represent the accused and take credit for the thousands of black and white citizens who were parading and petitioning on Manhattan's streets. The *Eagle* temporarily abandoned its pro-Southern Democratic stance and joined in the criticism. An editorial declared that the state of Alabama had convicted itself, not the defendants. The Reverend George A. Crapullo of the Brooklyn-Nassau Presbytery dramatically compared the Scottsboro verdicts to the "misinformed, misguided public opinion [that] sent Jesus to His death." Rabbi A. M. Heller of Flatbush insisted that the phrase "miscarriage of justice" did not capture the Scottsboro fiasco. On Sunday, April 16, 1933, 4,000 people crowded into a Scottsboro rally at Arcadia Hall on Halsey Street in Bedford. The Reverend Thomas

Harten, president of the National Afro Protective League, organized the event. Brooklyn attorney Samuel Leibowitz, representing the Scottsboro defendants, promised to fight the case all the way to the Capital if justice was not restored. Mayor John P. O'Brien then proclaimed Leibowitz the "lion-hearted" champion of the nine young men for his front-line role in the case and urged the audience to "have faith in the country's institutions and in its leaders" because "justice will eventually triumph." Following the Mayor's lead, Boss McCooey distanced his machine from the Southern wing of the party. Before the Brooklyn protest, Leibowitz wrote a scathing article from Alabama to the *Eagle*:

> A crowd of lantern-jawed bigots calling themselves AMERICAN CITI-ZENS, stood yesterday with smirking faces and spat upon the tomb of the immortal Abraham Lincoln. They cheered a verdict that condemned an innocent boy whose only crime was that he had black skin to death in Alabama[']s electric chair, a verdict based on the uncorroborated word of a several times convicted harlot and in defiance of unanswerable proof that her yarn was an insult to the intelligence of any fair-minded human being.
>
> To look for justice for a black man here is futile—but the challenge hurled by these Negro haters into the faces of decent citizens of America will be met by the defense of these boys with every drop of blood in our veins and fiber in our bodies. We'll not quit—not till hell freezes over.[10]

Leibowitz was eventually replaced as the lead attorney, but he continued to raise funds for the defense. In December 1933 Harten held another rally at Arcadia Hall and almost 2,000 African Americans came to hear Leibowitz and to craft a resolution condemning Scottsboro and lynching.[11]

Mob hysteria was not peculiar to the South. The murder of Mary Robinson Case, a 25-year-old white woman from Queens, proved that Gotham's cosmopolitan set could also be moved to violence and excess when defending the privileges of race. Across the city, black people found themselves being punished for an event to which they were connected only in the minds of a rabid press and the fantasies of a white citizenry addicted to its words.

A biased investigation and public hysteria following Frank Case's discovery of his wife's body in their bathtub on the night of January 11, 1937 make it impossible to be sure that the man who was put to death on August 19, 1937 was a murderer. A *New York Times* article described Mary Robinson Case as a young dynamic figure in her hometown of Lancaster, Pennsylvania, and a standout at Skidmore College where she majored in fine arts, who married well, and who kept a spotless kitchen. There was an immediate public cry for the truth and an arrest. And, when the Police Commissioner announced that a culprit—"Major Green, 33 years old, colored, who for the last six years has been employed as a porter by the Bachelors Club, located at the scene of the crime"—had been arrested, many white New Yorkers took the suspect's skin color to be evidence of his guilt.[12]

Green was taken into custody shortly after the corpse was discovered. Authorities claimed to have bloodstains on clothing taken from the building's incinerator and fingerprints on the Cases' bathroom door that linked Green to the crime. The *Eagle*, having prepared readers in the preceding days with photographs of the crime scene, pasted a picture of a catatonic Green surrounded by several white detectives on its front page under the subtitle: " 'No. 1 Houseboy' Grilled in Slaying." Detectives and an assistant district attorney "worked on Green" for a full day, employing a "psychological approach" in which Green was denied access to food, family, and legal counsel. The suspect was repeatedly urged "to tell the truth." Authorities later proudly revealed that when they finally gave Green a cheap chicken dinner "he began to talk," and his wife and mother-in-law were brought in to keep him cooperative. Almost 30 hours after Green's arrest, the district attorney was satisfied enough with a "version" of the confession to have a stenographer take it down.[13]

New York City was ready to try Major Green. Security was increased to protect the accused from death threats after falsified copies of Green's confession were published in the press. To cloak the racial overtones of the case, presiding Judge Charles S. Colden assigned a black attorney, Henry C. Lipscomb, to assist in Green's defense. The trial began on Monday, February 8, 1937. By Tuesday the jury had been selected. On Wednesday Green's lawyers entered an admission of guilt and simply worked to save him from the electric chair. A black undercover detective testified that he heard Green brag of the Case murder from a neighboring prison cell. On Thursday the trial of Major Green ended. "The blue-ribbon jury," boasted the *Times*, "required three hours and two minutes, of which an hour and ten minutes was spent at dinner, to find the 33 year-old Negro porter guilty." A week later Green was transferred to Sing Sing Prison where upon his arrival he sighed, "So this is 'up the river.' " On the night of August 19, after several months of appeals and pleas for clemency, Major Green was executed.[14] New York's judicial system had brought him from arrest to electrocution with a speed that could shame any Southern court.

Many African Americans in New York were punished for the murder of Mary Case. Across the city discrimination against black people increased. Brooklyn's George Wibecan, Republican insider and president of the Crispus Attucks Community Council, organized thousands of residents to stem the rash of intolerance and affronts that followed Green's arrest. Wibecan, the Reverend Sylvester Corrothers of Ralph Avenue African Methodist Episcopal Church, and Elder Napoleon Johnston of the Council tried to visit Queens District Attorney Charles P. Sullivan to discuss the case. "We are not here to defend Green if he is guilty," explained Wibecan. "We are here to see that he gets a fair break. We want to get away from [the] racial animosities in this case. Almost every time a case of this kind happens, involving a white woman, the cry is raised that a colored man is involved." Wibecan also sought to publicize the fact that all the black employees in the Cases' apartment building were fired and 400 black workers across New York City were discharged in the rage surrounding the trial. A few days after Wibecan's protest, Oswald Garrison Villard wrote the *Times* in support. Judging the "wholesale dismissal" of African Americans to be appalling, Villard pointed to his apartment building as proof that black employees' "record is 100 per cent. clean. No group of men of any race, or nationality could have made a better showing . . . or shown greater fidelity, honesty and sobriety."[15]

The Depression exposed African Americans' weak hold on political patronage and jobs by increasing the interethnic competition for such power, but the same forces that were causing havoc among black people were at work among white ethnics. In the 1930s jockeying within the local Democratic party showed the depth of ethnic division in the city. Jews stepped forward to challenge Irish domination of the local Democratic machine and municipal payroll. Ironically, the election of Fiorello LaGuardia, a Republican and an Italian, brought Jews into the city government. The mayoralty of the "Roosevelt Republican" sapped the strength of Tammany Hall, provided Jews, Italians, and African Americans a wedge into local politics, and forced Democratic Tammany to become more reliant upon New York's crime families.[16]

Many Irish leaders and organizations reacted to the new political challenges by slandering Jews as disloyal and Italians as organized criminals.

The heavily Irish Christian Front, formed from the Flatbush Anti-Communist League and the Flatbush Common Cause League, was a product of such pressures. Under Brooklyn's John Cassidy, the Christian Front took its moral direction from anti-Semite, radio personality Father Charles E. Coughlin and gained national attention by exposing and inventing connections between Jews and communism. The Front's leadership included many prominent Catholics. Father Edward Lodge Curran of Brooklyn was a visible Front supporter and the Diocesan organ, the *Brooklyn Tablet*, "praised and defended" the organization and reported its meetings. Brooklyn's Bishop Molloy, suggests a historian of the group, gave a subtle nod to the Front and "at least tacit approval to the pro-Coughlin stand of the *Tablet* and such priest as Father Curran." By 1939 the leadership of the Front was trying to turn its Rifle Club into a paramilitary corps, while a similar Bronx group, the Christian Mobilizers, actually established a military division.[17]

In the 1930s chapters of the German-American Bund were established in Brooklyn. The Bund was a working-class organization that supported Nazism and fancied itself the ultimate check on the supposed designs of domineering, communist Jews. In 1934 a single Brooklyn local had 450 members, most of whom were immigrants or recently naturalized citizens.[18]

The United States' entry into World War II brought a temporary calm to the city as defense jobs increased and conscription tightened the labor pool. The borough's shipping yards became a conduit for federal funds. The Brooklyn Navy Yard (BNY) employed two-thirds of all the yard workers in the borough, but racial discrimination limited African Americans' employment opportunities. When Roosevelt took office 500 of the 4,105 Yard workers were due to be laid off. A few months later millions of dollars were funneled into the Yard as its officials and local Democratic politicians successfully attracted work orders from Washington. The Navy Yard experienced minor labor struggles over attempts to lower wages and shorten work weeks to maximize employment; however, the Yard remained the greatest employer in the borough. By 1936 there were more than 8,000 people working at the facility. Four years later, as the United States escalated military production in preparation for the war in Europe, there were 20,000 workers at the BNY and 60 new hires each day. As the war closed it had 75,000 employees. The borough's other yards experienced equally dramatic growth. In July 1941 Brooklyn's shipyards had 32,948 workers. A year later there were 60,548, and, by the summer of 1943, 96,090 were working at the Brooklyn yards.[19]

Converting New York City to wartime production was not a simple task since the Metropolis was the center of paper capitalism and not heavy industry. More than 40 percent of Gotham's manufacturing workers were in the garment industry, 10 percent were in food production, and as many worked in printing and publishing. State and federal officials, looking to maximize the city's role in the war effort, estimated that less than a quarter of its industries could be easily moved to defense production. Yet, as the nation prepared for war, New York City outranked all but five states in the value of its defense products.[20] That was largely due to the industrial capacity of Brooklyn.

Labor-starved industries pulled in previously excluded groups as tens of thousands of young men were activated and sent overseas. In the summer of 1939 the National Youth Administration (NYA) offered black women courses in clerical, secretarial, switchboard, and reception occupations at the Brooklyn Urban League. New York NYA director Helen M. Harris agreed to cooperate with the League but limited training to fifteen women at a time. In the winter of 1941 the Brooklyn Urban League/Lincoln Settlement, the Carlton YMCA, and the National Urban League issued a report, published by the Brooklyn Coordinating Committee on Defense Employment (BCCDE), on the impact of defense industry work on New York's black population. The report called on the NYA and the Board of Education to provide more opportunities for African Americans in defense industries. Over a six-month period the coalition surveyed black applicants from every borough. It found that less than one-fourth of all solicitors received jobs and almost a third were assigned to training. Forty-one percent of the applicants were women.[21]

African Americans did not gain the number or type of jobs and training programs that they needed (see table 8.1). In 1941 85 percent of the 13,400 black workers at United States Navy Yards were laborers, helpers, or apprentices; moreover, black people made up less than 3 percent of the New York Metropolitan-area defense workers, the lowest rate of any major defense-production region. The nonwhite proportion of the defense labor force did increase as the war progressed, but the employment and assignment process remained discriminatory. In November 1942 95 percent of the 28,853 people being trained in New York State were white. If they escaped exclusion, black laborers still had difficulty getting desirable assignments. The United States Employment Service (USES) placed 70,056 nonwhite people in jobs in New York State between October and December of 1942, but more than 97 percent of these placements were unskilled, semiskilled, or service positions.[22] While government agencies complimented themselves for the increasing number of black laborers in defense work, the concentration of black people in low-skill categories, the strategic rather than open employment of women, and the finite tenure of these jobs provided no security beyond the war years.

TABLE 8.1

Race and Employment at Brooklyn's Shipbuilding and Repair Yards, 1942

Yard	Total	Women	Non-White	% Non-white
Brooklyn Navy Yard	39,654	1,462	NA	—
Bethlehem (2 yards)	6,552	NA	180	2.7
Robins Dry Dock/Repair	6,596	65	NA	—
Sullivan Dry Dock/Repair	2,075	25	56	2.7
Atlantic Basin Iron Works	2,035	7	0	0.0
Marine Basin Co.	1,050	0	0	0.0
A. Tickle Eng. Works	509	0	1	0.2
Ira S. Bushey & Sons Inc.	502	0	4	0.8
Wheeler Shipyard, Inc.	454	4	0	0.0
Dekom Shipbuilding Corp.	275	4	0	0.0
Tollefsen Brothers	250	3	0	0.0
Liberty Drydock Co., Inc.	237	3	10	4.2
Oceanic Ship Scaling Co.	200	0	0	0.0
Cardinal Engineering Co.	91	5	0	0.0
D. Costagliola & Co., Inc.	68	0	0	0.0
Total	60,548	1,578	251	0.4

Source:United States Employment Service, "The Employment Situation in the Shipbuilding and Repair Industry in New York City" (September 1942), in the Records of the War Manpower Commission, Office of the Assistant Executive Director for Program Development, General Records of Julius J. Joseph, 1942–1943, RG 211, Entry 94, Box No. 2, National Archives.

Federal agencies exaggerated the opportunities that wartime production brought African Americans (see table 8.2). Black men remained a marginal force in the wartime economy, although they were frequently the subjects of propaganda photos. "In the current reorganization of industry," wrote W. E. B. Du Bois of the New Deal, "there is no adequate effort to secure us a place in industry, to open opportunity for Negro ability, or to give us security in age or unemployment." African Americans never received their share of the benefits from the federal funds that inflated New York City's defense industries during World War II. In October 1940 the Brooklyn Council of the National Negro Congress alerted the press that the Sperry Gyroscope Company forbade the employment of black people under its national defense contracts. Sperry's officials were unmoved and exercised their right not to respond. By the winter of 1941 more than 120,000 New Yorkers were engaged in defense work, yet less than 3 percent of them were black. Moreover, people of color were concentrated in the least attractive and worst paid jobs with few opportunities for advancement. That fit a broader pattern; for 85 percent of the nation's black Navy Yard workers were in unskilled jobs. In Brooklyn the huge Navy Yard and its resident and neighboring defense contractors were at the center of labor discrimination. Beginning in 1943 the War Manpower Commission and the Fair Employment Practices Commission (FEPC) repeatedly investigated and accused the Arma Corporation of Brooklyn of discrimination against nonwhite workers. As the War was drawing to a close Arma was still blatantly ignoring federal mandates by employing African Americans in only the most menial capacities. In 1944 the FEPC questioned Yard Commandant Rear Admiral Kelly after Herman Boykin complained of discrimination against black workers seeking promotions. The Admiral never revealed the formula for being promoted at the Yard, but he did send a memo assuring Boykin of an advancement in the near future. The promotion was not forthcoming. Indeed, Boykin almost lost his job at the Navy Yard during a wave of cutbacks. An embarrassed administration instead appointed him to instruct in mechanics. That same year all the black women on the night shift of the Naval Clothing Depot were laid off although many had seniority over white day-shift workers. The company did not rethink its cost-cutting scheme until the Federal Workers Union of the Congress of Industrial Organizations (CIO) intervened. Percival Legall's case, filed with the FEPC in 1945, exposed the two-tier wage scale used at the Yard—black people were routinely paid less than white people for the same work.[23]

TABLE 8.2

Racial Criteria for Hiring at 202 New York City Defense Firms, 1941

Specification	No. of Firms	% of Firms
"White required"	66	32.7
"White preferred"	74	36.6
"Open"	62	30.7

Source: Meredith B. Givens, Director, Bureau of Research and Statistics, and Milton O. Loysen, Executive Director, Division of Placement and Unemployment Insurance, "The Employment Situation in New York City with Special Reference to National Defense Labor Requirements," May 1941, Appendix 13, in Records of the War Manpower Commission, Office of the Assistant Executive Director for Program Development, General Records of Julius J. Joseph, 1942–1943, RG 211, Entry 94, Box No. 2, National Archives.

New York City's defense industries selected employees by race although they were hiring under government contracts and spending public money, just as restricted unions continued to pursue the exclusion of African-American workers (see table 8.3). On June 10, 1943 three shop stewards at the Acme Backing Corporation in Brooklyn led white workers on a wildcat strike to protest the employment of a black man in the Key Department. Because of the swift intervention of the FEPC and the CIO, the shop stewards were fired and the walkout lasted only one day.[24] However, the incident clearly revealed white workers' ability to threaten wartime production goals in defense of their labor privilege.

The combination of white unions and calculating industrialists ensured that African Americans did not gain a stronghold on skilled jobs. Across Brooklyn public money was being used to bolster production but not all of the public was benefiting. White women were the preferred substitute laborers as the pool of white men receded and plant managers often chose women when resorting to employing black laborers. That simple formula kept nonwhite workers from challenging the division of the labor market after the War. Whatever their gender, African-American laborers remained unskilled and they remained vulnerable.

TABLE 8.3

Black Employees at Select Brooklyn Defense Firms, 1941–2

Company	Total	Black	Category	% Black
Sperry Gyroscope	17,000	300	low skilled	1.76
Arma Corporation	3,000	20	trainees	0.67
Julius Kayser & Co.a	740	75	mostly women	10.1
Micamold Corp.	610	0	—	0.00
C. Fisher Springa	300	25	skilled	8.33
Zip-A-Bag Corp.	100	70	women	70.0
Matam Corp.	85	1	—	1.18
U.S. Tool Co.	85	1	skilled woman	1.18
ESMCO Co.	77	0	—	0.00
Shearon Metallic Co.a	NA	6	—	—

a Ordnance plants.
Source:Records of the War Manpower Commission, Records of the Bureau of Training, Records of the Training within Industry Service, General Records, 1940–1945, Negro Employment, RG 211, Entry 227, Box No. 11, National Archives.

Robert C. Weaver, the most consistent analyst of black labor in the defense industry, argued that people of color had their best employment opportunities with ordnance manufacturers because the plants were constructed for the war and were not the strongholds of segregated unions. "In order to supply explosives, powder, and small arms for a rapidly expanding army, there are today in this country scores of ordnance plants under construction and in operation," postulated Weaver. "Practically all of these establishments are new factories, and they offer a desirable area for expanding the scope of Negro employment." Ordnance plants did offer wider opportunities to Brooklyn's black defense employees; however, it had little to do with federal policy. "There was no force of compulsion that made it necessary for the contractor to employ Negroes," noted an ordnance inspector assigned to examine the records of the Murray Manufacturing Corporation of Brooklyn. The gesture toward fairness was the result of a cold assessment of Murray's wartime needs that led executives to admit previous discriminatory practices: "During the tight labor market of 1943, the situation in regard to Negroes was studied in detail by the contractor's management, the decision being reached that Negroes could be trained and up-graded beyond the lower classification in which they had been heretofore used." The inspector noted that black workers were hired and promoted under the same rules as white workers, remarked that there was no difficulty with "assimilation," and then declared that the "employment of Negroes can be beneficial to employers and the fact that they contributed so much to the war effort at this plant should be an object lesson."[25] The day the War ended, 40 percent of Murray Manufacturing's employees were African American, but black women, white women, and white men outnumbered black men (see table 8.4).

TABLE 8.4

Race and Gender of Employees at Murray Manufacturing Corporation

Year	White Men	White Women	Black Men	Black Women	% Black	% Women
June 1942	373	248	8	2	1.6	39.6
Aug. 1945	529	513	289	434	41.0	53.7

Source: Harry M. Whittleton (Associate Head Inspector, Ordnance Materiel, War Department, Army Service Forces, New York Ordnance District), "Historical Data— Murray Manufacturing Corporation; 60 m/m, M49A2, 81 m/m, M43A1; Welded Type, Trench Mortar Shell" (Brooklyn: New York Ordnance District, 15 November 1945), 28–9, collection of the Brooklyn Historical Society.

TABLE 8.5

Black Representation in Skilled Trades (National), 1950

Occupation	Total	Black	% Black
Blacksmiths	40,770	1,980	4.9
Boilermakers	34,950	810	2.3
Cabinetmakers	71,280	1,680	2.4
Carpenters	898,140	34,860	3.9
Electricians	302,340	3,090	1.0
Excavation[a]	104,760	3,300	3.2
Foremen NEC	773,100	9,450	1.2
Glaziers	10,380	300	2.9
Inspectors NEC	86,310	1,320	1.5
Job Setters	24,120	360	1.7
Line/Servicemen	205,230	2,040	1.0
Machinists	496,320	7,530	1.5
Plumbers	271,530	8,880	3.3
Stat. Engineers	212,580	4,650	2.2
Stonecutters	8,880	270	3.0
Structural Metal	48,180	1,320	2.7
Tinsmiths[b]	117,270	990	0.8
Toolmakers[c]	152,940	420	0.3

[a]Excavating, grading, and road machinery operators.
[b]Includes coppersmiths and sheet metal workers.
[c]Includes diemakers and setters.
Source: Labor Department, National Association for the
Advancement of Colored People, *The Negro Wage-Earner
and Apprenticeship Training Programs: A Critical Analysis
with Recommendations* (New York: NAACP, 1960), 8–9.

Toward the end of 1945 FEPC regional director Edward Lawson declared war on segregated work units. His action was meaningless. As white veterans returned, black women were swept from the employment rolls of defense plants and along with them went the threat of nonwhite skilled workers integrating unions and trades. Government contracts were terminated, the Navy Yard curtailed production, and white workers replaced black workers. As Robert C. Weaver had warned in 1942, after a brief reprieve of three years African Americans found themselves again trying to wedge into closed unions.[26]

An avalanche of federal money expanded Brooklyn's labor market; however, government funds were channeled into industries and trades that white laborers dominated. While the Navy Yard became the largest employer in the borough and led the defense industries in a wartime boom and the building trades gorged themselves on a feast of federal subsidies to housing and public works construction, people of color were left to fight for inclusion while fending off the hardships of depression. The few jobs and training programs that black Brooklynites won lasted only as long as the war. The removal of nonwhite defense employees was completed as white veterans returned to their jobs, nonwhite industrial workers were laid off as the nation returned to peacetime production, and the defense industries began a steady migration to the segregated suburbs. Black women seized the opportunity in defense industries to sustain their families and communities, but they had virtually no opportunity to jump from defense work to organized labor. The same was true for black men, except for a *lucky* few who fought for entrance into construction unions and became laborers, helpers, and apprentices, not full members. In 1946, while federal money continued to fuel the construction industry, the National Urban League found only twenty-two licensed black electricians (six of whom held membership in the International Brotherhood of Electrical Workers), six black men in the plumbers' local, and two unionized black plasterers in all of New York City (see table 8.5). Even black veterans faced rampant discrimination. At the end of the war the Urban League, in a study of fifty cities, called the employment prospects of black veterans "most disheartening." "The movement of Negroes into peacetime employment lags far behind the movement of white veterans," the report concluded.[27]

There could be no stability in Brooklyn so long as black workers were excluded, and the Great Depression left white Brooklynites more determined to labor under the covenant of color.

CHAPTER NINE

Vulnerable People, Undesirable Places

—

**The New Deal
and the Making of
the Brooklyn Ghetto,
1920–1990**

—

There is not a single, thoughtful person living in the Bedford-Stuyvesant area who will condone lawlessness or criminality, whether committed by white or black people. By the same token these same thoughtful people don't want to find that the area in which they live is designated as a crime belt, in which persons from other parts of the city may fear to travel. Reasoning people of the area should get together and peacefully discuss ways and means to keep and preserve this much maligned area as a desirable section in which persons of all racial groups and of all religious persuasions may live in peace and harmony in the true democratic American way.

—Henry K. Ashcroft

The urban negro problem exists all over the country. It has been aggravated by the war. It is not confined to New York City or to the Bedford-Stuyvesant neighborhood. The City can't do everything. Individuals, families, churches and social organizations must do their part.

—Robert Moses

On July 16, 1964 a building superintendent sprayed three black boys with water near their Manhattan junior high school. They chased him into his building. Police Lieutenant Thomas Gilligan of the Fourteenth Division of Brooklyn was shopping in the area and responded to the commotion. He saw the three youths pounding on an apartment door with a garbage can top. He identified himself as a policeman and demanded that they cease. One boy drew a knife and charged the lieutenant, who would claim that he drew his revolver after giving the boy a warning, after which he shot the boy in the hand and several times in the torso. Eyewitnesses contradicted Gilligan's version of the incident. The boys were sprayed with water on purpose, said Beulah Barnes, an African-American woman, housewife, and nurse. A scuffle broke out and they chased the superintendent into the building, but only stayed a short while. As the kids came out of the building, Gilligan shot one of them, then "stood there for maybe 10 minutes just staring at the body. The boy never had any words with the [police]man." Within minutes students from the junior high school were on the scene responding with rocks and bottles. It was several hours before calm returned to the area.[1]

In the following days protest rallies in response to the shooting turned into riots during which participants looted stores, taunted passersby, and clashed with police. The police killed at least one other Harlem resident and injured hundreds. Chants of "killer cops" pierced the air, bricks and bottles rained down from apartment buildings onto the authorities, and downtown precincts shifted police officers to upper Manhattan.[2]

On July 18, 1964 the turmoil spread to Brooklyn. African Americans and Puerto Ricans demonstrated in the Brownsville section. A Congress of Racial Equality (CORE) rally in Bedford-Stuyvesant, to protest the killing of young James Powell, turned violent. Onlookers ignored the rally organizers' pleas to disperse and return home. About one thousand people remained at the intersection of Nostrand Avenue and Fulton Street, harassed the police, and sacked area stores. A few hours later quiet was restored. That day the local precinct captain met with thirty-five community leaders in his office, which had a photo of the captain shaking hands with Martin Luther King Jr. on one wall. Violence and rioting were repeated on Tuesday, July 21. Two Brooklyn residents were shot and sixty-five others were arrested. "Last night in Bedford-Stuyvesant, it was a time for the 'have nots' to get even," declared a *New York Post* article. Wednesday night brought damage to ninety stores in a ten-block area of Bedford-Stuyvesant. The cost to the business district was estimated at more than $300,000.[3]

"Now, I want to address remarks directly to the people of Harlem, Bedford-Stuyvesant, South Jamaica, East Harlem and all of the other areas of our city marked by congestion, unemployment, slum housing and other adverse social conditions," said Mayor Robert F. Wagner in a speech carried on most of the city's television and radio stations. Wagner eloquently asked the city for peace and offered verbal empathy to the suffering that urban life so frequently imposed on citizens. As if the riots were expected, he gave voice to the myriad of inequalities that affected the residents of New York's ghettos, and he pledged to bring on change:

> We must go all out to remedy injustice, to reduce inequality and to remove all conditions and practices which are a source of resentment and recrimination among these fellow citizens of ours.
>
> We are no richer than our poorest citizen, no stronger than the weakest among us.[4]

Calm returned to New York, but the citizens the Mayor had addressed so skillfully that evening soon discovered that his promises were not contractual and that he could do little to relieve their plight.

The conditions that brought on the 1960s riots were rooted in the New Deal era, when Bedford-Stuyvesant was an overwhelmingly white and fairly affluent district. While the physical separation of black Brooklynites was the most dramatic result of New Deal policy in the borough, that isolation was only the lubricant of oppression. Racial concentration set the foundation for a broader social agenda that put the black population at the mercy of their white co-citizens. Segregation allowed white Brooklynites to shift the burden of their social system to the minority of the population, and eventually permitted a transfer of social inequality irrespective of public policy.

When Franklin Delano Roosevelt took office, black people were spatially less segregated than white ethnics. In 1930 James Weldon Johnson could still call Brooklyn the place where "most of the upper class and well-to-do coloured people had lived." That same year the Bureau of the Census found that most (13 of 23) of Brooklyn's statistical areas had more than a thousand black residents, while only four had fewer than a hundred. Historian Harold X. Connolly, looking for the antecedents of Brooklyn's isolated black district, could find "no contiguous, compact ghetto such as existed in Harlem or South Side Chicago." Only "given hindsight" could one find even "in skeletal form by 1930 the outline of the future Brooklyn ghetto." Yet, by the time of Roosevelt's death in 1945, Central Brooklyn was the primary locale of nonwhite residency in the borough. And, in 1953, when President Truman left office, a vast black ghetto stretched across Brooklyn and was becoming the largest concentration of its kind. "Racial barriers blocked their access to a diverse range of urban institutions, socioeconomic necessities, and opportunities: labor unions, manufacturing jobs, housing facilities, churches and public accommodations of various sorts," writes Joe William Trotter, Jr. of African Americans in the prewar city. "These developments had roots in tangible issues such as competition for better-paying jobs, scarce housing resources, and the struggle for control over the city's government and other urban institutions."[5] Drawing its harshest divisions along white-black racial lines, the New Deal blurred the boundaries of European ethnicity and provided Brooklyn with a potent *whitening* experience (see table 9.1).

TABLE 9.1

Population of Brooklyn by Race, 1900–1990

Year	White	Black	Latino[a]	Chinese	Total
1900	1,146,909	18,367	—	—	1,166,582
1910	1,610,487	22,708	—	799	1,634,351
1920	1,984,953	31,912	—	811	2,018,356
1930	2,488,815	68,921	—	1,405	2,560,401
1940	2,587,951	107,263	—	1,251	2,698,285
1950	2,525,118	208,478	—	2,268	2,738,175
1960	2,245,859	371,405	—	4,636	2,627,319
1970	1,905,788	656,194	—	11,779	2,602,012
1980	1,265,769	723,748	393,103	26,067	2,230,936
1990	1,079,762	873,620	447,605	68,905	2,300,644

[a]Included in the white and black populations before 1980.
Source: Bureau of the Census, *Census of Population, 1900–1990*.

Brooklyn entered the Great Depression already suffering a serious shortage of affordable housing. In 1918 the Brooklyn Bureau of Charities' Tenement House Committee was still waging its war against the overcrowded slum by trying to reform its residents. "Our education of the tenant has heretofore been entirely by moral suasion," admitted the frustrated Committee, "and we need a good dose of compulsion in many cases to impress the lesson on his mind." Flatbush, East New York, Bushwick, Williamsburg, and Brownsville were all problem areas. Bushwick ranked with the Bronx and Manhattan's Lower East Side and Washington Heights for overcrowding. From 1906 to 1915 one of every four residences built in Brooklyn was a tenement and Kings County absorbed 47 percent of all the tenements constructed in the city. Handing out "For You" folders to children in the public schools, the Committee worked to spread the gospel of good home life. Model flats in Williamsburg gave a "concrete illustration" of decent housekeeping. In April 1914 the Committee began educating slum dwellers "in cleanliness, order, ventilation, and proper waste disposal in relation to health, fire prevention, and safety." Perhaps its most interesting tool was a "Ten Housing Commandments" card designed to correct the religious and domestic deficiencies that white Protestants so frequently observed in ethnics. A 1918 report on 3,227 working-class families, 17,737 people, noted that 56 percent lived in "discredited old law tenements."[6]

Brooklyn's old, affluent sections, including Brooklyn Heights, Park Slope, Fort Greene, and Bedford, were showing physical fatigue. Expansion into the outlying areas of the borough followed the extension of subway and elevated service and altered property values in the inner city. New, accessible, and competitively priced housing in South and East Brooklyn was attractive to the 4 million riders who used the city's trains each day. Subways and els sped past the older brownstone neighborhoods of the borough and into the newer areas. In older districts many homeowners hoped to replace elevateds with subways for beautification, but the short-term result was the addition of heavy construction to already unsightly avenues. In the 1930s in Bedford, where the removal of the el was one of many schemes to shore up the housing market, residents were more than disappointed when the subway finally opened and people from Harlem had direct access to their community via the "A train."[7] While the Heights' view of and proximity to Manhattan and the Slope's Prospect Park buoyed property values, Fort Greene and Bedford were at the beginning of a long period of decline.

In 1919 the Brooklyn Urban League surveyed its constituents' housing and found much of it to be substandard and congested. "The houses in which the great bulk of colored people are forced to live are totally unsatisfactory as homes in which to bring up healthy, moral families," the League reported. Many were made of wood, sheltered multiple families, and lacked light and ventilation. The 1918 Tenement House Committee investigation of working-class housing identified seventy black families, six of whom were West Indian. The black laboring class was distributed across North and Central Brooklyn, but they tended to live in sections with the highest concentration of old law tenements and the oldest physical plants. The only noticeable concentration of black families was in the St. Marks district, Central Brooklyn, where about a third of the families lived and where rental costs were highest. African-American workers concentration in service jobs explains their being gathered in high-rent districts, but they also paid a premium for being black. The Urban League reported that black families paid more for their accommodations than white families. League investigators found that rents increased as much as ten dollars per month when black tenants replaced white occupants. In 1929 the League examined housing along Fleet Street near its headquarters. "The buildings are old, and outside of those facing Myrtle Avenue and a few on Hudson Avenue, all are frame and two or three stories high. In many of the frame buildings the toilets are in the yard. In only one building are there baths . . .," it reported.[8]

Housing for the white working-class was not considerably better. Thousands of apartments had toilets in the yards and in public hallways. Thousands of rear tenements that admitted little air or light were still in use. "There are millions of people living under these conditions," warned A. F. Hinrichs of the State Housing Bureau. "There are now houses standing and occupied that were condemned as unfit for habitation in 1885." Reformers campaigned against the slums and the Brooklyn Chamber of Commerce pushed for the demolition of all blighted areas, but the destruction of tenements and dilapidated frame structures worsened the housing shortage. There was "no new construction available in Brooklyn for a person earning less than $45 per week," Hinrichs continued. Developers concentrated on middle-income housing. From 1917 to 1927 Brooklyn's land values increased 89 percent, double the gain for the city as a whole. Even the "older sections" became more expensive. In 1926 the city announced plans for the construction of Brooklyn College (originally to have been called the University of Brooklyn) and speculation ran wild about its possible site. None of Brooklyn's developers seemed greatly interested in providing living space for laborers so long as the construction of middle-class communities remained profitable. As well-to-do newcomers were drawn to the perimeter, the poor struggled for space and the middle class in Bedford, Park Slope, and Fort Greene organized to make sure that they would not find it. Race and ethnicity delineated that contest. For instance, the Gates Avenue Association, organized in the 1920s, and the Midtown Civic Club, established in the following decade, existed for the sole purpose of stopping black people's movement into Bedford.[9] They were joined by a number of similar organizations.

Luther Johnson, an African American and realtor in Brooklyn, noted the positive effect of black families purchasing properties in the borough. While many white families worried about the value of their homes as neighborhoods changed demographically, they tended to ignore the threat of a sagging real estate market. Black renters and buyers shored up rents and real estate prices throughout Central Brooklyn. "Our consistent buying of property for the past five years more or less has kept the market value of old Brooklyn property up to a satisfactory standard," Johnson said. Bedford and Stuyvesant were particularly dependent upon black in-migration to stabilize prices. Abraham Staub found that out when he tried to rent out a restricted apartment house. Located just outside Bedford, the apartments attracted so few white applicants that Staub appealed to the Brooklyn Supreme Court to overturn the racially restrictive clause in his mortgage agreement. Justice Selah Strong refused the plea.[10]

Still, African Americans were physically less segregated than most new immigrants. "The gregariousness of the newly arrived immigrants," argued a former secretary of the Brooklyn Tenement House Committee, "is shown by the fact that Italians, Hebrews and Slavs are confined for the most part to two or three localities." Black Brooklynites were also being depicted as undesirable. Advertising the racial and ethnic purity of new neighborhoods was standard procedure. In 1925 John Edmead, a black real estate broker, publicized the case of a black woman who bought a three-family brownstone home on the corner of Classon Avenue and Madison Street. A Catholic priest led an interdenominational white protest outside the Building Department, causing such a scene that the priest was reassigned. He went on to further infamy when he called the Reverend George Frazier Miller a "saucy nigger" after Miller defended the integrity of black women. In 1929 W. E. B. Du Bois discovered the restrictive covenants governing real estate developer Alexander Bing's Sunnyside Gardens in New York and Radburn in New Jersey, and reminded Bing of the harmful national results of segregation. Bing returned the impotent apologia, "We have in mind embarking shortly on a separate negro community." Robert De Forest and the directors of the Sage Foundation development refused Du Bois application to buy a home in exclusive Forest Hills, Queens, because of his race. That same year a white woman seeking revenge on her neighbors highlighted the restrictions on black Brooklynites' housing choices. The Lefferts Manor owners association questioned Ellen Morris, a resident, about guests staying in her home. In anger, Morris placed a large sign in front of her house announcing that it was for sale to "colored people only." Her white neighbors then camped outside her house and threatened her by phone.[11]

In 1935 the racial geography of Brooklyn began to shift. That year, the New Deal was dramatically altered when the owners of a slaughterhouse in Brownsville, Brooklyn, sued the United States government. "We are of the opinion that the attempt through the provisions of the Code to fix the hours and wages of employees of defendants in their intrastate business was not a valid exercise of federal power," wrote Justice Hughes in the unanimous

Schechter Poultry Corp. v. United States decision. With those words the legality of the National Industrial Recovery Act was destroyed and the era of the New Deal was neatly divided into two phases. Before *Schechter*, Roosevelt's cabinet had focused on reviving a stalled economy, easing the financial crisis, and controlling unemployment. Now New Dealers were faced with a decision that was as much an opportunity as it was a setback, and so began the "Second Hundred Days."[12]

A Roosevelt landslide in the election of 1936 seemed inevitable, and, with four more years of rule, Democrats looked forward to finishing the New Deal. This meant government spending for military expansion, public works, and housing construction. There were immediate benefits: public money could be used to shore up weak financial institutions and a faltering real estate market, government loans could spark consumer spending, affordable housing could reduce radical impulses, job patronage to Democratic voters could continue, government spending could drive the economy, and housing loans to white ethnics could help weaken the Republicans' suburban strongholds.

In New York the latter required changing the building trends of the metropolitan area. By the mid 1920s it was aphoristic that a neighborhood was judged as much on the ethnic background of its residents as it was on its housing stock, the convenience of its location, and the quality of its services. The Brooklyn Real Estate Board, which included virtually all of the borough's realtors and many of its major corporations (see table 9.2), made ethnic segregation its official policy. When the *New York Times* announced the publication of the Board's *Annual Year Book and Diary* of 1933, it reminded its audience that the book included interesting tidbits about taxes, zoning, and postage. The paper failed to mention that the *Diary* also contained a copy of the Board's Code of Ethics, which was adopted from the National Association of Real Estate Boards on November 1, 1927. Article 34 of the Code read: "A Realtor should never be instrumental in introducing into a neighborhood a character of property or occupancy, members of any race or nationality, or any individuals whose presence will clearly be detrimental to property values in that neighborhood."[13]

Black Brooklynites pooled their money and provided each other with the secure loans that banks and realtors denied them. About 1932 Barbadian men in the Bedford section of Brooklyn began addressing the economic hardships in the black community through an informal credit society. On July

18, 1939 they organized the Paragon Progressive Community Association. On January 29, 1941 the Paragon Progressive Federal Credit Union was established with an initial investment of $225. Garveyite in its structure, the Association employed a practical economic nationalism, taking deposits, providing home and business loans at reasonable rates, and giving black people control of their own resources. The Paragon Women's Auxiliary raised funds to purchase a Fulton Street headquarters. Paragon's growth was remarkable. At the end of 1941 the credit union had 187 members and was approved to sell government bonds. By 1945 it counted 1,117 members and extended over $200,000 in loans. Paragon expanded each decade thereafter and even moved its credit union to a more spacious site at 1471–1477 Fulton Street. When Paragon closed four decades later, it had assets of more than $15 million. It had also lent or secured more than $75 million in loans to its patrons. Churches also formed credit associations. Under the ministry of the Reverend Milton A. Galamison, Siloam Presbyterian in Bedford established a credit union in response to bank discrimination.[14]

TABLE 9.2
Major Corporations on the Brooklyn Real Estate Board, 1935

Abraham & Straus, Inc.	Green Point Savings Bank
Bay Ridge Savings Bank	Hamburg Savings Bank
Bond & Mortgage Guarantee	Home Insurance Company
Breevort Savings Bank of B'klyn.	Home Title Guarantee Company
Brooklyn Borough Gas Co.	Kings County Trust Company
Brooklyn Edison Company	Kingsboro Mortgage Corporation
Brooklyn Savings Bank	Lafayette National Bank
Brooklyn Trust Company	Lawyers Mortgage Guarantee
Brooklyn Union Coal Co.	Lawyers Title Corporation
City Bank Farmers Trust Co.	Lawyers Title & Guarantee Co.
City Savings Bank of B'klyn.	Lincoln Savings Bank of B'klyn.
Dime Savings Bank of B'klyn.	Manufacturers Trust Co.
Dime Savings Bank of W'msbg.	Metropolitan Life Insurance Co.
East Brooklyn Savings Bank	National Liberty Insurance Co.
East New York Savings Bank	New York Telephone Co.
Equitable Life Assurance Society	New York Title Insurance Co.
Flatbush Savings Bank	Roosevelt Savings Bank
Fulton Savings Bank of K.C.	South Brooklyn Savings Bank
Great Atlantic & Pacific Tea Co.	Title Guarantee & Trust Co.
Greater New York Savings Bank	Williamsburgh Savings Bank

Source: Brooklyn Real Estate Board, *Year Book and Diary for 1935* (Brooklyn: privately published, 1935), 39–60.

However Brooklyn's white business community was intent on profiting from the physical segregation and financial quarantine of people of color. Brooklyn Edison was more aggressive than the Real Estate Board in guiding the ethnic geography of the borough. Its *Market Survey* was filled with maps and information about housing construction and values. Edison divided Brooklyn into twenty-eight neighborhoods and catalogued the ethnic mixture of each along with more detailed descriptions of the specific locations of less desirable groups: Jews, Italians, and Negroes.[15]

The older areas of the borough had been losing population since the 1920s[16] because of the discriminatory actions of local financial institutions that were heavily invested in South Brooklyn and constricting their activities in North Brooklyn. This was not simply a matter of focusing resources. Denying loans to North Brooklyn decayed its communities and forced many residents to move. They were likely to relocate to South Brooklyn where new housing and ample credit could be found. In Bedford, or Bedford-Stuyvesant as the area was increasingly called,[17] frustrated citizens were publishing the *Bedford Home Owners News* to protest the financial crunch in their district. "The housing situation was brought about ... by many profiteers," declared one editorial. Writers for the *News*, while at times scattered in their attempt to find the source of their woes, frequently charged that unreasonably high mortgage rates in the district, high taxes, and banks which refused to grant them "financial aid" to keep their homes in good order were the causes of Bedford's decline. Most were tired of hearing polite bank officers tell them that their houses were too old or that "too much money has already been loaned in that particular section." A group of desperate Bedford homeowners asked President Roosevelt and Congress to extend the legislation that protected farm owners and rural communities "to include in its benefits the urban and city home owners."[18]

Some North Brooklyn residents resorted to gimmicks to save their homes from devaluation. Many Bedford residents believed that the razing of the Fulton Street el and the construction of a subway line was the road to the revitalization. Brooklyn Chamber of Commerce president William Kennedy promised that "the removal of the elevated road on Fulton Street would have a definite bearing on the real estate value of the section." Other residents of the area began a buy-in-Bedford campaign to circulate money in the community and support local businesses. But elevated trains and commercial sales were not the problem. Banks were manufacturing the financial crisis. Rather than holding on to declining property, white homeowners in North Brooklyn sold to local realtors, probably at a loss, and signed government mortgages in the new developments. Signs "to let," "for sale," and "for rent" sprouted across the region. Savvy investors bought properties at low prices and offered them at high rents to poorer groups who were barred from the more desirable sections. By 1936 it was irrational for middle-class white residents to remain in North Brooklyn.[19]

However, Brooklyn was not racially segregated until the federal government armed banks, insurance companies, and developers with public money and government authority. Banks and their government allies had ignored a simple caveat of Bedford's residents: "To prevent slums is better than having to clear them." In the 1920s Brooklyn's northern communities felt financial strains from the development of the borough's southern perimeter. In the 1930s an alliance of government, bank, real estate, and insurance interests destroyed the internal stability of North Brooklyn. Much of this damage took place under the direction of the Home Owners' Loan Corporation (HOLC). Established in the summer of 1933 as one of the New Deal's emergency measures, HOLC was charged with intervening in the mortgage market to prevent widescale foreclosures and bank failures. At its high point it had a national staff of 20,000. In New York State, the Loan Corporation focused on suburban areas, helping families of modest incomes purchase and keep one- and two-family homes. Only 30.2% of HOLC's state loans were made to New York City.[20]

HOLC was a failure in spite of its early rush of activity. In 1937 the Corporation had a 40 percent foreclosure rate and was losing money in New York State. When it liquidated its assets in 1951, the Loan Corporation showed a "slight profit." That turnaround was a result of the Corporation's regional lending policies and a closer marriage of its interests with those of financial institutions and realtors. By the late 1930s HOLC agents were surveying and mapping urban communities across the nation and working with banks and building investors to enact mortgage guidelines that guaranteed profit. The Loan Corporation's federal mandate insulated the process from local politics and protests. "The [Brooklyn] map and area descriptions were first made with the assistance of a representative of the HOLC Appraisal Department. They were then carefully checked with competent real estate brokers and mortgage lenders," wrote an agent. The borough's leading corporations were involved (see table 9.3). HOLC's Brooklyn consultants included George S. Horton, a three-term president, and Joseph W. Catharine, a two-term vice president and seven-term treasurer of the Brooklyn Real Estate Board while it was under its racially restrictive Code of Ethics.[21]

TABLE 9.3

Affiliations of Select Brooklyn Security Map Consultants

Atlantic Savings & Loan Association
Bowery Savings Bank
Dime Savings Bank
East New York Savings Bank
Emigrant Industrial Savings Bank
Equitable Life Assurance Society
Franklin Society for Home Building and Savings
Greater New York Savings Bank
Greenpoint Savings Bank
Group V Mortgage Information Bureau
Lincoln Savings Bank
New York City Housing Authority
Prudential Insurance Company of America
Railroad Federal Savings Bank
Regional Planning Association
South Brooklyn Savings and Loan
Williamsburgh Savings Bank

Source: "Explanation of Security Area Map," Section V of
"Brooklyn-New York Security Map and Area Description
Folder," in the Records of the Federal Home Loan Bank
Board, Home Owners' Loan Corporation, Records Relating
to the City Survey File, 1935–40, New York, RG195, Box
No. 58, National Archives, Washington, D.C.

"The purpose of the Residential Security Map [see map 2] is to reflect graph-ically the trend of desirability in neighborhoods from a residential view-point," explained its creators. HOLC agents divided Brooklyn into sixty-six communities, surveyed them, and gave each one of four grades. Areas coded "A" and colored green on the map were "new well-planned sections, not yet fully developed." Grade "B" districts were colored blue. They "remain desir-able places in which to live" but "as a rule are completely developed" and "have reached their peak." Zones that had old and obsolete housing, "inad-equate transportation, insufficient utilities, heavy special assessments, poor maintenance of homes" or disagreeable populations were graded "C" and colored yellow on the map. Communities that received the fourth rating, "D," suffered run-down houses, "undesirable" residents, vandalism, and poverty. The legend on an earlier generation Security Map described "D" grade areas as "hazardous." Colored red, these neighborhoods were judged unsafe and unfit for mortgage investment, and the resulting financial boycott acquired the opprobrious label "redlining."[22]

At first glance HOLC's course of action seems judicious. If the government were going to use public money to bolster faltering financial corporations then it was logical, even responsible, to gather information on the areas in which these institutions operated, consult with "experts," publish the results, and hold participants to practical and cautious lending policies. However, the Loan Corporation was never a disinterested steward of the nation's mortgage industry. From its inception HOLC operated under the assumption that the concerns of lenders and developers were paramount. The Corporation reflected the profit interests and prejudices of business, but it never created a legitimate mechanism for including the concerns of homeowners and homebuyers.

Moreover, the formulation and application of HOLC's criteria for grading neighborhoods were far from scientific. Most loans went to suburbs where the Loan Corporation used public moneys to underwrite private risk and to ensure the success of private developments. HOLC directed its loans in Brooklyn toward outer neighborhoods where developers held most of their investments. North Brooklyn was judged too risky for further investment, and on the Security Map most of that area was given the lowest grade "D," while most South Brooklyn neighborhoods managed at least "C" ratings.

In 1938 HOLC agents prepared sixty-six Area Descriptions to explain their evaluations. Each gave justifications for the grades given to every Brooklyn neighborhood. In addition to topography, housing age and condition, demand for unit purchases and rentals, and location, agents surveyed the occupations of area residents, median incomes, and relief levels. Question 2C asked for the percentage of foreign-born people in a community; 2D the percentage of Negroes; and 2E if one of these was *infiltrating*.

That HOLC sheltered the investments of real estate and financial institutions can be seen in its selection of Brooklyn's best neighborhoods; only on these surveys did agents consistently impose a reasonable standard (if a singular concern for profit can be described as reasonable public policy) for judging urban districts. Since most of New York State's housing construction was suburban, the Loan Corporation gave its A rating to only one of the borough's neighborhoods, Bay Ridge, which received that nod because local developers had concentrated their investments there. Brooklyn Heights received a "B" grade in spite of its affluence and its unrivaled view of Manhattan. Surveyors saw no chance for large-scale housing construction in the built-up Heights and developers were not deeply invested there, so its

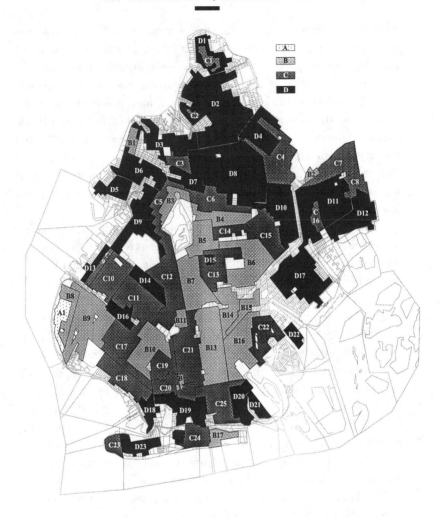

Map 2. Security Map of the Home Owners Loan Corporation

	GRADE A	GRADE B	GRADE C	GRADE D
1	Bay Ridge (A)	Brooklyn Heights (B)	Greenpoint (C-)	Greenpoint (D)
2		Highland Park (B)	Williamsburg (C-)	Williamsburg (D)
3		Park Slope (B)	Ft. Greene Hill (C+)	Navy Yd., B'klyn Bridge (D-)
4		Crown Heights (B)	Bushwick, Ridgewood (C)	Bushwick (D)
5		Upper Flatbush (B)	Lower Park Slope (C)	Red Hook (D)

6	Flatbush, Holy Cross (B-)	Eastern Parkway (C)	Gowanus Cnl., S. B'klyn (D)
7	Prospect Park, South (B+)	Arlington (C)	Hill Section (D)
8	Bay Ridge (B)	East New York (C-)	Bedford-Stuyvesant (D)
9	B.R. & Dyker Heights (B-)	West Sunset (C-)	West Park Slope (D)
10	Bensonhurst (B-)	Sunset (C)	Brownsville (D)
11	Midwood Manor (B-)	Borough Park (C+)	East New York (D)
12	Flatbush, Gravesend (B)	Prospect Park, SW (C)	New Lots (D)
13	Flatbush, E. Midwood (B)	Flatbush, Farragut (C)	West Suset, Bay Ridge (D)
14	Flatbush, Southeast (B)	North Flatbush (C-)	Kensington (D)
15	Flatbush, Kings Hwy. (B-)	West Brownsville (C-)	Flatbush (D)
16	Marine Park (B-)	East New York (C-)	New Utrecht (D)
17	Manhattan Beach (B)	West Bensonhurst (C-)	Canarsie (D)
18		Upper Bath Beach (C-)	Lower Bath Beach (D)
19		Bensonhurst, Malverne (C+)	Gravesend (D)
20		Gravesend (C-)	East Sheepshead (D)
21		Flatbush, Midwood (C+)	Gerritson Beach (D)
22		Flatlands (C)	Bergen Beach (D)
23		Sea Gate (C)	Coney Island (D)
24		Brighton Beach (C)	
25		Sheepshead Bay (C)	

Source: Reconstructed by author from an original color map in "Brooklyn-New York Security Map and Area Description Folder," in the Records of the Federal Home Loan Bank Board, Home Owners' Loan Corporation, Records Relating to the City Survey File, 1935–40, New York, RG195, Box No. 58, National Archives, Washington, D.C. Base map courtesy of the New York Department of City Planning.

"rows of large old-fashioned brown stone singles" were listed as "Detrimental Influences." Park Slope suffered a similar fate. Prospect Park and the area's large white Protestant and Irish Catholic population earned only a B because they had little room for new construction, although Loan Corporation representatives preferred to claim that the in-migration of Jews caused the conservative valuation. Elegant Crown Heights was given a B grade because of "traffic," and a Jewish concentration. Beautifully located Manhattan Beach, perched on Brooklyn's Atlantic shore, earned the same mark because surveyors objected to the "slow infiltration of somewhat poorer class Jewish" people. A section of Flatbush got a B<ms> because canvassers disapproved of the mixture of Jewish, Irish, and Italian residents. HOLC's representatives were also willing to upgrade communities to secure investments. To protect private investments in top-rated Bay Ridge, agents gave neighboring Dyker Heights a liberal B<ms> although it had a mixed Irish, Jewish, and Italian population, a federal reservation, railroad scars, industrial sites, some obsolete housing, and was adjacent to a "very poor area." Strategically located Bensonhurst was also awarded a B<ms>, overcoming "mixed races," a Jewish cemetery, and its poorer neighbors.[23]

The areas that received C-level ratings were more frequently judged on their ethnic compositions. This was partly an attempt to cover up the manipulation of federal money to secure private investments, partly an effort to cash in on housing segregation, and part meanspiritedness. These peculiar motivations forced HOLC staff to become more random in their accusations and more creative in their justifications but the underlying intent remained quite clear. Fort Greene, where Walt Whitman had built a brownstone a century before, had experienced decades of decline, but HOLC staff still gave it a gracious C+ because they approved of the "British" ancestry of its inhabitants. "German residents keep homes neat and orderly"—so Bushwick-Ridgewood was given a C in spite of the "infiltration" of Italians, a noisy elevated train, surrounding slum areas, and, paradoxically, its general shabbiness. In contrast, a more handsome section of Lower Park Slope, within a short distance of Prospect and containing "substantial houses," was given the same grade because of the "infiltration of lower grade [Italian] population." Also near Prospect Park and enjoying "substantial row brick construction" and convenient transportation, the Eastern Parkway district was punished with a C rating because of its Jewish majority and a tiny black colony. "Formerly a fine residential section of brick and stone singles," wrote the agent who surveyed Eastern Parkway, the "area is being adversely affected by [the] infiltration of lower grade [black] people from the north." Actually, only 2 percent of the community's citizens were nonwhite. Sea Gate was nicer than Flatlands, which lacked sewers and paved streets and was filled with dumps and vacant lots, but both received C grades—Sea Gate being penalized for its Jewish majority and Flatlands rewarded for its Irish and British residency and its unimproved lands. Greenpoint's C<ms> was a result of the age of its buildings, the absence of construction space, and a population which, while "frugal" and "home loving," was, unfortunately, Polish. The same rating was given to nearby Williamsburg where an unhealthy combination of Jewish, Italian, and Polish residents offended the raters. "Mixed races"— Scandinavian, Italian, and Irish—in West Sunset led graders to slap it with a C<ms>; and similar ethnic combinations in Upper Bath Beach and Southwest Prospect Park caused each to get that same grade. The Italian presence in North Flatbush was all that representatives needed to hit it with a C<ms> and dismiss it as a collection of "makeshift houses," "shacks," and "junk yards." The Jews of West Brownsville depended upon government relief and "in the past [some] joined together in a rent strike." The image of tenants making demands on owners and lenders was abhorrent. A harsh C<ms> rating was given to the district, and government employees warned potential mortgagors that, while there was "no agitation . . . at present," a "communistic type of Jewish population" inhabited West Brownsville.[24]

The lowest-grade areas of Brooklyn exposed the potential profits of residential segregation. Here, race, religion, and national origin were central concerns in HOLC's determinations. While the map does not portray it, true slums were juxtaposed with neighborhoods that had once been Brooklyn's most fashionable. HOLC agents stooped to stereotypes and name calling to support these decisions. For instance, surveyors ignored the fact that Brownsville was the home of Murder Inc., the crime gang which included the future lord-of-thugs Joseph "Joe Adonis" Doto, and which, in the 1930s, was responsible for perhaps 200 unsolved killings in Brooklyn and another 800 across the nation and in Canada. Rather, Brownsville's pushcarts, curbside markets, and "mixture of races" disturbed HOLC. They were particularly concerned with Jews: "Communistic type of people, who agitated 'rent strikes' some time ago."[25]

"Bodies were constantly being discovered in our neighborhood, guys were constantly being killed. Neighbors were leaving for prison and coming back. We didn't produce anything except robbery and gambling and fencing and hot goods," wrote Jerry Della Femina of his childhood in Gravesend. Loan Corporation agents graded the area harshly because they objected to its large and growing Italian community, who were "poor laboring class" and often found themselves on public relief. Warehouses, manufactories, old docks, and older houses earned the Navy Yard and pieces of Greenpoint and Williamsburg D and D- marks. The western section of Bushwick-Ridgewood received a D for its old-law tenements and growing Italian population. Irish, Italian, and Scandinavian Red Hook and Gowanus Canal, "slum type areas for many years," were both given D ratings. The old black district in Clinton Hill was listed with the borough's worst zones although it had few serious problems. Historic Bedford-Stuyvesant was condemned for its black population. Similarly, poor and working class Italians and Poles in West Park Slope explained its D grade. Assessors found nothing redeeming in the mingling of Italian, Danish, Polish, Swedish, and Jewish people in Kensington and, therefore, dubbed it a "very undesirable neighborhood of mixed races." Mappers carved a small Italian and black enclave out of handsome Flatbush, assigned it the fourth grade, and insulted it as "distinctly undesirable" for its "mixture of low grade races." When the Loan Corporation found poor Italians in New Utrecht, it blasted them as prideless, "low class," "low grade," and "of questionable occupation and income," while gratuitously predicting that the community had "very little likelihood of improvement." The public servants of HOLC called the laboring Jews and Italians of Canarsie "poor grade population" and rated that area D. "The low grade Italian population" of Lower Bath Beach was impoverished and "many [of them were] living in shacks and make-shift houses scattered throughout the area without plan or design," so HOLC wrote off the district.[26]

The Home Owners' Loan Corporation used public money to remove risk from the construction and real estate investments of private financial institutions and builders, and positioned the federal government as the primary agent of segregation in the borough. Even as federal surveyors were compiling the Brooklyn Security Map, Joseph Sanner, HOLC's counsel in New York State, was coyly assuring the residents of preferred Bay Ridge that they could expect continued federal financial support.[27] Under the guise of protecting investments, surveyors targeted Jews and Italians as the white ethnics most frequently, consistently, and severely discriminated against through HOLC policies. But the victimization of African Americans was unparalleled.

Bensonhurst and a portion of Flatbush, with sizable Italian populations, managed at least B- grades, just as a number of Jewish areas received B or better ratings. In contrast, not one of the eighteen neighborhoods that received a B- or better had any black residency, except for Crown Heights where the black population was described as "Nil," meaning "2 or 3 families between Nostrand and Schenectady Ave., there for 15–20 years." Only four of the twenty-five zones that received C ratings had nonwhite residency, the largest of which was Upper Bath Beach's 5 percent. Black people were disproportionately represented in those districts that were given HOLC's lowest ratings, D- and D. More than half of these areas (13 of 25) had black populations. In fact, according to the Loan Corporation's Security Map, the simplest rule for determining a "hazardous" community was any with more than 5 percent black residency.

The Brooklyn Security Map was not intended to mirror contemporaneous prejudices. For instance, mappers did not mention Brooklyn's small Chinese population, although New York's popular culture regularly disparaged Asians and they were marginalized in labor and politics. Black Brooklynites were victimized in the late nineteenth century when they were less than 2 percent of the total population, and anti-Asian sentiment was rife in twentieth-century Brooklyn. Policymakers ignored Chinese residents because their small numbers made systematic exploitation unprofitable. Similarly, federal surveyors for HOLC did not punish Brooklyn Heights because "Latins" were one of its "predominanting" populations;[28] however, less than a decade later, state authorities began to aggressively redline Latinos as that community increased. The catalyst of both policies was not attitudes but greed. HOLC policies were intended to guarantee the development and stability of newer neighborhoods and suburbs. White North Brooklyn residents were forced to choose between holding on to devalued properties in declining areas or selling out and fleeing to perimeter districts with government guaranteed mortgages. Financially choked and hemorrhaging middle-class residents, North Brooklyn's decay was written into government policy. The drain of municipal services that occurred as the local government moved to meet the needs and demands of the growing areas of South Brooklyn and their powerful backers finally sealed North Brooklyn's fate.

Discriminatory lending practices drew middle-class white people to South Brooklyn and the suburbs and forced African Americans and Caribbeans into North Brooklyn, drawing a line of racial separation across the heart of the borough. New Deal policies pushed targeted groups into limited areas and artificially increased the demand for and rental prices of the city's least desirable housing. On the other hand preferred groups were charged for the luxury of ethnic homogeneity. On both ends of the redlining process, banks, insurance companies, and realtors profited.

HOLC increased racialism in Brooklyn. The population of the ghetto and the perimeter remained fairly steady, increasing moderately each decade, but that constancy hid the fact that tens of thousands of black people were pouring into Central Brooklyn as white residents were streaming out. In fact, from 1930 to 1950 the only Brooklyn neighborhoods to experience net population losses were those white areas in North Brooklyn where white outmigration actually outpaced black residential growth (see table 9.4).[29] To relieve family fiscal pressures, white Brooklynites had to move to homogeneous communities, rid their neighborhoods of people who were different, and ensure that other groups did not *penetrate* their districts. The Security Map put the imprimatur of the federal government behind the proposition that the presence of some human beings was harmful. Jews were communistic and too many of them could injure a community. Italians were a threat to any neighborhood and their presence could retard property sales and assessments. HOLC policy not only made areas with large Italian and Jewish populations less attractive to buyers, it also made it difficult for those groups to move because few neighborhoods were willing to risk their presence. And no population was more dangerous than black people. No bank would lend them money to relocate to the newer areas, and the residents of those districts did not want black settlers. In zones that already had large nonwhite populations, white homeowners rushed to sell before banks stopped lending and property values plummeted. In areas with few people of color, white people maneuvered to make them leave. White families were punished for having black neighbors. They could lose their investment in their homes or they might be forced to sell them at a loss or ride them into worthlessness. If they chose to remain, the area around them was destined to decline. According to the federal authorities and local financial interests, black people were dangerous neighbors. That whole process was neither rational nor inevitable.

Many mansions still punctuate the stately brownstone rows of Bedford-Stuyvesant in a combination that forms a visual rebuttal to the suggestion that the area could ever be a slum; however, in two short decades those willing to draw wealth off misery destroyed the neighborhood. Bedford-Stuyvesant lies at the center of the vast redlined district of North Brooklyn, and HOLC predicted that it "probably will be the center of [the] colored population in the Borough within the next twenty five years." In fact, HOLC's prophecy was self-fulfilling. Its activities guaranteed that African Americans would become the majority group. The Area Description warned of their "steady" influx, and included the contradictory rider: "Colored infiltration [is] a definitely adverse influence on neighborhood desirability although Negroes will buy proper-ties at fair prices and usually rent rooms." It did not take long for the effects of the Loan Corporation's policies to manifest. By the early 1940s the *Times* was regularly referring to Bedford-Stuyvesant as "roughly analogous to the Harlem district in Manhattan" or, more concisely, "Brooklyn's 'Harlem.'"[30]

TABLE 9.4

Population of Brooklyn Neighborhoods, 1930–50

Area	1930	1940	1950
Bay Ridge	290,080	311,976	316,218
Bedford	284,371	301,118	306,632
Brownsville	298,122	296,930	278,840
Bushwick	240,909	240,220	231,003
Flatbush	356,096	438,073	478,110
Fort Greene	217,004	207,867	220,337
Gravesend	212,196	262,296	278,636
Red Hook	185,474	176,229	170,693
Sunset Park	224,997	231,413	219,589
Williamsburg	251,152	232,163	216,249

Source: Brooklyn Council for Social Planning, *Growing Up in Brooklyn: A Report of Brooklyn's Little White House Conference on Children and Youth* (Brooklyn: 1951), 80.

Media, realtors, and politicians obnoxiously tried to explain the social disorder that resulted from segregation by inventing the borough's growing inequali-ties as racially, not socially, determined. In an arrogant inversion of historical truth, they claimed that New Deal relief programs had coddled black people, making them lazy and criminal. "Government handouts for the past decade have been all this new generation has ever seen," Midtown Real Estate Association president Thomas H. Doyle smugly stated. "They know nothing of the strength and independence derived from working for a living." Bedford-Stuyvesant's Monsignor John L. Belford, entering his third decade of accusing black people of destroying the area, pleaded that his neighborhood needed "not only protection but salvation." Harlemites, he continued, were flooding into his district on the "A-train" and preying on white people. Combining his stereotypes, the Monsignor then complained that black public school children were attacking white parochial school kids. The community had become so violent that four area Catholic churches had canceled evening services. A Brownsville resident concurred, stating that he was tired of the "robberies, gambling, assaults and other criminal acts of all sorts [that] take place."[31]

Job and housing discrimination bred crime and unrest, but equally important in North Brooklyn's decline was the stretching of public services toward the newly built areas of South Brooklyn. As black Brooklynites were being thrust into Bedford-Stuyvesant, municipal services were shifting to protect and administer the new South Brooklyn developments. A *Brooklyn Eagle* headline in 1937 dubbed Bedford-Stuyvesant a "Copless, City Stepchild." Two years later George Wibecan and Sumner Sirtl, the latter of the Midtown Civic League, thought the situation in Central Brooklyn volatile enough to warrant a tolerance committee. In November 1941 Riis House, which was based on the Lower East Side of Manhattan, announced its plans to begin providing services to Bedford-Stuyvesant in response to crime, disease, overcrowding, and unemployment figures. Paul Blanshard, executive director of the Society for the Prevention of Crime, urged the Board of Estimate to provide funds to keep schools open at night for recreation in Bedford-Stuyvesant. Of the forty Brooklyn schools that had night activities for youngsters only one was in a district suffering high delinquency rates.[32]

"This area at one time was one of the finest residential sections of this Borough," began the August 1943 Kings County Grand Jury report on Bedford-Stuyvesant. The Jury, which was convented in response to the growing media coverage and public outcry over conditions in central Brooklyn, pilloried Mayor LaGuardia and his top officials for neglecting the district, allowing crime to go unchecked, and denying responsibility for the conditions in Central Brooklyn. Gangs roamed wild, crime escalated, social conditions decayed, and lives were being ruined but no official was acting to prevent it. In response to the Grand Jury's precise questions, Mayor LaGuardia deflected the blame by introducing *race*: "Let's be more frank about it—this is the negro question we are talking about." "When a neighborhood changes its *complexion* that way there is bound to be trouble," he insisted.[33]

"This is in no sense a race problem," the Jury retorted, criticizing the Mayor's attitude and inaction. Police Commissioner Valentine's testimony was filled with so many cavalier statements that the Jury berated his stance as "equivalent to confessing anarchy." The Grand Jury resisted the suggestion that the crime problem in Bedford-Stuyvesant was racial, and concluded, "the fault lies with the responsible public officials, and particularly, with the Mayor of this City in failing to invoke all the powers in his command and take all the steps necessayy [sic] to prevent the lawlessness we have referred to."[34]

Federal officials never received full blame for the social turmoil that resulted from the discriminatory use of government funds and authority, nor were local officials ever held accountable for following those policies, gleaning every chance to benefit their voters at the expense of other citizens, and adding schemes and manipulations of their own. The mayor easily won the battle for public opinion. As the Grand Jury was conducting its business, LaGuardia made a point of publicly dismissing people who accused the City of neglecting Central Brooklyn as "liars" and "crackpots." When the Report hit the media, the Mayor dismissed it as "entirely political." Race remained the most effective defense. White Brooklynites had already decided that the logical cause of the disorder in Central Brooklyn was its black residents and that the Grand Jury was simply being polite in not directly accusing them. Understanding that prejudice, African Americans immediately objected to the Report's failure to discuss the social and economic causes of the conditions in Bedford-Stuyvesant. So LaGuardia and his top officials instructed white New Yorkers that there was a causal connection between color and decay. Parks Commissioner Robert Moses wrote the Mayor shortly after the Report broke in the press, declaring that any suggestion that Bedford-Stuyvesant had been neglected was erroneous. Moses used an exaggerated definition of the area, which included most of North Brooklyn, to defend the district's park services. The real problem was race, he too insisted. "The urban negro problem exists all over the country," Moses proudly declared. "It has been aggravated by the war. It is not confined to New York City or to the Bedford-Stuyvesant neighborhood. The City can't do everything. Individual families, churches and social organizations must do their part." In a few lines, Moses had penned the position paper of New York City and most municipalities when confronted with the social results of their policies: If we are not the only ones who discriminate, we should not feel guilty about our discriminations.[35]

On November 21, 1943, 500 (mostly white) residents of Bedford-Stuyvesant gathered at the Bedford YMCA to call for the Mayor's ouster and to cheer the suggestion that an "influx of sunburned citizens who come up from the South mistaking liberty for license" had turned Central Brooklyn into "Little Harlem." Policeman David Liebman enthralled and mesmerized the audience with stories of "muggings" by the "sunburnt elements" and biological thieves in his precinct. Monsignor John Belford, who had probably never in his life turned down a chance to publicly slur other races, then stoked the flames of hatred. The white citizens in the audience were so convinced that black people were the source of their woes that when Henry S. Ashcroft, an African American and a lawyer, stood to defend them against the parade of slurs that had crossed and recrossed the room, he was "hissed and booed" while "more than half of those at the meeting started for the doors." Nonetheless, Ashcroft insisted that Bedford-Stuyvesant organizations had been struggling to get modern health, recreation, and educational facilities for more than a decade and that all the community's residents, black and white, were committed to seeing and end to criminality. "Every one knows that lawlessness and other unfortunate features of urban life are to some extent the result of poor economic conditions, lack of education—and lack of hope—which is no more than the result of frustration in the efforts of people to better themselves," Ashcroft concluded.[36]

Reaction to the Bedford hysteria was mixed. LaGuardia continued to deny all wrongdoing. Sumner Sirtl was so disgusted with the Mayor's response to the problems in Central Brooklyn that he challenged Governor Thomas E. Dewey to investigate the section, the local government's actions, the records of borough banks and insurance companies, and the books of the Federal Housing Authority and the Home Owners Loan Corporation. The City tried police officer Liebman for his role in arousing hatred in Bedford-Stuyvesant. Herbert T. Miller, executive secretary of the Carlton YMCA, charged that people of color were being used as a "political football" and called for a fact-finding committee to investigate the claims of the Grand Jury, to examine employment discrimination, and to look into the lack of recreational facilities in Central Brooklyn. Branches of the NAACP and the CIO tried to calm fears in the area. The radical American Labor Party's local arm declared the whole incident a "renewed plot to employ organized anti-Negro attacks as a method of real estate business and a strategy for political power." Judge Nathan Sobel, while giving instructions to another Brooklyn Grand Jury, challenged the public:

What are we to do about it? Are we to erect a fence around the Bedford-Stuyvesant [section]? I think we have done enough. We have welcomed our Negro brethren from the cabins in the South to the slums of New York. We have extended to them the privilege of paying the highest rents for the rottenest roosts out of the poorest wages for the dirtiest jobs. Now let us deny them relief! Let's punish the poor for being poor and the ignorant for being ignorant! Maybe we can create a smoke screen that will hide the real culprits—ourselves.[37]

Beneath the vulgarisms of North Brooklyn's white residents was proof that their neighborhoods were viable and that they were not looking to abandon them. Bedford-Stuyvesant's homeowners had waged a decade-long war against the unfair distribution of mortgage funds. In 1938 the Bedford and Stuyvesant Ministers' Associations compiled a document describing neighborhood needs. The ministers linked black and white churches to address the problems of a neglected district with a growing population and rapid residential turnover. Noting that ethnic succession "occurs again and again in metropolitan centers," the ministers assured themselves that "no one is to blame, no one can be censured; it is one of those inevitable things that come with growth and economic change." After giving a full accounting of institutional resources and a description of needs, the report called for an end to labor discrimination: "equal opportunity to those of equal merit."[38]

TABLE 9.5

Growth of the Paragon Progressive Federal Credit Union, 1941–1969

Year	Total Assets	Outstanding Loans
1941	n/a	$2,185.63
1945	$156,575.92	60, 476.93
1949	493,888.93	276,256.51
1954	1,269,975.32	892,570.66
1959	2,219,181.88	1,348,336.48
1964	3,128,074.69	2,014,678.80
1969	4,716,477.55	3,492,929.95

Source: Clyde G. Atwell, *The Paragon Story (1939–1969)*
(Brooklyn: privately printed, ca. 1976), 63–86.

Evidence of black Brooklynites' commitment to affordable and decent housing is also buried in the records of the Paragon Progressive Federal Credit Union (PPFCU) and its parent association. Both were born out of the housing and financial crisis. A president of the PPCA later recalled the sociohistorical environment of its founding:

Where there is greed there is no conscience. The strong will take advantage of the weak. The rich will continue to milk the blood of kindness from the poor. And so the great chasm widens between mankind. Then as now fair trade did not include the poor. Prices were high. Schemes for fleecing the blacks were rampant. Being poor but ambitious our people were most vulnerable. With an eye on self-preservation some ventured their life savings in the purchase of two family brownstones. In many instances the intended investment became a misfortune.

In its first decades the PPFCU served a largely Anglophone West Indian clientele. Clyde Atwell put it politely when he wrote that the membership "comes from the five continents with the heaviest preponderance from the Caribbean area." However, in time, Paragon's leadership could boast that a significant number of its clients were other West Indians, native-born black people, and a few Puerto Ricans. Paragon even assisted the formation of other credit unions among people of color and provided the Small Business Administration free office space to encourage entrepreneurship in Bedford-Stuyvesant.[39]

Other community organizations were also looking for solutions to Bedford-Stuyvesant's problems. In late 1945 the Stuyvesant Community Center opened, under the direction of Albert Edwards, in a three-story building at 265 Decatur Street. It was a product of the cooperation of St. Philip's Church, the Bureau of Social Service, the Boy and Girl Scouts, the Urban League, and the YMCA and YWCA; it served all residents regardless of color. Brownsville Neighborhood Council chairman Milton J. Goell prepared a plan of action to meet area needs as the nation emerged from World War II and confronted "a war against poverty, discomfort, disease, [and] crime, in our country." Issuing a strong plea for racial harmony, Goell and the Council included two practical efforts to meet the needs of African Americans in Brownsville: an integrated nursery to support working mothers and an integrated recreation center in the heart of the black district. These were to bolster the "scant facilities which the heroic pastors of their churches seek to create for them out of straw." Integration was key, but integration with respect rather than condescension. "They [black people] would not be admitted by sufferance—they would be admitted because the building belonged to them as citizens." The plan also called for closed markets to reduce outdoor trade and crowding, transit upgrades to rid Brownsville of its two-fare zones and trolleys, well-designed public housing, a casework center to deal with family problems, and the cleaning of Jamaica Bay.[40]

Brownsville's was a modest plan when contrasted with the grandiose schemes of local public works commissioners, but Brooklyn banks, insurance companies, utilities, and realtors had declared Brownsville a slum, and because many of its residents were Jews who wished to revitalize their community and save their homes, HOLC labeled the neighborhood "communistic." The fact that some of these people were willing to live in harmony with their black neighbors made that epithet even more fitting in the eyes of mortgage lenders.

Post-World War II Brownsville was typical of North Brooklyn neighborhoods. The Brooklyn Council for Social Planning warned the city that Brownsville was a cauldron of racial tensions. Still predominantly Jewish, Brownsville had 25,000 black residents who "have very little of anything." The district's continued decline affected everyone. Eventually, of all the Neighborhood Council's proposals, the only improvement given to the area in a timely fashion was public housing. In 1945 plans for the Brownsville Houses were made with accommodations for more than 1,300 families.[41] But, bank mortgage policies continued to draw middle-class residents to South Brooklyn and drain municipal services. That process isolated Brownsville's public housing projects in a falling neighborhood.

Brooklyn needed housing. Early in 1946 the Navy Yard chaplain warned that returning servicemen needed homes. That same year barracks at Manhattan Beach were converted into housing units for veterans. More than 20,000 Brooklyn applicants were waiting for government housing. Most new construction was in South Brooklyn, where George Gray, president of the Brooklyn Real Estate Board, set a goal of 30,000 new units for 1946. Yet, a year later 2,000 units of veterans' housing remained unsold because builders were using the crisis to continue their cozy relationship with government money.[42]

The postwar building boom allowed real estate interests to complete the development of South Brooklyn and the ghettoization of nonwhite citizens. Local banks and insurance companies aggressively pursued both these goals. In January 1945 thirty-seven financial and insurance institutions (see table 9.6), already joined under the rubric of the Mortgage Conference of New York (MCNY), published a *Population Survey* that divided Brooklyn into twenty-seven mapped sections. The Conference controlled 60 percent of the mortgage funds in Greater New York and had been in operation since the depression year 1932–1933. It traced the movement of people of color in the borough through the preceding decade and mapped the block-by-block residency of African Americans and Puerto Ricans for 1937, 1941, and 1945. That latter year the Savings Bank Trust Company of New York at No. 14 Wall Street—founded in 1933 to act as a central bank and general trust company for the state's mutual savings banks, and holding $646 million—took control of the Mortgage Conference's records and at its own expense continued to distribute the *Survey* to lenders.[43]

TABLE 9.6

Corporations in the Mortgage Conference of New York

Aetna Life Insurance Co.	Home Life Insurance Co.
Bankers Trust Co.	Home Title Guaranty Co.
Bronx Savings Bank	Irving Trust Company
Brooklyn Savings Bank	Lawyers Mortgage Corporation
Brooklyn Trust Co.	Manhattan Savings Bank
Canada Life Assurance Soc.	Manufacturers Trust Company
Central Savings Bank	Mutual Life Insurance Co. of NY
Chase National Bank of NYC	New England Mutual Life Ins.
City Bank Farmers Trust Co.	New York Life Insurance Co.
Dime Savings Bank of B'klyn.	New York Trust Company
Dollar Savings Bank of NYC	North River Savings Bank
Dry Dock Savings Institution	Prudential Insurance Company
Emigrant Industrial Savings Bank	Seamen's Bank for Savings
Empire City Savings Bank	Title Guarantee and Trust Co.
Franklin Savings Bank of NYC	Union Central Life Insurance Co.
Greenwich Savings Bank	Union Square Savings Bank
Guaranty Trust Co. of New York	West Side Savings Bank
Guardian Life Insurance Co.	

Source: *The New York Times*, 7 August 1946.

The Mortgage Conference betrayed the racist progression of public and private collusion over housing. MCNY fully extended the protections of whiteness to Jews and Italians—lesser victims of HOLC's work—and compensated with an increasing concern over the growth of Brooklyn's Latino population. However, the *Survey*'s primary purpose was to plot the locations of black citizens, concentrate them in convenient districts, and force them out of areas of investment. A single black resident became the basis for drawing a zone of caution around an entire city block; an exception being made for "Negro superintendents or servants" in white residences. Districts like Park Slope, Sunset Park, Borough Park, Flatbush, Canarsie, Bay Ridge, Bensonhurst, and Gravesend received the tribute "no residential

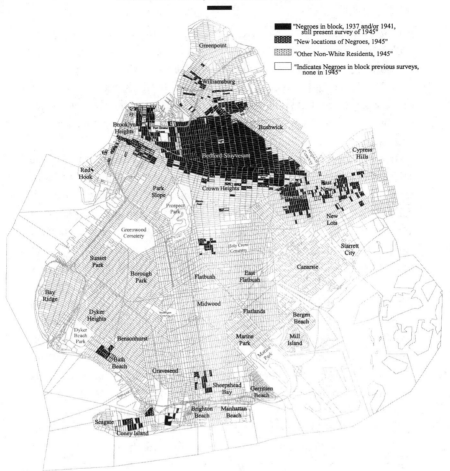

Mortgage Conference of New York, Brooklyn Population Survey

Source: Reconstructed by author from the Mortgage Conference of New York, "Population Survey No. 3-B, Brooklyn" (New York: The Mortgage Conference, 1945). BAse map courtesy of New York Department of City Planning.

negroes." The map created a distorted perception of the nonwhite population. At the time of the 1945 canvass, black people were barely 5 percent of
the borough's 2.5 million citizens; still, the *Survey*'s sole objective was to
record and control the residential patterns of "Negroes." In fact, MCNY's
documentation of "Other Non-White Residents" and its interest in the location of public housing were subordinate and complementary to a patholog-
ical assault on the civil liberties of black Brooklynites.[44]

In the late summer of 1946 the United States Justice Department sued the
Mortgage Conference, listing all the participating institutions as defendants,
for conspiracy to monopolize mortgage lending in New York State, using their
collective influence to prevent construction that might lower the value of
areas in which members had extended loans, and violating the civil rights of
African American and Puerto Rican citizens. The Conference fixed mortgage
rates, established uniform appraisal procedures, and set rents to eliminate
competition and drive up profits. To benefit from racial segregation, reported
the *Times*, the defendants "prepared, published, kept current and distributed
maps of each section of New York City showing blocks on which Negroes and
Spanish-speaking persons resided; refrained from making mortgage loans on
properties in such blocks, and induced owners of real estate in certain
sections of New York City to refuse to permit Negroes and Spanish-speaking
persons to move into such sections." The suit charged that rent gouging in
nonwhite neighborhoods was one of the results of this unilateral decision to
limit African-American and Latino mobility. In a public statement, MCNY
officials insisted that they had only worked "to place the mortgage lending
business in New York City on a more *scientific* basis for the good both of the
lender and the borrower." Conference president Harold Rutan took personal
offense at the Justice Department's unprovoked suit which slandered as
"conspiracy" what New York State preferred to describe as "cooperation."[45]

The Justice Department only sought to dissolve the Mortgage Conference
and to enjoin its members from re-creating similar combinations in the
future. Department officials did not involve themselves in the fact that these
activities damaged the lives and life chances of hundreds of thousands of
Brooklyn residents nor were they particularly interested in pursuing the
Conference's defense that it had received its moral and legal authority during
the Depression. The latter would bring them to the door of the Home
Owners' Loan Corporation from which the Mortgage Conference of New
York learned its trade.

African Americans in Brooklyn came to blame white people for their isolation but rarely did they focus their anger on Washington. Similarly, Ernest Quimby has noted, for white Brooklynites "no longer was the destabilization of Bedford-Stuyvesant seen as the result of official policy; rather it was seen as *caused* by the presence of nonwhites. That is, the stigma of decline was shifted from official hands to the hands of the Black population."[46]

National and local Democrats hid their role in the segregation of the city behind a web of financial institutions and complex policies, and were always quick to use the "attitudes" of white constituents as their ultimate defense. Democrats even gained the loyalty of black Brooklynites whose infrequent political victories came through that party. On the eve of the 1944 election, Rev. Harten called Franklin Roosevelt the "greatest friend of the Negroes," as 10,000 black residents prayed and fasted for the president's and Senator Robert Wagner's re-election.[47] For such dedication, black Brooklynites did receive rewards, however slight. The local Democracy sold itself as the dynamic force of change in the borough. Since the housing shortage affected African Americans most, Democrats pointed to Brooklyn's public housing to show their responsiveness to the needs of black citizens and their sincere desire to ease the shortage of "Negro housing." Public housing already had a stigma, one reinforced by the banks and insurance companies that carefully held it outside their areas of investment and one enhanced by New Dealers who used it as proof that their party cared for and watched over people of color as they struggled against a vague force called *racism*.

"If you are looking for filth and juvenile delinquency, you can find your quota in Brooklyn," commented Gertrude Tanneyhill, director of the Brooklyn branch of the Greater New York Urban League. Two years earlier the Brooklyn Urban League–Lincoln Settlement and the New York Urban League merged to better focus the struggle for economic and political justice in New York City. Of particular interest to the League was the growing segregation of black New Yorkers (see table 9.7). "Checks must be placed upon the suicidal trend toward racial ghettos observed in the spread of restrictive property owners' covenants," forcing public housing into already segregated areas, and eliminating people of color from the pool of home buyers.[48]

But the man who was in charge of New York's municipal construction had no tolerance for those who hungered for equality. Robert Moses, in his role as City Construction Coordinator, declared during an August 1947 radio interview that he had enough of radical minorities who delayed the city's building plans with demands for "impossibly low rent ceilings and anti-discrimination clauses." Moses was tired of being victimized and being made the "scapegoat." In fact, he continued, he only kept his position because of the Administration's support and a "naive stubbornness."[49]

TABLE 9.7

Concentration of the Black Population in Bedford-Stuyvesant, 1930–1957

Year	Black Bed-Stuy	% All Bed-Stuy	% All Bklyn.
1930	31,215	12	45
1940	65,166	25	61
1950	136,834	51	66
1957	166,213	66	—

Source: The Community Council of Greater New York, *Brooklyn Communities: Population Characteristics and Neighborhood Social Resources*, 2 Vols. (Brooklyn: September 1959), I: xviii-xxi, 100–1.

Moses was typical of a generation of "public servants" who felt that the Great Depression had given them the reason and the New Deal had given them the authority to inflict their view of progress upon the city without regard for the wishes of its citizens. "In less than ten years," predicted Moses in the summer of 1949, "one person out of every ten in New York City will look to the City Housing Authority as his landlord." A year later Thomas Farrell, chairman of the Housing Authority, praised the New York's public projects as a lesson in interracial living because all of the sites built after 1939 were integrated. A few months later Mayor O'Dwyer concurred, speaking at an Urban League luncheon at the Theresa Hotel in Harlem he complimented the city's public housing as a model of desegregated living. Both officials depended upon a loose definition of interracial. For instance, Brooklyn's Red Hook Houses were the first integrated projects in the New York, but less than one percent (24 of 2,545) of the original families were black.[50]

Moreover, integration was not the pivotal issue. As the Justice Department's suit against the Mortgage Conference exposed, the borough's banks and insurance companies worked to keep public housing away from new developments. Most of Brooklyn's projects were located in the redlined sections of North Brooklyn and were, therefore, destined to become segregated as Puerto Ricans and African Americans flooded into these neighborhoods and white people flowed from them. Projects also placed additional strains on North Brooklyn's dwindling public services, quickening rather than halting its decline.[51]

New York City's Slum Clearance Committee—created by Mayor William O'Dwyer in December 1948 in anticipation of Washington's Title-1 "urban renewal" funds—used its public authority and federal money to aid banks and investors in further segregating the borough, a manipulation that earned this program the pejorative label "Negro removal." Title 1 was intended to help cities acquire slum areas and discount them to private investors for rede- velopement. It did not take long for business to learn the power that the Committee wielded. By naming sites and approving developments, the Committee controlled the displacement and relocation of urban residents who sat in the path of targeted projects. The city's financial institutions had already mastered the art of keeping nonwhite people out of areas of invest- ment, control of the Slum Clearance Committee allowed them to uproot black people and Puerto Ricans already living in neighborhoods that were otherwise ripe for loans. From its beginning the Committee described its goals as being parallel to those of developers. Its organization was fully unde- mocratic. The City Controller did not audit the Slum Clearance Committee because its staff salaries were drawn from the budgets of other municipal departments. The Committee met irregularly, it was convened at the chairman's will, and averaged several one-hour meetings a year. A greater cause for concern was the transformation of the Slum Committee's member- ship. When O'Dwyer established the body it was composed of the Controller, the Housing Authority chair, the Corporation Counsel, the Board of Estimate's chief engineer, and, later, the State Power Authority chair; within a few years the first three resigned and were replaced by the Real Estate commissioner, the Building commissioner, and Thomas J. Shanahan, who the *Times* described as a "politician-banker." Having always been under the chairmanship of Robert Moses, the reconstituted Slum Committee sustained even closer ties to New York's financial and real estate interests and many of its staff were borrowed from city agencies that the chairman once headed or still led. Shanahan was the president of the Federation Bank and Trust Company and George E. Spargo, Moses' assistant, was a director of Federation Bank and a trustee of New York Savings Bank. Spargo and Shanahan were invited to govern the Clearance Committee although their institutions extended mortgage loans to the city's Title 1 projects. On three occasions the Slum Clearance Committee unilaterally dismissed a federally mandated New

York City Planning Commission report on blighted areas. The Planning Commission eventually acquiesced and amended its original guidelines to fit the Slum Committee's. By the summer of 1955 the SCC had handled almost $150 million in federal and local grants and a half billion dollars in private investments. Adding the power to designate slums to their restraint of mortgage funds, New York's financial institutions now exercised the extraordinary ability to whiten or darken any neighborhood at will.[52]

Local Democrats shamelessly used public housing to prove their responsiveness to the needs of African-American and Caribbean citizens, and to strengthen that impression they also engaged in a number of symbolic appointments and gestures. In 1939 Carolyn Dublin, a black resident of Bedford-Stuyvesant and an active member of St. Peter Claver's Church, became the first black probation officer in Brooklyn's higher courts. A year later 200 residents of Bedford-Stuyvesant and Williamsburg met at the First African Methodist Episcopal Church to demand the appointment of a black person to the Board of Education. Barely two months later, Mayor O'Dwyer named the Reverend John M. Coleman, pastor of St. Philip's Protestant Episcopal Church in Bedford, to a seven-year term. Coleman was the first black citizen to sit on the Board since 1918. That same summer Leonard Stanford, an African-American boy from Brooklyn, joined fifty other children in a ceremony at City Hall where a deputy mayor expressed great joy to see them and great shock that the young school patrol guards were barred from a function in Washington, D. C. because no hotels would take integrated groups. Few politicians went as far as O'Dwyer, who declared September 23, 1946 to be "End Lynching Day."[53]

It is a twisted irony that Brooklyn's politicians offered more vocal protests against segregated sports than they had against the construction of a black ghetto. By attacking Jim Crow in professional sports, local officials were able to grandstand as champions of racial equality without tackling the politically costly issues of employment and housing discrimination. In 1939 State Senator Charles Perry of Manhattan introduced a resolution condemning race prejudice in Major League baseball. Perry continued to push the issue. The following year the sports editors of twenty-five area college papers joined the protest. During the summer of 1942 the CIO entered an objection to racial restrictions in the professional game. Commissioner Kenesaw M. Landis made his position clear in the winter of 1943: "Each club is entirely free to employ Negro players to any extent it pleases and the matter is solely for each club's decision without any restrictions whatsoever." In the summer of 1945 two black players received tryouts with the Dodgers but were not signed. That same summer, New York representative Vito Marcantonio brought the issue of segregated professional baseball to the House of Representatives. Not to be outdone, Mayor LaGuardia asked Branch Rickey, president of the Dodgers, and Larry S. McPhail, president of the Yankees, to head up a committee to investigate sports discrimination. The Republican mayoral candidate, Judge Jonah Goldstein, took LaGuardia's challenge and publicly reminded the Major Leagues that "baseball is an American game, played in the American spirit of fairness and democracy. Baseball is not a Nazi game based on the hateful rules of so-called racial superiority. Every American, every true lover of clean and wholesome sports, loves baseball because it symbolizes our democratic national spirit. There should be only one test, the ability to play ball."[54]

In October 1945 Branch Rickey signed Jack Roosevelt Robinson of the Negro League's Kansas City Monarchs to the Montreal Royals, the Brooklyn Dodgers' farm team. Robinson, then 26, was a graduate of the University of California at Los Angeles. During the war he rose from the rank of private to lieutenant. In April 1947 Jackie Robinson was called up to the Brooklyn Dodgers and, as a subdued *Eagle* reporter insultingly stated, became "the first Negro boy ever to reach the big leagues."[55] Yet, the integration of its famous baseball team was a mild accomplishment when measured against Brooklyn's extraordinary social divisions.

In Brooklyn and across the nation a dramatic restructuring of residential patterns had occurred. In 1955 the Federal Commission on Race and Housing began tracing public money in the housing industry. Three years later it reported that local, state, and national action was necessary to correct the patterns of segregation and ghettoization in the United States. Listing recommendations for every level of government, the Commission challenged builders, realtors, and mortgage lenders to take oaths to build and sell without regard to race, extend mortgages without racial or religious restrictions, and allow nonwhite business people into their professional associations. The Commission also called on the National Association of Real Estate Boards to make integration a goal rather than a possibility.[56]

The borough of Queens, reported the Mayor's Committee for Better Housing, was the central location for recent housing construction in the city, and it competed with Staten Island for the smallest growth in nonwhite population. Because black residency was already low, Queens and Richmond Counties were favored sites for real estate developers. Similarly, from 1946 to

1955 Brooklyn received 200,000 units of new private housing, only 900 of which (less than half a percent) were sold to nonwhite people. Public housing was the only new construction available for black and Puerto Rican people, the report continued, but even that was normally constructed in segregated areas and therefore only served to reinforce ghettoization. The Committee demanded that the city face discrimination in housing "squarely" and take "positive steps" to open the housing market, that public housing be placed in open areas or slum areas that were not overwhelmingly nonwhite, that public housing officials make integration a goal, that the city begin to educate and regulate realtors, builders, and lenders on these aims, that statutes prohibiting such discrimination actually be enforced, and that mortgage lenders be asked to review their routines to remove discriminatory practices.[57] None of those recommendations were acted upon.

By 1950 it made sense to speak of "Negro neighborhoods" and "Negro housing," for both had been created in the Roosevelt years. In the following decades African Americans and Puerto Ricans pushed northward from Central Brooklyn toward Williamsburg and Bushwick and southward into Crown Heights while a growing population of black Caribbeans marched southward from Bedford-Stuyvesant through Crown Heights and into Flatbush. The northward pull was in part a result of concentrations of public housing, tenements, and houses divided for rental, while the southward draw was single-family homes (see table 9.8). As late as 1990 black Caribbeans' homeownership rates remained high, especially among Anglophone West Indians. For instance, people of Barbadian and Jamaican ancestry owned homes at about the rate for New York State (44%) and all black Caribbean communities owned homes at higher proportions than the state's total black population (24%). Moreover, West Indian homeownership in New York State, concentrated largely in the New York Metropolitan area, was far higher than that of Brooklyn's black (18%) and Latino (13%) communities, and competitive with white Brooklynites' rate (36%).[58]

Bank and government policies ensured that the old, glamorous sections of the borough struggled and that segregation continued. As late as 1980 South Brooklyn neighborhoods like Bay Ridge, Bensonhurst, and Sheepshead Bay were more than 90 percent white while black and Latino families concentrated in North Brooklyn's Bedford-Stuyvesant, Brownsville, and Bushwick. A decade later Bensonhurst's black population had grown to half a percent and Bedford-Stuyvesant's white population had fallen to less than a percent.[59]

TABLE 9.8

Black West Indian Population and Homeownership Rates, 1990

Nationality	Brooklyn Population	Homeownership Rate*
Barbadian	13,651	40%
Belizean	2,543	29
British West Indian	13,040	27
Dutch West Indian	452	31
Guyanese	27,220	36
Haitian	53,448	33
Jamaican	61,214	38
Trinidadian/Tobagonian	25,883	32

*Owner-occupied units as a percentage of all units in the state per group.

Source: Bureau of the *Census, Census of Population,* 1990, CP-2–34, 335; Caribbean Research Center, *Statistical Analysis of Persons of Caribbean Ancestry: Basic Demographic, Social and Economic Profile Based on 1990 Census Data,* Part 1 (Brooklyn: CRC, Medgar Evers College, 1993), 81–99.

"Brooklyn cannot well compete with the suburbs for capturing big and well-established manufacturers seeking a location," wrote the distinguished urban observer Jane Jacobs in 1961. Each year, because of its infrastructure and the lure of outlying areas, the borough lost factories and was relegated to being an "incubator" of new industries which in their early life needed inexpensive old buildings and the other assets of the city to establish themselves, but would as they expanded then relocate to perimeter areas. Brooklyn, Jacobs concluded, for too long had failed to construct new buildings, creating a visible and inefficient disparity between old and new structures and leaving it to function as an industrial halfway house for the suburbs.[60]

Brooklyn was in its adolescence when compared to the world's great metropolises. The decline of its industrial base and the illogic of its building stock were results of the manipulation of construction in the city. In 1962 President Kennedy ended the use of racial segregation as a criterion for federal housing authorities but nothing was done to reverse the effects of decades of discriminatory public building and spending.[61] Businesses—frightened by the radical shifts in population, harmed by the loss of middle-class residents, disturbed by escalating crime and decreasing public services, reacting to the problems of protecting workers and insuring property in red-lined areas, and seduced by the thriving government-subsidized suburbs—abandoned North and Central Brooklyn and finished the task of creating blight.

Segregated suburbs encircling isolated cities were not normal patterns of urban development. Across the nation, argued Harry P. Sharp of the University of Michigan, the division between white suburbs and nonwhite inner cities was growing. By 1960 twelve metropolitan areas had suburbs that were 93% white, Sharp continued. Prejudice, wrote the *Times* in agreement, was the catalyst beneath "the whole design of white residential suburbs around urban Negro slums [that] has been shaping up with unmistakable clarity in the North in recent years." The borders of cities were the fastest growing urban spaces in the nation. Between 1950 and 1966 the suburban United States absorbed more than 27 million white residents, and the percentage of nonwhite people outside cities dramatically declined. In the New York Metropolitan area the rate of suburban growth far outpaced that of the city core.[62]

From 1950 to 1970 more than a half million white residents left Brooklyn while the borough gained about 20,000 nonwhite people every twelve months. The influx of African Americans and Puerto Ricans reached 1,000 newcomers each week in the late 1950s.[63] Between 1940 and 1990 Kings County had a net loss of 1.5 million white people and a net gain of 1.3 million people of color. The movement came to be labeled "white flight," which captured the visible flow of white people out of the city and the simultaneous entrance of people of color into it, but included the mistaken suggestion that dark-skinned people were driving white people from urban neighborhoods. In fact, white Brooklynites were not running from people of color as much as they were chasing down government subsidies in outlying communities. Moreover, the in-migration of nonwhite people was the only stabilizing force in Brooklyn and prevented the collapse of the housing market and the disappearance of the tax base.

Brooklyn could already predict its fate by the things lost and the number of "lasts" it experienced. On March 6, 1944 the last elevated train crossed the Brooklyn Bridge, packed with memory seekers; exactly six years later, the Bridge had its final trolley crossing. In 1947 one of the borough's two daily newspapers, the *Brooklyn Citizen*, founded in 1886, folded. Only eight more years would pass before the *Brooklyn Daily Eagle* ceased publication. "A great borough lost its voice," Robert Moses sighed. In June of 1955 the bronze eagle from the top of the newspaper's plant was removed to a local community college, and in October the wrecking ball leveled the site. In the years that followed there were at least two unsuccessful attempts to revive the *Eagle*. In 1952 the pioneer Brooklyn Children's Museum, located in Brower Park in Crown Heights, was soliciting funds from the city to relocate to a safer neighborhood to protect its young clientele. While the museum would remain in Crown Heights, the sense of desperation that had led it to seek a new home prevailed. In 1960 W. E. B. Du Bois, now 92, applied for membership in the Communist party from his Brooklyn home and then defected to Ghana, where he died three years later. In 1962 the legendary Brooklyn Paramount Theater was closed and sold to Long Island University. Most disruptive to borough life, was the decommissioning of the Brooklyn Navy Yard, the largest industrial complex in the county, which resulted in the slow but steady transformation of the facility into a vast stretch of rusty buildings and rotting piers. While military spending in the United States continued to climb, the life of the urban yard had ended. At the same time, Brooklyn's sugar and brewing industries were collapsing. By 1960 only four major beer manufacturers—Rheingold, Schaefer, Piels, and Schlitz—remained.[64]

The most painful symbol of the decline of urban life was the apostasy of the Brooklyn Dodgers following the 1957 baseball season. The Dodgers were the borough's greatest promoters. As the masters of a peculiar brand of baseball and the ambassadors of bad English, the Dodgers made Brooklyn internationally famous for its sport, its ethnic mix, and its accent. In January 1960 Ebbets Field, the legendary park in which "the Bums" had played since 1913, was sold to the Kratter realty firm. In February the New York City Planning Commission approved a $22 million low-cost housing project for the site. That same month demolition of the park began for a September groundbreaking ceremony.[65]

Brooklyn fell loudly. Beneath the symbols the real evidence of urban decline was written across the borough. The residential division of people in the county had resulted in the tacit segregation of public schools that served white children in white areas and black children in black areas. Local buses and trains turned either all white or all brown as they passed the various zones of the city; schools, parks, libraries, and recreational facilities lacked diversity because of their circumscribed neighborhoods; and business districts found themselves catering to increasingly monolithic populations. African-American and Puerto Rican Brooklynites fared worse. A 1953 Hospital

Council of Greater New York study of Bedford-Stuyvesant's health needs disclosed that gap:

> Their income is low. Their housing is old and overcrowded. Their infant and neonatal death rates and other vital statistics indicate that health conditions need improvement. The Hospital Council is well aware of the unfavorable conditions under which the residents of Bedford-Stuyvesant live, particularly the Negro half of the population, and views with sympathy all efforts aimed at the mitigation and eventual removal of these conditions.[66]

By 1957 one of ten Brooklyn residents lived in Bedford-Stuyvesant, the heart of the Central Brooklyn ghetto and the borough's largest neighborhood. Almost 86 percent of all black Brooklynites lived in "Bed-Stuy" and its adjacent neighborhoods. At the beginning of the decade, "the lowest median [income in Brooklyn]—$2,338—was found in Health Area 28 . . . where almost 90 percent of the residents were Negro," noted the Community Council of Greater New York. Every Health Area in Bedford-Stuyvesant was beneath the median income for Brooklyn and the neighborhood's highest average incomes were in its predominantly white border areas. Bedford-Stuyvesant accounted for a quarter of the borough's relief cases although it housed only 10 percent of Brooklyn's population. It suffered an infant mortality rate a third higher than the borough-wide rate, four times the venereal disease cases, twice the tuberculosis occurrences, and a juvenile delinquency rate seven times Brooklyn's average.[67]

The year of the Bed-Stuy riots, 1964, Rev. Galamison contributed an essay on Bedford-Stuyvesant to a book on Harlem. The Brooklyn ghetto was, to quote the minister, a "Land of Superlatives." In "The Box," as Bedford-Stuyvesant was called, profiteering and abusive landlords, realtors, and banks were free to violate any and all laws. Men and women were kept from honest employment. Children were persecuted in an inferior, segregated, overcrowded, and "ethnomaniacal" school system. Gerrymandering left the borough's most populous district politically impotent. The government pursued an inhumane and destructive "policy of littering an already deprived community with low-income housing projects." Politicians resigned themselves to the hopelessness of the situation and sought only their own advancement. And flocks of vultures including check cashers and liquor dealers descended to pick the flesh from the corpse.[68]

But it was already axiomatic that black people were destructive. Oliver Pilat and Jo Ranson blamed the extension of the Independent Subway line, connecting Harlem to Brooklyn, for the decline of the Coney Island amusement park and beach. (Several subway lines end their runs at the Coney Island station.) "Coney was continuing to attract the most depressed layers of the urban population, particularly the Negroes, whose proportion on the clean white sand steadily grew," they lamented. Similarly, in his history of Jewish suburbanization, Isaac I. Gordon repeated the argument that African American and Puerto Rican movements into previously white neighborhoods was forcing the white exodus to the perimeter areas. Looking at New York City, Gordon anticipated the popular defense for white flight: "because standards and habits are different and because people like to live among their own kind."[69]

In 1969 African Americans and Puerto Ricans attempted to force Mayor John Lindsay to exercise his authority over the NYC Planning Commission to ensure equal housing opportunities. The Committee for Minority Representation on the City Planning Commission was incensed that the policymaking board had never had a nonwhite member and insisted that "the Mayor can no longer appoint outsiders to positions from which they can determine how black and Puerto Rican people are going to live." The Committee included scholars Kenneth Clarke, John Henrik Clarke, and Herbert Gans; Eric Arroyo and Roberto Cassablanca of the Puerto Rican Citizens Committee on Housing; Robert Bodrick of the Brownsville Community Council; J. Max Bond, Jr. of Bond, Johnson, Ryder Architects; Amalia Betanzos, executive director of the Puerto Rican Community Development Project; and Telesforo Del Valle, chair of the Harlem-East Harlem Model Cities Policy Committee. But Lindsay was unwilling to confront the powerful interests that operated through the Planning Commission.[70]

White residents began a decade-long, violent campaign throughout the five boroughs to control nonwhite homebuyers with fear and force. Every borough saw firebombings, cross burnings, and other terrorist acts. Canarsie, Brooklyn, became infamous because of its white residents' willingness to attack black homeowners and any real estate agents who sold to black people. Jonathan Rieder found that they also fled from New Deal liberalism and the Democratic party. Canarsie residents first looked to Southern Democrat, fringe presidential candidate, and rabid segregationist, George Wallace of Alabama for leadership, and, later, to the Republican party for a political message that kept people of color in their appropriate place. They described the presence of black and Latino people as a physical and biological threat, a danger displayed in their alleged preference for ghetto life, their refusal to "get ahead," and their role as spoilers in white people's struggle for mobility.[71] One need only look at their history to understand why white Brooklynites expected and demanded a right to social dominance.

In his sardonic novel, *The Brooklyn Book of the Dead*, Michael Stephens traced the journey of an Irish family reintroduced to Brooklyn during the father's funeral, and, in doing so, he captured the transfer of social inequality from white to black people in the borough. The matriarch was born in Bedford-Stuyvesant, the patriarch had immigrated to Manhattan's Hell's Kitchen and Irishtown, but lived most of his life among the thugs of Brooklyn's East New York. The parents eventually retired to Florida, the children to South Brooklyn and to the suburbs. Decades later the family returned to Brooklyn to bury their father in his former haunt, only to find:

> The old ghetto in Brooklyn. East New York. That mythical land between Bushwick and Bed-Stuy, between hell and Brownsville. High crime, low rent, none of the buildings more than a few stories except the projects—and not a familiar face on the street. This neighborhood hadn't seen their kind since Kennedy became president, two or three junkyard dogs' lifetimes ago.[72]

The formation of the Central Brooklyn ghetto ensured that race would be propelled into the future; for, the ghetto gave color an unmistakable, undeniable, and unavoidable daily reality, a reality that black people were accused of creating.

Segregation was the initial stride of domination. The Central Brooklyn ghetto allowed white people to hoard social benefits while people of color became the primary consumers of social ills. Its residents underwrote the life chances of those outside its borders. The ghetto guaranteed white Brooklynites a monopoly in public services and perpetual control of the local government, quality schools, cleaner and safer streets, more efficient transportation, a greater share of government subsidies, superior medical and health facilities, and greater access to parks, pools, and playgrounds. Those conditions, when coupled with white Brooklynites' power to limit the pool of nonwhite labor competitors, forcibly volunteered black Brooklynites for unemployment, crime, disease, and mortality. So people at the borough's periphery and in the suburbs quickly defended the ghetto as a product of black people's nature and culture and, therefore, fixed, and as quickly denied that it was socially established and, therefore, changeable. White Brooklynites embraced these racial beliefs as they fought to preserve a milieu of discrimination in politics, housing, and employment against the more potent assaults of the borough's escalating nonwhite populations.

The treacherous nature of human affairs manifests most often in the habit of dishonoring the victims of injustice rather than its agents; for, as Clyde Atwell of the PPCA wrote, "the system under which we live reserves little dignity for the poor."[73]

CHAPTER TEN

"A Society Such as Our Own"

▬

Education and
Labor in the
Brooklyn Ghetto,
1950—1990

▬

There are many ways of destroying children, ways of interfering with their growing up. There are barbaric methods like warfare and human sacrifice. But there are also subtle, more refined ways like discrimination, segregation, depriving their parents and, of course, through educational preparation, so essential in a society such as our own. . . .

There are those in our society who are coming more and more to understand that not only are our children being destroyed, but that the destruction is connived and deliberate and inevitable unless Negroes call a halt to this inhuman process. . . .

—Rev. Dr. M. A. Galamison

The dying groan in the city, and the souls of the wounded cry out; yet God does not punish them with wrong.

—Job 24:12

In a 1967 poll of Bedford-Stuyvesant residents the top civil rights priorities were housing, jobs, and education. These were interesting choices because many of the respondents were not parents. Education proved to be the most combustible issue in ghetto politics. Of the nearly 3,000 black, white, and Latino people surveyed, African Americans were far more likely to give poor ratings to the local schools and teachers and were particularly dissatisfied with the treatment that their children received. They sought greater community control, not absolute authority. Only a minority of black interviewees looked to hire and fire teachers but half demanded the power to transfer teachers and to replace principals.[1] On the eve of a wrenching battle over community control, black Brooklynites' preferences were clearly more contentious than their neighbors because, education was the cornerstone of black people's strategy for advancement. The lack of progress on school equality had shaken a long pattern of black people crossing ethnic, class, religious, and social barriers to unify under a local leadership dedicated to securing quality schooling. Brooklyn's black community was reacting to education's place in their historical and immediate struggle for advancement. The problem of segregated and inferior schools caused a crisis in black Brooklyn, a crisis that could only be answered with greater militancy.

"Negroes don't need segregated or integrated schools in themselves. What Negroes do need is an equal education and it happens that this is impossible in a segregated school," declared the Reverend Milton A. Galamison in a sermon at Siloam Presbyterian Church. In a few words, the minister captured the growing concerns of black parents as the physical and political isolation of their neighborhoods allowed for a hemorrhage of public resources. In 1943 PTAs from across North and Central Brooklyn formed the Bedford-Stuyvesant-Williamsburg Schools Council. Five years later, at the age of 25, Rev. Galamison came to Siloam. Charismatic and adventurous, the young minister quickly became a media favorite. By the 1950s he was featured on Christian television broadcasts. In 1956 he was appointed to the Education Committee of the Brooklyn branch of the National Association for the Advancement of Colored People (NAACP). Over the next three years he served as its president. "Under the leadership of Galamison," writes Clarence Taylor in his recent study of the school integration struggle, "the Brooklyn branch of the NAACP emerged, between the years 1956 and 1959, as a militant civil rights association organizing working-class parents who grappled with school officials to provide decent education for black and Puerto Rican children."[2] In just a few years after his arrival, Galamison achieved both celebrity and leadership of Brooklyn's most explosive civil right-era campaign.

Galamison, Annie Stein, Winston Craig, and Clair Cumberbatch established the grassroots NAACP Schools Workshop and moved the association to the foreground of the movement for equal education. The Education Committee alone had fifty-five members and the workshops, conducted every six weeks, drew 400 parents and the PTA presidents of more than sixty Bedford-Stuyvesant area schools. By the end of 1956 Galamison and Craig, writing for the Committee, declared that they had "in this one year made the issue of desegregation of the schools in N.Y. the # 1 civil rights issue of the day." Their early victories included the establishment of advanced classes, parent consultations, mandatory homework, remedial courses, and school libraries; physical repairs to some local schools; the acquisition of new text books that children could take home; and investigations into acts of discrimination against black students. More broadly, the Workshop moved to make maximum integration a variable in site selection for new schools and to force the Board of Education to take advantage of imbalanced enrollments to achieve desegregation. By 1958 they were demanding a halt to construction in segregated areas and publicly criticizing the Board for ghettoizing public schools and guaranteeing unequal education. That year Galamison appeared before the City Planning Commission and charged that Jim Crow schools had multiplied in the four years since the Brown v. Topeka Board of Education decision and the New York City Board of Education's resolution to end segregation.

> It is alarming to observe that, over so long a period of time, and in the face of so many resolutions, not a single Negro school in Brooklyn has been desegregated; that the number of segregated junior high schools has increased from 17 to 25; and that the pattern of segregation is rising rather than diminishing. It is equally disturbing to observe that of the 8 schools proposed in the new Capital Budget for construction or site selection to serve the Negro and Puerto Rican population, five are inevitably doomed to segregation by the proposed site selection; one may possibly enjoy integration and only two show evidence of avoiding the segregated pattern.[3]

As Galamison led the school struggle his Siloam Church became one of the largest black Presbyterian churches in the nation.

"The Presbyterian pastor criticized a school system designed to protect the privileges of teachers while neglecting the needs of children," writes Taylor. Blasting City Hall and the Board of Education for perpetuating school segregation, Galamison and the grassroots parents organizations sustained the broad appeal of equal-education initiatives in Central Brooklyn. Taylor asserts that much of their success came from the decision to remain grassroots, continually involve parents, and do public information campaigns, which meant that, while Galamison attracted much of the attention, black women were doing the day-to-day community organizing. In 1960, Galamison wrote an open letter to Mayor Robert Wagner and chided the decision to build yet another school in a segregated area as "reprehensible and a manifestation of absolute disregard for the welfare of all the children of New York City." The city-wide Parents Workshop for Equality followed with a public call to attend to the needs of the "more than 125,000 families of the ghetto schools."[4]

Frustration with increasing school segregation in the face of protests and in spite of official promises to integrate shoved the activists toward more militant demonstrations. Galamison gained the full support of Brooklyn CORE, the local branch of the NAACP, the Parents Workshop for Equality, the Harlem Parents Committee, the National Association for Puerto Rican Civil Rights, and the Urban League of Greater New York for a fantastic scheme to resist the de facto segregation of city schools. Galamison courted Bayard Rustin, the mastermind of the 1963 March on Washington, to coordinate the school boycott because he considered Rustin, "without exception, the best civil rights organizer in the country." Comedian and social activist Dick Gregory was a prominent supporter. On Monday, February 3, 1964, a boycott crippled the New York City school system (see table 10.1). More than 44 percent of the entire student body was absent, which was four percentage points higher than the combined population of nonwhite students. Organizers bragged that more people participated in their boycott than the March on Washington. "We feel that the boycott was the greatest civil rights demonstration on record," boasted Galamison. Thousands of protesters surrounded the headquarters of the Board of Education at 110 Livingston Street in Brooklyn, encircled 300 city schools, and established "Freedom Schools" in several neighborhood churches to give children and parents an education in nonviolent direct action.[5]

A second boycott, six weeks after the first, would again flex the muscles of African-American and Caribbean people in the city. Confident from the success of his first major action, Galamison predicted that the March boycott would spark a wave of nonviolent direct action campaigns in the city, bring tangible gains to his constituents, and remove the last of the "Negro Uncle Tom[s]" from office. (The minister also struck back at Congressman Emanuel Celler of Brooklyn, who accused Galamison of being a self-centered militant, and labeled him and Malcolm X obnoxious.) Taylor convincingly asserts that Galamison's unilateral decision to declare a second mass action and his need to be the central figure in the movement destroyed the coalition. The second boycott was a comparative failure. A hundred thousand fewer students participated. Two years later Galamison and his followers continued the fight alone; carrying signs that read "Happiness Is This Thing Called Equal Education" outside the homes of Board of Education members.[6]

TABLE 10.1

Absenteeism During the First Brooklyn School Boycott

School District	Students	Absent	% Absent
Bed-Stuy, Crown Hts., Park Slope (25, 27)	36,722	27,269	74.0
Red Hook (26, 28)	23,785	12,275	51.5
Greenpoint and Williamsburg (29–31)	24,530	16,627	67.7
Bedford-Stuyvesant and Bushwick (32–4)	44,703	34,559	77.0
Flatbush (35, 40)	49,861	8,099	16.2
Bath Beach and Bensonhurst (36, 37)	21,596	4,055	18.8
Coney Island (38, 39)	28,419	6,784	23.8
East Flatbush and East New York (41–42)	42,818	16,972	39.0
East Flatbush and East New York (43–44)	26,376	16,472	62.0

Source: *The New York Times*, 4 February 1964.

In 1968 the Ocean Hill-Brownsville section of Brooklyn experienced a series of teachers' strikes and the rise of local governance over schools. The People's Board of Education was the creation of politically active ministers, parents, and teachers in the Ocean Hill-Brownsville district. They hoped to make fundamental improvements in the quality of education. The collapse of the experiment in decentralization came on August 31 with the New York City teachers' decision to strike. Brownsville parents and local leaders turned against the teachers as they remained out of the classrooms and administrators transferred out of the district. In the months that followed the local Board took control of hiring and firing the professional staff. The struggle to control Ocean Hill schools pitted the parents and local Board against the United Federation of Teachers (UFT) with its heavily Jewish membership. Some black leaders were willing to exploit anti-white and anti-Semitic sentiments to dramatize the need for community control and there were UFT members and officials who were comfortable invoking racist stereotypes to attract and keep the support of New York's white majority. The result was a painful and prolonged conflict in the city and a deep rift in African American-Jewish relations.[7]

The furor of the 1960s school campaign can obscure its primary cause. Black and Latino residents were not just fighting about the quality of education and the condition of the schools at that moment, rather they were engaged in a broader conflict over the inability of communities of color to secure their children's future given ghettoization. Just as the labor subjugation of black people made them a target of neglect in New Deal housing policy, ghettoization made black people more vulnerable to white Brooklynites' control of educational resources. In Savage Inequalities, Jonathan Kozol documented the New York City public school system's failure to serve children of color. Alarmed at the absence of public outrage over the cyclical discoveries of manipulations calculated to generate these disparities, Kozol questioned why white parents so feared having their children placed in a fair educational competition. But the perversions of the school system, like the perversions of the housing market, are means to achieving a greater end: social domination. Ghettoization was not a simple issue of black people's access to housing, argues Joe William Trotter Jr. Physical isolation and the political issues specific to that segregation emanated from deeply rooted patterns of economic discrimination. Clarence Taylor found that the integration movement reacted in part to hiring discrimination against black teachers and the fact that many Bedford-Stuyvesant schools limited class time because of overcrowding. The question in Central Brooklyn was whether black parents were willing to allow their children's fate to become a function of the political power and whim of the hostile white regions that surrounded the ghetto—a question that already applied to other areas of life. Those political maneuvers meant that nonwhite neighborhoods had older facilities, fewer veteran teachers, poorer administration, greater numbers of provisional instructors, disrepair in the physical plant, program shortages, and the use of their schools as halfway houses for teachers being disciplined, trained, or transferred out of other areas.[8] The rapid decline of inner-city schools in the past three decades justifies the emotion and ferocity of the struggle of the late 1960s.

Ghettoization meant that the school system had to compensate for the economic and political vulnerabilities of the black community; or, as white Brooklynites had long demanded, social equality could only come if African Americans overachieved. The prevalence of discrimination and exclusion in the regular job market forced people of color to outperform white people in order to reach similar levels of well being. Black college graduates found that their material rewards resembled those of white high school graduates rather than their white peers while the artificially restricted job market of black underachievers and those of average accomplishment sentenced them to the dole or the ranks of the unemployed. Black parents reacted to the failure of their public schools with appropriate paranoia.

The segregation of the public and private labor markets worsened the pressure on public education. New York City's politicians aggravated racial segmentation in the municipal labor force and reinforced racial divisions in the private sector. City officials found themselves in the ridiculous position of having to address racial discrimination in hiring without tampering with white dominance in the labor market. Their solution was to incorporate black workers into a separate and unequal tier of clerical and service positions and then explain the resultant gap in wages and benefits as a product of that holy spirit of urban social relations, white racism. However cowardly, the policy was successful. It allowed politicians to increase the number people of color in the municipal force and invent a progressive political tradition, while never confronting white control of the most powerful unions and the pool of better-paying positions.

When Mayor Robert Wagner celebrated the more visible role of Puerto Ricans and African Americans in the municipal service, he conveniently ignored the fact that nonwhite public workers were grouped in the least lucrative and most tenuous jobs and categories. The mayor had not even achieved parity in his own office. In 1963, when the data were collected, most ethnic minorities working for New York City were doing semi-skilled, clerical, service, or labor jobs (see table 10.2). The City had over 25,000 black and Puerto Rican service workers. Clerical work provided about 7,000 minorities with municipal jobs concentrated in public agencies and departments, while the clerical staffs in the more prestigious administrative agencies were, by rule, white. The most striking discrimination was in the skilled ranks of City employees. Black workers did not dominate a single skilled craft in any municipal agency or department. City departments did not come close to hiring nonwhite craftsmen in proportion to their population. A few agencies even broadened the definition of skilled labor rather than hire and promote nonwhite workers.[9]

The bulk of the municipal government's Puerto Rican and African-American professionals were employed in agencies that dealt directly with the public, particularly the nonwhite public (see table 10.3). The departments of Health, Hospitals, and Welfare were the largest single employers of minority professionals. Black and Latino professionals had difficulty finding employment in the City's administrative agencies and departments. The Mayor's Office set the bar with not a single black or Puerto Rican professional on its staff. So while Mayor Wagner pledged that the city would rise to the challenge of equality, his administration was assuring that the quality of life in New York City would remain glaringly different across the color line.[10]

TABLE 10.2

NYC Municipal Craftsmen[a] by Race and Agency, 1963

Agency	White[b]	Black	Puerto Rican	% Nonwhite
Board of Education	1,186	28	5	2.7
Board of Estimate	8	0	0	0.0
Board of Higher Education	99	2	1	2.9
Department of Correction	94	6	2	7.8
Department of Finance	9	0	0	0.0
Department of Health	12	0	0	0.0
Department of Highways	1,082	16	1	1.5
Department of Hospitals[c]	676	74	22	12.4
Department of Marine & Aviation	327	3	5	2.4
Department of Markets	16	0	0	0.0
Department of Parks	598	5	0	0.8
Department of Public Works	729	17	2	2.5
Department of Purchase	19	3	1	17.4
Department of Sanitation	2,143	35	5	1.8
Department of Traffic	251	10	3	4.9
Water Supply, Gas, Electricity	321	6	0	1.8
Department of Welfare	53	2	0	3.6
Fire Department	2,432	38	1	1.6
Housing Authority	1,203	194	27	15.5
Office of Civil Defense	5	0	0	0.0
Real Estate Assessment	5	0	0	0.0
City Register	4	0	0	0.0
Triboro Bridge/Tunnel Authority	35	0	0	0.0

a. Craftsmen, foremen, and kindred workers. Only those municipal agencies that were significant employers of craftsmen are included. The most gross disparities were in this category, but no municipal occupational category had equal employment.
b. Includes all City workers who are not black or Puerto Rican.
c. Includes maintenance personnel.
Source: New York City Commission on Human Rights, *The Ethnic Survey: A Report on the Number and Distribution of Negroes, Puerto Ricans and Others Employed by the City of New York* (New York: 1964), Tables 1.1–1.68.

Wagner's mayoral heirs did little to challenge this peculiar municipal math. A federal study of Latinos in Bedford-Stuyvesant, Central and East Harlem, and the South Bronx found that they "were the most deprived of all workers residing in the city's major poverty neighborhoods. They were far more likely than others to be unemployed or to hold lower paying jobs." The Puerto Rican concentration in low-skill manufacturing was far higher than other groups. In part that was produced by language barriers and education but it was also the result of a closed labor market. A 1974 Equal Employment Opportunity Commission examination disclosed that white men controlled

New York's high-paying municipal jobs while black and Latino workers were crowded into "the two lowest-paying functions." White dominance was greatest in the city's managerial, professional, and skilled craft ranks and white workers were dramatically underrepresented in the low-salaried labor and service jobs. Moreover, white men earned higher salaries than nonwhite and white women workers in virtually every job category. In 1977 black and Puerto Rican workers in the municipal service remained concentrated in clerical positions. Half of the city's 25,000 clerks were black, and such work was the largest single job field for people of color. Latinos were underrepresented in virtually every major municipal employment category. Black Caribbeans and African Americans were added to the city payroll but almost always as clerks. About 70 percent of the new clerks were nonwhite and an even greater percentage were women. Almost a decade later black municipal workers achieved proportional representation only in agencies with a public face and Latinos still had a minimal presence in the pool of municipal employees. The major employers of Puerto Ricans were the Human Resources Administration, Commission of Human Rights, Correction, Juvenile Justice, and Social Services. Most new Latino hires were clerks. In 1987 black people's share of municipal jobs actually surpassed their proportion of New York City's population, but African-American civil servants remained in the most-insecure and least-lucrative titles. In the preceding ten year period the number and proportion of black clerks increased although the number of city clerks actually declined by three thousand. Eight of ten newly hired municipal clerks were women and an even greater proportion were now nonwhite.[11]

In contrast white men monopolized the better municipal jobs; keeping their stronghold on skilled and semi-skilled occupations in spite of their declining population in the city. The Police and Fire Departments were among New York's worst offenders, both were bastions of white male supremacy (see tables 10.4 and 10.5). In 1978 almost 90 percent of all police officers were white, and 98 percent were men. White men exercised even greater domination in the Fire Department, where women and nonwhite men being virtually barred. Over the next decade the Police proved somewhat vulnerable to the changing demographics of New York but still better than three of four officers were white and almost nine of ten were male. That change, significant given the racial history of the NYPD, was in no small way a product of the negative publicity that the department attracted from acts of brutality against the city's minority communities. The Fire Department experienced no such fluctuations in public prestige and continued to operate as a well-paid, white men's fraternity. In 1988 more than ninety percent of New York's firemen were white, the number of black uniformed workers had declined, and women remained grossly underrepresented.[12]

TABLE 10.3

Primary Municipal Employers of Minority Professionalsa,

1963

Agency	Whiteb	Black	Puerto Rican	% Nonwhite
Board of Education	40,468	3,690	239	8.8
Board of Education (non-educ.)	589	47	3	7.8
Commission on Human Rights	14	12	2	50.0
Department of Correction	128	41	4	26.0
Department of Finance	438	28	1	6.2
Department of Health	1,398	566	22	29.6
Department of Hospitals	5,439	2,063	281	30.1
Department of Parks	493	159	1	24.5
Department of Public Works	696	62	12	9.6
Department of Relocation	59	22	5	31.4
Department of Welfare	3,213	2,170	162	42.1
Housing Authority	478	88	18	18.2
Youth Board	93	115	22	59.6

a"Professional, technical and kindred workers."
bIncludes all City workers who are not black or Puerto Rican.
Source: New York City Commission on Human Rights, *The Ethnic Survey: A Report on the Number and Distribution of Negroes, Puerto Ricans and Others Employed by the City of New York* (New York: 1964), Tables 1.1–1.68.

TABLE 10.4

New York Police Department Uniformed Officers by Race, 1978–1988

Year	White	%	Black	%	Latino	%	Other	%
1978	21,847	89	1,914	8	801	3	18	.1
1988	21,229	77	3,014	11	3,003	11	178	.7

Note: The total number of uniformed officers in 1978 was 24,580 and in 1988 it was 27,424.
Source: [New York City Mayor's] Citywide Equal Employment Opportunity Committee, *Equal Employment Opportunity in New York City Government 1977–1987* (October 1988), 37.

TABLE 10.5

New York Fire Department Uniformed Personnel by Race, 1979–1988

Year	White	%	Black	%	Latino	%	Asian	%
1979	10,848	94	537	5	160	1	3	.3
1988	11,273	93	486	4	272	2	10	.8

Note: The total number of uniformed officers in 1979 was 11,548 and in 1988 it was 12,084.
Source: [New York City Mayor's] Citywide *Equal Employment Opportunity Committee, Equal Employment Opportunity in New York City Government 1977–1987* (October 1988), 42.

The racial segmentation of the municipal labor force had real effects on standards of living (see tables 10.6 and 10.7). A 1986 investigation of municipal workers revealed that the overwhelming proportion of black and Latino civil servants were hired in jobs that paid under $20,000 dollars a year while for white men the situation was reversed. Among provisional (temporary, noncompetitive) employees almost half of all white men were in the upper salary echelon while few people of color or women earned that income. White men alone held 4,087 (51%) of the municipality's 8,092 higher-salaried jobs. Women, of every background, were locked in lower-salaried positions. As late as 1997 New York's black women municipal employees were most likely to be in clerical work, white women in administrative positions, and black men in service and maintenance jobs, while white men remained grossly overrepresented in the municipality's high-salaried occupations. White men were most dependent upon the protective service positions, which included the lucrative jobs in the police and fire departments. Latinos and Asians remained underrepresented in the civil service.[13]

New York City's official hiring practices complemented the racial logic of the private market. A 1968 Look magazine exposé on racial discrimination in unions highlighted the plight of Vincent J. Whylie, his wife, and five daughters. In 1966 Whylie was a member of the Wood, Wire, and Metal Lathers' integrated local (AFL-CIO) in Daytona Beach, Florida. That year he moved to Brooklyn where "New York Local 46 (with only a single, inactive Negro among its 6,000 members) refused to accept his transfer card," wrote Jack Star, Look senior editor. The NAACP took Whylie's case; however, Whylie received only one job and was quickly laid off and replaced with a white man. Whylie's experience typified the African-American encounter with trade organizations. "Union control of apprenticeship programs remains a major bar to black progress today, there are fewer union Negro plumbers or electricians than Negro Ph.D.'s," Star decried. They reclassified lower-level job titles to achieve tacit integration and, thereby, skirt federal and state anti-discrimination statutes. That type of recategorization allowed white men to continue dominating the high-salary occupations while black men were either excluded or limited to the lowest-paid, most-demeaning tasks. Unions also forced non-white members into segregated locals in order to achieve statutory integration while limiting black workers' numbers and power. NAACP labor director Herbert Hill summarized the problem, noting that while labor should be fighting for black people's equality, "most unions have become instruments of racial oppression."[14]

TABLE 10.6

Salary Differentials in the New York Civil Service by Race,
1983–1986

Salary	White	%	Black	%	Latino	%	Other	%
Over 20K	1,171	70	287	17	97	6	138	8
Under 20K	1,552	29	3,052	56	625	12	201	4

Note: Data was collected from May 1983 to June 1986. It does not include uniformed personnel. Other is a close approximation of Asian representation.
Source: *Report of the Mayor's Commission on Hispanic Concerns* (December 10, 1986), 95.

TABLE 10.7

Salary Differentials of Provisional Employees by Race, 1983–1986

Salary	White	%	Black	%	Latino	%	Other	%
Over 20K	4,225	66	1,404	22	489	8	281	4
Under 20K	3,629	36	4,561	46	1,526	15	254	3

Note: Data was collected from May 1983 to June 1986. It does not include uniformed personnel. Other is a close approximation of Asian representation.
Source: *Report of the Mayor's Commission on Hispanic Concerns* (December 10, 1986), 95.

Across New York City, union discrimination continued unchecked. "Blacks and Hispanics are virtually excluded from 130 out of 193 industries in the city's private sector," read a 1985 report of the Community Service Society of New York. "The 130 industries in which blacks and Hispanics are minimally represented constitute a large part of the city's financial, manufacturing, communications, and cultural base." For black men this produced a far greater dependence upon clerical work than their white counterparts. They were barred from supervisory and nonsupervisory positions in New York's core industries. African-American and West Indian women suffered the most severely restricted job market. "In 1982, five industries accounted for 53 percent of the employment of black females in New York City, and they had the highest nonsupervisory concentration of any group in the study," CSS uncovered. The economic picture for Latinos, men and women, was as bleak. Their jobs were at the bottom of the occupational ladder in fields that had little opportunity for advancement. "White males retained their dominance in higher-paying jobs although their share of employment declined in the private sector," but that was not a function of education or training. The report noted an increase in white men's control of well-paid construction jobs in spite of their declining proportions, a dominance that worked to exclude men of color from this traditional avenue of mobility. In the high-paying blue-collar construction industries six of seven fields were limited to white men and their strength was increasing in at least half of those categories. In the white-collar finance, insurance, and real estate occupations, white people exercised what CSS labeled "hegemony," adding that the modest gains in nonwhite employment were at the lowest levels. Thus as the city's private and municipal employment rolls expanded to include a growing black and Latino labor force, white men managed to hold on to the best positions at all levels. The Society then noted the crux of the problem:

> Although the inaccessibility of supervisory jobs (i.e., managerial and professional) is a serious deterrent for minorities, their inability to find nonsupervisory employment is perhaps even more crucial. A major problem is their inability to obtain nonsupervisory employment in a wide variety of industries, particularly core industries that offer opportunities for advancement. A key aspect of occupational segmentation is that although whites have retained a strong base in core industries, they also are in increasing competition with blacks and Hispanics for nonsupervisory positions in peripheral industries.

In the 1990s race was still shaping the city's private labor market. Half of all white men were managers or professionals while women were clustered in clerical work and black men in service jobs.[15]

New York City continues to transfer public money to racially restricted industries. Officials have found government contracts useful tools for influencing private employment and voting behavior. Thus, injustice continues to deliver tangible benefits to broad segments of Brooklyn's white population. At the top of this racial hierarchy white men enjoy greater rewards for their individual accomplishments while people of color have such returns retarded. But the effects are far more damaging at the bottom of the social structure. Racial discrimination in employment, apprenticing, training, recruitment, and promotion works to shield white men from competition in the high-paying occupations at all skill and education levels, but no equivalent barriers protect women and nonwhite men in fields into which they have been forced. Tens of thousands of jobs in the municipal service and the private sector—offering high salaries, attractive benefits, and security—are reserved for white men of minimal educational achievement. The effect of limiting access to these occupations to a racially defined segment of the population should not be underestimated. The social effects of white male underachievers are muted in Brooklyn's white communities just as the negative impact of black people of marginal accomplishment are exaggerated in black communities (see table 10.8).

TABLE 10.8

Poverty and Unemployment by Race in Brooklyn, 1990

Race	Families Below Poverty Level	Unemployment Rate
White	11.1%	6.6%
Asian	17.7	7.1
Black	23.0	13.2
Latino	35.3	14.1

Source: Bureau of the Census, *Census of Population: 1990: Social and Economic Characteristics, New York,* Section 2, 1343,1571.

In a 1989 study of teenagers in three Brooklyn neighborhoods—one black, one Latino, and one white—Mercer Sullivan argued that the different results of their residents' lives did not correlate well with ambition or education. The white youths, and their parents, viewed completing vocational high school as an avenue to well-paid, blue-collar jobs; black teens and adults had a greater commitment to education because of the types of "good jobs" available to them and the political culture of their community. Not a single black youth in the sample enrolled in a vocational or technical high school; their ambitions were channeled toward the regular academic course and the clerical and service occupations open to black adults. Poorly paid factory jobs awaited Latino youths who often opted for this work because of the hostility of the public school system. Even with the minimum educational achievement Latino teens were unlikely to get manual or clerical work. They dropped out of school earliest. White teenagers were regularly introduced to blue-collar employment, enjoying opportunities to work on loading docks, handle machinery, and supervise in local factories. They had flexible hours and were often paid off the books; still, half of the white teens dropped out of high school and relied on the "connections" of family, friends, and local institutions to help them find work.[16]

With ample sarcasm, Jerry Della Femina described the importance of trades in Gravesend: "Getting a trade meant that the neighborhood sent its youth to either the New York School of Printing, the New York School of Textiles, or the school that attracted most of us, Grady High School, where we were taught how to become an airplane mechanic." Sullivan asserts that these networks have tremendous impact. For instance, the intellectual ambitions and achievements of black and white teens were similar, but young white underachievers suffered less for leaving school and they had a greater chance for redemption. "Teddy Haskell," who left school at sixteen, decided to get a GED two years later so that he could join his father's construction union. Conversely, black teenagers depended upon odd jobs and low-paying youth employment programs to make money. "The single most striking contrast" between the three communities is that the white "group did not report a single government-subsidized summer youth job," writes Sullivan. Race even determined criminal records. The neighborhoods had similar rates of noneconomic violence; however, the types of jobs that white teens did gave them "much greater opportunity for theft from the workplace." It was unlikely that white youth criminality would be expressed in street crimes, so they avoided "protracted involvement with the criminal justice system." Unemployment in minority neighborhoods pointed black and Latino youths toward "predatory crimes" which evolved into crime as a short-term career. Thus, the white district had a median income twice that of the black and Latino areas and higher than Brooklyn's average, it suffered far lower crime rates, had greater family stability, and generally maintained better schools.[17]

The personal, community, and institutional networks, or "connections," that white Brooklynites use exist because people of color—the majority of the borough's population—are excluded from whole categories of employment. As white workers in Brooklyn and its surrounds pass jobs in the skilled trades and better municipal unions along hereditarily, people of color are locked out of these occupations, kept from employment opportunities that are intergenerational, and left to fill lower-paying jobs as menials, in factory and service work, and in clerical positions as the municipal bureaucracy increases.

After all, the ghetto is not so much a place as it is a relationship—the physical manifestation of a perverse imbalance in social power. The ghetto is not the cause of social pathology, it is its destination. It is not the set of ever-changing, ever-negotiated disparities that dominate it but the financial, physical, and legal coercion that give rise to them. It cannot be defined by the people who occupy it but by the struggles that place them there. It is not social inequality but the attempt to predetermine the burden of social inequality. Thus, ghettos are different sizes, have different demographics, and suffer different conditions. They have in common only the lack of power that allows their residents to be physically concentrated and socially targeted. In the absence of the black ghetto, white ghettos would not necessarily appear; but there would be a more random distribution of social disparities which would fall in any number of ways depending upon the resistance of individuals and groups. That is what shapes white New Yorkers' moral choices and political behavior when confronted with the realities of a Harlem or a Bedford-Stuyvesant.

Ghettos do not lend themselves to reform.

Epilogue:

―――

A Fair
Interpretation

―――

An invented past can never be used; it cracks and crumbles under the pressures of life like clay in a season of drought.

—James Baldwin, *The Fire Next Time*

Several weeks ago when President Johnson spoke at the opening of the World's Fair, he compared the present fair to the fair of a few decades ago. He contended in his speech that the current fair is an example of progress. The fair was poorly attended because of a threatened stall-in. Jesse Gray had proposed to conduct bus trips from the fair to Harlem and sight-seeing tours through the roach and rat-infested tenements. There stood the president making speeches about progress. Several hundred young people from across the country were arrested for demonstrating inside the fair. Several youngsters were arrested and brutalized by the police for sitting on subway track. But there stood the President talking about progress.
. . . Whatever he was talking about he was not speaking the same language as the hundreds of people who gathered at the fair to protest and to go to jail. Obviously, in alluding to the scientific wonders of the fair the president was talking about what we have. The demonstrators were trying to call attention to what we are.

—Rev. Dr. M. A. Galamison

In the spring of 1964 the Brooklyn Congress on Racial Equality (CORE) publicized a plan to protest violations of civil rights at the grand opening of the World's Fair that threw the city into a fury. New York City's excitement about hosting the World's Fair was evident as early as 1960. In March of that year city officials selected Robert Moses as president of the 1964 Fair because Moses had an enviable reputation for getting things done and his prestige as master city builder was at its peak. His projects crushed objectors and were almost always completed before organized resistance could be mounted. The Fair was also the type of event to which a man with Moses' ego was drawn. He juggled his many titles and freed himself up to take charge of the planning. The city's chief builder did not disappoint. The organization of the Fair was meticulous and New York was bathing in the expectations of praise long before opening day. In February 1962 former president Harry S. Truman visited the site at Flushing Meadows Park, Queens. Moses handed the president a gold pass and then escorted the entourage down "Truman Walk," a path under construction that cut through the grounds.[1]

When the Brooklyn branch of CORE announced its intent to intrude upon the opening day celebrations to publicize the nation's injustices, most white New Yorkers felt that disruptive Negroes were holding them hostage. On April 9, 1964 CORE released its plan to tie up traffic on the five major arteries—the Grand Central Parkway, the Brooklyn-Queens Expressway, the Interborough Parkway, the Belt Parkway, and the Van Wyck Expressway— leading to the Fair grounds. CORE members and sympathizers were to fill cars with enough gas to reach the main roads and then allow them to stall. White New Yorkers found it difficult to accept that the display of their city and its gilding before President Johnson and 16,000 diplomats, politicians, business people, and socialites, might be turned into a nightmare of congested highways. Robert Moses insisted that he would protect the Fair from the "irresponsible interference" of civil rights organizations. The World's Fair, he continued, had not discriminated against anyone, and, therefore, the attempt to use it to stage demonstrations was an outrage. Moses assured reporters that hundreds of Pinkerton guards, armed with nightsticks and pistols, had been hired to make protesters submit.[2]

Less than a week before the CORE announcement, the Reverend Milton A. Galamison was arrested with nearly thirty other demonstrators who blocked one of the entrances to the Fair in a protest of segregation. Brooklyn CORE's plan carried the support of the local NAACP and other borough organizations. In the days that followed the announcement, the city was divided over the scheme to target the Fair. "The World's Fair has not been discriminating against anybody," read a *Times* editorial which shared Moses' indignation. "It is not a seat of government. It has no authority to bring about civil rights reforms or correct wrongs in the social order." CORE's national organization was under pressure to check its local chapter. President James

Farmer suspended the Brooklyn arm only two days after their announcement, asserting that the local's protest interfered with a national organizing program that included a more traditional demonstration inside the Fair. Taking the whole affair rather lightly, NAACP executive director Roy Wilkins dismissed the planned "stall-in" as "strictly Brooklynese," one of a long series of odd episodes that the borough had provided. Nonetheless, the press and the city's officials trotted out a number of prominent African Americans to condemn the planned action, or, as Louis Lomax jabbed, they showed their faith in the assumption that "if you can keep one or two big Negroes under control, you can keep all the little Negroes under control."[3]

As the city moved to stop the CORE plot against the Fair, the organization's support among African Americans, Caribbeans, and activists grew. Within days, the Harlem, Bronx, Yonkers, Columbia University, and Long Island (Mineola) chapters of CORE joined in support of the stall-in and declared the Brooklyn unit's suspension illegal. Queens CORE had not yet met to discuss the situation, but a chapter official gave his personal support for the Brooklyn group. Galamison publicly praised the protest and opened his church so that CORE could map out its final plans. The Brooklyn chapter of the NAACP was also in league with CORE, and nationally the NAACP was sympathetically silent. The Sanitation Workers' Union announced that its 10,000 employees would remain home on opening day if they were asked to tow cars from the highways. A week before the planned celebration, Brooklyn CORE angered its detractors further by announcing a plan to waste water and create a drought if the stall-in did not result in integration.[4]

City officials simply walked away from negotiations when CORE made demands that struck at the very heart of inequality in the borough. The city's human rights commissioner met with CORE representatives to try to avert the stall-in, and he was told that all city construction sites were to be closed and that a grand jury investigate discriminatory unions, that the city authorize rent strikes in slum buildings, that a grand jury investigate slum landlords, that all high schools be immediately desegregated, that the building of schools in ghetto areas be halted, and that a public review board be formed to investigate police brutality. Negotiations ended. The city hired private tow trucks, authorized public trucks to be manned by the police, and local officials entrenched themselves to wait out CORE. Only three days before the opening, Galamison was again arrested when he held a minor protest at the World's Fair site to test security. The following day CORE announced its plans to tie-up subway lines in addition to highways. Mayor Wagner dramatically responded that CORE held "a gun to the heart of the city."[5]

However, on April 22, 1964, opening day, the traffic on the major arteries leading to Flushing, Queens, ran smoothly, and there was little evidence of a massive conspiracy to ruin the Fair. CORE activists did temporarily block subway lines, several were dragged into bloody clashes with the police, and a score were arrested. Fifty CORE demonstrators picketed Gracie Mansion. The furor over the boycott hurt attendance at the Fair. Earlier that morning, a State Supreme Court judge issued an injunction against CORE, but the real cause of the protest's failure was the fact that the organizers were far better at publicizing their actions than coordinating them. Many people were undoubtedly frightened by the court injunction, but CORE never had an accurate estimate of the number of people who were committed to the protest. Isaiah Brunson, leader of Brooklyn CORE, "is no Bayard Rustin," sighed Rev. Galamison. A protest on the grounds during which demonstrators shouted down President Johnson, organized by national CORE for the sole purpose of countering the Brooklyn group, was more successful. Truman, Francis Cardinal Spellman, Governor Nelson A. Rockefeller, Mayor Wagner, and Bob Moses accompanied Johnson.[6]

Although many issues collided in the Fair crisis, it is worth noting that the authority of the state could be marshaled so easily and effectively to stop a protest of racial inequalities but was not available to prevent those injustices. The incident exposed the depth of racial disparity; for, not only did white New Yorkers dominate social resources, they also determined the appropriate moments, venues, and methods for the airing of grievances. They lived under the delusion that their society had reasonable mechanisms for addressing social injustices. Thus, the Fair could be declared a success while there were hundreds of thousands of Brooklynites whose children went to segregated schools, whose families lived in government-established ghettos, whose chances for fair and honest employment were restricted, and who were daily assaulted by the callousness of the society. A Galamison sermon mocked President Johnson for standing in a den of misery and offering a speech on progress. Mayor Wagner insultingly thanked black and Latino citizens for behaving, condemned the protesters who disrupted President Johnson's speech, and, with an air of paternalism, confessed that "there are civil wrongs which need to be righted."[7]

The events around the opening of the Fair created one of those historical moments when New Yorkers were forced to admit the stark injustices of their city and lament its racial divide. To expose the illusion of the latter, W. E. B. Du Bois used the analogy of the plate which, once cracked, seared ever after along the original break.[8] In time it became easy to believe that the old fracture caused the new damage and to forget that the plate had been repeatedly dropped. In fact, the recurrent falls caused the harm while the first schism only distributed the effects. Similarly, the longevity of racism has led some to suspect that color drives history and to ignore the events and conditions that give it meaning. They examine the past and regret the presence of racial division. Ultimately they make history the outcome of racism by forgetting the moments in which social power has determined the pattern of social injustice. Or, to continue Du Bois' metaphor, they look at the shattered plate and curse the crack while neglecting the forces of destruction.

At the nexus of race and labor, at the nexus of race and housing, and at the nexus of race and education is power. Having demanded that African Americans be ghettoized in housing, subordinated in employment, gerrymandered in politics, and isolated in social space, white residents necessarily knew that their life chances were antagonistic to those of black people. They could even create themselves as the victims of racial inequality by rhetorically inverting the power relations of their city. They determined that all social inequalities were legacies of a bygone era and, thus, made themselves innocent of wrongdoing. In order to deny benefiting from any systematic discrimination, they resorted to cyclical and often contradictory claims that inequality resulted from nature, history, or irrational forces. And all attempts to assist black Brooklynites became infringements upon white rights and white privileges or *unfair advantages* for people of color.

The assumption that United States history is progressive—evolving more just political and economic institutions, and, therefore, more humane social relations—clouds our understanding of race by obscuring the harshest realities of the past and present. Unarguably the nation has seen economic and political advances in the transformation from colony to sovereign state, from enslaved to free labor, from caste to democratic pluralism; however, what has remained strikingly consistent through those evolutionary processes is white people's ability (and expectation) to define the social place of black people, a capacity expressed in political discourse and action. Although American political economy has progressed, it has not delivered African Americans from the power of the white majority. The substance of "whiteness" is volatile, but the category has consistently and accurately described the exploitative capacity of the majority.

Race is the reflection of that power in ideology. Social power determines the varied characteristics and conditions of "racial groups" in our society. National and cultural communities get racialized because they enter into the society at similar moments and under similar conditions. They come to see themselves and are seen as a mass because the context of their incorporation is similar. Cultural or physiological similarities then reinforce the logic of their group status. When the historical situations change, race concepts change. That race is not neatly tied to geographic origins or culture is seen in the contrasting situations of the Protestant and Catholic Irish, German and Russian Jews, and native-born black people and black West Indians. Although in each comparison a group characteristic was shared, it still produced different and contradictory racial and ethnic imagery. Moreover, these conceptualizations can be imposed on groups without a common cultural or biological characteristic because of their comparable social circumstances, for instance the application of the word "nigger" to both antebellum African Americans and Irish Catholics. A social group can even simultaneously exist in different racial categories; for, contemporary racialism captures the power relations of disparate groups through biological and cultural metaphors. Not all white people benefit from racial exploitation to the same degree, while "minorities" are neither oppressed in the same way nor are they prevented from participating in each other's persecution.

Arguments for bipolar "racial progress" depend upon meaningless comparisons: the contemporary condition of black workers juxtaposed with that of enslaved Africans, levels of prejudice measured across historical periods, and overt acts and mechanisms of dominance compared through time. Here, progress is measured by white people's treatment of (or behavior toward) black people to the exclusion of the more important issue of black people's emancipation from white authority. Social relations can undergo revolutionary change without impacting the power dynamics of the society. Absent from formulations of racial progress is the variable of social power, which allows for different levels of persecution and methods of oppression limited only by the needs of the moment.

In *Hierarchical Structures and Social Value*, Richard Williams argues that African Americans occupy at every historical moment a "labor category" which determines "their economic and political power in a specific social

structure." Changes in historical periods and social relations produce requi-
site shifts in the labor categories, but do not necessarily disturb relative social
power.[9] For example slavery in Kings County made Africans' skin color a
symbol of oppression in ideology, but that truth should not obscure the more
important fact that Africans and African Americans emerged from slavery
with fewer defenses against further exploitation. The idea of race did not
make people more likely victims but those vulnerabilities did. Color seemed
to be the social determinant of injustice because Africans and African
Americans were least protected. In fact, real power relations shaped their fate
while color helped only to tie successive persecutions through time and vest
them with an air of inevitability. As African Americans disproportionately
bore these new inequities, white Brooklynites came to depend more heavily
upon color as a rationale for injustice and history as proof of its validity. In
fact, only two things have remained constant in the history of race in
Brooklyn: the social symbolism of color and the extraordinary maldistribution of power. The former has faithfully followed the career of the latter.

Racism continues to reflect a disparity of power and it is as egregious today
as it was in the eighteenth century because the advent of less dramatic forms
of dominance is *not* progress. More insidious in modern social relations is
the fact that white people do not have to expressly target black people in order
to exploit them. They only have to locate their interests in private and public
policies that have disparate impact. Freed from involvement in color-specific
political decisions and specific acts of racial oppression, white Americans can
more easily imagine the injustices of their society to be natural or irrational.

At no point in the history of Brooklyn has the dominant population
suffered full exposure to the actual risks and burdens generated by the social
system. It is that fact that gives race its power; it is that fact that creates the
necessity of race. The social realities described by color have changed dramatically and often, and that can be the basis of celebration. But one need only
travel to the expansive ghettos of Brooklyn, observe its racially-tiered labor
force, or mark the results of its separate and unequal educational system to
comprehend the inappropriateness of the term "progress."

Two centuries after the Whistelo trial, we still cannot explain race without
invoking social evidence. The notion is social and it reflects the relative well-
being of groups. There lay the roots of the "white backlash," a term that
describes the trepidation that many white voters have with politicians who
seem too greatly concerned with the plight of minorities, a term that,

according to the *Times*, came into general use as a warning to black people during Brooklyn CORE's protests of the 1964 World's Fair. On April 26, 1965 CORE demonstrators returned to Flushing Meadows Park, the site of the Fair, and were met by a collection of angry white young adults and teens calling themselves SPONGE: the Society for the Prevention of Negroes' Getting Everything.[10]

Inequality has its malcontents, so too it breeds its defenders.

Notes

PROLOGUE

1. General Sessions—New York, August Term, 1808, *The Commissioners of the Almshouse v. Alexander Whistelo (a black man)*, Schomburg Collection, NYPL.

2. Ibid., 1–5.

3. Ibid., 9–23.

4. General Sessions—New York, August Term, 1808, *The Commissioners of the Almshouse v. Alexander Whistelo (a black man)*, Schomburg Collection, NYPL.

Ibid., 1–5.

Ibid., 9–23.

Ibid., 24–42.

CHAPTER 1

1. Oscar and Mary F. Handlin, "Origins of the Southern Labor System," *William and Mary Quarterly*, 7, No. 2 (April 1950), 199.

2. The encounter was in Gravesend Bay. Henry Reed Stiles, ed., *The Civil, Political, Professional and Ecclesiastical History and Commercial and Industrial Record of the County of Kings and the City of Brooklyn, N. Y., From 1683 to 1884* (hereafter Stiles, *History of Kings County*), 2 Vols. (New York: W. W. Munsell, 1884), 1:22; Mrs. [Mariana Griswold] Schuyler Van Rensselaer, *History of the City of New York in the Seventeenth Century*, 2 Vols. (New York: Macmillan, 1909), 1: 4. On the origins and culture of the Canarsee, see Clark Wissler, ed., *The Indians of Greater New York and the Lower Hudson* (1909; New York: AMS Press, 1975), 47–48. A slightly different and more detailed version of these origins is given in Robert Steven Grumet, *Native American Place Names in New York City* (New York: Museum of the City of New York, 1981), 5–7; and Allen W. Trelease, *Indian Affairs in Colonial New York: The Seventeenth Century* (1960; Port Washington, N.Y.: Kennikat Press, 1971), 5–7, 26–27.

3. Stiles, *History of Kings County*, 1: 10.

4. The Canarsee controled today's Brooklyn, Governor's Island, the eastern portion

of Staten Island, and perhaps even the southern tip of Manhattan. See Trelease, *Indian Affairs in Colonial New York*, 7, 156n. A number of competing names and spellings were in use: Sewanhacky, Meitowax, Wamponomon, Paumanake, and Mattanwake are but a few. Stiles, *History of Kings County*, 1: 22, 25.

5. Ibid., 1: 25; Gabriel Furman, *Notes Geographical and Historical Relating to the Town of Brooklyn in Kings County on Long-Island* (1824; Brooklyn: Renascence, 1968), 58; Van Rensselaer, *History of New York*, 1: 419. A nineteenth century pastor of the Dutch Reformed Church of Flatbush recorded that the area was purchased from the Native Sachem for

> 10 Fathoms of black seawant or (wampum.)
> 10 Fathoms of white seawant or (wampum.)
> 5 Match coats of Duffells.
> 4 Blankets.
> 2 Gunners sight guns.
> 2 Pistols.
> 5 Double handfulls of Powder, (gispen bunches of powder.)
> 5 Bars of Lead.
> 10 Knives.
> 2 Secret aprons of Duffels, (Cuppas of Duffell.)
> 1 Half fat or half barrell of Stong Beer.
> 3 Cans of Brandy.
> 6 Shirts.

Seawant and wampum are "Indian money." Thomas M. Strong, *The History of the Town of Flatbush, in Kings County, Long-Island* (New York: Thomas R. Mercein, Jr., 1842), 32.

6. "Freedoms and Exemptions Granted by the West India Company to all Patroons, Masters, or Private Persons Who will Plant Colonies in New Netherland, 7 June 1629," in E. B. O'Callaghan, compiler, *Laws and Ordinances of New Netherland, 1638–1674* (Albany: Weed, Parsons, 1868), 7–10.

7. "Freedoms and Privileges Granted by the Director and Council of New Netherland to English Settlers, 6 June 1641," in Ibid., 27–28.

8. Ibid; Furman, *Notes on Brooklyn*, 15; Edgar J. McManus, *A History of Negro Slavery in New York* (Syracuse: Syracuse University Press, 1966), 3–4; Thomas Adams, *The Design of Residential Areas: Basic Considerations, Principles, and Methods* (Cambridge: Harvard University Press, 1934); Stiles, *History of Kings County*, 1: 24. This follows Pope Alexander VI's logic which in 1493, after Columbus' "discovery," brought the vertical division of the Atlantic and the granting of all of the "unknown world" to the west to Spain and the east to Portugal to prevent strife between the two powers. Van Rensselaer, *History of New York*, 1: 7–8. Letters from Dirck Storm, secretary, et. al. to the the Right Honorable Governor, 17 November 1671 and 25 January 1673, in Victor Hugo Paltsits, ed., *Minutes of the Executive Council of the Province of*

New York: Administration of Francis Lovelace, 1668–1673, 2 Vols. (Albany: State of New York, 1910), 2: 619–26.

9. Thomas J. Davis, "New York's Long Black Line: A Note on the Growing Slave Population, 1626–1790," *Afro-Americans in New York Life and History* (hereafter *AANYLH*), (January 1978), 41, 45; McManus, *Negro Slavery in New York*, 7, 5, 8, 13; Richard Shannon Moss, *Slavery on Long Island: A Study in Local Institutional and Early African-American Communal Life* (New York: Garland, 1993), 12–13.

10. "Ordinance of the Director and Council of New Netherland Against Fugitives from Service . . ., Passed 9 August 1640" and "Ordinance of the Director and Council of New Netherland, Against Harboring Fugitive Servants, Passed 13 April 1642," in O'Callaghan, *Laws and Ordinances of New Netherland*, 24, 32; Declaration of Peter Stuyvesant, 8 April 1654, in Charles T. Gehring, ed., *New York History Manuscripts: Dutch* (Baltimore: Genealogical Publishing, 1983), 5: 129–30.

11. Trelease, *Indian Affairs in Colonial New York*, 62–63, 73, 79; "Ordinance of the Director of New Netherland, Prohibiting the Sale of Firearms, etc., to Indians . . . Passed 31 March, 1639," in O'Callaghan, *Laws and Ordinances of New Netherland*, 18–19; Henry Reed Stiles, *A History of the City of Brooklyn. Including the Old Town and Village of Brooklyn, the Town of Bushwick, and the Village and City of Williamsburgh* (hereafter Stiles, *History of Brooklyn*), 3 Vols. (Brooklyn: published by subscription, 1867–1870), 1: 29; Stiles, *History of Kings County*, 1: 23. Sixty-seven people were killed during the Staten Island conflict. Governor Stuyvesant imposed fines on areas of Long Island that had failed to maintain adequate fortifications. Dutch Long Island, especially Midwout (Flatbush), was particularly slack in defense. Furman, *Notes on Brooklyn*, 56–57n.

12. Alden T. Vaughan, "Blacks in Virginia: A Note on the First Decade," *William and Mary Quarterly*, 29 (3) (July 1972), 469; Winthrop D. Jordan, *White over Black: American Attitudes Toward the Negro, 1550–1812* (1968; New York: Norton, 1977), passim.

13. Handlin, "Origins of the Southern Labor System," 206; Edmund S. Morgan, *American Slavery, American Freedom: The Ordeal of Colonial Virginia* (New York: Norton, 1975), 297; George M. Fredrickson, *The Arrogance of Race: Historical Perspectives on Slavery, Racism, and Social Inequality* (Middletown, CT: Wesleyan University Press, 1988), 5; Winthrop D. Jordan, "Modern Tensions and the Origins of American Slavery," *Journal of Southern History*, 28 (1) (February 1962), 29.

14. "Act of the Director and Council of New Netherland Emancipating Certain Negro Slaves therein Mentioned, Passed 25 February 1644," in O'Callaghan, *Laws and Ordinances of New Netherland*, 36–37.

15. Barbara J. Fields, "Ideology and Race in American History," in J. Morgan Kousser and James M. McPherson, eds., *Region, Race, and Reconstruction: Essays in Honor of C. Vann Woodward* (New York: Oxford University Press, 1982), 143–77.

16. "An Ordinance of the Director and Council Exempting Jews from Military Service, Passed 28 August 1655" and "An Ordinance of the Director and Council Prohibiting the Bringing of Quakers and Other Strollers into New Netherland, Passed 17 May 1663," in O'Callaghan, *Laws and Ordinances of New Netherland*, 191–92, 192–94n, 439–40.

17. Theodore W. Allen, *The Invention of the White Race*, 1 (New York: Verso, 1994), 7; Jordan, *White over Black*, 85–86.

18. Directors in Holland to Peter Stuyvesant, 7 April 1648, in Hugh Hastings, ed., *Ecclesiastical Records of the State of New York*, 8 Vols. (Albany: James B. Lyons, 1901–5), 1: 228–29; "Resolution of the Director and Council of New Netherland Opening the Trade to Brazil and Angola, and Authorizing the Importation of Slaves into New Netherland, Passed 20 January 1648," "Conditions and Regulations for the Importation of Negroes from Africa into New Netherland, Granted 4 April 1652," and "Ordinance of the Director General and Council on New Netherland, Imposing a Duty on Exported Negroes, Passed 6 August 1655," in O'Callaghan, *Laws and Ordinances of New Netherland*, 81–82, 127, 191.

19. Stiles, *History of Kings County*, 1: 10; William MacDonald, ed., *Select Charters and Other Documents Illustrative of American History, 1606–1775* (New York: Macmillan, 1906), 137.

20. *Ibid.*; Stiles, *History of Kings County*, 1: 10–11; James Baldwin, "Preface," to Roi Ottley and William J. Weatherby, eds., *The Negro in New York: An Informal Social History, 1626–1940* (New York: Praeger, 1967), xvi; Davis, "Long Black Line," 42; Stiles, *History of Brooklyn*, 1: 199.

21. Allen, *Invention of the White Race*, 32; Moss, *Slavery on Long Island*, 10–11; Daniel Denton, *A Brief Description of New-York: Formerly Called New-Netherlands, With the Places Thereunto Adjoyning. Together with the Manner o' its Scituation, Fertility of the Soyle, Healthfulness of the Climate, and the Commodities thence Produced. Also Some Directions and Advice to Such as Shall Go Thither: An Account of What Commodites They Shall Take with Them; The Profit and Pleasure that May Accrew to Them Thereby. Likewise a Brief Relation of the Customs of the Indians There* (1670; Ann Arbor: University Microfilms, Inc., 1966), 6–7. A brief biography of Denton, who was born on Long Island and was one of the first settlers of Jamaica, Queens, is available in Cornell Jaray, ed., *Historic Chronicles of New Amsterdam, Colonial New York and Early Long Island*, Second Series (Port Washington, New York: Ira J. Friedman, 1968?).

22. While there were fewer extended conflicts between Natives and Europeans on Long Island than in the surrounding areas, tensions and feuds did exist. Silas Wood, *A Sketch of the First Settlement of the Several Towns on Long-Island; With Their Political Condition, To the End of the American Revolution* (1828) in Jaray, *Historic Chronicles of New Amsterdam*, 64–65, 71–75.

23. Ralph Foster Weld, *Brooklyn Is America* (New York: Columbia University

Press, 1950), 24; Peter Ross, *A History of Long Island, From Its Earliest Settlement to the Present Time*, 2 Vols. (New York: The Lewis Publishing Company, 1902), 1: 119; McManus, *Negro Slavery in New York*, 23.

24. Allen, *Invention of the White Race*, 14; Morgan, *American Slavery, American Freedom*, 297.

25. Moss, *Slavery on Long Island*, 17, 18, 94; Carl Nordstrom, "The New York Slave Code," *AANYLH* (January 1980), 9–14; "Answers of Gov. Andros to Enquiries About New York; 1678," in E. B. O'Callaghan, *The Documentary History of the State of New York; Arranged Under the Direction of the Hon. Christopher Morgan, Secretary of State*, 4 Vols. (Albany: Weed, Parsons, 1849), 1: 91.

26. Ibid., New York State Library, *Calendar of Council Minutes, 1668–1783* (Albany: University of the State of New York, March 1902), 55, 61; John Cadman Hurd, *The Laws of Freedom and Bondage in the United States*, 2 Vols. (1858; New York: Negro Universities Press, 1968), 1: 278–79, 280, 281; also see *The Journal of the Legislative Council of the Colony of New-York. Began the 9th day of April, 1691; and Ended the 27 of September, 1743*, Published by Order of the Senate of the State of New-York (Albany: Weed, Parsons & Company, 1861), xxii, 227, 243, 386. One scholar has examined the legal difficulty and confusion of tying ancestry and social status in the antebellum South. Martha Hodes, *White Women, Black Men: Illicit Sex in the Nineteenth-Century South* (New Haven: Yale University Press, 1997), 96–122.

27. Trelease, *Indian Affairs in Colonial New York*, 156–66, 202–03; "Will of Jan Miserol [Jr.]," 10 October 1712, in F. R. Tillou, attorney (NYS Supreme Court) *Samuel I. Hunt vs. James Cunningham, Jabez Williams, John T. Williams, and Samuel Sneden* (New York: privately bound and printed by Banks, Gould & Co., Law Publishers, 1855), 37, Meserole Family Papers, Box 3, New York State Archives; *The New York Evening Post*, 30 June 1746, 13 March 1749, 8 May 1749.

28. Ibid., 4 August 1746, 15 June 1747, 25 March 1751, 20 April 1752.

29. "Number of Negroes Imported from 1701–1726," in O'Callaghan, *Documentary History of the State of New-York*, 1: 707; *The New York Evening Post*, 17 December 1744, 31 December 1744; *The Daily Advertiser, Political, Commercial, and Historical*, 20 December 1785.

30. David Brion Davis, *The Problem of Slavery in Western Culture* (Ithaca, NY: Cornell University Press, 1966), 443.

31. George Livermore, *An Historical Research Respecting the Opinions of the Founders of the Republic on Negroes as Slaves, as Citizens, and as Soldiers* (1863; New York: Augustus M. Kelley, 1970), 127–28; Davis, "Long Black Line," 56–57, 41.

32. *The Independent Gazette; or the New-York Journal Revived*, 20 December 1783, 27 December 1783; *The Daily Advertiser, Political, Commercial, and Historical*, 22 September 1785, 20 December 1785; Alexander C. Flick, *History of the State of New York*, 10 Vols. (New York: Columbia University Press, 1933–7), 4: 262, 265; Harold X.

Connolly, "Blacks in Brooklyn from 1900 to 1960" (Doctoral dissertation, New York University, 1972), 7; *Return of the Whole Number of Persons within the Several Districts of the United States, According to "An Act Providing for the Enumeration of the Inhabitants of the United States," Passed March the First, One Thousand Seven Hundred and Ninety-One* (Philadelphia: Childs and Swaine, 1791), 36.

33. Nordstrom, "New York Slave Code," 17, 20; Ross, *History of Long Island*, 1: 121; Moss, *Slavery on Long Island*, 149–51; Bureau of the Census, *Negro Population, 1790–1915* (Washington, DC: Government Printing Office, 1918), 57.

CHAPTER 2

1. Henry Reed Stiles, *A History of the City of Brooklyn. Including the Old Town and Village of Brooklyn, the Town of Bushwick, and the Village and City of Williamsburgh* (hereafter Stiles, *History of Brooklyn*), 3 Vols. (Brooklyn: published by subscription, 1867–1870), 1: 232–33, 2: 406; Stephen A. Ostrander, *A History of the City of Brooklyn and Kings County*, 2 Vols. (Brooklyn: Annie A. Ostrander, 1894), 1: 172–73; Gertrude Lefferts Vanderbilt, *The Social History of Flatbush, and Manners and Customs of the Dutch Settlers in Kings County* (New York: D. Appleton, 1881), 249. Written between the 1820s and the early twentieth century, these histories include: Gabriel Furman, *Notes Geographical and Historical Relating to the Town of Brooklyn in Kings County on Long-Island* (1824; Brooklyn: Renascence, 1968); Gabriel Furman, *Antiquities of Long Island* (1874; edited by Frank Moore, Port Washington, Long Island: Ira J. Friedman, 1968); Silas Wood, *A Sketch of the First Settlement of the Several Towns on Long-Island; With Their Political Condition, To the End of the American Revolution* (1828) in Cornell Jaray, ed., *Historic Chronicles of New Amsterdam, Colonial New York and Early Long Island*, Second Series (Port Washington, New York: Ira J. Friedman, 1968); Henry Reed Stiles, ed., *The Civil, Political, Professional and Ecclesiastical History and Commercial and Industrial Record of the County of Kings and the City of Brooklyn, N. Y., From 1683 to 1884* (hereafter Stiles, *History of Kings County*), 2 Vols. (New York: W. W. Munsell, 1884); Thomas M. Strong, *The History of the Town of Flatbush, in Kings County, Long-Island* (New York: Thomas R. Mercein, Jr., 1842); Eugene L. Armbruster, *The Eastern District of Brooklyn* (New York: 1912); J. T. Bailey, *An Historical Sketch of Brooklyn, and the Surrounding Neighborhood, Including the Village of Williamsburgh, and the Towns of Bushwick, Flatbush, Flatlands, New Utrecht, and Gravesend. To Which is Added an Interesting Account of the Battle of Long Island* (Brooklyn: J. T. Bailey, 1840); James H. Callender, *Yesterdays on Brooklyn Heights* (New York: Dorland, 1927). Also see those histories sponsored by institutions: Bits of Old Brooklyn (Brooklyn: J. A. Davidson, 1881); Brooklyn Trust Company, *Historic Brooklyn: A Collection of the Facts, Legends, Traditions and Reminiscences that Time has Gathered About the Historic Homesteads and Landmarks of Brooklyn* (Brooklyn: Brooklyn Trust Company, 1941); John V. Jewell, *Historic Williamsburgh: An Account of the Settlement and Development*

of Williamsburgh and its Environs, from Dutch Colonial Days to the Present (Brooklyn: Williamsburgh Savings Bank, 1926). After the Civil War, Stiles was a general promoter of genealogy. See Henry Reed Stiles, A.M., M.D., *The Stiles Family in America. Genealogies of the Connecticut Family Descendants of John Stiles, of Windsor, Conn., and of Mr. Francis Stiles, of Windsor and Stratford, Conn., 1635–1894; Also the Connecticut New Jersey Families, 1720–1894; and the Southern (or Bermuda-Georgia) Family, 1635–1894. With Contributions to the Genealogies of Some New York and Pennsylvania Families. And an Appendix, Containing Information Concerning the English Families of the Name* (Jersey City: Doan & Pilson, 1895); Henry Reed Stiles, *A Hand-Book of Practical Suggestions for the Use of Students in Genealogy* (Albany, NY: Joel Munsell's Sons, 1899).

2. The Meserole name underwent a series of spelling changes as did many Dutch names in the Colonial period. The surname appears as Miserol, Miserole, Mescerool, Mescerooll, etc. Jan Meserole and his son's first names were often recorded as Jean and John.

3. Walter Monfort Meserole's handwritten genealogical manuscript of the Meserole family (hereafter Meserole Genealogy); Letter from W. M. Meserole to C. Fuller Williams, Esq., 27 April 1910, Meserole Family Papers, Box 1, New York State Archives.

4. Ibid.; *Brooklyn Daily Eagle*, 25 May 1919.

5. As the name evolved, the Lefferts adopted a common intergenerational tradition of naming one male youngster Leffert Lefferts. Stiles, *History of Brooklyn*, 2: 174–75n. Bedford is one of the oldest Europe-inflicted divisions on the island. It was first designated in 1667, and in 1670 the Natives sold it for "100 Guilders of Seawant, Half a tun of strong Beer, 2 half tuns of good Beer, 3 Guns, long barrells, with each a pound of powder, and lead proportionable—2 bars of a gun, 4 match coates."

It enclosed an area of land that stretched from the border of Breuckelen, near today's Borough Hall to what is today Stuyvesant Avenue. It competed with Flatbush in importance. Furman, *Notes on Brooklyn*, 15–17, 36; Henry M. Christman, ed., *Walt Whitman's New York: From Manhattan to Montauk* (New York: Macmillan, 1963), 26. An anonymous sketched map of Long Island (ca. 1770, available at the Library of Congress) noted that the distance from Brooklyn to Bedford is about two miles and the terain "is open & not very Hilly." Bedford became a part of the City of Brooklyn at its incorporation in 1834.

6. Gravesend was the only "English town" established in the county and it had a population that was only half British. On the dominance of Dutch slaveholders in Kings County, see Shane White, *Somewhat More Independent: The End of Slavery in New York City, 1770–1810* (Athens: The University of Georgia Press, 1991), 21. Few families kept hogs because cheap pork was imported from the southern colonies. "Rate List of New Utrecht; 28th Sept'r. 1683," in E. B. O'Callaghan, *The Documentary History of the State of New York; Arranged Under the Direction of the Hon. Christopher Morgan, Secretary of State*, 4 Vols. (Albany: Weed, Parsons, 1849), 2: 506–07. Meserole

Genealogy; "Will of Jan Miserol [Jr.]," 10 October 1712, in F. R. Tillou, attorney (NYS Supreme Court) *Samuel I. Hunt vs. James Cunningham, Jabez Williams, John T. Williams, and Samuel Sneden* (New York: privately bound and printed by Banks, Gould, 1855), 36–37, Meserole Family Papers, Box 3.

7. Harold X. Connolly, *A Ghetto Grows in Brooklyn* (New York: New York University Press, 1977), 3–4. The Director General granted Van Sale and Lord Werckhoven two lots in the draw for the meadows of Utrecht. O'Callaghan, *Documentary History of the State of New York*, 1: 639–40; Stiles, *History of Kings County*, 1: 10; Furman, *Notes on Brooklyn*, 73; Stiles, *History of Brooklyn*, 2: 329–30; Mrs. [Mariana Griswold] Schuyler Van Rensselaer, *History of the City of New York in the Seventeenth Century*, 2 Vols. (New York: Macmillan, 1909), 1: 353, 419–20, 2: 466; Richard Shannon Moss, *Slavery on Long Island: A Study in Local Institutional and Early African-American Communal Life* (New York: Garland, 1993), 94, 175–76.

8. "Census of Kings County; About 1698. A List of All the Freeholders Their Wives Children Apprentices and Slaves Within the Kings County on Nassauw Island" in O'Callaghan, *Documentary History of the State of New York*, 3: 133–38.

9. *Ibid.*

10. "Will of Christina Cappoens," 17 June 1687, in Tillou, *Hunt vs. Cunningham*, 15–20, Meserole Family Papers, Box 3.

11. Stiles, *History of Brooklyn*, 1: 232–33; Moss, *Slavery on Long Island*, 80–82.

12. "Census of Kings County; About 1698," 135, *passim*.

13. Knickerbocker families prefered marrying into other Dutch lines. The Meserole genealogy includes unions with the Praa, Monfort, Martense, Schenck, Beekman, Bennett, Van Cott, Strycker, Rapalje, Remsen, Pierrepont, Joosten, Nostrand, Varick, Young, Low, Jansen, Carman, Seaman, Laurens, Reyersen, Mulhem, and Fordham families. Meserole Genealogy, Meserole Family Papers, Box 1.

14. *Collections of the New-York Historical Society, for the Year 1893* (New York: privately published, 1894), 6–7.

15. "Will and Testament of Peter Praa, Esq.," 1739, in Tillou, *Hunt vs. Cunningham*, 29, Meserole Family Papers, Box 3.

16. "Last Will and Testament of Leffert Lefferts," 15 April 1799, in Henry C. Murphy, Jr., comp., *The North Farm of Leffert Lefferts. Supreme Court, County of Kings. James Carson Brevoort against Elizabeth Dorothea Brevoort, and Others* (Brooklyn: privately printed, 1 November 1880), 213–18.

17. "Last Will and Testament of Denyse Denyse," 1 May 1801, in Mrs. [Charlotte Rebecca] Bleecker Bangs, *Reminiscences of Old New Utrecht and Gowanus* (New York: privately printed, 1912), 66–67, 124–25.

18. "Last Will and Testament of Leffert Lefferts," 215; "Last Will and Testament of Dina Rapalje," 27 February 1750, entry 8, Papers of John Rapalje, the Rapalje Papers, New-York Historical Society; Bureau of the Census, *Heads of Families at the First Census*

of the United States taken in the Year 1790: New York (Washington, DC: Government Printing Office, 1908), 96–98; Jessica Kross, *The Evolution of an American Town: Newtown, New York, 1642–1775* (Philadelphia: Temple University Press, 1983), 92.

19. *The New York Evening Post*, 15 April 1745, 20 July 1747, 31 October 1748, 28 November 1748, 25 March 1751, 1 July 1751; Kross, *Evolution of an American Town*, 92.

20. Theodore W. Allen, *The Invention of the White Race*, 1 (New York: Verso, 1994), 35–36; Moss, *Slavery on Long Island*, 95–99; Ostrander, *History of Brooklyn*, 1: 171–72, 177; Furman, *Antiquities of Long Island*, 221–22.

21. Moss *Slavery on Long Island*, 113. "Will of Jan Miserol (Jr.);" "Will of Jacob Miserol," 18 July 1782, in Tillou, *Hunt vs. Cunningham*, 37, 41–43, Meserole Family Papers, Box 3.

22. T. J. Davis, *A Rumor of Revolt: The "Great Negro Plot" in Colonial New York* (New York: Free Press, 1985), 54–57, 224–27; Stiles, *History of Brooklyn*, 2: 119–22; Daniel Horsmanden, *The New-York Conspiracy, or a History of the Negro Plot, with the Journal of the Proceedings Against the Conspirators at New-York in the Years 1741–2* (1810; Westport, Connecticut: Negro Universities Press, 1969), 102, 353–72, 386.

23. Moss, *Slavery on Long Island*, 113–14; *The New York Evening Post*, 29 September 1746; Graham Russell Hodges and Alan Edward Brown, eds., *"Pretends to Be Free": Runaway Slave Advertisements from Colonial and Revolutionary New York and New Jersey* (New York: Garland, 1994), 140–41, 186–87, 196–97, 216–17, 299.

24. Connolly, *Ghetto Grows in Brooklyn*, 4–5; *The New York Evening Post*, 14 August 1749, 1 April 1751, 20 May 1751, 17 June 1751, 5 August 1751; Ostrander, *History of Brooklyn*, 24–26, 27–29, 38; Moss, *Slavery on Long Island*, 33, 39–42; Stiles, *History of Kings County*, 1: 93.

25. Office of the Treasurer, New York (colony), *Manifest Books*, 27, in "Reports of Goods Imported to New York, 1740–1775," New York State Archives, Albany.

26. Thomas L. Purvis, "The National Origins of New Yorkers in 1790," *New York History*, 67 (2) (April 1986), 135; Stiles, *History of Brooklyn*, 2: 38–39.

27. Bureau of the Census, *Heads of Families in the Year 1790*, 96–98; Moss, *Slavery on Long Island*, 70–71; *Census of Brooklyn, 1801. Long Island, New York Census, 1801, Census of Kings County*, colllection of the New York Historical Society.

28. "Copy Probate of the Last Will and Testament of David Van Cotts, Dec'd.," 11 February 1806, in Tillou, *Hunt vs. Cunningham*, 57–63, Meserole Family Papers, Box 3. Census, *Heads of Families in the Year 1790*, 96–98. Nicholas Schenck was the great-grandson of seventeenth century colonists Jan Martense Schenck and Jannetje Van Voorhees. Indenture of Peter, 15 May 1811; Indenture of Albert, 1 January 1819, Schenck Family Papers (misc. mss.), New York Historical Society.

29. "Report of the Standing Committee," 19 May 1800, Vol. 5, Records of the New York Manumission Society, New-York Historical Society; *The Long-Island Star*, 9 January 1812, 15 July 1812, 28 April 1813, 19 January 1814, 20 January 1819; Census,

Heads of Families in the Year 1790, 96–98; Moss, *Slavery on Long Island*, 55–60; Connolly, *Ghetto Grows in Brooklyn*, 6; *The Liberator*, 13 February 1836. In 1827, Sojourner Truth, the Dutch-accented freedwoman who descended from the Hudson Valley to join the national antislavery crusade, had to escape from her master in Upstate New York when he forced her to continue laboring after state emancipation. Truth then had to go to court to have her son returned from Alabama where her former owner had sold him in direct opposition to New York's laws. Sojourner Truth, *Narrative of Sojourner Truth; A Bondswoman of Olden Time, Emancipated by the New York Legislature in the Early Part of the Present Century; With a History of Her Labor and Correspondence Drawn from Her "Book of Life"* (1878; New York: Arno and The New York Times, 1968), 39–46.

30. Indentures between Mary McCrea and William Bodle, 9 May 1798, and Mary McCrea and Samuel Sackett, 12 June 1800, in Folders 33 and 34, Box 13, Duyckinck Family Papers, New York State Archives.

31. Harry B. Yoshpe, "Record of Slave Manumissions in New York During the Colonial and Early National Periods," *Journal of Negro History* (January 1941), 83, 88, 99.

32. White, *Somewhat More Independent*, 49; Manumission agreement between Nicholas Schenck and Harry Ferguson, 7 June 1819, Schenck Family Papers (misc. mss.). Emphasis mine.

33. *The Long-Island Star*, 23 October 1811, 1 January 1812.

34. Ibid., 29 April 1812, 3 June 1812, 14 April 1813, 21 April 1813, 26 May 1813.

35. Ibid., 10 February 1819, 9 June 1819, 16 June 1819, 30 June 1819, 8 September 1819.

36. Stiles, *History of Kings County*, 1: 620.

CHAPTER 3

1. *Brooklyn Daily Times*, 2 September 1859; *New-York Daily Tribune*, 3 September 1859.

2. *Ibid.; New York Times*, 2 September 1859; *New York Evening Post*, 2 September 1859.

3. All of these could pass for large towns in England. In 1801 New York's population was approximately 75,000, Manchester's 75,000, Liverpool's 82,000, Birmingham's 71,000, and Glasgow's 77,000. See B[rian]. R. Mitchell, *Abstract of British Historical Statistics* (London: Cambridge University Press, 1962), 24. It was only after the War of 1812 that New York clearly overtook the rest of the cities of the United States and began its century-long march to overtake London in population. Robert Ernst, *Immigrant Life in New York City, 1825–1863* (New York: King's Crown Press, Columbia University, 1949), 14. Smith noted the dramatic imbalance of trade between England and the colonies, but did not connect it to the size of their respective cities. Adam Smith, *An Inquiry Into the Nature and Causes of the Wealth of Nations* (1776; New York: Modern Library, 1937), 534–35, 894–95.

4. James H. Callender, *Yesterdays on Brooklyn Heights* (New York: Dorland, 1927),

11; "Plan for an attack on New York" and "On the Proposed Conference at Hartford with the Count de Rochambeau and the Chevalier de Ternay," in Harold C. Syrett, ed., *The Papers of Alexander Hamilton* (New York: Columbia University Press, 1961), 2: 389–91, 391–96; on Captain Alexander Hamilton in the Battle of Long Island see, Henry Cabot Lodge, *Alexander Hamilton* (Boston: Houghton, Mifflin, 1895). One historian has claimed that the name "Brooklyn" was first used in the will of Sarah De Bevoise. See Watson Burdette O'Connor, *Bedford in Breuckelen Town, from 1667 to 1868, an historical sketch, with map* (New York: 1926), 5, copy available in the Brooklyn Collection, Main Branch, Brooklyn Public Library.

5. Ralph Foster Weld, *Brooklyn Is America* (New York: Columbia University Press, 1950), 43.

6. W. J. Cornell, "Assets on Hand at Date of Last Accounting as Their then Valuation, 1853," in Folder, 21, Box 14, Duyckinck Family Papers, New York State Archives; John Jay Knox, *A History of Banking in the United States* (New York: Bradford Rhodes, 1903), 423–24.

7. Henry Reed Stiles, *A History of the City of Brooklyn. Including the Old Town and Village of Brooklyn, the Town of Bushwick, and the Village and City of Williamsburgh* (hereafter Stiles, *History of Brooklyn*), 3 Vols. (Brooklyn: published by subscription, 1867–1870), 2: 227; Maury Klein and Harvey A. Kantor, *Prisoners of Progress: American Industrial Cities, 1850–1920* (New York: Macmillan, 1976), 208; Kenneth T. Jackson, *Crabgrass Frontier: The Suburbanization of the United States* (New York: Oxford University Press, 1985), 32; Blake McKelvey, *The Urbanization of America, 1860–1915* (New Brunswick, New Jersey: Rutgers University Press, 1963), 4, 32; Elizabeth Leavitt Howe, "My Early and Later Days: Their Story for My Children and Grandchildren" (unpublished manuscript, 1898), 16–18, Fisher Howe Papers, New York Historical Society; Cornell, "Assets on Hand at Date of Last Accounting, 1853," Folder 21, Box 14, Duyckinck Family Papers; Joshua Brown and David Ment, *Factories, Foundries, and Refineries: A History of Five Brooklyn Industries* (Brooklyn: The Brooklyn Educational & Cultural Alliance, 1980), 6; Henry Reed Stiles, ed., *The Civil, Political, Professional and Ecclesiastical History and Commerical and Industrial Record of the County of Kings and the City of Brooklyn, N.Y., From 1683 to 1884* (hereafter Stiles, *History of Kings County*), 2 Vols. (New York: W. W. Munsell, 1884), 1: 522–23; Ralph Foster Weld, *Brooklyn Village, 1816–1834* (New York: Columbia University Press, 1938), 6; Edward K. Spann, *The New Metropolis: New York City, 1840–1857* (New York: Columbia University Press, 1981), 49, 151; Sean Wilentz, *Chants Democratic: New York City & the Rise of the American Working Class, 1788–1850* (New York: Oxford University Press, 1984), 36; Ernst, *Immigrant Life in New York City,* 20. Some evidence of the disposal of Brooklyn real estate in this period is available in the deeds, logs, and contracts in the Van Nostrand Family Papers, 1 Folder, New York State Archives. The Navy Yard was easily the biggest thing in the County, followed by the neighboring hospital and ceme-

tery. There was also the sizeable James Street Market in the Heights. See Alex'r. Martin, "Map of Brooklyn, Kings County, Long Island, from an Entire New Survey" (New York: 1834). Daniel Haskell's "Map of the City of Brooklyn" (1835) details the bulk of the improved area of the city which extended about fifteen blocks from the shore. For Broooklyn this was tremendous growth. In 1816 Brooklyn Village stretched only five blocks inland and much of that was still farm land. Neighboring Williamsburg had an even smaller improved area. See "The Village of Brooklyn in 1816, Compiled from the First Village Map of that date by Jeremiah Lott, and from Poppleton and Lott's Map of the Pierrepont Estate of 1819" (New York: F. Mayer, 1819).

8. Hezekiah Beers Pierrepont was the first to reclaim the original spelling of the surname. R. Burnham Moffat, *Pierrepont Genealogies, from Norman Times to 1913, with Particular Attention Paid to the Line of Descent from Hezekiah Pierpont, Youngest Son of Rev. James Pierpont of New Haven* (New York: privately printed, 1913), 35–36, 78–81, 159–65; Stiles, *History of Brooklyn*, 2: 147–51; Jackson, *Crabgrass Frontier*, 30–31. A map of the Pierrepont lots is available in the Map Division of the New York Public Library.

9. Stiles, *History of Brooklyn*, 2: 137–39.

10. Lefferts was the bank's president for twenty-two years. Stiles, *History of Brooklyn*, 2: 175–77; Henry Wysham Lanier, *A Century of Banking in New York, 1822–1922* (New York: Gilliss, 1922), 142–50.

11. Stiles, *History of Brooklyn*, 2: 287–88.

12. Rev. John W. Chadwick, "Brooklyn: The Greatest of the Five Boroughs of Greater New York," in *King's Views of New York, 1896–1915 & Brooklyn, 1905* (New York: Benjamin Blom, 1974). Brooklyn had counter-claims to the river and the shore but New York had too much political strength to lose such a key privilege. Jackson, *Crabgrass Frontier*, 31–32; Moffat, *Pierrepont Genealogies*, 159–65; Gabriel Furman, *Notes Geographical and Historical Relating to the Town of Brooklyn in Kings County on Long-Island* (1824; Brooklyn: Renascence, 1968), 22; Callender, *Yesterdays on Brooklyn Heights*, 36; Walt Whitman, *Autobiographia, or The Story of a Life* (1875; New York: Charles L. Webster, 1892), 27–28; Walt Whitman, "Crossing Brooklyn Ferry," *Leaves of Grass: Comprehensive Readers Edition* (New York: New York University Press, 1965), 159–60; J. T. Bailey, *An Historical Sketch of Brooklyn, and the Surrounding Neighborhood, Including the Village of Williamsburgh, and the Towns of Bushwick, Flatbush, Flatlands, New Utrecht, and Gravesend. To Which is Added an Interesting Account of the Battle of Long Island* (Brooklyn: J. T. Bailey, 1840), 5; Weld, *Brooklyn Village*, 16–17, 39; Raymond A. Mohl, *The New City: Urban America in the Industrial Age, 1860–1920* (Arlington Heights, Illinois: Harlan Davidson, 1985), 29; James Blaine Walker, "Old-Time Ferry Boats to Brooklyn: Quaint and Curious Customs Before the Days of Bridges and Tunnels," in Henry Collins Brown, ed., *Valentine's Manual of Old New York* (New York City: Gracie Mansion, 1924), 271–78; Thomas Leslie & John W. Leslie, comp., *Brooklyn (Alphabetical and Street) Directory and Yearly Advertiser for*

1841–2 (Brooklyn: The House and General Agency Office, 1842); letter dated 9 September 1841 in L. Maria Child, *Letters From New-York* (New York: Charles S. Francis, 1843), 15–16. The ferry regulations of 1654 are in *Bits of Old Brooklyn* (Brooklyn: J. A. Davidson, 1881), 5. The Meseroles also profited from the ferry improvements. See letter to C. Fuller Williams, Esq., 27 April 1910, Meserole Family Papers, Box 1, New York State Archives.

13. Letter dated 30 September 1841 in Child, *Letters From New-York*, 35–37.

14. George Hall enjoys the distinction of being the first mayor of the city of Brooklyn (under the 1834 charter) and the first mayor of the consolidated city of Brooklyn (1854). Stiles, *History of Brooklyn*, 2: 387, 395, 418; "An Act to Consolidate the Cities of Brooklyn and Williamsburgh and the Town of Bushwick into One Municipal Government, and to Incorporate the Same," Passed April 17, 1854 (Brooklyn: I. Van Anden, 1854); John V. Jewell, *Historic Williamsburgh: An Account of the Settlement and Development of Williamsburgh and its Environs, from Dutch Colonial Days to the Present* (Brooklyn: Williamsburgh Savings Bank, 1926), 16, 21, 37, 38.

15. Walter Monfort Meserole's handwritten genealogical manuscript of the Meserole family (hereafter Meserole Genealogy); "Abstract of th Title of Adrian Meserole, to a lot of land on the Northwest Corner of Norman and Manhattan Avenues in the 17th Ward of the City of Brooklyn, Kings County, and State of New York," 27 March 1883, in Meserole Family Papers, Box 1; James Guthrie to Herman J. Redfield, Collector of New York, 2 September 1856, *Letter Book 1856–7*, in General Correspondence, Customs, New York, NY, Records of the Bureau of Customs, RG 36, Box T282225, US National Archives (New York).

16. George Templeton Strong, entry for 5 October 1850, *The Diary of George Templeton Strong*, Allan Nevins and Milton Halsey Thomas, eds., 4 Vols. (New York: Macmillan, 1952), 2: 22; Jacob Judd, "The History of Brooklyn, 1834–1855: Political and Administrative Aspects" (Doctoral dissertation, New York University, 1959), 73–74; Whitman, *Autobiographia*, 44. A biography of Van Anden–"Isaac Van Anden: Proprietor of the 'Brooklyn Daily Eagle' "–is available in *Brooklyn Monthly*, May 1869, 189–98.

17. Phillip S. Foner, *Business & Slavery: The New York Merchants & The Irrepressible Conflict* (Chapel Hill: The University of North Carolina Press, 1941), 148–68; "Report of the Standing Committee," 19 May 1800, Vol. 5, Records of the New York Manumission Society, New-York Historical Society; Anthony Gronowicz, *Race and Class Politics in New York City before the Civil War* (Boston: Northeastern University Press, 1998), 81, 118–19, 135; Robert Trent Vinson, "The Law as Lawbreaker: The Promotion and Encouragement of the Atlantic Slave Trade by the New York Judiciary System, 1857–1862," *Afro-Americans in New York Life and History* (hereafter, *AANYLH*) (July 1996), 35, passim; Kenneth M. Stampp, *The Peculiar Institution: Slavery in the Ante-Bellum South* (New York: Vintage, 1956), 271–72; John R. Spears, *The American Slave-Trade: An Account of its Origin, Growth and Suppression* (New

York: Charles Scribner's Sons, 1900), 225–28.

18. David Brion Davis, *Slavery and Human Progress* (New York: Oxford University Press, 1984), 78–79; Gavin Wright, *The Political Economy of the Cotton South: Households, Markets, and Wealth in the Nineteenth Century* (New York: Norton, 1978), 90–91; Harold D. Woodman, *King Cotton and His Retainers: Financing and Marketing the Cotton Crop of the South, 1800–1925* (1968; Columbia: University of South Carolina Press, 1990), 170–71; Lanier, *A Century of Banking in New York*, 197; Callender, *Yesterdays on Brooklyn Heights*, 77.

19. Stiles, *History of Brooklyn*, 2: 128–31, 201, 3: 575; also see, the Records of the Pierrepont Stores, Brooklyn Historical Society.

20. Stiles, *History of Kings County*, 1: 646; Stiles, *History of Brooklyn*, 3: 577–80n; "The New York City Commercial Register, Containing the Cards of the Principal Merchants, Manufacturers & c., in the City and Vicinity, Classified According to the Business, Forming a Business Directory of Reliable Parties in All the Various Branches," 153, in H. Wilson, comp., *Trow's New York City Directory, for the Year Ending May 1, 1866* (New York: John F. Trow, 1866).

21. Sam'l. B. Ruggles (for Edward Curtis and himself) to Hon Corn. Lawrence, Collector, 18 May 1848, *Letter Book, August 7, 1845–June 21, 1849*, 98–99; James Guthrie to Herman J. Redfield, 9 October 1856, H. J. Redfield to Howell Cobb, 13 June 1857, and H. Cobb to H. J. Redfield, 15 June 1857, *Letter Book 1856–1857*, 27–28, 172–73, 176–77, both in General Correspondence, Records of the Bureau of Customs, Box T282225.

22. Harry W. Havemeyer, *Merchants of Williamsburgh: Frederick C. Havemeyer, Jr., William Dick, John Mollenhauer, Henry O. Havemeyer* (privately published, 1989), 13–34; Stiles, *History of Kings County*, 1: 672; R. W. Beachey, *The British West Indies Sugar Industry in the Late 19th Century* (1957; Westport, CT: Greenwood, 1978), 129. For a contemporaneous and first-hand account of the refining process, see Charles A. Goessmann's *Contribution on the Manufacture and Refining of Cane-Sugar* (New York: Holman, 1864) and *Notes on the Manufacture of Sugar in the Island of Cuba* (Syracuse: Journal Book and Job Office, 1865).

23. For instance, sugar industry production was four times that of petroleum refineries in Brooklyn. United States Department of Commerce, *Historical Statistics of the United States: Colonial Times to 1970*, Part II (Washington, DC: Government Printing Office, 1975), 691; *Monthly List, 1867, July to December*, Collection District No. 3 of the State of New York, Internal Revenue Service Tax Assessment Lists, 1862–1917, Records of the Internal Revenue Service, RG 58, US National Archives (New York); Havemeyer, *Merchants of Williamsburgh*, 34–36; John Disturnell, comp., *New York As It Was and As It Is; Giving an Account of the City from its Settlement to the Present Time; Forming a Complete Guide to the Great Metropolis of the Nation, Including the City of Brooklyn and the Surrounding Cities and Villages; Together with a Classified Business Directory* (New York: D. Van Nostrand, 1876), 293; Stiles, *History of Kings*

County, 1: 105, 2: 669–73; Klein and Kantor, *Prisoners of Progress*, 112–13; *Boyd's Brooklyn Business Directory, 1860* (New York: Appleton, 1860), 130, 133, 137; David M. Ellis, et. al., *A Short History of New York State* (Ithaca: New York: Cornell University Press, 1957), 175–76; Foner, *Business & Slavery*, passim. On the Sugar Trust in Brooklyn, see Daniel Catlin Jr., *Good Work Well Done: The Sugar Business Career of Horace Havemeyer, 1903–1956* (New York: privately printed, 1988).

24. Stiles, *History of Kings County*, 1: 672; Havemeyer, *Merchants of Williamsburgh*, 16, 43–62; Gronowicz, *Race and Class Politics in New York City*, 127, 155; Jeremiah Whipple Jenks and Walter E. Clark, *The Trust Problem* (Garden City, NY: Doubleday, 1929), 353–58. On production levels, see Myer Lynsky, *Sugar Economics, Statistics, and Documents* (Washington, DC: US Sugar Cane Refiners' Association, 1938), and Robert R. Nathan Associates, Inc., *Cane Sugar Refining in the United States: Its Ecomonic Importance* (Washington, DC: US Sugar Cane Refiners' Association, 1971).

CHAPTER 4

1. Richard Shannon Moss, *Slavery on Long Island: A Study in Local Institutional and Early African-American Communal Life* (New York: Garland, 1993), 173; "On the Condition of the Free People of Color in the United States," *The Anti-Slavery Examiner*, No. 13 (New York, 1839), 3–23.

2. George E. Walker, *The Afro-American in New York City, 1827–1860* (New York: Garland, 1993), 6–7.

3. The artisans split from Tammany partly because of the machine's pro-bank stance. Anthony Gronowicz, *Race and Class Politics in New York City Before the Civil War* (Boston: Northeastern University Press, 1998), 60–65; Noel Ignatiev, *How the Irish Became White* (New York: Routledge, 1995), 68–69, passim.

4. Irish Catholics and priests were accused of participating in the 1741 conspiracy. In 1700 the first anti-Catholic law was passed in New York. It called for the "perpetual imprisonment" of any Catholic priest caught in the colony. Death was prescribed for priests caught attempting to escape. Rev. J. R. Bayley, *A Brief Sketch of the Early History of the Catholic Church on the Island of New York*, 2nd ed. (New York: Catholic Publication Society, 1870), 38–47.

5. David R. Roediger, *The Wages of Whiteness: Race and the Making of the American Working Class* (New York: Verso, 1991), 147–50; Theodore W. Allen, *The Invention of the White Race*, Vol. 1 (New York: Verso, 1994), 19.

6. Harold Zink, *City Bosses in the United States: A Study of Twenty Municipal Bosses* (Durham, NC: Duke University Press, 1930), 178–79; Peter Ross, *A History of Long Island, From Its First Settlement to the Present Time*, 2 Vols. (New York: Lewis Publishing, 1902), 2: 93.

7. Ibid., 2: 92, 93; Zink, *City Bosses*, 189, 180, 181, 179; *Brooklyn Sunday Sun*, 12

July 1874.

8. Zink, *City Bosses*, 180; *Brooklyn Sunday Sun*, 7 December 1873; *The New-York Tribune*, 6 November 1893. On the Republican fidelity of the *Tribune*, see Richard Kluger, *The Paper: The Life and Death of the New York Herald Tribune* (New York: Knopf, 1986), 13–167.

9. Graham Hodges, " 'Desirable Companions and Lovers': Irish and African Americans in the Sixth Ward, 1830–1870," in Ronald H. Bayor and Timothy J. Meagher, eds., *The New York Irish* (Baltimore: The Johns Hopkins University Press, 1996), 117.

10. *The Liberator*, 3 February 1854, 10 February 1854.

11. Ibid., 17 August 1855.

12. Emil Olbrich, *The Development of the Sentiment on Negro Suffrage to 1860* (1912; New York: Negro Universities Press, 1969), 29–38; Alden Spooner, *Spooner's Brooklyn Directory, For the Year 1822* (Brooklyn: Office of the Long Island Star, May 1822), 57.

13. Olbrich, *Development of the Sentiment on Negro Suffrage*, 72–78.

14. A number of contradictory descriptions of this church's formation exist; this one, gleaned from several sources, seems most likely. The African Wesleyan Methodist Episcopal Church, Inc., *146th Annual Anniversary Commemorative Journal, 1818–1964* (Brooklyn: A. Q. Martin-Funn Funeral Home, 1964); Harold X. Connolly, *A Ghetto Grows in Brooklyn* (New York: New York University Press, 1977), 9–10, 11; Henry Reed Stiles, ed., *The Civil, Political, Professional and Ecclesiastical History and Commerical and Industrial Record of the County of Kings and the City of Brooklyn, N.Y., From 1683 to 1884* (hereafter Stiles, *History of Kings County*), 2 Vols. (New York: W. W. Munsell, 1884), 2: 1029–31; Henry Reed Stiles, *A History of the City of Brooklyn. Including the Old Town and Village of Brooklyn, the Town of Bushwick, and the Village and City of Williamsburgh* (hereafter Stiles, *History of Brooklyn*), 3 Vols. (Brooklyn: published by subscription, 1867–1870), 3: 704–07; Rev. Edwin Warriner, *Old Sands Street Methodist Episcopal Church, of Brooklyn, N.Y.: An Illustrated Record, Historical and Biographical* (New York: Phillips & Hunt, 1885), 15–16, 21–22; Clarence Taylor, "The Formation and Development of Brooklyn's Black Churches, from the Nineteenth to the Early Twentieth Century," *Long Island Historical Journal*, 5 (2): 212; Moss, *Slavery on Long Island*, 172–73; Spooner, *Spooner's Brooklyn Directory, For the Year 1822*; *The Brooklyn Sunday Sun*, 28 December 1873. The "African Ch." is included on Alex'r. Martin, "Map of Brooklyn, Kings County, Long Island, from an Entire New Survey" (New York: 1834). Alexander M'Caine continued to publish his pro-slavery ideas. See *The Liberator*, 14 October 1842. Philadelphia's independent African-American church was begun by Richard Allen and Absalom Jones of the Free African Society and bore fruit early in the 1790s as the African Church of Philadelphia. Richard Allen broke with the established hierarchy to plant the seeds of the African Methodist Episcopal Church in 1817, the year before the Brooklyn experiment. See Gary B. Nash, *Forging Freedom:*

The Formation of Philadelphia's Black Community, 1720–1840 (Cambridge: Harvard University Press, 1988), 109–33.

15. Taylor, "Formation and Development of Brooklyn's Black Churches," 214; Clarence Taylor, *The Black Churches of Brooklyn* (New York: Columbia University Press, 1994), 14–24.

16. Willis Augustus Hodges, *Free Man of Color: The Autobiography of Willis Augustus Hodges*, edited with an introduction by Willard B. Gatewood, Jr. (Knoxville: University of Tennessee Press, 1982), 46; Maritcha Remond Lyons, "Memories of Yesterdays, All of Which I Saw and Part of Which I Was: An Autobiography" (unpublished manuscript, ca. 1924), 26, 46, Williamson [Lyons] Family Papers, Schomburg Collection, NYPL.

17. James W. C. Pennington, *The Fugitive Blacksmith; or, Events in the History of James W. C. Pennington, Pastor of A Presbyterian Church, New York, Formerly a Slave in the State of Maryland, United States*, 2nd. ed. (London: Charles Gilpin, 1849), in *Five Slave Narratives: A Compendium* (New York: Arno Press and The New York Times, 1968), 1, 43, 50–51, 55–56; *The Liberator*, 6 August 1831; R. J. M. Blackett, *Beating Against the Barriers: The Lives of Six Nineteenth-Century Afro-Americans* (1986; Ithaca, New York: Cornell University Press, 1989), 1, 6, 10; C. Peter Ripley, et. al., eds., *The Black Abolitionist Papers*, 6 Vols. (Chapel Hill: The University of North Carolina Press, 1991–2), 3: 17; Rev. William J. Simmons, *Men of Mark: Eminent, Progressive and Rising* (1887; New York: Arno and The New York Times, 1968), 913–15; William Wells Brown, *The Black Man, His Antecedents, His Genius, and His Achievements* (1863; New York: Arno and The New York Times, 1969) 276–78. Austin Steward, an African-American merchant in Rochester, New York, was one of the early promoters of temperance in that city. See, Paul E. Johnson, *A Shopkeeper's Millennium: Society and Revivals in Rochester, New York, 1815–1837* (New York: Hill and Wang, 1978), 117–18. In 1837 the Reverend J. C. Beman, an African American, founded the State Temperance Society of Colored People in New Haven, Connecticut. *The Weekly Advocate*, 28 January 1837. Harriet Beecher Stowe, *Uncle Tom's Cabin* (1852; New York: Norton, 1994), 387–88.

18. *The Liberator*, 2 July 1831.

19. Hodges, *Free Man of Color*, 39, 43.

20. *The Liberator*, 13 August 1831.

21. Ripley, ed., *Black Abolitionist Papers*, 4: 144–45n; *The Weekly Anglo-African*, 9 March 1861; *The Anglo-African Magazine*, 1 (2) (February 1859).

22. *The Liberator*, 21 April 1832.

23. *The Colored American*, 11 March 1837, 28 August 1841.

24. Ralph Foster Weld, *Brooklyn Village, 1816–1834* (New York: Columbia University Press, 1938), 118, 173; Martin Robinson Delany, *The Condition, Elevation, Emigration, and Destiny of the Colored People of the United States, Politically Considered*

(1852; New York: Arno and The New York Times, 1968), 34; Lyons, "Memories of Yesterdays," 26.

25. *The Liberator*, 7 April 1832; Carter G. Woodson, *The Mind of the Negro as Reflected in Letters Written During the Crisis, 1800–1860* (Washington, D. C.: The Association for the Study of Negro Life and History, 1926), 238; "Prospectus of the Ninth Volume of Frederick Douglass' Paper," in Phillip S. Foner, ed., *The Life and Writings of Frederick Douglass*, 5 Vols. (New York: International Publishers, 1975), 5: 381; *Frederick Douglass' Paper*, 9 November 1855, in Ripley, ed., *Black Abolitionist Papers*, 4: 310–14; Carter Godwin Woodson, *The Negro Professional Man and the Community with Special Emphasis on the Physician and the Lawyer* (1934; New York: Negro Universities Press, 1969), 17.

26. *The Liberator*, 5 April 1834, 6 August 1836, 21 April 1837; *American Anti-Slavery Reporter* (June 1834) 92–94.

27. *The Liberator*, 18 October 1850, 25 October 1850, 9 April 1852; Rhoda Golden Freeman, *The Free Negro in New York City in the Era Before the Civil War* (New York: Garland, 1994), 61–62.

28. *The Liberator*, 10 May 1844, 14 February 1851, 4 April 1851.

29. *The Liberator*, 2 July 1831; *The Weekly Advocate*, 14 January 1837; Connolly, *Ghetto Grows in Brooklyn*, 13; Freeman, *Free Negro in New York City*, 97.

30. Smith was a graduate of the University of Glasgow, where he received three degrees including a doctor of medicine. William Wells Brown, the nation's first black novelist, wrote of Smith, "history, antiquity, bibliography, translation, criticism, political economy, statistics,—almost every department of knowledge,—receive emblazon from his able, ready, versatile, and unwearied pen." *The Colored American Magazine* later declared Smith the most eminent of the New York African Society's members. In addition to a Manhattan practice, he owned one of that city's finest drug stores. Using the pseudonym "Communipaw," Smith regularly contributed to *Fredrick Douglass' Paper*. In 1851, he prepared the report for the Committee on the Social Conditions of the Colored Race, which detailed the increasing poverty and poor health of New York's African-American population. Brown, *Black Man*, 205; Harold X. Connolly, "Blacks in Brooklyn from 1900 to 1960" (Doctoral dissertation, New York University, 1972), 53; "New York African Society for Mutual Relief–Ninety-Seventh Anniversary," *The Colored American Magazine* (December 1905), 689; Mary White Ovington, *Half a Man: The Status of the Negro in New York* (1911; New York: Negro Universities Press, 1969), 27; Robert Ernst, *Immigrant Life in New York City, 1825–1863* (New York: King's Crown Press, Columbia University, 1949), 104–05; David W. Blight, "In Search of Learning, Liberty, and Self Definition: James McCune Smith and the Ordeal of the Antebellum Black Intellectual," *Afro-Americans in New York Life and History* (July 1985), 10. Author's emphasis. James McCune Smith, M.A., M. D., "Toussaint L'Ouverture and the Haytian Revolutions," in Alice Moore Dunbar, ed.,

Masterpieces of Negro Eloquence: The Best Speeches by the Negro from the Days of Slavery to the Present Time (New York: Bookery Publishing, 1914), 19, 31.

31. *The Colored American*, 4 March 1837; William Seraile, *Voice of Dissent: Theophilus Gould Steward (1843–1924) and Black America* (Brooklyn: Carlson, 1991), 60.

32. Frederick Douglass, *My Bondage and My Freedom* (1855; New York: Dover, 1969), 451–56; Daniel O'Connell and Theobald Mathew, "Address from the People of Ireland, To Their Country-men and Country-women in America!" *The Liberator*, 11 March 1842.

33. Hodges' first name is given as William in the publication. William H. Smith, comp., *The Brooklyn City and Kings County Record: A Budget of General Information; with a Map of the City, an Almanac, and an Appendix, containing the New City Charter* (Brooklyn: William H. Smith, 1855), 200–202.

34. Kenneth L. Roff, "Brooklyn's Reaction to Black Suffrage in 1860," *AANYLH* (January 1978), 27–29, 35, 30–32, 35–36; *The Liberator*, 2 November 1860; Walker, *Afro-American in New York City*, 130; Benjamin Quarles, *Black Abolitionists* (New York: Oxford University Press, 1969), 173; Olbrich, *Development of the Sentiment on Negro Suffrage*, 126–27.

35. *The Liberator*, 12 May 1865.

CHAPTER 5

1. *The Liberator*, 19 July 1861.

2. James Brewer Stuart, *Holy Warriors: The Abolitionists and American Slavery* (New York: Hill and Wang, 1976), 68–69; Lewis Tappan, *The Life of Arthur Tappan* (1871; Westport, Connecticut: Negro Universities Press, 1970), 174–76; *The Liberator*, 14 December 1833, 21 December 1833.

3. Anthony Gronowicz, *Race and Class Politics in New York City before the Civil War* (Boston: Northeastern University Press, 1998), 70–72; *The Liberator*, 12 October 1833; Tappan, *Life of Arthur Tappan*, 207–17; *American Anti-Slavery Reporter* (July 1834), 111–12; Rhoda Golden Freeman, *The Free Negro in New York City in the Era Before the Civil War* (New York: Garland, 1994), 149.

4. Bertram Wyatt-Brown, *Lewis Tappan and the Evengelical War Against Slavery* (Cleveland: The Press of Case Western Reserve University, 1969), 152–53; Tappan, *Life of Arthur Tappan*, 249–50. An intersting biography of Child is available in Seth Curtis Beach, *Daughters of the Puritans: A Group of Brief Biographies* (1905; Freeport, New York: Books for Libraries Press, 1967), 79–119.

5. Stuart, *Holy Warriors.*, 160; Newell Dwight Hillis, *The Battle of Principles: A Study of the Heroism and Eloquence of the Anti-Slavery Conflict* (1912; New York: Negro Universities Press, 1969), 146; Frederick Douglass, "The Meaning of July Fourth for the Negro," delivered at Rochester, New York, 5 July 1852, in Phillip S. Foner, ed., *The Life*

and Writings of Frederick Douglass, 5 Vols. (New York: International Publishers, 1975), 2: 199; Lyman Abbott, *Henry Ward Beecher* (1903; New York: Chelsea House, 1980), 26.

6. *The Liberator*, 5 April 1834; *American Anti-Slavery Reporter* (April 1834) 52–53 (May 1834) 76–77. Lewis Tappan credited his brother Arthur with Lyman Beecher's appointment at Lane. See Tappan, *Life of Arthur Tappan*, 225.

7. Thomas W. Knox, *The Life and Work of Henry Ward Beecher, An Authentic, Impartial and Complete History of His Public Career and Private Life from Cradle to Grave, Replete with Anecdotes, Incidents, Personal Reminiscences and Character Sketches, Descriptive of the Man and His Times* (Hartford: Hartford Publishing, 1887), 66–68; *The Liberator*, 30 September 1853; Andrew A. Freeman, *Abraham Lincoln Goes to New York* (New York: Coward-McCann, 1960), 59.

8. Benjamin Quarles, *Black Abolitionists* (New York: Oxford University Press, 1969), 61; Knox, *Life and Work*, 133; Abbott, *Henry Ward Beecher*, 162. On the Edmondson sisters journey to New York, see James W. C. Pennington, *The Fugitive Blacksmith; or, Events in the History of James W. C. Pennington, Pastor of A Presbyterian Church, New York, Formerly a Slave in the State of Maryland, United States*, 2nd. ed. (London: Charles Gilpin, 1849), in *Five Slave Narratives: A Compendium* (New York: Arno and The New York Times, 1968), viii–ix.

9. Walt Whitman, *Autobiographia, or The Story of a Life* (1875; New York: Charles L. Webster, 1892), 35.

10. *The Liberator*, 31 May 1850; Mary White Ovington, *The Walls Came Tumbling Down* (1947; New York: Schocken, 1970), 5.

11. *The Liberator*, 23 August 1850.

12. Ibid., 11 May 1853.

13. There is a discrepancy over the date of this auction. *The Liberator*, 18 July 1856; Brooklyn Trust Company, *Historic Brooklyn: A Collection of the Facts, Legends, Traditions and Reminiscences that Time has Gathered About the Historic Homesteads and Landmarks of Brooklyn* (Brooklyn: Brooklyn Trust Company, 1941), 50.

14. Knox, *Life and Work*, 299–300. Plymouth later provided for Rose Ward's education at Howard University. *Historic Brooklyn*, 50.

15. Ray Allen Billington, ed., *The Journal of Charlotte L. Forten: A Free Negro in the Slave Era* (1953; New York: Collier, 1961), 68.

16. *The Brooklyn Sunday Sun*, 30 November 1873.

17. *The Brooklyn Monthly*, March 1869, 1; Knox, *Life and Work.*, 130–31; *The Liberator*, 11 November 1853, 29 February 1856, 11 April 1856; *Historic Brooklyn*, 49.

18. George Templeton Strong, Sunday, 19 October 1856, *The Diary of George Templeton Strong*, Allan Nevins and Milton Halsey Thomas, eds., 4 Vols. (New York: Macmillan, 1952), 2: 304. On 28 June 1830, less than a year after the publication of his radical antislavery pamphlet, David Walker was found dead outside his Boston clothing shop. See David Walker, *An Appeal, in Four Articles, Together with a Preamble,*

to the Coloured Citizens of the World, But in Particular, and Very Expressly, to Those of the United States of America, ed. with an intro. by Charles M. Wiltse (1829; New York: Hill and Wang, 1965), viii–xi. Stuart, *Holy Warriors*, 71; Knox, *Life and Work*, 150–51; Abbott, *Henry Ward Beecher*, 189.

19. Strong, Monday, 25 November 1850 and Thursday, 29 May 1856, *Diary* 2: 30, 375.

20. George M. Fredrickson, *The Inner Civil War: Northern Intellectuals and the Crisis of the Union* (New York: Harper & Row, 1965), 19, 20–22; Henry Reed Stiles, ed., *The Civil, Political, Professional and Ecclesiastical History and Commerical and Industrial Record of the County of Kings and the City of Brooklyn, N.Y., From 1683 to 1884* (hereafter Stiles, *History of Kings County*), 2 Vols. (New York: W. W. Munsell, 1884), 2: 1171; Whitman, *Autobiographia*, 41.

21. Joseph Jay Rubin and Charles H. Brown, eds., *Walt Whitman of the New York Aurora: Editor at Twenty-Two* (State College, Pennsylvania: Bald Eagle, 1950), 57–58.

22. Stiles, *History of Kings County*, 2: 1171; Henry Reed Stiles, *A History of the City of Brooklyn. Including the Old Town and Village of Brooklyn, the Town of Bushwick, and the Village and City of Williamsburgh* (hereafter Stiles, *History of Brooklyn*), 3 Vols. (Brooklyn: published by subscription, 1867–1870), 3: 933, 938; *White Man's Newspaper*, June 1851.

23. Walt Whitman, *The Eighteenth Presidency!* (Lawrence,: University of Kansas Press, 1956), 28–36.

24. Ibid.

25. J. N. Gloucester to Captain Brown, 9 March 1858, in Benjamin Quarles, ed., *Blacks on John Brown* (Urbana: University of Illinois Press, 1972), 4–5; Mrs. E. A. Gloucester to "Esteemed Friend," 18 August 1859, *The Anglo-African Magazine*, 1 (12) (December 1859).

26. See W. E. Burghardt Du Bois, *John Brown* (1909; New York: International Publishers, 1987), 173; Knox, *Life and Work*, 157, 155.

27. Beecher questioned the varacity of some of his trustees who he suspected disapproved of the invitation to Phillips. He later apologized. *The Liberator*, 11 November 1859, 18 November 1859, 27 April 1860.

28. James Redpath, *Echoes of Harper's Ferry* (1860; New York: Negro Universities Press, 1970), 417–18.

29. Ibid., 419.

30. Freeman, *Free Negro in New York City*, 156; *The Liberator*, 6 January 1860.

31. Hillis, *Battle of Principles*, 181–82; Stiles, *History of Brooklyn*, 3: 787; Freeman, *Abraham Lincoln Goes to New York*, 15–17, 58–64; Clarence Winthrop Bowen quoted in James H. Callender, *Yesterdays on Brooklyn Heights* (New York: Dorland, 1927), 149–50. In 1843 David Leavitt built the mansion. In 1853 he sold it to Henry C. Bowen. Louis Kossuth was also entertained there while in Brooklyn. Leavitt retired to Great Barrington, Massachusetts. See Elizabeth Leavitt Howe, "My Early and Later

Days: Their Story for My Children and Grandchildren" (unpublished manuscript, 1898), 38, Fisher Howe Papers, New-York Historical Society. The following year Bowen paid $305 for his family pew. See *Brooklyn Daily Eagle*, 4 January 1861.

32. Kenneth L. Roff, "Brooklyn's Reaction to Black Suffrage in 1860," *AANYLH* (January 1978), 27–29, 35, 30–32, 35–36; *The Liberator*, 2 November 1860; George E. Walker, *The Afro-American in New York City, 1827–1860* (New York: Garland, 1993), 130; Quarles, *Black Abolitionists*, 173; Emil Olbrich, *The Development of the Sentiment on Negro Suffrage to 1860* (1912; New York: Negro Universities Press, 1969), 126–27.

33. Donald E. Simon, "Brooklyn in the Election of 1860" (Master's thesis, City College, City University of New York, May 1965), 41, 72–73.

34. *The Liberator*, 14 October 1864; "Mayor Fernando Wood's Recommendation for the Secession of New York City," 6 January 1861, in Henry Steele Commager, ed., *Documents of American History*, 5th Ed. (New York: Appleton Century Crofts, 1943), 374–76; Gronowicz, *Race and Class Politics in New York City*, 144, 156–58.

35. *The Brooklyn Daily Times*, 13 April 1861, 22 April 1861.

36. *The Liberator*, 23 November 1860, 7 December 1860.

37. *The Weekly Anglo-African*, 12 January 1861, 10 August 1861; *The Liberator*, 7 June 1861.

38. Ibid., 26 April 1861.

39. Whitman, *Autobiographia*, 49; Walt Whitman to George Washington Whitman, 12 July 1861, in Edwin Haviland Miller, ed., *Walt Whitman: The Correspondence* (New York: New York University Press, 1961), 1: 56–57; Foner, ed., *Life and Writings of Frederick Douglass*, 3: 435n. The Regiment was largely drawn from the members of Plymouth Church as were two companies of the Fourteenth Regiment. Knox, *Life and Work*, 169–70, 173–78; Stiles, *History of Kings County*, 1: 487–92; Stiles, *History of Brooklyn*, 2: 443, 445–46; *The Liberator*, 19 July 1861; *Brooklyn Times*, 22 April 1861.

40. *The Weekly Anglo-African*, 4 May 1861.

41. *The Liberator*, 13 December 1861, 24 January 1862, 24 October 1862.

42. Frederick Douglass, *Douglass's Monthly*, September 1862, in Phillip S. Foner and Ronald L. Lewis, eds., *The Black Worker: A Documentary History from Colonial Times to the Present* (Philadelphia: Temple University Press, 1978), 1:277–79; Phillip Shaw Paludan, *"A People's Contest": The Union and the Civil War, 1861–1865* (New York: Harper & Row, 1988), 182.

43. *Eagle*, 2 January 1863, 3 January 1863; *The New York Times*, 1 January 1863, 4 January 1863, 6 January 1863; *The Liberator*, 26 December 1862, 16 January 1863.

44. *NY Times*, 6 January 1863; Knox, *Life and Work*, 183–208; Abbott, *Henry Ward Beecher*, 244–63; Hillis, *Battle of Principles*, 212–41.

45. Walt Whitman to George Washington Whitman, 12 July 1861, *Correspondence*, 1: 56–57.

46. *Eagle*, 10 July 1863, 13 July 1863; Iver Bernstein, *The New York City Draft Riots:*

Their Significance for American Society and Politics in the Age of the Civil War (New York: Oxford University Press, 1990), 18–19; Strong, Monday, 13 July 1863, *Diary*, 3: 335–36.

47. Maritcha Remond Lyons, "Memories of Yesterdays, All of Which I Saw and Part of Which I Was: An Autobiography" (unpublished manuscript, ca. 1924), 3, 8–10, Williamson [Lyons] Family Papers, Schomburg Collection, NYPL.

48. *Eagle*, 10 June 1951; Lyons, "Memories of Yesterdays," 77.

49. *Eagle*, 14 July 1863.

50. Bernstein, *New York Draft Riots*, 20–29, 282, 66; *The Liberator*, 31 July 1863; Stiles, *History of Kings County*, 1: 491–92; Strong, Thursday, 16 July 1863, *Diary*, 3: 341.

51. Letters from John W. Rode, Sergt., 4th Precinct, to Mr. [Albro] Lyons, 17 July 1863, Williamson Family Papers.

52. Hillis, *Battle of Principles*, 131; *Eagle*, 14 July 1863; *The Liberator*, 24 July 1863; Bernstein, *New York Draft Riots*, 34, 20–21, 32; Strong, Monday, 20 July 1863, *Diary* 3: 343.

53. *The Liberator*, 24 July 1863.

54. Ibid., 24 July 1863; James M. McPherson, *The Negro's Civil War: How American Negroes Felt and Acted During the War for the Union* (New York: Vintage, 1965), 72–73. Nonetheless, Henry Reed Stiles insisted that "the law abiding disposition of the citizens of Brooklyn was shown in the universal observance of the peace throughout the city. A few trifling manifestations of ill will to the negro were exhibited." Stiles, *History of Brooklyn*, 2: 452.

55. Walt Whitman to Louisa Van Velsor Whitman, 15 July 1863, *Correspondence*, 1: 117–18.

56. *Ibid.*; Stiles, *History of Brooklyn*, 2: 458; author's emphasis, Whitman to Louisa Van Velsor Whitman, 30 June 1863, *Correspondence*, 1: 111–14; *New York Age*, 19 October 1905; J. Lain, comp., *The Brooklyn City Directory for the Year Ending May 1st, 1865* (Brooklyn: J. Lain and Company, 1864); Luis F. Emilio, *History of the Fifty-Fourth Regiment of Massachusetts Volunteer Infantry, 1863–1865* (Boston: Boston Book, 1894), 57–58, 330; William Seraile, *Voice of Dissent: Theophilus Gould Steward (1843–1924) and Black America* (Brooklyn: Carlson, 1991), 60.

57. *The Liberator*, 28 April 1865, 5 May 1865.

58. Stiles, *History of Brooklyn*, 2: 477–78; Harold D. Woodman, *King Cotton and His Retainers: Financing and Marketing the Cotton Crop of the South, 1800–1925* (1968; Columbia: University of South Carolina Press, 1990), 246–47.

CHAPTER 6

1. Philip N. Racine, ed., *Piedmont Farmer: The Journals of David Golightly Harris, 1855–1870* (Knoxville: University of Tennessee Press, 1990), 360–64; Charles White Kellogg, entries for 19 November, 25 December, 26 December, *Diary, 1865*; and entries for 28 February, 13 March, 20 March, *Diary, 1866*, in Kellogg Diaries, Diaries

of Charles White Kellogg, 1863–1888, New-York Historical Society.

2. Kellogg, entries for 13 March, 20 March, *Diary, 1866.*

3. Ibid., passim.

4. Noel Ignatiev, *How the Irish Became White* (New York: Routledge, 1995), 173, 174–75.

5. Eric Foner, *Nothing But Freedom: Emancipation and Its Legacy* (Baton Rouge: Louisiana State University Press, 1983), 40; George Templeton Strong, 7 December 1867, *The Diary of George Templeton Strong,* Allan Nevins and Milton Halsey Thomas, eds., 4 Vols. (New York: Macmillan, 1952), 4: 172; Phillip Shaw Paludan, *"A People's Contest":* *The Union and the Civil War, 1861–1865* (New York: Harper & Row, 1988), 392.

6. *Brooklyn Daily Eagle,* 28 March 1880, 31 March 1880.

7. Ronald E. Butchart, " 'We Best Can Instruct Our Own People': New York African Americans in the Freedmen's Schools, 1861–1875," *Afro-Americans in New York Life and History* [hereafter, *AANYLH*] (January 1988), 30–32.

8. David R. Roediger, *The Wages of Whiteness: Race and the Making of the American Working Class* (New York: Verso, 1991), 176–77; C. Vann Woodward, *Origins of the New South, 1877–1913* (1951; Baton Rouge: Lousiana State University Press, 1971), 291–320.

9. Alexander C. Flick, *History of the State of New York,* 10 Vols. (New York: Columbia University Press, 1933–37), 7: 203; Maritcha Remond Lyons, "Memories of Yesterdays, All of Which I Saw and Part of Which I Was: An Autobiography" (unpublished manuscript, ca. 1924), 32, Williamson [Lyons] Family Papers, Schomburg Collection, NYPL.

10. Roger Alan Cohen, "The Lost Jubilee: New York Republicans and the Politics of Reconstruction and Reform, 1867–1878" (Doctoral dissertation, Columbia University, 1976), 6, 27, 56–76.

11. C. Vann Woodward, *Reunion & Reaction* (1951; Garden City, New York: Doubleday Anchor, 1956), 1–18, 201–20, passim.

12. Not until the twentieth century did more than ten percent of black Americans live in the Northern states and their percentage of the North's population decline every decade of the nineteenth century (see table).

13. On the end of Reconstruction see Eric Foner, *Reconstruction: America's Unfinished Revolution, 1863–1877* (New York: Harper & Row, 1988), passim; W. E. Burghardt Du Bois, *Black Reconstruction in America: An Essay Toward a History of the Part Which Black Folk Played in the Attempt to Reconstruct Democracy in America, 1860–1880* (1935; New York: Russell & Russell, 1962), 670–708; George C. Rable, *But There Was No Peace: The Role of Violence in the Politics of Reconstruction* (Athens: The University of Georgia Press, 1984). J. Morgan Kousser, *The Shaping of Southern Politics: Suffrage Restriction and the Establishment of the One-Party South, 1880–1910* (New Haven: Yale University Press, 1974), 36–40, 47–59, *passim*; C. Vann Woodward, *The Strange Career of Jim Crow,* 3rd Rev. Ed. (New York: Oxford University Press, 1974), *passim.*

Black Population in the United States, 1790-1900

Year	National Black	Northern Black	% in North	% of North
1790	757,208	67,424	8.90	3.55
1800	1,002,037	83,701	8.35	3.22
1810	1,377,808	109,309	7.93	2.98
1820	1,771,656	128,984	7.28	2.53
1830	2,328,642	166,757	7.16	2.39
1840	2,873,648	231,671	8.06	2.34
1850	3,638,808	285,369	7.84	2.08
1860	4,441,830	340,240	7.66	1.76
1870	4,880,009	452,818	9.28	1.82
1880	6,580,793	615,038	9.35	1.97
1890	7,488,676	701,018	9.36	1.80
1900	8,833,994	880,771	9.97	1.90

Source: Bureau of the Census, *Negro Population, 1790–1915*(Washington, DC: Government Printing Office, 1918), 33.

14. Gwendolyn Mink, *Old Labor and New Immigrants in American Political Development: Union, Party, and State, 1875–1920* (Ithaca: Cornell University Press, 1986), 90. Stewart, an established lawyer, preacher, professor, and author, finished his career as a justice of the Liberian Supreme Court. Harold X. Connolly, *A Ghetto Grows in Brooklyn* (New York: New York University Press, 1977), 47n; William Wells Brown, *Men of Mark: Eminent, Progressive and Rising* (1887; New York: Arno and The New York Times), 1052–54. Some evidence of the place of Asians in nineteenth-century Brooklyn is given in the *Eagle*'s listing under "Chinamen in Brooklyn," which made an immediate connection between Asian residents and laundry work: "It is estimated that there are over 700 Chinamen in the city of Brooklyn, and about 800 laundries. In the State of New York there are about 10,000 Chinamen." *Brooklyn Daily Eagle Almanac, 1894*, 197. However, Brooklyn's Chinese community was politically active. In 1892 six hundred Chinese Brooklynites organized to oppose federal anti-Asian legislation. In September of that year the Chinese Equal Rights League hosted a protest meeting at New York's Cooper Union. Charles J. McClain, *In Search of Equality: The Chinese Struggle against Discrimination in Nineteenth-Century America* (Berkeley: University of California Press, 1994), 205–6.

15. Emphasis mine. *Eagle*, 30 July 1873, 14 August 1873.

16. Ibid.

17. Mary White Ovington, *The Walls Came Tumbling Down* (1947; New York: Schocken, 1970), 6; *New York Age*, 31 August 1905.

18. Lyons, "Memories of Yesterdays," 1–2. During the Civil War the Reverend John Gloucester of Brooklyn sent his daughter to collect the rents on his Manhattan prop-

erties and she was refused transportation on two omnibuses. The progressive papers objected because her father was a major property owner in the two cities and a heavy taxpayer, as if caste should be sensitive to wealth. *The Liberator*, 28 August 1863.

19. Lyons, "Memories of Yesterdays," 25; Samuel R. Scottron, "New York African Society for Mutual Relief—Ninety-Seventh Anniversary," *The Colored American Magazine* (December 1905), 685.

20. Albro Lyons, Sr., Henry Albro Williamson, et. al., compilers, "Record of the Family of George Lyons 1783 — to — and its Branches as Follows: Marshall ___ to 1861/ Burrill 1871 to ___/ Kingsland 1888 to ___/ Hiram Lyons branches" (typed manuscript, comp. on 18 July 1851 and 5 October 1894), *passim*, Williamson Family Papers.

21. *Brooklyn Sunday Sun*, 21 December 1873.

22. James Weldon Johnson, *Along This Way: The Autobiography of James Weldon Johnson* (1933; New York: Penguin, 1990), 46–50, 202.

23. New York Amsterdam News, 21 February 1923.

24. Calvin B. Holder, "The Causes and Composition of West Indian Immigration to New York City, 1900–1952," *AANYLH*, 11 (1) (January 1987), 7, 10; Henry Etzdowitz and Gerald Schaflander, *Ghetto Crisis: Bureaucracy vs. Progress in Bedford-Stuyvesant* (Boston: Little, Brown, 1969), 3.

25. Mary White Ovington, *Half A Man: The Status of the Negro in New York* (1911; New York: Negro Universities Press, 1969), 173; Connolly, *Ghetto Grows in Brooklyn*, 30–31. Ovington's family were disciples of Henry Ward Beecher. During the Civil War they held two pews at Plymouth. See *Eagle*, 4 January 1861.

26. Clarence Taylor, "The Formation and Development of Brooklyn's Black Churches, from the Nineteenth to the Early Twentieth Century," *Long Island Historical Journal*, 5 (2): 209–26; Clarence Taylor, *The Black Churches of Brooklyn* (New York: Columbia University Press, 1994), 14–28.

27. Ovington, *Walls Came Tumbling Down*, 6; *Twenty-Ninth Annual Report of the Brooklyn Howard Colored Orphan Asylum Society* (Brooklyn: G. A. Pulis, 1898), *passim*; *Hand Book of the Howard Orphan Asylum of Brooklyn* (1898); Henry Reed Stiles, ed., *The Civil, Political, Professional and Ecclesiastical History and Commerical and Industrial Record of the County of Kings and the City of Brooklyn, N.Y., From 1683 to 1884* [hereafter, Stiles, ed., *History of Kings County*], 2 Vols. (New York: W. W. Munsell & Co., 1884), 2: 983; Henry Reed Stiles, *A History of the City of Brooklyn. Including the Old Town and Village of Brooklyn, the Town of Bushwick, and the Village and City of Williamsburgh* (hereafter, Stiles, *History of Brooklyn*), 3 Vols. (Brooklyn: published by subscription, 1867–1870), 3: 836; David Ment and Mary Donovan, *The People of Brooklyn: A History of Two Neighborhoods* (Brooklyn: The Brooklyn Educational & Cultural Alliance, 1980), 20.

28. Jervis Anderson, *This Was Harlem: 1900–1950* (New York: Noonday, 1981), 42–44; The Citizens' Protective League, *Persecution of Negroes, by Roughs and Policemen,*

in the City of New York, August 1900; Louis R. Harlan, *Booker T. Washington: The Making of a Black Leader, 1856–1901* (New York: Oxford University Press, 1972), 311–13, 314.

29. Brooklyn incorporated New Lots in 1886, Flatbush, Gravesend, and New Utrecht in 1894, and Flatlands in 1896, making it the nation's fourth largest city. Two years later, Brooklyn, most of Queens, the Bronx (then part of Westchester County), and Staten Island, were annexed by New York City. In Brooklyn, the advisory vote of 1894 favored consolidation with New York City by only 277 votes, 65,744 to 65,467. A few months before the merger, *The Century Magazine* announced the significance of consolidation: "On January 1, 1898, the city of New York will become in population the second city of the world, yielding precedence to London alone, Paris being third in the scale, and Berlin fourth." New Lots' history begins in the 1670s when a section of its land was purchased by the Dutch. On 21 March 1677, British Governor Andros chartered the area as a separate village and its lots were laid out. It was a village in the town of Flatbush until 1852 when it gained independence. Alter F. Landesman, *Brownsville: The Birth, Develoment and Passing of a Jewish Community in New York* (1969; New York: Bloch, 1971), 17–18; John V. Jewell, *Historic Williamsburgh: An Account of the Settlement and Development of Williamsburgh and its Environs, from Dutch Colonial Days to the Present* (Brooklyn: Williamsburgh Savings Bank, 1926), 16, 21, 37, 38; Kenneth T. Jackson, *Crabgrass Frontier: The Suburbanization of the United States* (New York: Oxford University Press, 1985), 142–44; Roger S. Tracey, M.D., "The Growth of Great Cities," *The Century Magazine* (November 1897), 79.

30. Connolly, *Ghetto Grows in Brooklyn*, 67, 89; Cheryl Lynn Greenberg, *Or Does It Explode?: Black Harlem in the Great Depression* (New York: Oxford University Press, 1991), 58.

31. *The New York Times*, 6 October 1915; W. E. B. Du Bois, *Dusk of Dawn: An Essay Toward an Autobiography of a Race Concept* (1940; New Brunswick, New Jersey: Transaction, 1992), 317.

32. *NY Times*, 4 January 1917; 20 July 1918.

33. Ibid., 5 May 1921, 6 May 1921, 1 March 1926.

34. *Amsterdam News*, 5 August 1925.

35. *NY Times*, 25 April 1926, 4 July 1926, 27 February 1926.

36. *Age*, 25 November 1922, 9 December 1922; Kenneth T. Jackson, *The Ku Klux Klan in the City, 1915–1930* (New York: Oxford University Press, 1967), 175, 176–77; *Amsterdam News*, 13 December 1922. Plymouth's liberal tradition toward African Americans continued. Hillis was even involved in the "Circle for Negro Relief," which operated from the church. *Age*, 20 December 1919.

37. Jackson, *Ku Klux Klan in the City*, 176–78; Connolly, *Ghetto Grows in Brooklyn*, 68; *Amsterdam News*, 20 December 1922, 14 March 1923; also see Charles Haley, "The Klan in the Midst: The Ku Klux Klan in Upstate New York Communities," *AANYLH* (January 1983), 41–51.

38. On the spy scares, see *NY Times*, 13 July 1915, 15 July 1915, 21 July 1915, 21

April 1917, 22 April 1917, 23 April 1917, 16 May 1917, 17 May 1917. On the spread of the racial hysteria, see Du Bois, *Dusk of Dawn*, 246; *NY Times*, 9 April 1918, 30 June 1918, 9 September 1918. On the communist threat and race, see *NY Times*, 8 January 1924, 26 April 1925.

39. *Revolutionary Radicalism, Its History, Purpose and Tactics, with an Exposition and Discussion on the Steps Being Taken and Required to Curb It: Being the Report of the Joint Legislative Committee Investigating Seditious Activities, Filed April 24, 1920, in the Senate of the State of New York*, Part 1 (of 2), 2 Vols. (Albany: J. B. Lyon, 1920), 1476–78, 1482, *passim*. *Age*, 13 December 1919.

40. *NY Times*, 30 June 1918; Harry Jerome, *Migration and the Business Cycles* (New York: National Bureau of Economic Research, 1926), 35; NUL, *Negro Membership in American Labor Unions*, 8; W. E. B. Du Bois, "The Migration of Negroes," *Crisis* (June 1917), 63–66. For biographies of the migrants, see "Letters of Negro Migrants of 1916–1918," *Journal of Negro History* (July 1919), 290–340; "Additional Letters of Negro Migrants of 1916–1918," ibid. (October 1919), 412–65; T. J. Woofter, Jr., "Migration of Negroes from Georgia, 1916–17," in U. S. Department of Labor, *Negro Migration in 1916–17* (1919; New York: Negro Universities Press, 1969), 82–86. The better histories of the migration include Peter Gottlieb, *Making Their Own Way: Southern Blacks' Migration to Pittsburgh, 1916–30* (Urbana: University of Illinois Press, 1987); James R. Grossman, *Land of Hope: Chicago, Black Southerners, and the Great Migration* (Chicago: The University of Chicago Press, 1989); Nell Irvin Painter, *Exodusters: Black Migration to Kansas After Reconstruction* (New York: Norton, 1976).

41. Pennsylvania's black population also had a Southern majority and in New Jersey a plurality of the colored population was Southern. U. S. Bureau of the Census, *Negro Population, 1790–1915* (Washington, DC: Government Printing Office, 1918), 83; Allan H. Spear, *Black Chicago: The Making of a Negro Ghetto, 1890–1920* (Chicago: The University of Chicago Press, 1967), 138.

42. Clyde Vernon Kiser, *Sea Island to City: A Study of St. Helena Islanders in Harlem and Other Urban Centers* (1932; New York: Antheneum, 1969), 127; Robert B. Grant, *The Black Man Comes to the City: A Documentary Account from the Great Migration to the Great Depression*, 1915–1930 (Chicago: Nelson-Hall, 1972), 16–17; W. E. Burghardt Du Bois, *Darkwater: Voices from Within the Veil* (1920; New York: AMS Press, 1969), 89; *NY Times*, 23 April 1923, 24 April 1923, 4 May 1923, 23 May 1923, 5 September 1916.

43. Ibid., 11 September 1915, 29 March 1917, 9 March 1925, 10 March 1925.

44. Bureau of the Census, *Negroes in the United States, 1920–32* (Washington, DC: Government Printing Office, 1935), 32–35; *Amsterdam News*, 14 July 1926; Virginia E. Sanchez Korrol, *From Colonia to Community: The History of Puerto Ricans in New York City* (1983); Berkeley: The University of California Press, 1994), 173; Calvin B. Holder, "The Rise of the West Indian Politician in New York City, 1900–1952,

AANYLH, 4 (1) (January 1980), 46–49. Also see, Jeffrey Nathan Gerson, "Building the Brooklyn Machine: Irish, Jewish and Black Political Succession in Central Brooklyn, 1919–1964" (Doctoral Dissertation, City University of New York, 1990), 179–80, passim.

45. Holder, "Causes and Composition of West Indian Immigration," 9, 11, 14–16; Paule Marshall, *Brown Girl, Brownstones* (1959; New York: Feminist Press, 1981), 222; Ira De Augustine Reid, *The Negro Immigrant: His Background, Characteristics and Social Adjustment, 1899–1937* (New York: Columbia University Press, 1939), 107–8, 121; Clyde G. Atwell, *The Paragon Story (1939–1969)* (Brooklyn: privately printed, ca. 1976), 11–12.

46. *Age*, 18 November 1922; Sanchez Korrol, *From Colonia to Community*, 40, 44–46, 54–55.

47. *NY Times*, 24 April 1920.

48. *Eagle*, 24 April 1920; *Age*, 1 May 1920.

49. Final stanza of Gwendolyn B. Bennett's "Heritage," *Opportunity* (December 1923), 371; *Eagle*, 23 April 1920; Jessie Carney Smith, ed., *Notable Black American Women* (Detroit: Gale Research, 1992), 1: 77–80.

50. John Purroy Mitchel, Mayor of New York City, "The Public Schools of New York," *The Crisis: A Record of the Darker Races*, July 1917, 132; Gilbert Osofsky, *Harlem: The Making of a Ghetto: Negro New York, 1890–1930*, 2nd ed. (New York: Harper & Row, 1971), 5; Connolly, *Ghetto Grows in Brooklyn*, 24; Ment and Donovan, *People of Brooklyn*, 21–22; Nicholas Marlow, "Bedford-Stuyvesant Place-Names" (Master's thesis, Brooklyn College, 1963), 8; Mary Manoni, *Bedford-Stuyvesant: The Anatomy of a Central City Community* (New York: Quadrangle, 1973), 2. By 1871, there were four colored schools: (1) at Willoughby near Raymond Street, No. 2 at Troy Avenue near Bergen (Weeksville), No. 3 at Union Avenue near S. Third Street, and No. 4 at High near Jay Street. *Manual of the Common Council of the City of Brooklyn for 1871*, compiled by William C. Bishop (Brooklyn: Arthur Brown, 1871), 311–13.

51. *Amsterdam News*, 16 May 1923; Connolly, *Ghetto Grows in Brooklyn*, 67.

52. *Amsterdam News*, 17 March 1926.

53. See St. Augustine's Protestant Episcopal Church, "Financial Report for the Year 1930," *passim*.

54. Connolly, *Ghetto Grows in Brooklyn*, 89–90.

55. *NY Times*, 23 August 1928, 15 March 1929.

56. *Eagle*, 16 September 1929, 17 September 1929; *NY Times*, 17 September 1929.

57. *Amsterdam News*, 5 September 1929, 2 October 1929; *Eagle*, 17 September 1929, 23 September 1929; *NY Times*, 18 September 1929; *Age*, 21 September 1929; Connolly, *Ghetto Grows in Brooklyn*, 60–67.

58. *NY Times*, 19 September 1929, 20 September 1929; 22 September 1929; *Amsterdam News*, 25 September 1929.

59. *NY Times*, 23 September 1929, 25 September 1929, 29 September 1929, 2 October 1929, 24 September 1929, 27 September 1929, 30 September 1929; *Age*, 28 September 1929; *Eagle*, 23 September 1929.

60. *Amsterdam News*, 25 September 1929.

61. Ibid., 23 October 1929; *NY Times*, 8 October 1929, 9 October 1929, 18 October 1929, 19 October 1929, 14 October 1929.

62. W. E. B. Du Bois to Joseph B. Glenn, 24 March 1925, in Aptheker, ed., *Correspondence*, 1: 311; W. E. B. Du Bois, "The Color Line and the Church," *Crisis* (November 1929), 387–88.

CHAPTER 7

1. Memorandum from Spencer S. Hamilton, Asst. General Superintendent, to Philip E. Pfeifer, General Superintendent, 8 June 1944; memorandum from Philip E. Pfeifer, General Superintendent, to the Board of Transportation, 10 June 1944; promotional letter from Charles H. White, Chairman, B. M. T. Trolley Operators Unit, Brooklyn NAACP, 5 August 1944, in New York Board of Transportation Records, Discrimination 1938–1963, Box 18, Files 1–2, New York City Transit Museum Archives.

2. Official Communication from James Harten, Aide to the Mayor, to the Hon. John Delaney, 4 August 1943; memorandum from Wm. Jerome Daly to the members of the Board (of Transportation), 4 May 1945, in Board of Transportation Records, Box 18, Files 1–2.

3. Reeve Vanneman and Lynn Weber Cannon have provided an insightful analysis of class theory and the construction of American exceptionalism. See *The American Perception of Class* (Philadelphia: Temple University Press, 1987), 1–17, *passim*.

4. Olivier Zunz has convincingly argued that ethnic clusters in late-nineteenth-century Detroit were the result of "an irregular system of dominance" that linked labor and residential patterns. See *The Changing Face of Inequality: Urbanization, Industrial Development, and Immigrants in Detroit, 1880–1920* (Chicago: The University of Chicago Press, 1982), 47–59. Woodward dated the Jim Crow era in the South at 1890. The same date can be used in the North. C. Vann Woodward, *The Strange Career of Jim Crow*, 3rd Rev. Ed. (New York: Oxford University Press, 1974), *passim*. Vernon Lane Morton found that Mississippi's first Jim Crow law was passed in 1865, but this does not constitute a system of segregation. *The Negro in Mississippi, 1865–1890* (1947; New York: Harper & Row, 1965), 230. In Brooklyn there were many examples of segregation in public and private accommodations before 1890; yet, as Woodward and Du Bois argue, the patterns of segregation at the turn of the century are strikingly different and constitute a true system of racial division. For a

history of segregation in New York, see Seth M. Scheiner, *Negro Mecca: A History of the Negro in New York City, 1865–1920* (New York: New York University Press, 1965), 170–214. W. E. B. Du Bois, *The Philadelphia Negro* (1899; Millwood, New York: Kraus-Thomson, 1973), 5.

5. Domestics were not included and occupations were not provided for many people. A list of jobs of 260 black workers in Brooklyn, 1865 shows the following:

Laborer (59); Laundress (32); Seaman (32); Porter (28); Whitewash (23); Waiter (12); Cook (6); Coachman (6); Steward (5); Tailor (5); Barber (4); Candies (3); Ropemaker (3); Driver (3); Painter (3)Nurse (2); Seamstress (2); Carman (2); Teacher (2); Hairdresser (2); Shoemaker (2); Penman (1); Sexton (1); Stewardess (1); Paperhanger (1); Chair mender (1); Herbalist (1); Reverend (1): (This category is clearly underestimated. There were other ministers who did not give the ministry as their primary occupation. Black people's occupations were not always listed.) Gardener (1); Carpenter (1); Drygoods (1); Grocer (1); Expressman (1); Machinist (1); Packer (1); Boatman (1); Engineer (1); Photographer (1); Drover (1); Smith (1); Dressmaker (1); Janitor (1); Scourer (1); Fisherman (1).

Source: J. Lain, comp., *The Brooklyn City Directory for the Year Ending May 1st, 1865* (Brooklyn: J. Lain, 1864), passim.

6. Bureau of the Census, *Statistics of Women at Work* (Washington, DC: Goverment Printing Office, 1907), 266–71; Scheiner, *Negro Mecca*, 51; *Brooklyn Daily Eagle*, 3–5 January 1880, 1 April 1915, 1 April 1920

7. Gerda Lerner, ed., *Black Women in White America: A Documentary History* (New York: Pantheon, 1972), 229–34; Paule Marshall, *Brown Girl, Brownstones* (1959; New York: Feminist Press, 1981), 11; Clyde G. Atwell, *The Paragon Story (1939–1969)* (Brooklyn: privately printed, ca. 1976), 15.

8. *Brooklyn Sunday Sun,* 14 December 1873.

9. Harold X. Connolly, *A Ghetto Grows in Brooklyn* (New York: New York University Press, 1977), 21–22, 29; William Seraile, "Brooklyn's 'Colored Society:' A Minister's Observation, 1876–1877," *Afro-Americans in New York Life and History* (hereafter, *AANYLH*) (January 1991), 43, 46–48; William Seraile, *Voice of Dissent: Theophilus Gould Steward (1843–1924) and Black America* (Brooklyn: Carlson, 1991), 59.

10. Italics mine. *Eagle,* 23 September 1881.

11. Charles Green and Basil Wilson, *The Struggle for Black Empowerment in New York City: Beyond the Politics of Pigmentation* (New York: Praeger, 1989), 2–21; Calvin B. Holder, "The Rise of the West Indian Politician in New York City, 1900–1952," *AANYLH*, 4 (1) (January 1980), 46; Connolly, *Ghetto Grows in Brooklyn*, 29–30.

12. The United Colored Democracy published the hires as a campaign tool (see table).

Tammany Patronage to African Americans, 1897–1913

Agency	Black Employees
District Attorney's Office, NY	1 assistant district attorney
	1 diary clerk
	2 messengers
Corporation Counsel's Office	1 assistant corporation counsel
	1 confidential attendant
Tax Department	1 deputy commissioner of taxes
	2 clerks
	1 messenger
Finance Department	1 law clerk
	2 clerks
	1 messenger
Mayor's Office	2 sealers of weights and measures
	1 executive clerk
City Chamberlain's Office	1 bank messenger
	1 messenger
Department of Water Supply	1 assistant engineer
	2 inspectors of water meters
	1 inspector of hydrants
	3 clerks
	1 messenger
Borough President, Manhattan	1 inspector of highways
	1 inspector of vaults
	1 foreman
	5 corporation inspectors
	1 clerk
	1 cleaner
	1 elevator attendant
Sheriff's Office	1 assistant deputy sheriff
	3 cleaners
Fire Department	1 deputy inspector of combustibles
	1 inspector of oils
	1 clerk
	1 first grade fireman
	1 driver
Department of Health	4 sanitary inspectors
	1 clerk
	7 inspectors of disinfectant
	(several) nurses
	1 typewriting copyist
Police Department	2 patrolmen

Dock Department	2 stenographers
	2 clerks
	6 marine stokers
	30 laborers
Commissioner of Licenses	1 inspector of licenses
Register's Office	2 copyists
Tenement House Department	1 clerk
Bridge Department	1 engineman
	1 marine stoker
	1 marine sounder
	1 stenographer
	1 watchman
	6 laborers
Surrogate's Office	1 messenger
Department of Charities	1 messenger
Park Department	12 laborers
Department of Sewers	2 laborers
Street Cleaning Department	2 detail foremen
	1 inspector of mud scows
	1 inspector of garbage
	(over) 600 drivers and
	sweepers
Borough President, Bronx	1 messenger
Borough President, Queens and Richmond	(several) laborers
Register's Office, Brooklyn	1 clerk
Coroner's Office, Brooklyn	1 clerk
District Attorney's Office, Brooklyn	1 clerk
Board of Education	70 female teachers
	6 male teachers
	1 assistant music director

Tammany Hall United Colored Democracy of New York, *Tammany Hall vs. Fusion or Organized Democracy Against Disorganized Autocracy and Bastard Reform* (New York: 1913), 4–7, Schomburg Collection, NYPL; also see, Ira Katznelson, *Black Men, White Cities: Race, Politics, and Migration in the United States, 1900–30, and Britain, 1948–68* (London: Oxford University Press, 1973), 78–79.

13. Du Bois, *Philadelphia Negro*, 126–38; Seraile, "Brooklyn's 'Colored Society,' " 43; Maritcha Remond Lyons, "Memories of Yesterdays, All of Which I Saw and Part of Which I Was: An Autobiography" (unpublished manuscript, ca. 1924), 27–28, Williamson [Lyons] Family Papers, Schomburg Collection, NYPL.

14. *New York Age*, 10 August 1905.

15. Scheiner, *Negro Mecca*, 203–04; Melvyn Dubofsky, *When Workers Organize: New York City in the Progressive Era* (Amherst: University of Massachusetts Press, 1968), 3, 4; Harry Jerome, *Migration and the Business Cycles* (New York: National Bureau of Economic Research, 1926), 35; *New York Age*, 1 November 1919; *New York*

Amsterdam News, 11 December 1929, 18 December 1929.

16. Mary White Ovington, *Half A Man: The Status of the Negro in New York* (1911; New York: Negro Universities Press, 1969), 96–98; Charles Lionel Franklin, *The Negro Labor Unionist of New York: Problems and Conditions Among the Negroes in the Labor Unions of Manhattan with Special Reference to the N.R.A. and Post-N.R.A. Situations* (New York: Columbia University Press, 1936), 72–73; Robert B. Grant, *The Black Man Comes to the City: A Documentary Account from the Great Migration to the Great Depression, 1915–1930* (Chicago: Nelson-Hall, 1972), 96. In his study of black workers in Milwaukee, Joe William Trotter, Jr. notes the extent to which union exclusion paced the proletarianization of black people in that city. See *Black Milwaukee: The Making of an Industrial Proletariat, 1915–1945* (Urbana: University of Illinois Press, 1985), 3–33. On racial exclusion by unions in other cities, see Du Bois, *Philadelphia Negro*, 126–46; Peter Gottlieb, *Making Their Own Way: Southern Blacks' Migration to Pittsburgh, 1916–30* (Urbana: University of Illinois Press, 1987), 146–77; James R. Grossman, *Land of Hope: Chicago, Black Southerners, and the Great Migration* (Chicago: The University of Chicago Press, 1989), 181–85; Niles Carpenter, *Nationality, Color, and Economic Opportunity in the City of Buffalo* (1927; Westport, Connecticut: Negro Universities Press, 1970), 112–14; Kenneth L. Kusmer, *A Ghetto Takes Shape: Black Cleveland, 1870–1930* (Urbana: University of Illinois Press, 1976), 66–90; David M. Katzman, *Before the Ghetto: Black Detroit in the Nineteenth Century* (Urbana: University of Illinois Press, 1973), 104–34; Stephan Thernstrom, *The Other Bostonians: Poverty and Progress in the American Metropolis, 1880–1970* (Cambridge: Harvard University Press, 1973), 184–94.

17. Louise Venable Kennedy, *The Negro Peasant Turns Cityward: Effects of Recent Migrations on Northern Centers* (1930; New York: AMS Press, 1968), 80–83.

18. Henry Coffin Syrett, *The City of Brooklyn, 1865–1898: A Political History* (1944; New York: AMS Press, 1968), 241–42; Joshua B. Freeman, *In Transit: The Transport Workers Union in New York City, 1933–1966* (New York: Oxford University Press, 1989), 16.

19. Grant, *Black Man Comes to the City*, 88; Phillip S. Foner and Ronald L. Lewis, eds., *The Black Worker: A Documentary History from Colonial Times to the Present*, 5 Vols. (Philadelphia: Temple University Press, 1980), 5: 96; *Age*, 23 March 1905; Dubofsky, *When Workers Organize*, 122; quoted in Franklin, *Negro Labor Unionist of New York*, 61–62; Vernon H. Jensen, *Strife on the Waterfront: The Port of New York Since 1945* (Ithaca, New York: Cornell University Press, 1974), 232; Department of Research and Investigations, National Urban League, *Negro Membership in American Labor Unions* (New York: NUL, 1930), 49.

20. Foner, *Black Worker*, 5: 105–06; *The New York Times*, 7 October 1917; Ovington, *Half A Man*, 163–64; Mary White Ovington, *The Walls Came Tumbling Down* (1947; New York: Schocken, 1947), 27; Moses Rischin, *The Promised City: New York's Jews,*

1870–1914 (1962; New York: Harper & Row, 1970), 246–50; *The Survey*, 21 March 1914; Franklin, *Negro Labor Unionist of New York*, 94, 93.

21. *Age*, 14 September 1905; William P. Moore, "Progressive Business Men of Brooklyn," *The Voice of the Negro* (July 1904), 304–08; Bureau of the Census, *Negroes in the United States, 1920–32: Retail Business* (Washington, DC: Government Printing Office, 1934), 36–40.

22. Ovington, *Walls Came Tumbling Down*, 4–5, 8, 10; Mary White Ovington to W. E. B. Du Bois, 10 June 1904, in Herbert Aptheker, ed., *The Correspondence of W.E.B. Du Bois*, 3 Vols. (Amherst: University of Massachusetts Press, 1973), 1: 76–77.

23. Ovington, *Walls Came Tumbling Down*, 53–54; Mary White Ovington, *Portraits in Color* (New York: Viking, 1927), 78.

24. Scheiner, *Negro Mecca*, 128; Ovington to Du Bois, 20 May 1906, in Aptheker, *Correspondence*, 1: 118–20; Ovington, *Walls Came Tumbling Down*, 121.

25. Ibid., 43–46; Addie W. Hunton, "The Cosmopolitan Society of Greater New York," *The Voice* (May 1907), 185–86.

26. Ovington, *Walls Came Tumbling Down*, 43–46. Ovington, Du Bois, and James Weldon Johnson joined the Civic Club when it was established in 1917. Although the Club eventually had a tremendous impact on the lives of black New Yorkers, its founders actually debated, at length, allowing Negroes to join. James Weldon Johnson, *Along This Way: The Autobiography of James Weldon Johnson* (1933; New York: Penguin, 1990), 328–29.

27. Ovington, *Walls Came Tumbling Down*, 100–107; Aptheker, ed., *Correspondence of W. E. B. Du Bois*, 1: 144, 147; W. E. B. Du Bois, *Dusk of Dawn: An Essay Toward an Autobiography of a Race Concept* (1940; New Brunswick, New Jersey: Transaction, 1992), 94–95; Connolly, *Ghetto Grows in Brooklyn*, 88.

28. George E. Wibecan, "New York Negro Clubs," a pamphlet of The New York State Commission, National Negro Exposition, Richmond, Virginia (New York: 1915), Schomburg Collection, NYPL. One of the Garnet Club's major events is described in the *Age*, 1 June 1905. The Douglass Club is described in the *Age*, 3 May 1919.

29. *Amsterdam News*, 7 October 1925; *Age*, 20 April 1905.

30. N. Barnett Dodson, "Carlton Avenue Branch of the Brooklyn, N. Y., Young Men's Christian Association," *CAM* (February 1904), 117–18; Connolly, *Ghetto Grows in Brooklyn*, 88.

31. *Age*, 12 October 1905; "Young Women's Christian Association of Brooklyn—Lexington Avenue Branch," *CAM* (February 1906), 99–101.

32. *Age*, 12 October 1905; S. R. S[cottron]., "Evening Industrial School for Brooklyn: Result of the Efforts on the Part of Several Clergymen and Distinguished Citizens—Opposed by a Few," *CAM* (August 1907), 95–96.

The Association of Neighborhood Workers praised Buldley's school during a dinner for Jane Addams of Hull House: "That school in New York which perhaps more than any other does the best work for social service among its pupils is the school on Forty-first street. The principal of this school is Afro-American and so are many of his teachers. Ninety-eight percent of the pupils are Afro-Americans. It is here that we see the effort being made to make the school a social centre for the parent and the child, to stand for that neighborhood idea that this association emphasizes. And the effort has met with success."

See the *Age*, 6 April 1905. Bulkley provided a description of his evening school in a letter to the editor of the *New York Times*. He was responding to the portrayal of Thomas Dixon's *The Clansman* in a neighboring theater. After instructing the *Times* on African Americans' desire to educate and elevate themselves in the face of persistent hate, he noted that his evening program had a thousand men and women and "Not a room in the building is vacant. Even seats for baby pupils and kindergarten tables are occupied. Neither cold nor heat, snow nor moonshine, with all their attendant drawbacks or attractions, can keep these people away. In the theatre the audience is looking at the past; these people are looking into the future. To the one crowd despair; to the other hope." See Foner, *Black Worker*, 5: 37.

33. Calvin B. Holder, "The Causes and Composition of West Indian Immigration to New York City, 1900–1952," *AANYLH*, 11 (1) (January 1987), 7–11.

34. *Age*, 18 March 1909; Bert J. Thomas, "Historical Functions of Caribbean-American Benevolent/Progressive Associations," *AANYLH*, 12 (2) (July 1988), 45–51; Joyce Toney, "The Perpetuation of a Culture of Migration: West Indian American Ties With Home, 1900–1979," Ibid., 13 (1) (January 1989), 41–42, 43.

35. The West Indian Cricket Club won the 1904 title. *Age*, 25 May 1905, 1 June 1905; on sports and leisure, see the *Age* and the *Amsterdam News* throughout the period.

36. Brooklyn Urban League and Lincoln Settlement Association, *Annual Report, 1923*, passim.

37. *Eagle*, 1 April 1915; *Age*, 6 September 1919.

38. Brooklyn Urban League (BUL), *Annual Report, 1919* (Brooklyn: privately printed, 1919), 7–8.

39. BUL and Lincoln Settlement Association, *Annual Report, 1923*, 6–7.

40. BUL and LSA, *Annual Report, 1929*, 5, 17.

41. BUL and LSA, *Annual Report, 1931*, 10.

42. Freeman, *In Transit*, 28; Foner, *Black Worker*, 6: 39–42; *The Complete Report of Mayor LaGuardia's Commission on the Harlem Riot of March 19, 1935* (1935; New York: Arno Press & the New York Times, 1969), 124; *NY Times*, 31 March 1937, 2 November 1938, 8 June 1941.

43. Letter from Malcolm G. Martin, President, National Negro Congress (Brooklyn Council), to Board of Transportation, 22 May 1941; letter from Wm. Jerome Daly, Secretary, to City Council of the City of Chicago, 9 January 1943, in Board of Transportation Records, Box 18, File 1.

44. Office of the Personnel Clerk, Board of Transportation, "All Females (White) by Classification as of December 31, 1944" and "All Females (Negro) by Classification as of December 31, 1944," Board of Transportation Records, Box 18, File 2.

45. Freeman, *In Transit*, 151–54.

46. *Amsterdam News*, 9 September 1925.

47. Black Apprentices in Four National Trades, 1890–1920

Trade	1890	1900	1910	1920
Blacksmith	226	131	178	161
Carpenter	263	123	253	198
Painter	51	85	68	80
Brick Mason	113	83	171	127

Arthur Mann, *LaGuardia: A Fighter Against His Times, 1882–1933* (Chicago: The University of Chicago Press, 1959), 290–91; *NY Times*, 2 November 1938, 2 December 1944, 26 February 1946, 23 September 1946.

48. Both studies found the same pattern of systematic exclusion. NUL, *Negro Membership in American Labor Unions*, 13; Labor Department, National Association for the Advancement of Colored People, *The Negro Wage-Earner and Apprenticeship Training Programs: A Critical Analysis with Recommendations* (New York: NAACP, 1960), 10.

CHAPTER 8

1. *New York Age*, 29 September 1945.

2. Chart titled "RELIEF—OCTOBER, 1933," in the Records of the Bureau of Employment Security, U. S. Employment Service (USES), Records of Lawrence A. Oxley [hereafter Lawrence A. Oxley Papers], "Reports of Investigations of Negro Unemployment and Public Placement Facilities for Negroes, 1937–39, Missouri-North Carolina," RG 183, Box No. 3, United States National Archives.

3. *Brooklyn Daily Eagle*, 1 April 1933.

4. Ibid., 16 March 1931; *The New York Times*, 9 February 1933, 17 January 1933.

5. Mr. [Lawrence A.] Oxley to the Secretary through Dr. Lubin, "Statement on Negro Labor," November 9, 1935, 4–5, in the Lawrence A. Oxley Papers, "Applications and Letters Requesting Employment, 1934–37, A-R," RG 183, Box No. 2; Robert C. Weaver, *The Negro Ghetto* (New York: Harcourt, Brace, 1948), 77. We can forgive the slight geographical inaccuracy of the Urban League report. It was quite common to still refer to Manhattan as New York City and to Brooklyn as if it remained an independent municipality. *NY Times*, 11 June 1931, 18 March 1932, 11 December 1933; Harry Haywood, *Black Bolshevik: Autobiography of an Afro-American Communist* (Chicago: Liberator, 1978), 350; *Golden Jubilee Album of St. Philip's P. E. Church* (Brooklyn: 1949), 41.

6. Major Devine was born George Baker in Georgia around 1880. He came to

Harlem about 1910 and raised money to establish a church on Myrtle Avenue in Bedford, Brooklyn. In 1919, he purchased a home at Sayville, Long Island, and moved his congregation there but remained an active figure in Harlem and Bedford. Partly because of the controversy that followed him to Long Island, he returned to Harlem in 1931 as Father Divine and became a legend and mogul during the Depression. In the 1930s, Divine operated at least two store front Peace Missions in Bedford-Stuyvesant, one on Classon Avenue and Fulton Street and the other at Fulton and Downing Streets. See Rayford W. Logan and Michael R. Winston, eds., *Dictionary of American Negro Biography* (New York: Norton, 1982), 178–80; George H. Hobart, "Survey Bedford-Stuyvesant Area, Brooklyn, N.Y., February–March 1938, for the Bedford and Stuyvesant Ministers' Associations and the Brooklyn Church and Mission Federation" (Brooklyn: privately printed, 1938), 8; Robert Weisbrot, *Father Divine* (Urbana: University of Illinois Press, 1983), *passim*.

7. Arthur Mann, *LaGuardia Comes to Power, 1933* (Chicago: The University of Chicago Press, 1965), 127; *NY Times*, 11 October 1932, 7 November 1932, 11 October 1936, 27 October 1936.

8. Edwin R. Lewinson, *Black Politics in New York City* (New York: Twayne, 1974), 84–85; Jeffrey Nathan Gerson, "Building the Brooklyn Machine: Irish, Jewish and Black Political Succession in Central Brooklyn, 1919–1964" (Doctoral Dissertation, City University of New York, 1990), 183–215.

9. *NY Times*, 26 March 1931, 9 April 1931, 24 April 1931, 12 July 1931, 6 September 1931, 11 April 1933.

10. Mark Naison, *Communists in Harlem During the Depression* (Urbana: University of Illinois Press, 1983), 57–89; Dan T. Carter, *Scottsboro: A Tragedy of the American South* (New York: Oxford University Press, 1971), *passim*; *Eagle* 10 April 1933, 11 April 1933; *NY Times*, 10 April 1933, 11 April 1933, 17 April 1933.

11. Ibid., 12 December 1933.

12. Ibid., 12 January 1937, 13 January 1937, 14 January 1937.

13. *Eagle*, 12 January 1937, 13 January 1937; *NY Times*, 15 January 1937.

14. *Eagle*, 15 January 1937; *NY Times*, 16 January 1937, 7 February 1937, 9 February 1937, 10 February 1937, 11 February 1937, 12 February 1937, 20 February 1937, 20 August 1937.

15. Wibecan was Brooklyn's leading black Republican. In 1912 he formed a borough-wide political organization. He spoke German and was influential in Brooklyn's German community politics. In 1933 he retired as the supervisor of the inquiry department for the Post Office. From 1910 to 1940, he attended all the Republican state conventions and many national conventions and participated in the nomination of candidates. Lewinson, *Black Politics in New York*, 83–84; *NY Times*, 17 January 1937, 22 January 1937.

16. LaGuardia depended far less on "connections" to organized criminals, but one Brooklyn mobster, Joseph "Joe Adonis" Doto, was reported to hold influence over him. Ronald H. Bayor, *Neighbors in Conflict: The Irish, Germans, Jews, and Italians of New York City, 1929–1941*, 2nd ed. (Chicago: University of Illinois Press, 1988), 24–33, 42, 45.

17. Ibid., 98–100, 101, 106.

18. Ibid., 60–62.

19. *NY Times*, 5 February 1932, 15 July 1932, 19 November 1932, 7 July 1933, 23 July 1933, 24 July 1933, 15 April 1934, 6 July 1936, 23 August 1936, 24 May 1940, 29 May 1940, 20 November 1940; Alter F. Landesman, *Brownsville: The Birth, Development and Passing of a Jewish Community in New York* (1969; New York: Bloch, 1971), 321; United States Employment Service, "The Employment Situation in the Shipbuilding and Repair Industry in New York City" (September 1942), in the Records of the War Manpower Commission, Office of the Assistant Executive Director for Program Development, General Records of Julius J. Joseph, 1942–1943, RG 211, Entry 94, Box No. 2, National Archives.

20. M. P. Catherwood, Commissioner, New York State Division of Commerce, and Meredith B. Givens, Director of Research and Statistics, United States Employment Service for New York, "The Problem of War Production and Surplus Labor in New York City," 4, 6, 8, in Julius J. Joseph Papers, RG 211, Entry 94, Box No. 2.

21. *NY Times*, 20 August 1939, 9 November 1941.

22. Robert C. Weaver, "Racial Employment Trends in National Defense," *Phylon* (First quarter, 1942), 23–27; War Manpower Commission, Bureau of Program Planning and Review, Labor Market Division, "Placement Activities, December 1942," 8, 14, in Julius J. Joseph Papers, RG 211, Entry 94, Box No. 1.

23. W. E. B. Du Bois, *Dusk of Dawn: An Essay Toward an Autobiography of a Race Concept* (1940; New Brunswick, New Jersey: Transaction, 1992), 320; Weaver, "Racial Employment Trends in National Defense," 23, 27; Herman D. Bloch, "The Employment Status of the New York Negro in Retrospect," ibid. (Fourth quarter, 1959), 331–36; *NY Times*, 22 October 1940; David F. Noble, *Forces of Production: A Social History of Industrial Automation* (New York: Knopf, 1984), 22. In the Midwest, the war did bring real gains to black workers. See Edward Greer, *Big Steel: Black Politics and Corporate Power in Gary, Indiana* (New York: Monthly Review, 1979), 93–95.

24. Office memorandum from Joy P. Davis to Mr. John A. Davis, May 22, 1944, in Records of the Committee on Fair Employment Practices, Division of Review & Analysis, "Tension Files," 1943–45, Montana-New York, RG 228, Entry 37, Box No. 450, National Archives.

25. Weaver, "Employment Trends," 26; Harry M. Whittleton (Associate Head Inspector, Ordnance Materiel, War Department, Army Service Forces, New York Ordnance District), "Historical Data—Murray Manufacturing Corporation; 60 m/m, M49A2, 81 m/m, M43A1; Welded Type, Trench Mortar Shell" (Brooklyn:

New York Ordnance District, 15 November 1945), 29, collection of the Brooklyn Historical Society.

26. *Age*, 27 October 1945; Weaver, "Employment Trends," 29–30.

27. *NY Times*, 2 April 1946, 12 June 1946, 11 January 1947.

CHAPTER 9

1. *New York Post*, 17 July 1964; *The New York Times*, 17 July 1964; Langston Hughes, "The Harlem Riot—1964," in John Henrik Clarke, ed., *Harlem: A Community in Transition* (1964; New York: Citadell, 1969), 214–20.

2. *NY Times*, 19 July 1964; *Post*, 20 July 1964.

3. *NY Times*, 21 July 1964, 22 July 1964, 23 July 1964; *Post*, 22 July 1964, 23 July 1964.

4. *NY Times*, 23 July 1964.

5. James Weldon Johnson, *Black Manhattan* (1930; New York: Ayer, 1990), 59; Bureau of the Census, *Negroes in the United States 1920–32* (Washington, DC: Government Printing Office, 1935), 68; Harold X. Connolly, *A Ghetto Grows in Brooklyn* (New York: New York University Press, 1977), 54–55. Looking at Pittsburgh, Peter Gottlieb has also found that there was no delineated Negro ghetto before 1930. See *Making Their Own Way: Southern Blacks' Migration to Pittsburgh, 1916–30* (Urbana: University of Illinois Press, 1987), 67. Joe William Trotter, Jr., *Black Milwaukee: The Making of an Industrial Proletariat, 1915–45* (Urbana: University of Illinois Press, 1985), 3.

6. Brooklyn Tenement House Committee and Herbert S. Swan, *The Progress of Housing Reform in Brooklyn: A Report of the Tenement House Committee of the Brooklyn Bureau of Charities and a Study of Land Overcrowding in Brooklyn* (Brooklyn: Bureau of Charities, ca. 1918), 13, 22–23, 36–39, 14–15; *The Survey*, 28 April 1917; John C. Gebhart, *Housing Standards in Brooklyn: An Intensive Study of the Housing Records of 3227 Workingmen's Families* (Brooklyn: Bureau of Charities, 1918), 3, 59. In 1901 a then-new Tenement House Law was passed. It made "dumbell" tenements illegal.

7. *NY Times*, 1 January 1924, 3 April 1925, 17 May 1925, 16 January 1927; Oscar Handlin, *The Newcomers: Negroes and Puerto Ricans in a Changing Metropolis* (Cambridge: Harvard University Press, 1959), 31; Connolly, *Ghetto Grows in Brooklyn*, 73–74. Gilbert Osofsky noted the impact of public transportation decisions on Harlem real estate. See, *Harlem: The Making of a Ghetto: Negro New York, 1890–1930*, 2nd ed. (New York: Harper & Row, 1971), 87–89.

8. BUL, *Annual Report, 1919*, 2–3; Gebhart, *Housing Standards in Brooklyn*, 46–50; BUL-Lincoln Settlement, Inc., *Annual Report, 1929*, 12.

9. Beginning in 1917 extension courses of the City College of New York were offered at Brooklyn's Boys' High School. Two thousand people were registered in that program when plans for the new university were announced. *NY Times*, 25 April 1926,

16 May 1926, 21 December 1926, 17 July 1927, 31 July 1927, 7 August 1927; Connolly, *Ghetto Grows in Brooklyn*, 59, 69.

10. *New York Amsterdam News*, 19 August 1925, 9 September 1925.

11. Gebhart, *Housing Standards in Brooklyn*, 50; *Amsterdam News*, 5 August 1925, 4 December 1929; W. E. B. Du Bois to Alexander Bing, 24 April 1929, Alexander M. Bing to W. E. B. Du Bois, 29 April 1929, in Herbert Aptheker, ed., *The Correspondence of W.E.B. Du Bois*, 3 Vols. (Amherst: University of Massachusetts Press, 1973), 1: 401–2; W. E. B. Du Bois, *Dusk of Dawn: An Essay Toward an Autobiography of a Race Concept* (1940; New Brunswick, New Jersey: Transaction, 1992), 185–86.

12. *Schechter Poultry Corp. v. United States*, in Henry Steele Commager, ed., *Documents of American History*, 4th ed. (New York: Appleton-Century-Crofts, 1948), 463; Alter F. Landesman, *Brownsville: The Birth, Develoment and Passing of a Jewish Community in New York* (New York: Bloch, 1969), 313–15; William Leuchtenberg, *Franklin D. Roosevelt and the New Deal, 1932–1940* (New York: Harper & Row, 1963), 145–46, 150.

13. *NY Times*, 25 December 1932; Brooklyn Real Estate Board, *Year Book and Diary for 1935* (Brooklyn: privately published, 1935), 75, 78.

14. Bert J. Thomas, "Historical Functions of Caribbean-American Benevolent/Progressive Associations," *Afro-Americans in New York Life and History*, hereafter *AANYLH*, 12 (2) (July 1988), 51; Clyde G. Atwell, *The Paragon Story (1939–1969)* (Brooklyn: privately printed, ca. 1976), 13–21, 63–68. Information on the Siloam credit union is available in the Milton A. Galamison Papers, Schomburg Center, NYPL.

15. Brooklyn Edison, *Brooklyn Market Survey* (Brooklyn: Brooklyn Edison Company, Inc., 1936), 13–14.

16. Ibid., 20.

17. In 1931 the *Eagle* first referred to the area as Bedford-Stuyvesant. See Ernest Quimby, "Bedford-Stuyvesant," in Rita Seiden Miller, ed., *Brooklyn USA: The Fourth Largest City in America* (New York: Brooklyn College Press, 1979), 230.

18. *Bedford Home Owners News*, July 1936, September 1936, October 1936.

19. *NY Times*, 24 April 1932; *Bedford Home Owners News*, October 1936.

20. Ibid., September 1936; C. Lowell Harriss, *History and Policies of the Home Owners' Loan Corporation* (New York: National Bureau of Economic Research, 1951), 51–57.

21. Ibid., 3–6; Thomas J. Sugrue, *The Origins of the Urban Crisis: Race and Inequality in Postwar Detroit* (Princeton: Princeton University Press, 1996), 61; "Explanation of Security Area Map," Section V of "Brooklyn - New York Security Map and Area Description Folder," in the Records of the Federal Home Loan Bank Board, Home Owners' Loan Corporation, Records Relating to the City Survey File, 1935–40, New York, RG195, Box No. 58, United States National Archives.

22. Ibid.

23. "Security Area Descriptions," Section VI, HOLC Records.

24. Ibid.

25. Ibid; Burton B. Turkus and Sid Feder, *Murder Inc.: The Story of "the syndicate"* (New York: Farrar, Straus, and Young, 1951), 4, 13–14, 23, 27; Jenna Weissman Joselit, *Our Gang: Jewish Crime and the New York Jewish Community, 1900–1940* (Bloomington: Indiana University Press, 1983), 168–69; Landesman, *Brownsville*, 329–35.

26. Jerry Della Femina and Charles Sopkin, *An Italian Grows in Brooklyn* (Boston: Little, Brown, 1978), 63; "Security Area Descriptions," Section VI, HOLC Records.

27. *Brooklyn Daily Eagle*, 22 January 1937.

28. Security Area Descriptions," Section VI, HOLC Records.

29. Brooklyn Council for Social Planning, *Growing Up in Brooklyn: A Report of Brooklyn's Little White House Conference on Children and Youth* (Brooklyn: 1951), 80.

30. "Summary of a Survey of New York," "Security Area Descriptions," HOLC Papers; *NY Times*, 8 November 1941, 15 November 1941, 25 November 1941.

31. In fact, by 1941, almost 40% of the city's black population was dependent upon relief or temporary government jobs for support. That was largely due to discrimination in New Deal employment programs. *NY Times,* 17 March 1941, 8 November 1941, 26 November 1941.

32. Quimby, "Bedford-Stuyvesant," 231; *NY Times*, 13 March 1939, 15 November 1941, 25 November 1941.

33. Emphasis mine. Kings County Grand Jury, "Presentment of the August 1943 Grand Jury of Kings County In the Investigation of Crime and Disorderly Conditions of the Bedford-Stuyvesant Area of Brooklyn" (Brooklyn: 1943), 1, 2–3, 4–7, 12.

34. Ibid.

35. *NY Times*, 16 November 1943; Robert Moses, Commissioner to Hon. F. H. LaGuardia, Mayor of the City of New York, 19 November 1943, in "Recreation and Related Projects: Bedford-Stuyvesant Area," LIHS: Brooklyn Pamphlets, The Brooklyn Historical Society.

36. *NY Times*, 22 November 1943; *Eagle*, 23 November 1943.

37. Ibid., 1 November 1943, 22 November 1943, 23 November 1943; *NY Times*, 25 November 1943, 27 November 1943, 7 December 1943.

38. George H. Hobart, "Survey Bedford-Stuyvesant Area, Brooklyn, N.Y., February–March 1938, for the Bedford and Stuyvesant Ministers' Associations and the Brooklyn Church and Mission Federation" (Brooklyn: privately printed, 1938), 3, 16.

39. Atwell, *Paragon Story*, 15, 24–25, 89.

40. *New York Age*, 24 November 1945; Milton J. Goell, *A Post-War Plan for Brownsville* (Brooklyn: Brownsville Neighborhood Council, 1944), 7, 10–13, 16–27, 30.

41. *NY Times*, 31 July 1945, 21 April 1946.

42. Ibid., 6 January 1946, 21 Jaunuary 1946, 29 January 1946, 27 February 1946, 11 March 1947, 18 May 1947.

43. The Mortgage Conference of New York, "Population Survey No. 3-B, Brooklyn"

(New York: The Mortgage Conference, 1945); *Eagle*, 7 August 1946; *NY Times*, 7 August 1946.

44. MCNY, "Population Survey No. 3-B."

45. Italics mine. *Eagle*, 7 August 1946; *NY Times*, 7 August 1946.

46. Author's emphasis. Quimby, "Bedford-Stuyvesant," 232.

47. *NY Times*, 6 November 1944.

48. Ibid., 6 April 1944, 11 April 1946, 2 June 1946.

49. Ibid., 25 August 1947.

50. Ibid., 4 May 1949, 12 February 1950, 9 June 1950.

51. The Citizens Union demanded that Mayor Wagner and Housing Authority chair Phillip J. Cruise stop reinforcing segregation by placing public housing in Negro and Puerto Rican areas. Ibid., 30 July 1956. Joe William Trotter, Jr. has noted a similar relationship between public and private housing construction in Milwaukee. *Black Milwaukee*, 183. For an interesting critique of race and public housing, see Robert C. Weaver, "Racial Policy in Public Housing," *Phylon* (Second quarter, 1940), 149–61.

52. Sam Bass Warner, Jr., *The Urban Wilderness: A History of the American City* (New York: Harper & Row, 1972), 244; Sugrue, *Origins of the Urban Crisis*, 86; The Mayor's Committee for Better Housing of the City of New York, "Report of the Subcommittee on Urban Redevelopment, Including Slum Clearance, Neighborhood Conservation, and Rehabilitation" (August 1955), 5, in the Robert C. Weinberg Papers, Long Island University Library, Brooklyn Campus, Box LXXIV, Folder 1; *NY Times*, 30 June 1959. Through the 1960s African Americans and Puerto Ricans struggled to stop the Committee from further segregating the city. This conflict frequently played out in the Rockaways and the West Side and Lower East Side of Manhattan, see Ibid., 11 November 1959, 22 November 1959, 21 June 1961, 16 May 1962, 30 May 1962, 23 June 1962. Many Brooklyn and area organizations—including the Bedford-Stuyvesant Neighborhood Council, the Bedford YMCA and Professional Men's Luncheon Club, the Central Brooklyn Coordinating Council, the Congress of Puerto Rican Municipalities, the Puerto Rican Association for Community Affairs, the Puerto Rican-Hispanic Leadership Forum, the Stuyvesant Community Center, and the Urban League of Greater New York—combined to oppose the construction of fancy homes and luxury apartments at Breezy Point. They wanted a public park built there so that many ethnic and socioethnic groups could have access to the area. The city eventually agreed to the demands. Committee for a Park at Breezy Point, "Information Kit: Breezy Point Park"; also a pamphlet titled "Stop the Bulldozers!" Weinberg Papers, Box LXXXII, Folders 4–5. *NY Times*, 15 March 1960, 19 October 1962, 31 October 1962, 1 November 1962, 12 November 1962, 3 June 1963. On African Americans' early optimism over slum clearance, see B. T. McGraw, "The Housing Act of 1954 and Implications for Minorities," *Phylon* No. 2 (1940), 171–82.

53. *NY Times*, 20 August 1939, 22 September 1946, 31 January 1947, 15 May

1948, 16 May 1948, 22 July 1948.

54. Ibid., 17 May 1939, 23 January 1940, 14 April 1940, 30 July 1942, 4 December 1943, 7 April 1945, 8 April 1945, 25 April 1945, 12 August 1945, 24 September 1945.

55. Ibid., 24 October 1945, 11 April 1947; *Eagle*, 11 April 1947.

56. *NY Times*, 10 November 1958.

57. Final Report of the Mayor's Committee for Better Housing of the City of New York, "65 Steps Toward Better Housing For All New Yorkers" (September 1955), 16–19, and "63 Steps Toward Better Housing For All New Yorkers" (September 1955), 9–10, Weinberg Papers, Box LXXIV, Folder 1.

58. The homeownership rate is the owner-occupied units as a percentage of all units. Caribbean Research Center, *Statistical Analysis of Persons of Caribbean Ancestry: Basic Democgraphic, Social and Economic Profile Based on 1990 Census Data*, Part 1 (Brooklyn: CRC, Medgar Evers College, 1993), 81–99; Bureau of the Census, *1990 Census of Population and Housing*, 1990 CPH-3-245H (Washington, DC: 1993), 923.

59. Department of City Planning, New York City, *Demographic Profiles: A Portrait of New York City's Community Districts from the 1980 & 1990 Censuses of Population and Housing* (New York: Department of City Planning, 1992), 90–161.

60. Jane Jacobs, *The Death and Life of Great American Cities* (New York: Vintage, 1961), 196–97.

61. William K. Tabb, *The Political Economy of the Black Ghetto* (New York: Norton, 1970), 16–17.

62. *NY Times*, 25 April 1956, 15 November 1956, 7 May 1961; *Report of the National Advisory Commission on Civil Disorders* (New York: Bantam, 1968), 243; Karl E. Taeuber and Alma F. Taeuber, *Negroes in Cities: Residential Segregation and Neighborhood Change* (New York: Atheneum, 1969), 57.

63. Bureau of the Census, *Census of Population: 1960*, Vol. 1, Part 34, 16; New York Department of City Planning, *Bulletin* (22 November 1954), 8; *NY Times*, 27 December 1953, 29 July 1955, 18 August 1958.

64. Ibid., 30 August 1947, 6 March 1944, 6 March 1950, 23 August 1952, 4 June 1944, 23 June 1955, 29 June 1955, 25 October 1955, 23 October 1960, 23 November 1961, 23 August 1962, 13 October 1962; Joseph Palisi, "The Brooklyn Navy Yard," in Miller, *Brooklyn USA*, 122; Will Anderson, "The Breweries of Brooklyn: An Informal History," in Ibid., 133. On Du Bois return to Brooklyn in the early 1950s and his home at 31 Grace Court, see Shirley Graham Du Bois, *His Day is Marching On: A Memoir of W. E. B. Du Bois* (New York: Lippincott, 1971), 177–96; W. E. B. Du Bois, *The Autobiography of W. E. B. Du Bois: A Soliloquy on Viewing My Life from the Last Decade of Its First Century* (New York: International Publishers, 1968), passim.

65. *NY Times*, 1 January 1960, 18 February 1960, 24 February 1960, 21 September 1960.

66. Hospital Council of Greater New York, "Hospital Needs of the Bedford-Stuyvesant Area in Brooklyn" (December 1953), 2.

67. The Community Council of Greater New York, *Brooklyn Communities: Population Characteristics and Neighborhood Social Resources*, 2 Vols. (New York: 1959), I: xviii, 98–99, 105, 106–7. For instance, the census tracts at the north of the Bedford-Stuyvesant area were as much as 99% white while at the neighborhood's southernmost perimeter tracts with a 98% black population could be found. See *United States Census of Housing: 1950: Block Statistics, Brooklyn Borough, New York City*, Vol. 5, Part 127 (Washington, D. C.: Government Printing Office, 1952), 5–8.

68. Milton A. Galamison, "Bedford-Stuyvesant–Harlem Across the River," in John Henrik Clarke, ed., *Harlem USA* (1964; New York: Macmillan, 1971), 203–16.

69. Oliver Pilat and Jo Ranson, *Sodom by the Sea: An Affectionate History of Coney Island* (Garden City, New York: Doubleday, Doran, 1941), 333–34; Albert I. Gordon, *Jews in Suburbia* (1959; Connecticut: Greenwood, 1973), 9.

70. *Amsterdam News*, 5 April 1969.

71. Jonathan Rieder, *Canarsie: The Jews and Italians of Brooklyn Against Liberalism* (Cambridge: Harvard University Press, 1985), 57–131, passim. Thomas Sugrue has also found a reign of violence against black homebuyers and the rise of white anti-liberalism in Postwar Detroit. See, *Origins of the Urban Crisis*, 209–58.

72. Michael Stephens, *The Brooklyn Book of the Dead* (Norman, Illinois: Dalkey Archive, 1994), 11.

73. Atwell, *Paragon Story*, 97.

CHAPTER 10

1. The Center for Urban Education, *Community Attitudes in Bedford-Stuyvesant: An Area Study* (Summer 1967), 23, 65–69, 76.

2. Milton A. Galamison, "What Child is This?" sermon delivered 29 December 1963 at Siloam Presbyterian Church, Milton A. Galamison Papers, Box 5, File 26, Schomburg Collection, NYPL; Clarence Taylor, *Knocking at Our Own Door: Milton A. Galamison and the Struggle to Integrate New York City Schools* (New York: Columbia University Press, 1997), 47, 62.

3. Ibid., 60; Education Committee, Brooklyn Branch of the NAACP, "Annual Report," 29 November 1956; Minutes from a meeting of the Hon. Cecile Ruth Sands (and various Board of Education members) with the Brooklyn Branch NAACP and local parents, 9 June 1958; Milton A. Galamison, "Testimony," before the New York City Planning Commission, City Hall, 17 October 1958, all in Galamison Papers, Box 14, File 98.

4. Taylor, *Knocking at Our Own Door*, 79–83, 92–97, 104–08; Milton A. Galamison to Hon. Robert F. Wagner, 1 March 1960; Milton A. Galamison, "An Analysis of the Board of Education Open Enrollment Policy," in Galamison Papers, Box 14, File 99.

5. Taylor, *Knocking at Our Own Door*, 146; *New York Post*, 4 February 1964; *The New York Times*, 4 February 1964; Galamison, "Bedford-Stuyvesant," 196–97. In his

pioneer study following the 1963 Harlem riots, Kenneth B. Clark noted the segregation of inner-city schools and the detrimental impact they had on the life chances of black people. *Dark Ghetto: Dilemmas of Social Power,* 2nd ed. (1965; Middletown, Connecticut: Wesleyan University Press, 1989), 111–53.

6. *NY Times,* 16 March 1964, 23 March 1964, 3 April 1964, 19 May 1964, 11 November 1965; Taylor, *Knocking at Our Own Door,* 146–58.

7. Martin Mayer, *The Teachers Strike: New York, 1968* (New York: Harper & Row, 1969), passim; Taylor, *Knocking at Our Own Door,* 176–206; Charles Green and Basil Wilson, *The Struggle for Black Empowerment in New York City: Beyond the Politics of Pigmentation* (New York: Praeger, 1989), 23–26.

8. Jonathan Kozol, *Savage Inequalities: Children in America's Schools* (New York: Basic Books, 1991), 83–132; Joe William Trotter, Jr., *Black Milwaukee: The Making of an Industrial Proletariat, 1915–45* (Urbana: University of Illinois Press, 1985), xi; Taylor, *Knocking at Our Own Door,* 52, 66.

9. New York City Commission on Human Rights, *The Ethnic Survey: A Report on the Number and Distribution of Negroes, Puerto Ricans and Others Employed by the City of New York* (New York: 1964), table 1.1–1.68, passim.

10. Ibid.

11. U. S. Department of Labor, Bureau of Labor Statistics, *The New York Puerto Rican: Patterns of Work Experience* (Regional Reports, Poverty Area Profiles, no. 19, May 1971), 1, 21–22; Equal Employment Opportunity Commission, *Employment Profiles of Women and Minorities in 23 Metropolitan Areas, 1974* (Washington, DC: EEOC, 1976), 198–211; *Report of the Mayor's Commission on Hispanic Concerns* (December 10, 1986), 97; [New York City Mayor's] Citywide Equal Employment Opportunity Committee, *Equal Employment Opportunity in New York City Government 1977–1987* (October 1988), 5–6.

12. Ibid., 37, 42.

13. *Report of the Mayor's Commission on Hispanic Concerns,* 95; Equal Employment Opportunity Commission, *Job Patterns for Minorities and Women in State and Local Government: 1997* (Washington, DC: EEOC, 1998), 166–67, 252.

14. Jack Star, "A National Disgrace: What Unions do to Blacks," *Look* (November 12, 1968), 32, No. 23, 33–37.

15. Walter W. Stafford, *Closed Labor Markets: Underrepresentation of Blacks, Hispanics and Women in New York City's Core Industries and Jobs* (New York: Community Service Society of New York, January 1985), vii–xvi, 76–80, passim; Equal Employment Opportunity Commission, *Job Patterns for Minorities and Women in Private Industry: 1990* (Washington, DC: EEOC, 1991), 275.

16. Mercer L. Sullivan, *"Getting Paid": Youth Crime and Work in the Inner City* (Ithaca: Cornell University Press, 1989), 20–22, 32–52.

17. Jerry Della Femina and Charles Sopkin, *An Italian Grows in Brooklyn* (Boston:

Little, Brown, 1978), 29; Sullivan, "*Getting Paid*," 72–92, 96, 178–79, 206–11

EPILOGUE

1. *New York Times*, 1 March 1960, 1 February 1962.

2. *New York Post*, 10 April 1964; *NY Times*, 10 April 1964.

3. Ibid., 11 April 1964, 13 April 1964, 17 April 1964.

4. *Post*, 12 April 1964, 13 April 1964; *NY Times*, 11 April 1964, 12 April 1964, 13 April 1964, 14 April 1964, 15 April 1964.

5. Ibid., 16 April 1964, 19 April 1964, 20 April 1964, 21 April 1964; *Post*, 16 April 1964.

6. Ibid., 22 April 1964; *NY Times*, 22 April 1964, 23 April 1964.

7. Milton A. Galamison, "The World of Success," sermon delivered 14 June 1964 at Siloam Presbyterian Church, Galamison Papers, Box 5, File 26, Schomburg Collection, NYPL; *NY Times*, 24 April 1964.

8. W. E. Burghardt Du Bois, *Darkwater: Voices from within the Veil* (1920; New York: AMS Press, 1969), 94. See also, Barbara J. Fields, "Ideology and Race in American History," in J. Morgan Kousser and James M. McPherson, eds., *Region, Race, and Reconstruction: Essays in Honor of C. Vann Woodward* (New York: Oxford University Press, 1982), 143–77, from which this approach to the subject is adopted.

9. Richard Williams, *Hierarchical Structures and Social Value: The Creation of Black and Irish Identities in the United States* (New York: Cambridge University Press, 1990), 1–3, 131–32.

10. *NY Times*, 3 August 1964, 17 April 1965, 26 April 1965, 16 May 1965,

Bibliography

MANUSCRIPT AND ARCHIVAL COLLECTIONS

Brooklyn Collection, Brooklyn Public Library (Grand Army Plaza).
Brooklyn Pamphlets, Brooklyn Collection, The Brooklyn Historical Society.
(Records of the) Bureau of Customs, U. S. National Archives (New York).
(Records of the) Bureau of Employment Security, U. S. Employment Service, U.S. National Archives.
(Records of the) Committee on Fair Employment Practices, U.S. National Archives.
Duyckinck Family Papers, New York State Archives.
(Records of the) Federal Home Loan Bank Board, U.S. National Archives.
Fisher Howe Papers, New-York Historical Society.
(Records of the) Internal Revenue Service, U. S. National Archives-New York.
Kellogg Diaries/ Kellogg Papers, New-York Historical Society.
Meserole Family Papers, New York State Archives.
Milton A. Galamison Papers, Schomburg Collection, NYPL.
New York Board of Transportation Records, New York Transit Museum Archives.
(Records of the) New York Manumission Society, New-York Historical Society.
(Records of the) New York State Office of the Auditor of the Canal Department, New York State Archives.
(Records of the) Office of the Treasurer, New York Colony, New York State Archives.
Pierrepont Family Papers, New York State Archives.
The Rapalje Papers, New-York Historical Society.
(Records of the) War Manpower Commission, U.S. National Archives.
Robert C. Weinberg Papers, Long Island University Library, Brooklyn Campus.
Schenck Family Papers, New-York Historical Society.
Williamson [Lyons] Family Papers, Schomburg Collection, NYPL.
Van Nostrand Family Papers, New York State Archives.

PERIODICALS

The Anti-Slavery Examiner.
The Anti-Slavery Reporter.
Bedford Home Owners News.
Brooklyn Monthly.
The Brooklyn Daily Eagle.
The Brooklyn Daily Eagle Almanac.
The Brooklyn Daily Times.
The Brooklyn Sunday Sun.
The Century Magazine.
The Colored American.
The Colored American Magazine.
The Crisis.
The [New York] Daily Advertiser; Political, Commercial, and Historical.
The Independent Gazette; or the New-York Journal Revised.
The Liberator.
The Long-Island Star.
The New York Age.
The New York Amsterdam News.
The New York Daily Tribune.
The New-York Evening Post.
The New York Herald Tribune.
The New York Post.
The New York Times.
Opportunity.
The Survey.
Valentine's Manual of Old New York.
The Voice [of the Negro].
The Weekly Advocate.
The Weekly Anglo African.
The [New York] White Man's Newspaper.

GOVERNMENT PUBLICATIONS.

Acts Relating to the City of Brooklyn, and the Ordinances Thereof; Together with an Appendix, Containing the Old Charters, Statistical Information, &C. &C.. Brooklyn: A. Spooner & Son, 1840.

"An Act to Consolidate the Cities of Brooklyn and Williamsburgh and the Town of Bushwick into One Municipal Government, and to Incorporate the Same." Passed April 17, 1854. Brooklyn: I. Van Anden, 1854.

Bishop, William C. comp. *Manual of the Common Council of Brooklyn for 1859–60.* Brooklyn: George C. Bennett, 1859.

———. *Manual of the Common Council of the City of Brooklyn for 1861–2.* Brooklyn: George C. Bennett, 1861.

———. *Manual of the Common Council of the City of Brooklyn for 1871.* Brooklyn: Arthur Brown, 1871.

Bureau of the Census. *Census of Population: 1900–1990.*

———. *Statistics of Women at Work.* Washington, DC: Goverment Printing Office, 1907.

———. *Heads of Families at the First Census of the United States taken in the Year 1790: New York.* Washington, DC: Government Printing Office, 1908.

———. Bureau of the Census. *Negroes in the United States, 1920–32: Retail Business.* Washington, DC: Government Printing Office, 1934.

———. *United States Census of Housing: 1950: Block Statistics, Brooklyn Borough, New York City,* Vol. 5, Part 127. Washington, D. C.: Government Printing Office, 1952.

———. *Negro Population, 1790–1915.* Washington, DC: Government Printing Office, 1918.

———. *Negroes in the United States 1920–32.* Washington, DC: Government Printing Office, 1935.

———. *Statistical Abstract of the United States, 1971.*

———. *1990 Census of Population and Housing: Population and Housing Characteristics for Census Tracts and Block Numbering Areas: New York, NY PMSA,* Section 2. Washington, DC: Government Printing Office, 1993.

Census of Brooklyn, 1801. Long Island, New York Census, 1801, Census of Kings County, collection of the New York Historical Society.

[New York City Mayor's] Citywide Equal Employment Opportunity Committee. *Equal Employment Opportunity in New York City Government 1977–1987.* October 1988.

[Committee Investigating Seditious Activities,] *Revolutionary Radicalism, Its History, Purpose and Tactics, with an Exposition and Discussion on the Steps Being Taken and Required to Curb It: Being the Report of the Joint Legislative Committee Investigating Seditious Activities, Filed April 24, 1920, in the Senate of the State of New York.* 2 vols. Albany: J. B. Lyon, 1920.

The Community Council of Greater New York. *Brooklyn Communities: Population Characteristics and Neighborhood Social Resources.* 2 vols. New York: 1959.

Department of City Planning, New York City. *Demographic Profiles: A Portrait of New York City's Community Districts from the 1980 & 1990 Censuses of Population and Housing.* New York: Department of City Planning, 1992.

Equal Employment Opportunity Commission. *Employment Profiles of Women and Minorities in 23 Metropolitan Areas, 1974.* Washington, DC: EEOC, 1976.

———. *Job Patterns for Minorities and Women in Private Industry: 1990.* Washington, DC: EEOC, 1991.

———. *Job Patterns for Minorities and Women in State and Local Government: 1997.* Washington, DC: EEOC, 1998.

General Sessions–New York, August Term, 1808. *The Commissioners of the Almshouse v. Alexander Whistelo. a black man,* Schomburg Collection, NYPL.

Hospital Council of Greater New York. "Hospital Needs of the Bedford-Stuyvestant Area in Brooklyn." New York: December 1953.

[Kings County Grand Jury,] "Presentment of the August 1943 Grand Jury of Kings County In the Investigation of Crime and Disorderly Conditions of the Bedford-Stuyvesant Area of Brooklyn." Brooklyn: 1943.

[The Mayor's Commission on the Harlem Riots]. *The Complete Report of Mayor LaGuardia's Commission on the Harlem Riot of March 19, 1935.* 1935; New York: Arno & The New York Tmes, 1969.

[The Mayor's Commission on Hispanic Concerns]. *Report of the Mayor's Commission on Hispanic Concerns.* December 10, 1986.

The Mayor's Committee for Better Housing of the City of New York, "65 Steps Toward Better Housing For All New Yorkers." September 1955.

———. "63 Steps Toward Better Housing For All New Yorkers." September 1955.

Mayor's Office. "Civil Service Regulations of the City of Brooklyn." prescribed by the Hon. Seth Low 15 August 1884 and effected 12 September 1884.

McCloskey, Henry comp. *Manual of the Common Council of the City of Brooklyn for 1866.* Brooklyn: Arthur Brown, 1866.

Report of the National Advisory Commission on Civil Disorders. New York: Bantam, 1968.

New York City Commission on Human Rights. *The Ethnic Survey: A Report on the Number and Distribution of Negroes, Puerto Ricans and Others Employed by the City of New York.* New York: 1964.

New York Department of City Planning. *Bulletin.*

New York State Library. *Calendar of Council Minutes, 1668–1783.* Albany: University of the State of New York, March 1902.

E. B. O'Callaghan. *The Documentary History of the State of New York; Arranged Under Direction of the Hon. Christopher Morgan, Secretary of State.* 4 vols. Albany: Weed, Parsons, 1849.

———. comp. *Laws and Ordinances of New Netherland, 1638–1674.* Albany: Weed, Parsons, 1868.

Paltsits, Victor Hugo ed. *Minutes of the Executive Council of the Province of New York: Administration of Francis Lovelace, 1668–1673.* 2 vols. Albany: State of New York, 1910.

Return of the Whole Number of Persons within the Several Districts of the United States,

According to "An Act Providing for the Enumeration of the Inhabitants of the United States." *Passed March the First, One Thousand Seven Hundred and Ninety-One.* Philadelphia: Childs and Swaine, 1791.

[Senate of the State of New York,] *The Journal of the Legislative Council of the Colony of New-York. Began the 9th day of April, 1691; and Ended the 27 of September, 1743.* Published by Order of the Senate of the State of New-York. Albany: Weed, Parsons, 1861.

U. S. Department of Commerce. *Historical Statistics of the United States: Colonial Times to 1970,* Part II. Washington, DC: Government Printing Office, 1975.

U. S. Department of Labor, Bureau of Labor Statistics. *The New York Puerto Rican: Patterns of Work Experience.* Regional Reports, Poverty Area Profiles, Number 19, May 1971.

Whittleton, Harry M. Associate Head Inspector, Ordnance Materiel, War Department, Army Service Forces, New York Ordnance District. "Historical Data–Murray Manufacturing Corporation; 60 m/m, M49A2, 81 m/m, M43A1; Welded Type, Trench Mortar Shell." Brooklyn: New York Ordnance District, 15 November 1945, 29, collection of the Brooklyn Historical Society.

Wright, Carroll D. *The Slums of Baltimore, Chicago, New York, and Philadelphia: Seventh Special Report of the Commissioner of Labor.* 1894; reprint: New York: Negro Universities Press, 1969.

AUTOBIOGRAPHIES, DIARIES, LETTERS, AND JOURNALS

Aptheker, Herbert ed. *The Correspondence of W.E.B. Du Bois.* 3 vols. Amherst: University of Massachusetts Press, 1973.

Billington, Ray Allen ed. *The Journal of Charlotte L. Forten: A Free Negro in the Slave Era.* 1953; New York: Collier, 1961.

Child, L. Maria. *Letters From New-York.* New York: Charles S. Francis, 1843.

Della Femina, Jerry and Charles Sopkin. *An Italian Grows in Brooklyn.* Boston: Little, Brown, 1978.

Douglass, Frederick. *My Bondage and My Freedom.* 1855; New York: Dover, 1969.

Bois, Shirley Graham Du. *His Day is Marching On: A Memoir of W. E. B. Du Bois.* New York: J. B. Lippincott, 1971.

Bois, W. E. Burghardt Du. *Darkwater: Voices from within the Veil.* 1920; New York: AMS Press, 1969.

———. *Dusk of Dawn: An Essay Toward an Autobiography of a Race Concept.* 1940; New Brunswick, New Jersey: Transaction, 1992.

———. *The Autobiography of W. E. B. Du Bois: A Soliloquy on Viewing My Life from the Last Decade of Its First Century.* New York: International Publishers, 1968.

"Letters of Negro Migrants of 1916–1918." *Journal of Negro History.* July 1919.

"Additional Letters of Negro Migrants of 1916–1918." *Journal of Negro History.*

October 1919.

Haywood, Harry. *Black Bolshevik: Autobiography of an Afro-American Communist.* Chicago: Liberator, 1978.

Hodges, Willis Augustus. *Free Man of Color: The Autobiography of Willis Augustus Hodges,* edited with an introduction by Willard B. Gatewood, Jr. Knoxville: University of Tennessee Press, 1982.

Holloway, Emory and Vernolian Shwarz, eds. *I Sit and Look Out: Editorials from the Brooklyn Daily Times by Walt Whitman.* New York: Columbia University Press, 1932.

Howe, Elizabeth Leavitt "My Early and Later Days: Their Story for My Children and Grandchildren." unpublished manuscript, 1898, collection of the New-York Historical Society.

Johnson, James Weldon. *Along This Way: The Autobiography of James Weldon Johnson.* 1933; New York: Penguin, 1990.

Lyons, Maritcha Remond "Memories of Yesterdays, All of Which I Saw and Part of Which I Was: An Autobiography." unpublished manuscript, ca. 1924, Schomburg Collection, NYPL.

Miller, Edwin Haviland ed. *Walt Whitman: The Correspondence.* New York: New York University Press, 1961.

Nevins, Allan and Milton Halsey Thomas, eds. *The Diary of George Templeton Strong.* 4 vols. New York: Macmillan, 1952.

Ovington, Mary White. *The Walls Came Tumbling Down.* 1947; New York: Schocken, 1947.

Pennington, James W. C. *The Fugitive Blacksmith; or, Events in the History of James W. C. Pennington, Pastor of A Presbyterian Church, New York, Formerly a Slave in the State of Maryland, United States,* 2nd. ed. London: Charles Gilpin, 1849, in *Five Slave Narratives: A Compendium.* New York: Arno and The New York Times, 1968.

Racine, Philip N. ed. *Piedmont Farmer: The Journals of David Golightly Harris, 1855–1870.* Knoxville: University of Tennessee Press, 1990.

Redpath, James. *Echoes of Harper's Ferry.* 1860; New York: Negro Universities Press, 1970.

Tappan, Lewis. *The Life of Arthur Tappan.* 1871; Westport, Connecticut: Negro Universities Press, 1970.

Truth, Sojourner. *Narrative of Sojourner Truth; A Bondswoman of Olden Time, Emancipated by the New York Legislature in the Early Part of the Present Century; With a History of Her Labor and Correspondence Drawn from Her "Book of Life".* 1878; New York: Arno and The New York Times, 1968.

Whitman, Walt. *Autobiographia, or The Story of a Life.* 1875; New York: Charles L. Webster, 1892.

Woodson, Carter G. *The Mind of the Negro as Reflected in Letters Written during the Crisis, 1800–1860.* Washington, D. C.: The Association for the Study of Negro Life and History, Inc. 1926.

OTHER PUBLISHED PRIMARY SOURCES

The African Wesleyan Methodist Episcopal Church, Inc. *146th Annual Anniversary Commemorative Journal, 1818–1964.* Brooklyn: A. Q. Martin-Funn Funeral Home, 1964.

Andrews, Charles C. *The History of the New-York African Free-Schools, From Their Establishment in 1787, to the Present Time; Embracing a Period of More than Forty Years: Also a Brief Account of the Successful Labors of the New York Manumission Society: With an Appendix.* 1830; New York: Negro Universities Press, 1969.

Atwell, Clyde G. *The Paragon Story. 1939–1969.* Brooklyn: privately printed, ca. 1976.

Bailey, J. T. *An Historical Sketch of Brooklyn, and the Surrounding Neighborhood, Including the Village of Williamsburgh, and the Towns of Bushwick, Flatbush, Flatlands, New Utrecht, and Gravesend. To Which is Added an Interesting Account of the Battle of Long Island.* Brooklyn: J. T. Bailey, 1840.

Bits of Old Brooklyn. Brooklyn: J. A. Davidson, 1881.

Bangs, Mrs. [Charlotte Rebecca] Bleecker. *Reminiscences of Old New Utrecht and Gowanus.* New York: privately printed, 1912.

Bogert, Henry H. ed. *Year Book of the Holland Society of New York, 1906.* New York: Knickerbocker Press, 1908.

Boyd's Brooklyn Business Directory, 1860. New York: Appleton, 1860.

Brooklyn Council for Social Planning. *Growing Up in Brooklyn: A Report of Brooklyn's Little White House Conference on Children and Youth.* Brooklyn: 1951.

Brooklyn Edison. *Brooklyn Market Survey.* Brooklyn: Brooklyn Edison Company, Inc. 1936.

Brooklyn Real Estate Board. *Year Book and Diary for 1935.* Brooklyn: privately published, 1935.

Brooklyn Tenement House Committee and Herbert S. Swan. *The Progress of Housing Reform in Brooklyn: A Report of the Tenement House Committee of the Brooklyn Bureau of Charities and a Study of Land Overcrowding in Brooklyn.* Brooklyn: Bureau of Charities, ca. 1918.

Brooklyn Urban League. *Annual Report, 1919.* Brooklyn: privately published, 1919.

Brooklyn Urban League-Lincoln Settlement Inc. *Annual Report[s], 1923, 1929, 1931.* Brooklyn: privately published, 1923–31.

Brown, William Wells. *The Black Man, His Antecedents, His Genius, and His Achievements.* 1863; New York: Arno and The New York Times, 1969.

Caribbean Research Center. *Statistical Analysis of Persons of Caribbean Ancestry: Basic Democgraphic, Social and Economic Profile Based on 1990 Census Data,* Part 1.

Brooklyn: CRC, Medgar Evers College, 1993.

The Center for Urban Education. *Community Attitudes in Bedford-Stuyvesant: An Area Study.* Summer 1967.

Chadwick, Rev. John W. "Brooklyn: The Greatest of the Five Boroughs of Greater New York." in *King's Views of New York, 1896–1915 & Brooklyn, 1905.* New York: Benjamin Blom, 1974.

The Citizens' Protective League. *Persecution of Negroes, by Roughs and Policemen, in the City of New York, August 1900.*

Christman, Henry M. ed. *Walt Whitman's New York: From Manhattan to Montauk.* New York: Macmillan, 1963.

Commager, Henry Steele ed. *Documents of American History*, 4th ed. New York: Appleton-Century-Crofts, 1948.

Conkling, Alfred R. *City Government in the United States.* New York: D. Appleton, 1894.

Delany, Martin Robinson. *The Condition, Elevation, Emigration, and Destiny of the Colored People of the United States, Politically Considered.* 1852; New York: Arno and The New York Times, 1968.

Denton, Daniel. *A Brief Description of New-York: Formerly Called New-Netherlands, With the Places Thereunto Adjoyning. Together with the Manner o' its Scituation, Fertility of the Soyle, Healthfulness of the Climate, and the Commodities thence Produced. Also Some Directions and Advice to Such as Shall Go Thither: An Account of What Commodites They Shall Take with Them; The Profit and Pleasure that May Accrew to Them Thereby. Likewise a Brief Relation of the Customs of the Indians There.* 1670; Ann Arbor: University Microfilms, Inc. 1966.

Disturnell, John comp. *New York As It Was and As It Is; Giving an Account of the City from its Settlement to the Present Time; Forming a Complete Guide to the Great Metropolis of the Nation, Including the City of Brooklyn and the Surrounding Cities and Villages; Together with a Classified Business Directory.* New York: D. Van Nostrand, 1876.

Dripps, Mathew. *Map of the City of Brooklyn, Being the Cities of Brooklyn & Williamsburgh and the Town of Bushwick as Consolidated January 1st 1855 by an Act of the Legislature of the State of New York, Passed April 17th 1854, Showing the Same as Laid Out by Commissioners and Corected as Altered by Different Acts of the Legislature Up to Date, Showing Also a Part of the City of New York.* Brooklyn: M. Dripps, 1869.

Duncan, Russell ed. *Blue-Eyed Child of Fortune: The Civil War Letters of Colonel Robert Gould Shaw.* Athens: University of Georgia Press, 1992.

Foner, Phillip S. ed. *The Life and Writings of Frederick Douglass.* 5 vols. New York: International Publishers, 1975.

———. and Ronald L. Lewis, eds. *The Black Worker: A Documentary History from*

Colonial Times to the Present. 5 vols. Philadelphia: Temple University Press, 1980.

French, J. H. *Gazetteer of the State of New York: Embracing a Comprehensive View of the Geography, Geology, and General History of the State, and a Complete History and Description of Every County, City, Town, Village, and Locality.* Syracuse, New York: Pearsall Smith, 1860.

Furman, Gabriel. *Notes Geographical and Historical Relating to the Town of Brooklyn in Kings County on Long-Island* (1824; Brooklyn: Renascence, 1968.

———. *Antiquities of Long Island,* edited by Frank Moore. 1874; Port Washington, Long Island: Ira J. Friedman, 1968.

Galamison, Dr. Milton A. "Bedford-Stuyvesant–Harlem Across the River." in John Henrik Clarke, ed. *Harlem: USA.* 1964; New York: Macmillan, 1971.

Gebhart, John C. *Housing Standards in Brooklyn: An Intensive Study of the Housing Records of 3227 Workingmen's Families.* Brooklyn: Bureau of Charities, 1918.

Gehring, Charles T. ed. *New York History Manuscripts: Dutch.* Baltimore: Genealogical Publishing Co. 1983.

Goell, Milton J. *A Post-War Plan for Brownsville.* Brooklyn: Brownsville Neighborhood Council, 1944.

Goessmann, Charles A. *Contribution on the Manufacture and Refining of Cane-Sugar.* New York: Holman, 1864.

———. *Notes on the Manufacture of Sugar in the Island of Cuba.* Syracuse: Journal Book and Job Office, 1865.

Daniel Haskell's "Map of the City of Brooklyn." 1835.

Hastings, Hugh ed. *Ecclesiastical Records of the State of New York.* 8 vols. Albany: James B. Lyons, 1901–5.

Hillis, Newell Dwight. *The Battle of Principles: A Study of the Heroism and Eloquence of the Anti-Slavery Conflict.* 1912; New York: Negro Universities Press, 1969.

Hobart, George H. "Survey Bedford-Stuyvesant Area, Brooklyn, N.Y. February- March 1938, for the Bedford and Stuyvesant Ministers' Associations and the Brooklyn Church and Mission Federation." Brooklyn: privately printed, 1938.

Hodges, Graham Russell and Alan Edward Brown, eds. *"Pretends to Be Free": Runaway Slave Advertisements from Colonial and Revolutionary New York and New Jersey.* New York: Garland, 1994.

Horsmanden, Daniel. *The New-York Conspiracy, or a History of the Negro Plot, with the Journal of the Proceedings Against the Conspirators at New-York in the Years 1741–2.* 1810; Westport, Connecticut: Negro Universities Press, 1969.

[Howard Colored Orphan Asylum,] *Twenty-Ninth Annual Report of the Brooklyn Howard Colored Orphan Asylum Society.* Brooklyn: G. A. Pulis, 1898.

———. *Hand Book of the Howard Orphan Asylum of Brooklyn.* Brooklyn: 1898.

Hughes, Langston "The Harlem Riot–1964." in John Henrik Clarke, ed. *Harlem: A Community in Transition.* 1964; New York: Citadell, 1969.

Hurd, John Cadman. *The Laws of Freedom and Bondage in the United States*. 2 vols. 1858; New York: Negro Universities Press, 1968.

Jaray, Cornell ed. *Historic Chronicles of New Amsterdam, Colonial New York and Early Long Island*, Second Series. Port Washington, New York: Ira J. Friedman, Inc. 1968.

Johnson, James Weldon. *Black Manhattan*. 1930; New York: Ayer, 1990.

Knox, Thomas W. *The Life and Work of Henry Ward Beecher, An Authentic, Impartial and Complete History of His Public Career and Private Life from Cradle to Grave, Replete with Anecdotes, Incidents, Personal Reminiscences and Character Sketches, Descriptive of the Man and His Times*. Hartford: Hartford Publishing, 1887.

Lain, J. comp. *The Brooklyn City Directory for the Year Ending May 1st, 1865*. Brooklyn: J. Lain, 1864.

Lerner, Gerda ed. *Black Women in White America: A Documentary History*. New York: Pantheon, 1972.

Leslie, Thomas & John W. Leslie comp. *Brooklyn. Alphabetical and Street Directory and Yearly Advertiser for 1841–2*. Brooklyn: The House and General Agency Office, 1842.

Livermore, George. *An Historical Research Respecting the Opinions of the Founders of the Republic on Negroes as Slaves, as Citizens, and as Soldiers*. 1863; New York: Augustus M. Kelley, 1970.

Lott, Jeremiah "The Village of Brooklyn in 1816, Compiled from the First Village Map of that date by Jeremiah Lott, and from Poppleton and Lott's Map of the Pierrepont Estate of 1819." New York: F. Mayer & Sons, 1819.

MacDonald, William ed. *Select Charters and Other Documents Illustrative of American History, 1606–1775*. New York: Macmillan, 1906.

Martin, Alex'r. "Map of Brooklyn, Kings County, Long Island, from an Entire New Survey." New York: 1834.

Moffat, R. Burnham. *Pierrepont Genealogies, from Norman Times to 1913, with Particular Attention Paid to the Line of Descent from Hezekiah Pierpont, Youngest Son of Rev. James Pierpont of New Haven*. New York: privately printed, 1913.

The Mortgage Conference of New York. "Population Survey No. 3-B, Brooklyn." New York: The Mortgage Conference, 1945.

Murphy, Henry C. Jr. comp. *The North Farm of Leffert Lefferts. Supreme Court, County of Kings. James Carson Brevoort against Elizabeth Dorothea Brevoort, and Others*. Brooklyn: privately printed, 1 November 1880.

National Association for the Advancement of Colored People. *The Negro Wage-Earner and Apprenticeship Training Programs: A Critical Analysis with Recommendations*. New York: NAACP, 1960.

[Department of Research and Investigations of the] National Urban League. *Negro Membership in American Labor Unions*. New York: NUL, 1930.

New-York Historical Society. *Collections of the New-York Historical Society, for the Year 1893*. New York: privately published, 1894.

Ostrander, Stephen A. *A History of the City of Brooklyn and Kings County*. 2 vols. Brooklyn: Annie A. Ostrander, 1894.

Quarles, Benjamin ed. *Blacks on John Brown*. Urbana: University of Illinois Press, 1972.

Riis, Jacob A. *The Battle with the Slum*. 1902; Montclair, New Jersey: Patterson Smith, 1969.

Ripley, C. Peter et. al. eds. *The Black Abolitionist Papers*. 6 vols. Chapel Hill: The University of North Carolina Press, 1991–2.

Ross, Peter. *A History of Long Island, From its First Settlement to the Present Time*. 2 vols. New York: Lewis Publishing, 1902.

Rubin, Joseph Jay and Charles H. Brown, eds. *Walt Whitman of the New York Aurora: Editor at Twenty-Two*. State College, Pennsylvania: Bald Eagle, 1950.

St. Augustine's Protestant Episcopal Church. "Financial Report for the Year 1930."

[St. Phillip's P.E. Church,] *Golden Jubilee Album of st. Philip's P. E. Church*. Brooklyn: 1949.

Siloam Presbyterian Church. "Historical Sermon by the Pastor, Rev. W. A. Alexander, D.D." in *Siloam Presbyterian Church, Semi-Centenial, May 21st to July 25th, 1899*. Brooklyn: Nolan Bros. 1899.

Simmons, Rev. William J. *Men of Mark: Eminent, Progressive and Rising*. 1887; New York: Arno and The New York Times, 1968.

Smith, Adam. *An Inquiry into the Nature and Causes of the Wealth of Nations. 1776; New York: Modern Library, 1937*.

Smith, James McCune M.A. M. D. "Toussaint L'Ouverture and the Haytian Revolutions." in Alice Moore Dunbar, ed. Masterpieces of Negro Eloquence: The Best Speeches by the Negro from the Days of Slavery to the Present Time. New York: Bookery Publishing, 1914.

Smith, William H. comp. *The Brooklyn City and Kings County Record: A Budget of General Information; with a Map of the City, an Almanac, and an Appendix, containing the New City Charter*. Brooklyn: William H. Smith, 1855.

Spooner, Alden. *Spooner's Brooklyn Directory, For the Year 1822*. Brooklyn: Office of the Long Island Star, May 1822.

Stam, Harry E. *Looking Back at One Hundred Years of Progress in Anglo-Saxon Lodge, No. 137, Brooklyn, N. Y. Free and Accepted Masons of the State of New York and the Passing in Review of its Many Activities*. Brooklyn: Harry E. Stam, 1948.

Steffens, Lincoln. *The Shame of the Cities*. 1904; New York: Hill and Wang, 1957.

Sterling, Dorothy ed. *We Are Your Sisters: Black Women in the Nineteenth Century*. New York: Norton, 1984.

Stiles, Henry Reed. *A History of the City of Brooklyn. Including the Old Town and Village of Brooklyn, the Town of Bushwick, and the Village and City of Williamsburgh*. 3 vols.

Brooklyn: published by subscription, 1867–1870.

———. ed. *The Civil, Political, Professional and Ecclesiastical History and Commerical and Industrial Record of the County of Kings and the City of Brooklyn. N.Y. From 1683 to 1884.* 2 vols. New York: W. W. Munsell, 1884.

———. *The Stiles Family in America. Genealogies of the Connecticut Family Descendants of John Stiles, of Windsor, Conn. and of Mr. Francis Stiles, of Windsor and Stratford, Conn. 1635–1894; Also the Connecticut New Jersey Families, 1720–1894; and the Southern. or Bermuda-Georgia Family, 1635–1894. With Contributions to the Genealogies of Some New York and Pennsylvania Families. And an Appendix, Containing Information Concerning the English Families of the Name.* Jersey City: Doan & Pilson, 1895.

———. *A Hand-Book of Practical Suggestions for the Use of Students in Genealogy.* Albany, NY: Joel Munsell's Sons, 1899.

Strong, Thomas M. *The History of the Town of Flatbush, in Kings County, Long-Island.* New York: Thomas R. Mercein, Jr. 1842.

Stowe, Harriet Beecher. *Uncle Tom's Cabin.* 1852; New York: Norton, 1994.

Syrett, Henry Coffin ed. *The Papers of Alexander Hamilton.* New York: Columbia University Press, 1961.

Tammany Hall United Colored Democracy of New York. *Tammany Hall vs. Fusion or Organized Democracy Against Disorganized Autocracy and Bastard Reform.* New York: 1913.

Townsend, Reginald T. *Mother of Clubs: Being the History of the First Hundred Years of the Union Club of the City of New York, 1836–1936.* New York: Union Club, 1936.

Vanderbilt, Gertrude Lefferts. *The Social History of Flatbush, and Manners and Customs of the Dutch Settlers in Kings County.* New York: D. Appleton, 1881.

Walker, David. *An Appeal, in Four Articles, Together with a Preamble, to the Coloured Citizens of the World, But in Particular, and Very Expressly, to Those of the United States of America,* ed. with an intro. by Charles M. Wiltse. 1829; New York: Hill and Wang, 1965.

Warriner, Rev. Edwin. *Old Sands Street Methodist Episcopal Church, of Brooklyn, N.Y.: An Illustrated Record, Historical and Biographical.* New York: Phillips & Hunt, 1885.

Whitman, Walt. *Democratic Vistas, and Other Papers.* London: Walter Scott, 1888.

———. *The Eighteenth Presidency!,* Edward F. Grier, ed. Lawrence: University of Kansas Press, 1956.

———. *Leaves of Grass: Comprehensive Readers Edition.* 1855; New York: New York University Press, 1965.

Wibecan, George E. "New York Negro Clubs." a pamphlet of The New York State Commission, National Negro Exposition, Richmond, Virginia. New York: 1915.

Wilson, H. comp. *Trow's New York City Directory, for the Year Ending May 1, 1866.* New

York: John F. Trow, 1866.

Wilson, Joseph T. *The Black Phalanx: A History of the Negro Soldiers of the United States in the Wars of 1775–1812, 1861-'65.* 1890; New York: Arno and The New York Times, 1968.

Wood, Silas. *A Sketch of the First Settlement of the Several Towns on Long-Island; With Their Political Condition, To the End of the American Revolution.* 1828.

SECONDARY SOURCES.

Abbott, Lyman. *Henry Ward Beecher.* 1903; New York: Chelsea House, 1980.

Abelow, Samuel P. *History of the Brooklyn Jewry.* Brooklyn: Scheba, 1937.

Adams, Thomas. *The Design of Residential Areas: Basic Considerations, Principles, and Methods.* Cambridge: Harvard University Press, 1934.

Allen, Theodore W. *The Invention of the White Race,* Vol. 1. New York: Verso, 1994.

Anderson, Jervis. *This Was Harlem: 1900–1950.* New York: Noonday, 1981.

Anderson, Will "The Breweries of Brooklyn: An Informal History." in Rita Seiden Miller, ed. *Brooklyn USA: The Fourth Largest City in America.* New York: Brooklyn College Press, 1979.

Armbruster, Eugene L. *The Eastern District of Brooklyn.* New York: 1912.

Baldwin, James "Preface." to Roi Ottley and William J. Weatherby, eds. *The Negro in New York: An Informal Social History, 1626–1940.* New York: Praeger, 1967.

Bayley, Rev. J. R. *A Brief Sketch of the Early History of the Catholic Church on the Island of New York,* 2nd ed. New York: Catholic Publication Society, 1870.

Bayor, Ronald H. *Neighbors in Conflict: The Irish, Germans, Jews, and Italians of New York City, 1929–1941,* 2nd ed. Chicago: University of Illinois Press, 1988.

Beach, Seth Curtis. *Daughters of the Puritans: A Group of Brief Biographies.* 1905; Freeport, New York: Books for Libraries Press, 1967.

Beachey, R. W. *The British West Indies Sugar Industry in the Late 19th Century.* 1957; Westport, CN: Greenwood, 1978.

Bedford, Scott E. ed. *Readings in Urban Sociology.* New York: D. Appleton, 1927.

Bernstein, Iver. *The New York City Draft Riots: Their Significance for American Society and Politics in the Age of the Civil War.* New York: Oxford University Press, 1990.

Blackett, R. J. M. *Beating Against the Barriers: The Lives of Six Nineteenth-Century Afro-Americans.* 1986; Ithaca, New York: Cornell University Press, 1989.

Blight, David W. "In Search of Learning, Liberty, and Self Definition: James McCune Smith and the Ordeal of the Antebellum Black Intellectual." *Afro-Americans in New York Life and History.* July 1985.

Bloch, Herman D. "The Employment Status of the New York Negro in Retrospect." *Phylon.* Fourth quarter, 1959.

Brooklyn Trust Company. *Historic Brooklyn: A Collection of the Facts, Legends, Traditions and Reminiscences that Time has Gathered About the Historic Homesteads and Landmarks of Brooklyn*. Brooklyn: Brooklyn Trust Company, 1941.

Brown, Joshua and David Ment. *Factories, Foundries, and Refineries: A History of Five Brooklyn Industries*. Brooklyn: The Brooklyn Educational & Cultural Alliance, 1980.

Brown, William Wells. *Men of Mark: Eminent, Progressive and Rising*. 1887; New York: Arno and The New York Times.

Butchart, Ronald E. " 'We Best Can Instruct Our Own People': New York African Americans in the Freedmen's Schools, 1861–1875." *Afro-Americans in New York Life and History*. January 1988.

Callender, James H. *Yesterdays on Brooklyn Heights*. New York: Dorland, 1927.

Carpenter, Niles. *Nationality, Color, and Economic Opportunity in the City of Buffalo*. 1927; Westport, Connecticut: Negro Universities Press, 1970.

Carter, Dan T. *Scottsboro: A Tragedy of the American South*. New York: Oxford University Press, 1971.

Jr. Daniel Catlin. *Good Work Well Done: The Sugar Business Career of Horace Havemeyer, 1903–1956*. New York: privately printed, 1988.

Clark, Kenneth B. *Dark Ghetto: Dilemmas of Social Power*, 2nd ed. 1965; Middletown, Connecticut: Wesleyan University Press, 1989.

Cohen, Roger Alan "The Lost Jubilee: New York Republicans and the Politics of Reconstruction and Reform, 1867–1878." Doctoral dissertation, Columbia University, 1976.

Harold X. Connolly, *A Ghetto Grows in Brooklyn*. New York: New York University Press, 1977.

University Press, 1966.

———. dissertation, "Blacks in Brooklyn from 1900 to 1960." Doctoral New York University, 1972.

Davis, David Brion. *The Problem of Slavery in Western Culture*. Ithaca, NY: Cornell University Press, 1966.

———. *Slavery and Human Progress*. New York : Oxford University Press, 1984.

Davis, Thomas J. *A Rumor of Revolt: The "Great Negro Plot" in Colonial New York*. New York: Free Press, 1985.

———. "New York's Long Black Line: A Note on the Growing Slave Population, 1626–1790." *Afro-Americans in New York Life and History*. January 1978.

Massey, Douglas S .and Nancy A. Denton. *American Apartheid: Segregation and the Making of the Underclass*. Cambridge: Harvard University Press, 1993.

Dolan, Jay P. *The Immigrant Church: New York's Irish and German Catholics, 1815-1865*. Baltimore: The Johns Hopkins University Press, 1975.

Bois, W. E. B. Du. *The Philadelphia Negro*. 1899; Millwood, New York: Kraus-Thomson, 1973.

———. *John Brown*. 1909; New York: International Publishers, 1987.

———. *Black Reconstruction in America: An Essay Toward a History of the Part Which*

Black Folk Played in the Attempt to Reconstruct Democracy in America, 1860–1880. 1935; New York: Russell & Russell, 1962.

Dubofsky, Melvyn. *When Workers Organize: New York City in the Progressive Era.* Amherst: University of Massachusetts Press, 1968.

Ellis, David M. et. al. *A Short History of New York State.* Ithaca: New York: Cornell University Press, 1957.

Emilio, Luis F. *History of the Fifty-Fourth Regiment of Massachusetts Volunteer Infantry, 1863–1865.* Boston: Boston Book, 1894.

Ernst, Robert. *Immigrant Life in New York City, 1825–1863.* New York: King's Crown Press, Columbia University, 1949.

Etzdowitz, Henry and Gerald Schaflander. *Ghetto Crisis: Bureaucracy vs. Progress in Bedford-Stuyvesant.* Boston: Little, Brown, 1969.

Fields, Barbara J. "Ideology and Race in American History." in J. Morgan Kousser and James M. McPherson, eds. *Region, Race, and Reconstruction: Essays in Honor of C. Vann Woodward.* New York: Oxford University Press, 1982.

Fishman, Robert. *Bourgeois Utopias: The Rise and Fall of Suburbia.* New York: Basic Books, 1987.

Flick, Alexander C. *History of the State of New York*, 10 Vols. New York: Columbia University Press, 1933–37.

Foner, Eric. *Nothing But Freedom: Emancipation and its Legacy.* Baton Rouge: Louisiana State University Press, 1983.

———. *Reconstruction: America's Unfinished Revolution, 1863–1877.* New York: Harper & Row, 1988.

Foner, Phillip S. *Business & Slavery: The New York Merchants & The Irrepressible Conflict.* Chapel Hill: The University of North Carolina Press, 1941.

Franklin, Charles Lionel. *The Negro Labor Unionist of New York: Problems and Conditions Among the Negroes in the Labor Unions of Manhattan with Special Reference to the N.R.A. and Post-N.R.A. Situations.* New York: Columbia University Press, 1936.

Fredrickson, George M. *The Arrogance of Race: Historical Perspectives on Slavery, Racism, and Social Inequality.* Middletown, CN: Wesleyan University Press, 1988.

———. *The Inner Civil War: Northern Intellectuals and the Crisis of the Union.* New York: Harper & Row, 1965.

Freeman, Andrew A. *Abraham Lincoln Goes to New York.* New York: Coward- McCann, 1960.

Freeman, Joshua B. *In Transit: The Transport Workers Union in New York City, 1933–1966.* New York: Oxford University Press, 1989.

Freeman, Rhoda Golden. *The Free Negro in New York City in the Era Before the Civil War.* New York: Garland, 1994.

Gerson, Jeffrey Nathan "Building the Brooklyn Machine: Irish, Jewish and Black

Political Succession in Central Brooklyn, 1919–1964." Doctoral Dissertation, City University of New York, 1990.

Gordon, Albert I. *Jews in Suburbia*. 1959; Connecticut: Greenwood, 1973.

Gottlieb, Peter. *Making Their Own Way: Southern Blacks' Migration to Pittsburgh, 1916–30*. Urbana: University of Illinois Press, 1987.

Grant, Robert B. *The Black Man Comes to the City: A Documentary Account from the Great Migration to the Great Depression, 1915–1930*. Chicago: Nelson-Hall, 1972.

Green, Charles and Basil Wilson. *The Struggle for Black Empowerment in New York City: Beyond the Politics of Pigmentation*. New York: Praeger, 1989.

Greenberg, Cheryl Lynn. *Or Does It Explode?: Black Harlem in the Great Depression*. New York: Oxford University Press, 1991.

Greer, Edward. *Big Steel: Black Politics and Corporate Power in Gary, Indiana*. New York: Monthly Review, 1979.

Gronowicz, Anthony. *Race and Class Politics in New York City before the Civil War*. Boston: Northeastern University Press, 1998.

Grossman, James R. *Land of Hope: Chicago, Black Southerners, and the Great Migration*. Chicago: The University of Chicago Press, 1989.

Grumet, Robert Steven. *Native American Place Names in New York City*. New York: Museum of the City of New York, 1981.

Haley, Charles "The Klan in the Midst: The Ku Klux Klan in Upstate New York Communities." *Afro-Americans in New York Life and History*. January 1983.

Handlin, Oscar. *The Newcomers: Negroes and Puerto Ricans in a Changing Metropolis*. Cambridge: Harvard University Press, 1959.

Handlin, Oscar and Mary F. Handlin. "Origins of the Southern Labor System." *William and Mary Quarterly*, Vol. 7, No. 2. April 1950.

Harlan, Louis R. *Booker T. Washington: The Making of a Black Leader, 1856–1901*. New York: Oxford University Press, 1972.

Harriss, C. Lowell. *History and Policies of the Home Owners' Loan Corporation*. New York: National Bureau of Economic Research, 1951.

Havemeyer, Harry W. *Merchants of Williamsburgh: Frederick C. Havemeyer, Jr. William Dick, John Mollenhauer, Henry O. Havemeyer*. privately published, 1989.

Hodes, Martha. *White Women, Black Men: Illicit Sex in the Nineteenth-Century South*. New Haven: Yale University Press, 1997.

Hodges, Graham Russell " 'Desirable Companions and Lovers': Irish and African Americans in the Sixth Ward, 1830–1870." in Ronald H. Bayor and Timothy J. Meagher, eds. *The New York Irish*. Baltimore: The Johns Hopkins University Press, 1996.

Holder, Calvin B. "The Rise of the West Indian Politician in New York City, 1900-1952." *Afro-Americans in New York Life and History*, Vol. 4, No. 1. January 1980.

———. "The Causes and Composition of West Indian Immigration to New York City,

1900–1952." *Afro-Americans in New York Life and History*, Vol. 11, No. 1. January 1987.

Hosay, Philip Myron "The Challenge of Urban Poverty: Charity Reformers in New York City, 1835–1890." Doctoral dissertation, University of Michigan, 1969.

Ignatiev, Noel. *How the Irish Became White*. New York: Routledge, 1995.

Jackson, Kenneth T. *The Ku Klux Klan in the City, 1915–1930*. New York: Oxford University Press, 1967.

———. *Crabgrass Frontier: The Suburbanization of the United States*. New York: Oxford University Press, 1985.

Jacobs, Jane. *The Death and Life of Great American Cities*. New York: Vintage, 1961.

Jenks, Jeremiah Whipple and Walter E. Clark. *The Trust Problem*. Garden City, NY: Doubleday, 1929.

Jensen, Vernon H. *Strife on the Waterfront: The Port of New York Since 1945*. Ithaca, New York: Cornell University Press, 1974.

Jerome, Harry. *Migration and the Business Cycle*. New York: National Bureau of Economic Research, 1926.

Jewell, John V. *Historic Williamsburgh: An Account of the Settlement and Development of Williamsburgh and its Environs, from Dutch Colonial Days to the Present*. Brooklyn: Williamsburgh Savings Bank, 1926.

Johnson, Paul E. *A Shopkeeper's Millennium: Society and Revivals in Rochester, New York, 1815–1837*. New York: Hill and Wang, 1978.

Jordan, Winthrop D. *White over Black: American Attitudes Toward the Negro, 1550-1812*. 1968; New York: Norton, 1977.

———. "Modern Tensions and the Origins of American Slavery." *Journal of Southern History*, Vol. 28, No. 1. February 1962.

Joselit, Jenna Weissman. *Our Gang: Jewish Crime and the New York Jewish Community, 1900–1940*. Bloomington: Indiana University Press, 1983.

Judd, Jacob "The History of Brooklyn, 1834–1855: Political and Administrative Aspects." Doctoral dissertation, New York University, 1959.

Katzman, David M. *Before the Ghetto: Black Detroit in the Nineteenth Century*. 1973; Urbana: University of Illinois Press, 1975.

Katznelson, Ira. *Black Men, White Cities: Race, Politics, and Migration in the United States, 1900–30, and Britain, 1948–68*. London: Oxford University Press, 1973.

———. "Was the Great Society a Lost Opportunity?" in Steve Fraser and Gary Gerstle, eds. *The Rise and Fall of the New Deal Order, 1930–1980*. Princeton, New Jersey: Princeton University Press, 1989.

Kennedy, Louise Venable. *The Negro Peasant Turns Cityward: Effects of Recent Migrations on Northern Centers*. 1930; New York: AMS Press, 1968.

Kiser, Clyde Vernon. *Sea Island to City: A Study of St. Helena Islanders in Harlem and Other Urban Centers*. 1932; New York: Antheneum, 1969.

Klein, Maury and Harvey A. Kantor. *Prisoners of Progress: American Industrial Cities, 1850–1920*. New York: Macmillan, 1976.

Kluger, Richard. *The Paper: The Life and Death of the New York Herald Tribune*. New York: Knopf, 1986.

Knox, John Jay. *A History of Banking in the United States*. New York: Bradford Rhodes, 1903.

Kousser, J. Morgan. *The Shaping of Southern Politics: Suffrage Restriction and the Establishment of the One-Party South, 1880–1910*. New Haven: Yale University Press, 1974.

Kozol, Jonathan. *Savage Inequalities: Children in America's Schools*. New York: Basic Books, 1991.

Kross, Jessica. *The Evolution of an American Town: Newtown, New York, 1642–1775*. Philadelphia: Temple University Press, 1983.

Kusmer, Kenneth L. *A Ghetto Takes Shape: Black Cleveland, 1870–1930*. Urbana: University of Illinois Press, 1976.

Landesman, Alter F. *Brownsville: The Birth, Develoment and Passing of a Jewish Community in New York*. 1969; New York: Bloch, 1971.

Lanier, Henry Wysham. *A Century of Banking in New York, 1822–1922*. New York: Gilliss, 1922.

Lapham, James Sigurd "Ther German-Americans of New York City 1860–1890." Doctoral dissertation, St. John's University, 1977.

Lees, Andrew. *Cities Perceived: Urban Society in European and American Thought, 1820–1940*. Manchester, England: Manchester University Press, 1985.

Leuchtenberg, William. *Franklin D. Roosevelt and the New Deal, 1932–1940*. New York: Harper & Row, 1963.

Lewinson, Edwin R. *Black Politics in New York City*. New York: Twayne, 1974.

Litwack, Leon F. *North of Slavery: The Negro in the Free States, 1790–1860*. Chicago: The University of Chicago Press, 1961.

Lodge, Henry Cabot. *Alexander Hamilton*. Boston: Houghton, Mifflin, 1895.

Logan, Rayford W. and Michael R. Winston, eds. *Dictionary of American Negro Biography*. New York: Norton, 1982.

Lynsky, Myer. *Sugar Economics, Statistics, and Documents*. Washington, DC: US Sugar Cane Refiners' Association, 1938.

McClain, Charles J. *In Search of Equality: The Chinese Struggle Against Discrimination in Nineteenth-Century America*. Berkeley: University of California Press, 1994.

McCullough, David W. *Brooklyn . . . And How It Got That Way*. New York: Dial, 1983.

McGraw, B. T. "The Housing Act of 1954 and Implications for Minorities." *Phylon*. No. 2, 1940.

McKelvey, Blake. *The Urbanization of America, 1860–1915*. New Brunswick: Rutgers

University Press, 1963.

McManus, Edgar J. *A History of Negro Slavery in New York*. Syracuse: Syracuse University Press, 1966.

McPherson, James M. *The Negro's Civil War: How American Negroes Felt and Acted during the War for the Union*. New York: Vintage, 1965.

Mabee, Carleton. *Black Education in New York State*. Syracuse, New York: Syracuse University Press, 1979.

Mann, Arthur. *LaGuardia: A Fighter Against His Times, 1882–1933*. Chicago: The University of Chicago Press, 1959.

———. *LaGuardia Comes to Power, 1933*. Chicago: The University of Chicago Press, 1965.

Manoni, Mary. *Bedford-Stuyvesant: The Anatomy of a Central City Community*. New York: Quadrangle, 1973.

Marable, Manning "South African Nationalism in Brooklyn: John L. Dube's Activities in New York State, 1877–1899." *Afro-Americans in New York Life and History,*. January 1979.

Marlow, Nicholas "Bedford-Stuyvesant Place-Names." Master's thesis, Brooklyn College, 1963.

Marshall, Paule. *Brown Girl, Brownstones*. 1959; New York: Feminist Press, 1981.

Marx, Karl. *Capital*. 3 vols. reprinted: New York: International Publishers, 1967.

Meakin, Budgett. *Model Factories and Villages: Ideal Conditions of Labour and Housing*. Philadelphia: George W. Jacobs, ca. 1905.

Ment, David and Mary Donovan. *The People of Brooklyn: A History of Two Neighborhoods*. Brooklyn: The Brooklyn Educational & Cultural Alliance, 1980.

Mink, Gwendolyn. *Old Labor and New Immigrants in American Political Development: Union, Party, and State, 1875–1920*. Ithaca: Cornell University Press, 1986.

Mitchell, B[rian]. R. *Abstract of British Historical Statistics*. London: Cambridge University Press, 1962.

Mohl, Raymond A. *The New City: Urban America in the Industrial Age, 1860–1920*. Arlington Heights, Illinois: Harlan Davidson, 1985.

Morgan, Edmund S. *American Slavery, American Freedom: The Ordeal of Colonial Virginia*. New York: Norton, 1975.

Morton, Vernon Lane. *The Negro in Mississippi, 1865–1890*. 1947; New York: Harper & Row, 1965.

Moss, Richard Shannon. *Slavery on Long Island: A Study in Local Institutional and Early African-American Communal Life*. New York: Garland, 1993.

Naison, Mark. *Communists in Harlem During the Depression*. Urbana: University of Illinois Press, 1983.

Nash, Gary B. *Forging Freedom: The Formation of Philadelphia's Black Community, 1720–1840*. Cambridge: Harvard University Press, 1988.

Robert R. Nathan Associates, Inc. *Cane Sugar Refining in the United States: Its Ecomonic Importance.* Washington, DC: US Sugar Cane Refiners' Association, 1971.

Noble, David F. *Forces of Production: A Social History of Industrial Automation.* New York: Knopf, 1984.

Nordstrom, Carl "The New York Slave Code." *Afro-Americans in New York Life and History.* January 1980.

O'Connor, Watson Burdette. *Bedford in Breuckelen Town, from 1667 to 1868, an Historical Sketch, with Map.* New York: 1926.

Olbrich, Emil. *The Development of the Sentiment on Negro Suffrage to 1860.* 1912; New York: Negro Universities Press, 1969.

Osofsky, Gilbert. *Harlem: The Making of a Ghetto, Negro New York, 1890–1930,* 2nd ed. New York: Harper & Row, 1971.

Ovington, Mary White. *Half A Man: The Status of the Negro in New York.* 1911; New York: Negro Universities Press, 1969.

———. *Portraits in Color.* New York: Viking, 1927.

Painter, Nell Irvin. *Exodusters: Black Migration to Kansas After Reconstruction.* New York: Norton, 1976.

Palisi, Joseph "The Brooklyn Navy Yard." in Rita Seiden Miller, ed. *Brooklyn USA: The Fourth Largest City in America.* New York: Brooklyn College Press, 1979.

Paludan, Phillip Shaw. *"A People's Contest": The Union and the Civil War, 1861–1865.* New York: Harper & Row, 1988.

Park, Robert "The City: Suggestions for the Investigation of Human Behavior in the Urban Environment." in Robert E. Park, Ernest W. Burgess, Roderick D. McKenzie, eds. *The City.* 1925; Chicago: The University of Chicago Press, 1967.

Pilat, Oliver and Jo Ranson, *Sodom by the Sea: An Affectionate History of Coney Island.* Garden City, New York: Doubleday, Doran & Company, Inc. 1941.

Purvis, Thomas L. "The National Origins of New Yorkers in 1790." *New York History,* Vol. 67, No. 2. April 1986, 133–53.

Quarles, Benjamin. *Black Abolitionists.* New York: Oxford University Press, 1969.

Quimby, Ernest "Bedford-Stuyvesant." in Rita Seiden Miller, ed. *Brooklyn USA: The Fourth Largest City in America.* New York: Brooklyn College Press, 1979.

Rable, George C. *But There Was No Peace: The Role of Violence in the Politics of Reconstruction.* Athens, Georgia: The University of Georgia Press, 1984.

Reid, Ira De Augustine. *The Negro Immigrant: His Background, Characteristics and Social Adjustment, 1899–1937.* New York: Columbia University Press, 1939.

Rieder, Jonathan. *Canarsie: The Jews and Italians of Brooklyn Against Liberalism.* Cambridge: Harvard University Press, 1985.

Rischin, Moses. *The Promised City: New York's Jews, 1870–1914.* 1962; New York: Harper & Row, Publishers, 1970.

Roediger, David R. *The Wages of Whiteness: Race and the Making of the American*

Working Class. New York: Verso, 1991.

Roff, Kenneth L. "Brooklyn's Reaction to Black Suffrage in 1860." *Afro-Americans in New York Life and History*. January 1978.

Roff, Sandra "The Accessibility of Libraries to Blacks in Nineteenth Century Brooklyn, New York." *Afro-Americans in New York Life and History*. July 1981.

————."The Brooklyn African Woolman Benevolent Society Rediscovered." *Afro-Americans in New York Life and History*. July 1986.

A. N. Rygg. *Norwegians in New York, 1825–1925*. Brooklyn: Norwegian News, 1941.

Sanchez Korrol, Virginia E. *From Colonia to Community: The History of Puerto Ricans in New York City*. 1983; Berkeley, California: University of California Press, 1994.

Scheiner, Seth M. *Negro Mecca: A History of the Negro in New York City, 1865- 1920*. New York: New York University Press, 1965.

Scott, Mel. *American City Planning Since 1890: A History Commemorating the Fiftieth Anniversary of the American Institute of Planners*. Berkeley: University of California Press, 1969.

Seraile, William. *Voice of Dissent: Theophilus Gould Steward. 1843–1924 and Black America*. Brooklyn: Carlson, 1991.

————. "Susan McKinney Steward: New York State's First African-American Woman Physician." *Afro-Americans in New York Life and History*. July 1985.

————. "Brooklyn's 'Colored Society:' A Minister's Observation, 1876- 1877." *Afro-Americans in New York Life and History*. January 1991.

Sharp, Reverend John K. *Priests and Parishes of the Diocese of Brooklyn, 1820–1944*. New York: Roman Catholic Diocese of Brooklyn, 1944.

Simon, Donald E. "Brooklyn in the Election of 1860." Master's thesis, City College, City University of New York, May 1965.

Sitkoff, Harvard. *A New Deal for Blacks: The Emergence of Civil Rights as a National Issue: The Depression Decade*. New York: Oxford University Press, 1978.

Smith, Jessie Carney ed. *Notable Black American Women*. Detroit: Gale Research, 1992.

Spann, Edward K. *The New Metropolis: New York City, 1840–1857*. New York: Columbia University Press, 1981.

Spear, Allan H. *Black Chicago: The Making of a Negro Ghetto, 1890–1920*. Chicago: The University of Chicago Press, 1967.

Spears, John R. *The American Slave-Trade: An Account of its Origin, Growth and Suppression*. New York: Charles Scribner's Sons, 1900.

Stafford, Walter W. *Closed Labor Markets: Underrepresentation of Blacks, Hispanics and Women in New York City's Core Industries and Jobs*. New York: Community Service Society of New York, January 1985.

Stampp, Kenneth M. *The Peculiar Institution: Slavery in the Ante-Bellum South*. New York: Vintage, 1956.

Stephens, Michael. *The Brooklyn Book of the Dead*. Norman, Illinois: Dalkey Archive, 1994.

Stuart, James Brewer. *Holy Warriors: The Abolitionists and American Slavery*. New York: Hill and Wang, 1976.

Sugrue, Thomas J. *The Origins of the Urban Crisis: Race and Inequality in Postwar Detroit*. Princeton: Princeton University Press, 1996.

Sullivan, Mercer L. *"Getting Paid": Youth Crime and Work in the Inner City*. Ithaca: Cornell University Press, 1989.

Swan, Robert J. "Did Brooklyn. N.Y. Blacks Have Unusual Control Over Their Schools? Period 1: 1815–1845." *Afro-Americans in New York Life and History*. July 1983.

Syrett, Henry Coffin. *The City of Brooklyn, 1865–1898: A Political History*. 1944; New York: AMS Press, 1968.

Tabb, William K. *The Political Economy of the Black Ghetto*. New York: Norton, 1970.

Taeuber, Karl E. and Alma F. Taeuber. *Negroes in Cities: Residential Segregation and Neighborhood Change*. New York: Atheneum, 1969.

Taylor, Clarence. *The Black Churches of Brooklyn*. New York: Columbia University Press, 1994.

———. *Knocking at Our Own Door: Milton A. Galamison and the Struggle to Integrate New York City Schools*. New York: Columbia University Press, 1997.

———. "The Formation and Development of Brooklyn's Black Churches, from the Nineteenth to the Early Twentieth Century." *Long Island Historical Journal*, Vol. 5, No. 2.

Taylor, Philip. *The Distant Magnet: European Emigration to the U.S.A.*. New York: Harper Torchbooks, 1971.

Thernstrom, Stephan. *The Other Bostonians: Poverty and Progress in the American Metropolis, 1880–1970*. Cambridge: Harvard University Press, 1973.

Thomas, Bert J. "Historical Functions of Caribbean-American Benevolent/Progressive Associations." *Afro-Americans in New York Life and History*, Vol. 12, No. 2. July 1988.

Toney, Joyce "The Perpetuation of a Culture of Migration: West Indian American Ties With Home, 1900–1979." *Afro-Americans in New York Life and History*, Vol. 13, No. 1. January 1989.

Trelease, Allen W. *Indian Affairs in Colonial New York: The Seventeenth Century*. 1960; Port Washington, N.Y.: Kennikat, 1971.

Trotter, Joe William Jr. *Black Milwaukee: The Making of an Industrial Proletariat, 1915–1945*. Urbana: University of Illinois Press, 1985.

Turkus, Burton B. and Sid Feder. *Murder Inc.: The Story of "the syndicate"*. New York: Farrar, Straus, and Young, 1951.

Van Rensselaer, Mrs. [Mariana Griswold] Schuyler. *History of the City of New York in the Seventeenth Century*. 2 vols. New York: Macmillan, 1909.

Vanneman, Reeve and Lynn Weber Cannon. *The American Perception of Class.* Philadelphia: Temple University Press, 1987.

Vaughan, Alden T. "Blacks in Virginia: A Note on the First Decade." *William and Mary Quarterly*, Vol. 29, No. 3. July 1972.

Vinson, Robert Trent "The Law as Lawbreaker: The Promotion and Encouragement of the Atlantic Slave Trade by the New York Judiciary System, 1857–1862." *Afro-Americans in New York Life and History.* July 1996.

Walker, George E. *The Afro-American in New York City, 1827–1860.* New York: Garland, 1993.

Ward, David. *Poverty, Ethnicity, and the American City, 1840–1925: Changing Conceptions of the Slum and the Ghetto.* Cambridge: Cambridge University Press, 1989.

Warner, Sam Bass Jr. *The Urban Wilderness: A History of the American City.* New York: Harper & Row, 1972.

Weaver, Robert C. "Racial Employment Trends in National Defense." *Phylon.* First quarter, 1942.

———. "Racial Policy in Public Housing." *Phylon.* Second quarter, 1940.

———. *The Negro Ghetto.* New York: Harcourt, Brace, 1948.

Weisbrot, Robert. *Father Divine.* Urbana: University of Illinois Press, 1983.

Weld, Ralph Foster. *Brooklyn Village, 1816–1834.* New York: Columbia University Press, 1938.

Press, ———. *Brooklyn is America.* New York: Columbia University 1950.

White, Shane. *Somewhat More Independent: The End of Slavery in New York City, 1770–1810.* Athens: The University of Georgia Press, 1991.

Wilentz, Sean. *Chants Democratic: New York City & the Rise of the American Working Class, 1788–1850.* New York: Oxford University Press, 1984.

Williams, Richard. *Hierarchical Structures and Social Value: The Creation of Black and Irish Identities in the United States.* New York: Cambridge University Press, 1990.

Woofter, T. J. Jr. "Migration of Negroes from Georgia, 1916–17." in U. S. Department of Labor. *Negro Migration in 1916–17.* 1919; New York: Negro Universities Press, 1969.

Wissler, Clark ed. *The Indians of Greater New York and the Lower Hudson.* 1909; New York: AMS Press, 1975.

Woodman, Harold D. *King Cotton and His Retainers: Financing and Marketing the Cotton Crop of the South, 1800–1925.* 1968; Columbia: University of South Carolina Press, 1990.

Woodson, Carter Godwin. *The Negro Professional Man and the Community with Special Emphasis on the Physician and the Lawyer.* 1934; New York: Negro Universities Press, 1969.

Woodward, C. Vann. *The Strange Career of Jim Crow*, 3rd Rev. Ed. New York: Oxford

University Press, 1974.

———. *Origins of the New South, 1877–1913*. 1951; Baton Rouge: Lousiana State University Press, 1971.

———. *Reunion & Reaction*. 1951; Garden City, New York: Doubleday Anchor, 1956.

Wright, Gavin. *The Political Economy of the Cotton South: Households, Markets, and Wealth in the Nineteenth Century*. New York: Norton, 1978.

Wyatt-Brown, Bertram. *Lewis Tappan and the Evengelical War Against Slavery*. Cleveland: The Press of Case Western Reserve University, 1969.

Yoshpe, Harry B. "Record of Slave Manumissions in New York During the Colonial and Early National Periods." *Journal of Negro History*. January 1941, 78- 105.

Zink, Harold. *City Bosses in the United States: A Study of Twenty Municipal Bosses*. Durham: Duke University Press, 1930.

Zunz, Olivier. *The Changing Face of Inequality: Urbanization, Industrial Development, and Immigrants in Detroit, 1880–1920*. Chicago: The University of Chicago Press, 1982.

Index

The Columbia History of Urban Life
Kenneth T. Jackson, General Editor

François Weil, *A History of New York*   2004

Evelyn Gonzalez, *The Bronx*   2004

Jon C. Teaford, *The Metropolitan Revolution: The Rise of Post-Urban America*   2006